THOMAS HARDY

Selected Letters

Thomas Hardy in old age, photographed by Wheeler of Weymouth.
(Frederick B. Adams)

THOMAS HARDY

Selected Letters

EDITED BY

MICHAEL MILLGATE

CLARENDON PRESS · OXFORD

1990

Oxford University Press, Walton Street, Oxford OX2 6DP
Oxford New York Toronto
Delhi Bombay Calcutta Madras Karachi
Petaling Jaya Singapore Hong Kong Tokyo
Nairobi Dar es Salaam Cape Town
Melbourne Auckland
and associated companies in
Berlin Ibadan

Oxford is a trade mark of Oxford University Press

Published in the United States
by Oxford University Press, New York

British Library Cataloguing in Publication Data
Hardy, Thomas 1840–1928
Thomas Hardy: selected letters.
1. Fiction in English. Hardy, Thomas, 1840–1928.
Correspondence, diaries etc.
I. Title II. Millgate, Michael 1929–
823'.8
ISBN 0–19–818546–4

Library of Congress Cataloging in Publication Data
Hardy, Thomas, 1840–1928
[Correspondence. Selections]
Thomas Hardy: selected letters / edited by Michael Millgate.
p. cm.
Includes index.
1. Hardy, Thomas, 1840–1928—Correspondence. 2. Authors,
English—19th century—Correspondence. 3. Authors, English—20th
century—Correspondence. I. Millgate, Michael. II. Title.
PR4753.A4 1990
823'.8—dc20
[B] 89–8698 CIP
ISBN 0–19–818546–4

Set by CentraCet, Cambridge
Printed and bound in
Great Britain by Bookcraft Ltd.
Midsomer Norton, Bath

CONTENTS

INTRODUCTION

THE standard image of Thomas Hardy fixes him at the end of his long double career as major novelist and major poet, full of years and honours, recognized around the world as the greatest of living writers. Then as now, his extraordinary reputation rested primarily upon the sheer range and magnitude of his achievement and the persistence of his creativity into extreme old age, but it also reflected, especially within Britain itself, an appreciation of the distance he had travelled in order to arrive at his final eminence. Not, to be sure, a distance to be counted in miles, for Max Gate, the house in which he died on 11 January 1928, lies within an hour's easy walk of the cottage in which he was born on 2 June 1840. But certainly—given the rural obscurity and near-poverty of that beginning in the earliest years of Victoria's reign—a distance of immense historical scope and social significance.

Partly because he grew up in a world still dominated by an essentially oral culture, partly because he did no travelling—apart from one childhood absence in his mother's company—until his departure for London at the age of twenty-one, no letters from Hardy's youth are known to survive. The earliest in this volume—it is also the earliest extant—is dated 17 August 1862, when he was already twenty-two. Nor are there many examples from the next dozen years, a period spent almost entirely as an assistant architect either in London or in Dorset, with only the last two years devoted fully to his newly—and adventurously—adopted career as a novelist. He had few male acquaintances other than his office colleagues, and evidently gave insufficient promise of future distinction to ensure the preservation of such letters as he did send. He must have written to his close friend and mentor Horace Moule, but Moule's personal papers failed to survive the irregularity of his life and the scandal of his death. Also missing—doubtless for perfectly ordinary, understandable reasons—are Hardy's letters to the young women to whom he was successively, if not very profoundly, attracted during the 1860s and 1870s. Hardy's future wife Emma Lavinia

Gifford certainly did value and keep the letters he wrote to her during the four years of their courtship, only to destroy them—together with her own replies—some forty years later, when their marriage had deteriorated into bitterness and anger.

Hardy clearly regretted the loss of those particular letters—claiming on one occasion that they had been comparable to the love-letters of Robert Browning and Elizabeth Barrett—and he kept all his life a tiny packet of letters and notes received from Horace Moule. But he would have felt only gratitude and relief at the disappearance of other documentary witnesses to the thoughts and emotions of his early years. Dedicated as he became to both the principle and practice of personal privacy, Hardy sought to ensure that nothing of even a mildly compromising nature remained among the incoming correspondence he left behind him at his death. He could not, of course, exercise any such control over the letters he had himself sent out into the world, but his desire for discretion seems in general to have been respected. Florence Henniker fortunately preserved a good many of the lively letters she received from Hardy over the years, but she also destroyed many others. Florence Dugdale, who became Hardy's second wife, was less comprehensively destructive than her predecessor had been; even so, only a few letters to her survive, providing tantalizing glimpses of Hardy in a relaxed, confiding, and reminiscent mood that is all too rarely displayed elsewhere.

Though much is taken, much none the less abides. For the years subsequent to the publication in 1874 of *Far from the Madding Crowd*, the novel which first made his reputation, Hardy's letters exist in substantial numbers, illuminating a far broader range of his friendships, preoccupations, and moods. With only a few correspondents does he come close to seeming a 'natural' letter-writer, unhesitatingly generous of time, space, and imaginative sympathy, and there is no indication that the constant interplay and potential intimacy of epistolary exchange provided him—who had, after all, worked in so many different literary forms—with an otherwise unavailable medium of self-realization. But he emerges as an attractive—if sometimes a disconcertingly 'ordinary'—figure from the letters included in this volume, revealing on numerous occasions what Edmund Gosse once called 'a gaiety not quite consistent in the most pessimistic of poets'. There is perhaps some narrowing of his interests as he proceeds towards and into extreme old age, and some lessening of spontaneity after his second marriage as he falls into the habit—for all except his most personal communications—of writing in pencil, and often in the third person, the letters that his wife would then type up. But even his very last letter, written on what proved to be his deathbed, betrays no diminution of intellectual control, no slackening of active engagement with literature or with life itself.

In determining the contents of this volume it proved impracticable to arrange them in terms of a comprehensive series of topical headings. With rare exceptions (such as his protests against being labelled a pessimist), Hardy does not engage in 'set-piece' disquisitions on general themes but tends rather to confront specific practical situations—usually of a professional nature—or to respond, often with exhaustive thoroughness, to the subjects raised and concerns expressed in the letter (particularly if from an old friend) to which he happens to be replying. There seemed no satisfactory alternative, in fact, to the straightforward chronological sequence here adopted, especially since it enabled the final choice of letters to be made from among the full range of those available. Because, however, it seemed reasonable to assume that Hardy's letters to editors and publishers would in general be found less rewarding than those to family and friends, his very extensive professional correspondence is represented here only to the extent necessary to keep constantly alive the sense of his life as being primarily and continuously one of work— of sheer literary labour on the one hand and, on the other, of unremitting attention to the business aspects of authorship and to the relentless daily influx of yet more letters.

The texts for all the letters in this selected edition have been taken from those established in the seven volumes of *The Collected Letters of Thomas Hardy*, edited by Richard L. Purdy and Michael Millgate, and published by the Clarendon Press between 1978 and 1988. As in that earlier edition, the layout

of the original documents has to some extent been standard-
ized. Addresses, dates, valedictions, and postscripts are
always placed in the same locations, wherever they may have
occurred in the actual letter. Addresses are set out on a single
line, with vertical rules showing where the line-breaks
occurred, and small capitals are used to distinguish those
which were engraved, printed, or die-stamped—when Hardy,
that is to say, did not write the address in his own hand but
used some form of 'headed' stationery. When the date of a
letter has been supplied in whole or in part from a source
other than the letter itself, the supplied portions are placed
within square brackets; when a date remains in doubt, it is
followed by a question-mark.

All texts are reproduced in full (though the documents on
which they are based may occasionally be incomplete) and
Hardy's wording, spelling, and punctuation are precisely
followed, except for the silent insertion of periods accidentally
omitted from the ends of sentences and the silent correction
of erroneous repetitions of the same word (as in 'it was was').
In this selected edition, four editorial and three typographical
errors in the *Collected Letters* have also been corrected, together
with a few Hardyan spelling and capitalization errors of a
trivial kind (varying by a single letter only); six commas have
been supplied within lists for the sake of clarity; and a single
two-letter fragment of text torn away from the original
document has been restored—all without editorial signals of
any kind. It has not seemed necessary, as a general rule, to
distinguish here among letters and postcards, or among typed
letters and those written in Hardy's own hand, but these and
other such details (including the sources of original documents) are available in the apparatus to the *Collected Letters*
and have been included in the notes to this present volume
whenever they seemed relevant to a full understanding of
individual letters.

Those notes have been placed immediately following the
letters to which they refer, primarily as a means of making
quickly and conveniently available to interested readers the
information necessary to an understanding of Hardy's crowd-
ing allusions—especially in letters to his sisters, his wives,
and his closest friends—to specific people, animals, places,

objects, and events. Hardy's correspondents are identified in the notes to the first letter addressed to them; earlier mentions are normally referred forward to that main identification, which is in any case clearly signalled as such in the volume index. Other persons are identified the first time they are mentioned; references back are not normally provided, but the main identification, again, is readily traceable through the index. The biographical aspects of the volume are further reinforced by a chronology of the main events of Hardy's life and by a series of brief intercalated commentaries that seek to place particular letters or, more usually, sequences of letters within the broader contexts of Hardy's life and literary career.

Although *Thomas Hardy: Selected Letters* bears my name as sole editor, it is of course heavily dependent upon the editorial work previously conducted in collaboration with Richard Little Purdy, and I am glad to have this opportunity of registering once more the magnitude of my personal and professional indebtedness to him. In preparing, revising, and checking the volume I have been greatly assisted by Christine Bacque, Kate Lawson and Lesley Mann and especially by Catharine Carver and Pamela Dalziel, both of whom took time from their own work to look with their customary—and exemplary—thoroughness at mine.

LIST OF LETTERS

CHRONOLOGY

1840   Born, eldest child of Thomas and Jemima (Hand) Hardy, at Higher Bockhampton, Dorset (2 June).

1856   Articled to John Hicks, Dorchester architect (11 July).

1862   Goes to London (17 April); soon employed in architectural office of Arthur Blomfield.

1867   Returns to Dorset because of ill health (20 July); again employed by Hicks.

1868   Completes final draft of 'The Poor Man and the Lady' (later destroyed) (9 June).

1869   Employed by Weymouth architect G. R. Crickmay (May).

1870   Goes to St Juliot, Cornwall, to inspect church; meets Emma Lavinia Gifford for the first time (7 March).

1871   *Desperate Remedies* pub. (3 vols.) by Tinsley Brothers (25 March).

1872   In London lodgings, working for the architect T. Roger Smith (March). *Under the Greenwood Tree* pub. (2 vols.) by Tinsley Brothers (June). First instalment of *A Pair of Blue Eyes* in September number of *Tinsleys' Magazine* (15 August).

1873   *A Pair of Blue Eyes* pub. (3 vols.) by Tinsley Brothers (late May). Suicide of Horace Moule at Cambridge (21 September). First instalment of *Far from the Madding Crowd* in the *Cornhill Magazine* (December).

1874   Marries Emma Lavinia Gifford at St Peter's Church, Paddington (17 September); honeymoon in France. Takes rooms at St David's Villa, Hook Road, Surbiton (6 October). *Far from the Madding Crowd* pub. (2 vols.) by Smith, Elder (23 November).

1875   Moves to 18 Newton Road, Westbourne Grove, London (22 March). Moves to West End Cottage, Swanage, Dorset (15 August).

1876   Moves to 7 Peter (or St Peter) Street, Yeovil, Somerset (early March). *The Hand of Ethelberta* pub. (2 vols.) by Smith, Elder (3 April). Moves to Riverside (or Rivercliff) Villa, Sturminster Newton, Dorset (3 July).

1878   Moves to 1 Arundel Terrace, Trinity Road, Upper Tooting (22 March). *The Return of the Native* pub. (3 vols.) by Smith, Elder (4 November).

1880   Beginning of serious illness (23 October). *The Trumpet-Major* pub. (3 vols.) by Smith, Elder (26 October).

1881   Moves to Lanherne, The Avenue, Wimborne, Dorset (25 June). *A Laodicean* pub. (3 vols.) by Sampson Low (early December).

1882   *Two on a Tower* pub. (3 vols.) by Sampson Low (late October).

1883   Moves to Shire-Hall Lane, Dorchester (June).

1885   Moves to Max Gate (designed by himself), just outside Dorchester (29 June).

1886   *The Mayor of Casterbridge* pub. (2 vols.) by Smith, Elder (10 May).

1887   *The Woodlanders* pub. (3 vols.) by Macmillan (15 March). Visits Italy (March–April).

1888   *Wessex Tales* pub. (2 vols.) by Macmillan (4 May).

1891   *A Group of Noble Dames* pub. by Osgood, McIlvaine (30 May). *Tess of the d'Urbervilles* pub. (3 vols.) by Osgood, McIlvaine (late November).

1892   Death of Thomas Hardy, sen. (20 July).

1893   Visits Dublin; first meeting with Florence Henniker (19 May).

1894   *Life's Little Ironies* pub. by Osgood, McIlvaine (22 February).

1895   First vol. of Wessex Novels edn. pub. by Osgood, McIlvaine (4 April). *Jude the Obscure* pub. by Osgood, McIlvaine (1 November).

1897   *The Well-Beloved* pub. by Osgood, McIlvaine (16 March).

1898   *Wessex Poems* pub. by Harper & Brothers (December).

1901   *Poems of the Past and the Present* pub. by Harper & Brothers (mid-November).

1904   *The Dynasts*, Part I, pub. by Macmillan (13 January). Death of Jemima Hardy (3 April).

1906   *The Dynasts*, Part II, pub. by Macmillan (9 February).

1908   *The Dynasts*, Part III, pub. by Macmillan (11 February).

1909   *Time's Laughingstocks* pub. by Macmillan (3 December).

1910   Receives the Order of Merit (June).

1912 First two vols. of Wessex Edition pub. by Macmillan (30 April). Death of Emma Lavinia Hardy (27 November).

1913 *A Changed Man and Other Tales* pub. by Macmillan (24 October).

1914 Marries Florence Emily Dugdale at St Andrew's Church, Enfield (10 February). *Satires of Circumstance* (including 'Poems of 1912–13') pub. by Macmillan (17 November).

1915 Death of Mary Hardy, the elder of his sisters (24 November).

1917 *Moments of Vision* pub. by Macmillan (30 November).

1922 *Late Lyrics and Earlier* pub. by Macmillan (23 May).

1923 *The Famous Tragedy of the Queen of Cornwall* pub. by Macmillan (15 November).

1925 *Human Shows, Far Phantasies, Songs, and Trifles* pub. by Macmillan (20 November).

1927 Address at Dorchester Grammar School stone-laying: last public appearance (21 July).

1928 Dies at Max Gate (11 January). *Winter Words* pub. by Macmillan (2 October). *The Early Life of Thomas Hardy* pub. under the name of Florence Emily Hardy (2 November).

1930 *The Later Years of Thomas Hardy* pub. under the name of Florence Emily Hardy (29 April).

THE LETTERS

[In April 1862, following the completion of his apprenticeship to the Dorchester architect John Hicks, Hardy left Dorset for London. He quickly found lodgings in the northern suburb of Kilburn and employment in the busy and cheerful office of Arthur Blomfield, a prominent church architect of the day, remaining there until ill-health forced him back to Dorset in summer 1867. His earliest surviving letters are those in which he describes to his beloved sister Mary, always closer to him than any other member of the family, something of his professional and personal life and of his early interest in literature.]

To Mary Hardy

Kilburn 17 Aug. [1862] | 9.p.m.

My dear Mary,

"After the fire a still small voice"—I just come from the evening service at St. Mary's Kilburn & this verse, which I always notice, was in the 1st Lesson.

This Ch: of St. Mary is rather to my taste and they sing most of the tunes in the Salisbury hymn book there.

H.M.M. was up, the week before last. We went to a Roman Catholic Chapel on the Thursday evening. It was a very impressive service. The Chapel was built by Pugin. Afterwards we took a cab to the Old Hummums, an hotel near Covent Garden where we had supper. He may come & settle permanently in London in a few months, but is not certain yet.

I have found Martha Sparks & went one evening to the Exhibition with her. She is now gone home for a short time.

Ellis was up last week. I had half a day at the Exhibition with him. He is now living at home, looking out for a situation. I do not think he will get into anything yet.

I have not been to a theatre since you were here. I generally run down to the Exhibition for an hour in the evening two or three times a week, after I come out I go to the reading room of the Kensington Museum—

It has been pouring with rain all the day and last night;
such a disappointment for thousands of Londoners, whose
only holiday is Sunday—

I should like to have a look at the old Cathedral &c in about
a month or so. The autumn seems the proper season for seeing
Salisbury. Do you ever go to St Thomas's? Be careful about
getting cold again, and do not go out in evenings—

P.S. is reading extracts from Ruskins "Modern Painters" to
me which accounts for the wretched composition of this
epistle, as I am obliged to make comments &c on what he
reads.

Ever yours,
T.H.

I did not put the coffee in the bottle. It was bought as you
saw it.

Hardy: Mary Hardy (1841–1915), TH's elder sister, currently attending the
teachers' training college in Salisbury.   this verse: 1 Kings 19: 12; it
always retained a special significance for TH.   H.M.M.: TH's close
friend Horatio [Horace] Mosley Moule (1832–73), fourth son of the Revd
Henry Moule (see letter of 11 Feb. 1880); his tragically unfulfilled career
ended in suicide.   Sparks . . . Ellis: Martha Mary Sparks (1834–1916),
TH's first cousin, working in London as a lady's maid; Ellis was a former
pupil of John Hicks, the Dorchester architect to whom TH had been
apprenticed. TH made several visits to the International Exhibition of
1862, held mainly on the site now occupied by the Natural History
Museum, and notable for its displays of art and architecture as well as of
manufactured products.   Kensington Museum: correctly the South Kensington Museum, now the Victoria and Albert.   St Thomas's: a Salisbury
church with a richly carved roof.   P.S.: probably P. Shaw, TH's fellow
lodger at 3 Clarence Place, Kilburn.

To Mary Hardy

8. St M's Pl. C+. | 3/11/62 | (written overnight) | (at
Kilburn)

My dear Mary,

I suppose you are very glad that Xmas is coming.

Do not send back the Sat. Revs but take care of them and

put them in your box, so that I may have them when I want
them—

I wish you wd tell me how u.r. when u. write. I have a
"cowdid by head" so I have stayed in all day to be all right
to morrow.

Last Friday night there was a *conversazione* (pronounced—
kon-ver-sat-zi-on-e) at the Architectural Association's rooms.
There were about 300, or 400 present, including your humble
servant. Mr Blomfield, one of the Committee, gave me a
ticket, and Mr Bunker, another committee man, another, wh.
I gave to Shaw and we went together. After lots of speechify-
ing from learned professors, there was music &c, and coffee—
this last rather in small quantities. Many ladies were there,
and of course in full dress, Shaw lent me a dress
coat as I did not possess one. My name was
proposed amongst many others, for becoming a
member,—this only means paying 10s/- a year.

Miss A. and Father went off all right as you know. Do you
ever write to Eliza? Father enjoyed himself thoroughly. I took
them to hear the Opera of *Lurline* at Covent Garden, but
nothing would satisfy Father unless he went to see the Thames
Tunnel. This, you know, is 5 or 6 miles from Kilburn, and
lies in one of the lowest and most crowded parts of London.
Accordingly, one morning he started off alone, agreeing to
meet Miss A. at the foot of the Monument on Tower hill at 1
oclock. She had been somewhere out eastward during the
morning about her situation. What is to be wondered at is the
fact that they actually did meet to a minute but as Father was
there a little too soon, he went to the top of the Monument
(200 feet). "Just to pass away the time". He said he shd not
have gone up only "he zid a lot of other voke guane up". Well
they went to the T.T. together and came home all right.

I expect to come home Xmas. for a little time. Frank Lock
is living in London, & is coming to see me. Perhaps Shaw
may come down with me for a day or two Xmas. It wd be
good fun, he is such a "coddle" and wd enjoy the outing. He
wd be considered a great gun too in our parish.

I am very economical of paper as u. may see.

Goodbye. Harry wrote yesterday.

T.H.

C+: Charing Cross.   *Sat. Revs*: copies of the *Saturday Review*, to which TH subscribed.   *Architectural Association's*: a recently established professional body, less prestigious than the Royal Institute of British Architects.   *Blomfield*: Arthur William Blomfield (1829–99), from whose architectural office at 8 St Martin's Place, next to St Martin-in-the-Fields, TH was writing; J. A. Bunker was a senior member of the firm.   *Miss A. . . . Eliza*: apparently Eliza Amey and her niece, also named Eliza Amey, of Dorchester; the latter had been a classmate of Mary Hardy's at Salisbury. *Father*: Thomas Hardy senior (1811–92) ran a small building business from the Higher Bockhampton cottage in which TH had been born.   *Lurline*: by William Vincent Wallace   *Frank Lock*: his father's farm, Higher Kingston, was—like Higher Bockhampton—in 'our parish' of Stinsford.   *Harry*: Henry Hardy, TH's younger brother; see letter of 18 Sept. 1874.

To Mary Hardy

Kilburn 19th Feb. [1863]

My dear Mary,

I dont fancy that 'tis so very long since I wrote and the Saturdays have been sent regularly but I really intended to write this week.

You see that we have moved, so for the future my address will be as on the other side. We have not recovered from the confusion yet, and our drawings and papers are nohow.

The new office is a capital place—It is on the first floor and on a terrace that overlooks the river. We can see from our windows right across the Thames, and on a clear day every bridge is visible. Everybody says that we have a beautiful place.

To day has been wretched. It was almost pitch dark in the middle of the day, and everything visible appeared of the colour of brown paper or pea-soup.

There is a great deal of preparation for the approaching wedding. The Princess is to arrive on the 7th March and the wedding will be on the 10th. On her landing at Gravesend she will be received by the Prince, the Mayor, Mayoress &c. They will then go by train to the Bricklayers' Arms station, and then in procession over London Bridge, along Fleet Street, Strand, C+, Pall Mall, Piccadilly, through Hyde Park and up the Edgware Road to Paddington Station—thence to Windsor. The windows along the route are full of notices that seats to view the procession are to be let. There will be an illumination the evening of the 10th.

I went to Richmond yesterday evening to see Lee. He is better, but is going to Kent for a short time before coming back to the office.

I have not heard anything about the Essay yet. The name of the successful competitor will be known in about a fortnight. I am now very busy getting up a design for a Country Mansion for which a small prize is offered—£3 the best & £2 the second best—It has to be sent in by the 27th March—

I am glad you have got a drawing prize, but you dont say what—I think you have done very well altogether. Tell me about the organ and how the Sundays go off—I am uncommonly interested. How is your friend the blind man &c School, clergyman &c. *Say how you are*, don't forget—I am quite well. Horace Moule has been ill. So has H.A. as I daresay you know. Has she written yet—I sent a Valentine to Harry and Kate to please them. Harry wrote me a letter, and Kate printed one and sent—rather a curiosity in its way.

I sent Mrs Rolls's photographs and she sent me a paper & letter. She says that Parsons is postmaster in place of Lock who has resigned.

I tried the Underground Railway one day—Everything is excellently arranged.

Do you think to run up Easter? If so, you must not mind being left alone all day—but you know your way about.

P.S. has commenced the sketch of our house for you. He says it will soon be finished.

Is Katie coming up to live with you & when is Mother coming?

Ever your affectionate
Tom—

the other side: TH wrote most of this letter on the back of an engraved notice of Blomfield's move from St Martin's Place to 8 Adelphi Terrace. *wedding*: of the Prince of Wales (later Edward VII) and Princess Alexandra of Denmark.   *Lee*: John T. Lee, another member of Blomfield's firm. *Essay . . . small prize*: TH was awarded the Silver Medal of the RIBA for his essay 'On the Application of Coloured Bricks and Terra Cotta to Modern

Architecture'; he was also successful in the country mansion competition, open to members of the Architectural Association.   *School*: the National School at Denchworth, near Wantage, Berkshire, at which Mary Hardy was now teaching; she was also expected to play the organ in the local church.   *H.A.*: perhaps Henrietta Adams, a friend of TH's mother and once in service with the same family at Stinsford House.   *Kate*: Katharine Hardy (see letter of 7 Aug. 1897), the younger of TH's sisters, still only a child at this date.   *Mrs Rolls's*: Ann Rolls was the wife of a Stinsford farmer.   *Underground Railway*: the Metropolitan Railway, operated by steam locomotives, had just opened.

To Mary Hardy

8 Adelphi Terrace | 19 Dec. 1863

My dear Mary/

I was beginning to think you had given up writing altogether, when your letter came. Certainly try to get as long a time as you can Christmas.

I am glad you have been to Oxford again. It must be a jolly place. I shall try to get down there some time or other. You have no right to say that you are not connected with art. Everybody is, to a certain extent; the only difference between a profesor and an amateur being that the former has the (often disagreeable) necessity of making it his means of earning bread and cheese—and thus often rendering what is a pleasure to other people a "bore" to himself.

About Thackeray. You must read something of his. He is considered to be the greatest novellist of the day—looking at novel writing of the highest kind as a perfect and truthful representation of actual life—which is no doubt the proper view to take. Hence, because his novels stand so high as works of Art or Truth, they often have anything but an elevating tendency, and on this account are particularly unfitted for young people—from their very truthfulness. People say that it is beyond Mr Thackeray to paint a perfect man or woman—a great fault if novels are intended to instruct, but just the opposite if they are to be considered merely as Pictures. *Vanity Fair* is considered one of his best.

I expect to go home about Tuesday or Wednesday after

Xmas & shall then find you there of course—We must have
a "bit of a lark"—

Ever affectly

Tom—

[*several words obliterated*]
I am able to write 40 words a minute. The average rate of a
speaker is from 100, to 120 and occasionally 140; so I have
much more to do yet.

to Oxford again: Denchworth is only some 15 miles from Oxford.   *profesor*:
so spelled by TH, who seems in any case to have meant 'professional'.
40 words a minute: TH was learning shorthand with a view to undertaking
some form of literary journalism.

To Mary Hardy

Saturday. Oct 28. [1865]

My dear Mary,
    I sent *Barchester Towers* by B.P., & you are probably by this
time acquainted with Eleanor Bold &c. This novel is considered the best of Trollope's.
    Yesterday Lord Palmerston was buried—the Prime Minis-
ter. I & the Lees got tickets through a friend of a friend of Mr
B's, & we went of course. Our tickets admitted to the
triforium, or monk's walk, of Westminster Abbey, & we got
from there a complete view of the ceremony. You will know
wh. part of the Abbey I mean if you think of Salisbury
Cathedral & of the row of small arches over the large arches,
wh throw open the space between the roof of the aisles & the
vaulting.

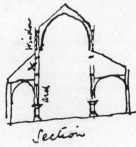

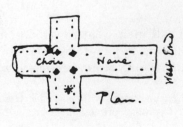

Where I have put the X in the section is where I stood; over the ✖ on the Plan. The mark ✤ shows where the grave is, between Pitt's & Fox's & close by Canning's. All the Cabinet ministers were there as pall bearers. The burial service was Purcell's. The opening sentences "I am the resurrection &c" were sung to Croft's music. Beethoven's Funeral March was played as they went from the choir to the vault, & the Dead March in Saul was played at the close. I think I was never so much impressed with a ceremony in my life before, & I wd not have missed it for anything. The Prince of Wales & Duke of Cambridge were present.

Ld John Russell, or Earl Russell as he is now, is to be Prime Minister in Pam's place. Only fancy, Ld P. has been connected with the govt off and on for the last 60 years, & that he was contemporaneous with Pitt, Fox, Sheridan, Burke &c. I mean to say his life overlapped theirs so to speak. I sent father a newspaper containing an account of his life, & to day one with an account of the funeral. As you are not a politician I didn't send you one, but since father has taken to reading newspapers these things interest him.

If you can get *Pelham*, read it when you next want something. Do not hurry over Barchester, for I have enough to do. I think Wells is the place intended. Will it be a good thing or will it be awkward for you if H.A. & I come down for Xmas day & the next? I am rather glad that hot close weather is gone & the bracing air come again. I think I told you I had joined the French class at King's College.

Ever sincerely

TH.

A tall man went to see Chang the Chinese Giant, & on his offering to pay, the doorkeeper said "Not at all Sir, we don't take money from the *profession!*" at least so *Punch* says.

B.P.: book post.   *Palmerston*: Henry John Temple, 3rd Lord Palmerston (1784–1865), prime minister 1855–65; the other political figures mentioned by TH are George Canning (1770–1827), William Pitt (1759–1806), Charles James Fox (1749–1806), Richard Brinsley Sheridan (1751–1816), Edward Burke (1729–97), and Lord John Russell, 1st Earl Russell (1792–1878).   *the Lees*: John Lee's brother was another of Blomfield's ('Mr B's') employees.   *Purcell's . . . Croft's*: the composers Henry Purcell (1658?–95) and William Croft (1677?–1727).   *Pelham*: the novel (1828) by Bulwer-Lytton (see letter of 15 July 1891).   *H.A.*: see letter of 19 Feb. 1863.   *so Punch says*: Chang, the subject of a pair of cartoons in the current issue of *Punch*, was 8 feet 2 inches tall.

[Ill-health forced Hardy back to his Higher Bockhampton home in the summer of 1867. He was still working as an architect, having abandoned as impracticable his long-cherished hopes of a university education (probably to be followed by ordination), but seeking simultaneously for some way of sustaining himself by his pen. He had written both poetry and prose during his years with Blomfield—publishing a humorous prose sketch, 'How I Built Myself a House', in *Chambers's Journal* in 1865—and upon his return to Dorset he began work on a novel, *The Poor Man and the Lady*, which if not quite 'socialistic', as he later claimed, was deeply hostile to the English class system. Introduced to the Macmillan publishing house by his friend Horace Moule, himself an aspiring though persistently failing man of letters, Hardy had the extraordinary experience, for an unknown writer, of having his first work read and criticized not only by Alexander Macmillan but also by John Morley and George Meredith. *The Poor Man and the Lady* remained unpublished, except in so far as sections of it were incorporated into later novels, but Hardy was sufficiently encouraged to proceed to the writing of *Desperate Remedies* (1871), *Under the Greenwood Tree* (1872), and *A Pair of Blue Eyes* (1873), his first significant success coming with Leslie Stephen's solicitation of *Far from the Madding Crowd* for serialization in 1873–4 in the prestigious pages of the *Cornhill Magazine*.]

To Alexander Macmillan

Bockhampton, | Dorchester, | July 25. 1868

Sir,

In writing the novel I wish to lay before you— "The Poor Man and the Lady" (sent by to-day's post) the following considerations had place.

That the upper classes of society have been induced to read, before any, books in which *they themselves* are painted by a comparative outsider.

That in works of such a kind, unmitigated utterances of strong feeling against the class to which these readers belong, may lead them to throw down a volume in disgust; whilst the very same feelings inserted edgewise so to say; half concealed beneath ambiguous expressions, or at any rate written as if they were not the chief aims of the book (even though they may be)—become the most attractive remarks of all.

That now a days, discussions on the questions of manners, rising in the world, &c (the main incidents of the novel) have grown to be particularly absorbing.

That as a rule no fiction will considerably interest readers poor or rich unless the passion of love forms a prominent feature in the thread of the story.

That novelty of *position* and *view* in relation to a known subject, is more taking among the readers of light literature than even absolute novelty of subject.

Hence the book took its shape, rightly or wrongly.

Mr Moule has very kindly written me a letter of introduction, which accompanies my own, and, I believe, sufficiently explains other points.

I am, Sir,

Your obedient servant
Thomas Hardy.

Macmillan: Alexander Macmillan (1818–96), co-founder with his brother Daniel of the Macmillan publishing house.

To Alexander Macmillan

Bockhampton | Dorchester | Sept 10. [1868]

Dear Sir,

I have become anxious to hear from you again. As the days go on, & you do not write, & my production begins to assume that small & unimportant shape everything one does assumes as the time & mood in which one did it recedes from the present I almost feel that I don't care what happens to the book, so long as something happens. The earlier fancy, that *Hamlet* without Hamlet would never do turns to a belief that it would be better than closing the house.

I wonder if your friend meant the building up of a story, & not English composition, when he said I must study composition. Since my letter, I have been hunting up matter for another tale, which would consist entirely of rural scenes & humble life; but I have not courage enough to go on with it till something comes of the first.

Faithfully yours
Thomas Hardy.

Would you mind suggesting the sort of story you think I could do best, or any literary work I should do well to go on upon?

your friend: John Morley (see letter of 20 Nov. 1885), the gist of whose reader's report on *The Poor Man and the Lady* Macmillan had conveyed to TH in a letter of 10 Aug.; TH asked his advice about his future career when they met in London early in 1869.

To Malcolm Macmillan

Bockhampton | Dorchester | Aug 17. 1871

Sir,

I have delayed my reply till I could send you perfect copies of the reviews which appeared—the extracts sent having been taken from notes I made in my pocketbook at the time. The novel was "Desperate Remedies"; & the MS. was submitted to you in the first place.

If you have time to read the reviews you will perceive that each takes for commendation a different element, & that they were therefore useless as guides to me for my second story. It seemed however that upon the whole a pastoral story would be the *safest* venture.

The article in the *Spectator* seemed strange enough to me— my object in the story having been *simply* to construct an intricate puzzle which nobody should guess till the end—& the characters were, to myself, mere puppets or pegs to weave the work upon—without reality or character enough in them to warrant their being denounced for want of moral attributes—the villain being in fact just about as human as the Giants slain by Jack, & capable of corrupting to the same degree. This the *Spectator* did not see—or would not, & produced an article which contradicts itself most noticeably. A novel which was good enough to justify two columns of lauded quotation could not possibly be so bad as to warrant opening remarks that are really little else than personalities. Still, being on the weaker side, I thought it just as well not to dabble in plot again at present, even though both *Athenæum* & *M. Post* thought the "power" lay there.

Yours faithfully
Thomas Hardy.

Macmillan: Malcolm Kingsley Macmillan (1853–89), eldest son of Alexander Macmillan, had written to acknowledge receipt of *Under the Greenwood Tree*, TH's 'second story', submitted ten days earlier.   *reviews*: *Desperate Remedies*, TH's first published novel, had been noticed by the *Spectator*, *Athenaeum*, and *Morning Post* in Apr. 1871.

To Geneviève Smith

Tuesday night [6 January 1874]

Dear Mrs Smith,

I send "Blue Eyes" which I beg you to keep till you have quite done with it. I shall be delighted if you or any of your household are impressed by anything the book contains as pleasantly as I was by your conversation last night. I cannot help thinking of your varied knowledge & experiences, which are of that precise kind that has a peculiar charm for all engaged in such pursuits as mine—& for myself doubly, from having been denied by circumstances until very lately the society of educated womankind, which teaches men what cannot be acquired from books, and is indeed the only antidote to that bearishness which one gets into who lives much alone.

Will you hand over the enclosed specimen of a proof to Mr B. S.?

Very sincerely yours
Thomas Hardy.

Smith: Emily Geneviève Smith, née Simpson (1816–77), wife of the Revd Reginald Southwell Smith, rector of West Stafford, a village just east of Dorchester; she sketched, spoke fluent French, and was an exceptionally accomplished singer.   *"Blue Eyes"*: *A Pair of Blue Eyes* (1873), TH's third published novel and the first to carry his name as author.   *Mr B. S.*: the Smiths' son Reginald Bosworth Smith (1839–1908), author and Harrow schoolmaster, one of TH's earliest and closest friends.

[In March 1870, when Hardy was working for a Dorset architect, he was asked to inspect a dilapidated church in the remote Cornish hamlet of St Juliot. There he met and was instantly attracted to the minister's sister-in-law, Emma Lavinia Gifford, daughter of a Plymouth solicitor. The romance survived a four-year engagement and the opposition of both families—class-conscious on the part of the Giffords, class-suspicious on the part of the Hardys—and Hardy and Emma were married in London in September 1874, shortly before the publication, in two volumes, of *Far from the Madding Crowd*. Hardy's literary and economic future now seemed secure, but his new standing was somewhat damaged by the relative failure of *The Hand of Ethelberta* (1876), his second novel for the *Cornhill*, and he did not immediately find an editor interested in serializing *The Return of the Native*.]

To Henry Hardy

Morton's Hotel | Queen's Road | Brighton | Friday.
[18 September 1874]

Dear Henry,

I write a line to tell you all at home that the wedding took place yesterday, & that we are got as far as this on our way to Normandy & Paris. There were only Emma & I, her uncle who married us, & her brother, my landlady's daughter signed the book as one witness.

I am going to Paris for materials for my next story. Shall return the beginning of October—& shall call at once at 4 Celbridge Place to see if there is any letter.

We sent an advertisement of the marriage to the Dorset Chronicle—Try to see it.

Yours in haste
Tom.

Thanks for your good wishes.

Hardy: Henry Hardy (1851–1928), TH's brother, who first assisted and then succeeded their father in the family building business. *uncle* . . . *brother*: the Revd Edwin Hamilton Gifford (1820–1905), later archdeacon of London, and Walter Edwin Gifford (1847–1904), minor civil servant; the landlady's daughter was Sarah Williams, of 4 Celbridge Place, Paddington. *next story*: *The Hand of Ethelberta*.

To Katharine S. MacQuoid

ST. DAVID'S: | HOOK ROAD: SURBITON. | November 17. 1874

My dear Madam,

I thank you very sincerely for your letter. The question whether women of ordinary types should or should not be depicted as the heroines of novels is such a nice one that it is difficult to discuss it in writing. I myself, I must confess, have no great liking for the perfect woman of fiction, but this may be for purely artistic reasons.

As regards the woman of real life, the whole gist of the

matter lies in what you summarize in the words "true & simple". The majority—or at any rate a respectable minor-ity—of women are quite worthy enough in nature to satisfy any reasonable being, but I venture to think that they too frequently do not exhibit that nature truly & simply—& thus the nature is condemned by their critics when the form of its manifestation only is in fault.

I had an idea that Bathsheba, with all her errors, was not devoid of honesty of this kind: it is however a point for readers to decide. I must add that no satire on the sex is intended in any case by the imperfections of my heroines, those qualities being merely portrayed in the regular course of an art which depends rather on picturesqueness than perfect symmetry for its effects.

I am much gratified to hear that my story has afforded you pleasure.

Very faithfully yours
Thomas Hardy.

Mrs Macquoid.

Macquoid: Katharine Sarah Macquoid (1824–1917), prolific novelist and travel writer. *St. David's*: the Hardys moved into lodgings at St David's Villa, Surbiton, in Oct. 1874, shortly after returning from their honeymoon, and continued to occupy furnished accommodation in London until July 1875.

To Leslie Stephen

18 Newton Road | Westbourne Grove | May 21 [1875]

My dear Mr Stephen,

I readily leave out the second title after your discovery of the effect it would be likely to have. My meaning was simply, as you know, that the story would concern the follies of life rather than the passions, & be told in something of a comedy form, all the people having weaknesses at which the superior lookers-on smile, instead of being ideal characters. I should certainly deplore being thought to have set up in the large joke line—the genteelest of genteel comedy being as far as ever I should think it safe to go at any time.

I shall have a little more MS. to send in a few days, & when you have looked it over I shall be glad to call & learn any improvement you may suggest.

Very truly yours
T. Hardy.

I have a good time for correcting the proofs of last portion just now. Probably I may expect them soon.

Stephen: Leslie Stephen (1832–1904), man of letters, philosopher, and editor of both the *Cornhill* and the *Dictionary of National Biography*.   *second title*: Stephen had objected to 'A Comedy in Chapters' as the subtitle of *The Hand of Ethelberta*, which began appearing in the *Cornhill* for July 1875.

To R. D. Blackmore

18 Newton Road | Westbourne Grove W. | June 8. 1875

Dear Mr Blackmore,

I have just read your finest book (as I think)—Lorna Doone, & I cannot help writing just one line to tell you how astonished I was to find what it contained—exquisite ways of describing things which are more after my own heart than the "presentations" of any other writer that I am acquainted with. It seems almost absurd that I had never read it before, considering the kind of work I attempted in Far from the Madding Crowd, & it has been a continual regret to me— since I have found out what the book contains—that I had not read it before meeting you. Little phases of nature which I thought nobody had noticed but myself were continually turning up in your book—for instance, the marking of a heap of sand into little pits by the droppings from trees was a fact I should unhesitatingly have declared unknown to any other novelist till now. A kindred sentiment between us in so many things is, I suppose, partly because we both spring from the West of England.

I congratulate you on the reception of your new book. I

always read far in the rear of the general public, & have therefore not got it yet. Believe me

Yours very truly
Thomas Hardy.

Blackmore: Richard Doddridge Blackmore (1825–1900), novelist; his *Lorna Doone: A Romance of Exmoor* was first published in 1869.   *new book*: *Alice Lorraine: A Tale of the South Downs* (1875).

To Evangeline Smith

Sturminster Newton | Dec 5. 1876

Dear Miss Smith,

I have read your charming little story with such a keen interest in its writer that my attempted position of frigid critic has been difficult to maintain. However, I will do my best to dismiss all thoughts of where it came from, & to estimate the work on its own merits, as you desire.

The story then, is one which would be called *promising* by experienced critics. The plot is well conceived, & well developed; but the writing itself shows want of practice in that department, which was probably the reason of its rejection by the editor you mentioned. The early pages show this particularly. I have ventured to make pencillings here and there on the MS. to draw your attention to doubtful portions, that you may reconsider them. The last two pages of Book No 1 consist of a digression which I should advise you to strike out: & the ill-feeling between Miss P. & the Lygon girls is scarcely veiled enough. Even Alice's repentance afterwards fails to remove this impression. On the other hand I have to congratulate you on your execution of the scene in the Church-porch on Midsummer night, which is really strongly written, & the best bit in the tale: Also, too, on the way in which you have managed to introduce the leading idea of the story, when it is nearly forgotten, by showing the refusal of the carthorses to pass the churchyard with Alice behind them. The weird reason of this comes into the mind in excellent contrast to the general happiness & sunlight of the hour.

Now you must not think it harsh of me to say what I am going to say—that if I were you I should rewrite the story from beginning to end, & condense it to about one half, or two-thirds, its present length. I do not absolutely advise you to do this, but were the story to turn up among my old manuscripts that is the treatment which would occur to me as best. As a literary exercise alone it is worth doing, even if you never attempt to print the story. It would be also a good thing if you were to write in a clear round hand in a first MS., though after you become known this does not matter so much.

With regard to the second MS. The story, or rather sketch, is a very fair specimen of light, farcical comedy. Should it be refused by an editor the reason will probably be the extreme slightness of the whole thing. There is some affectation in the expressions, which might be easily cured by excision. I cannot well express an opinion on the literary power or possibilities of the writer without knowing his or her age. There is a certain fluency in the wording which seems to show that the person is not altogether inexperienced in expressing him or herself: so that if it is the unassisted work of a writer under 25 he is to be praised. There is real humour in the characters, & the sketch altogether is amusing. As first attempts both this & the Midsummer eve story are far above the average.

Believe me to remain

Sincerely yours
Thomas Hardy.

═ MSS. returned by this same post.

Smith: Evangeline Frances Smith (1854–1945), sister of Reginald Bosworth Smith.   *Sturminster Newton*: the north Dorset village in which the Hardys rented a house from July 1876 to Mar. 1878.   *little story*: unpublished, although three novels by her subsequently appeared; the other manuscript was apparently by Evangeline's younger sister Blanche.

To John Blackwood

Sturminster Newton | Blandford, Dorset. | April 12. 1877

My dear Sir,

I have great pleasure in sending you the first 15 chapters of my new story—posted last night.

It occurred to me that it would be better thus to put the MS. into your hands, that you might look through it as far as written, than to attempt to give you an outline of the story by letter. Its length, as nearly as I can judge, will be about three times that of the portion sent—that is, it will contain matter enough for 10 or 12 parts in a magazine.

Should you think the story to be of a kind which will suit readers of your magazine I will give any further particulars. The only point at all conditional in my offer of the MS. to you as editor, would have reference to the time at which, in the event of your liking it, the first part could appear, my wish being, if possible, to get the book issued complete not later than 1st May 1878.

I will just add that, should there accidentally occur any word or reflection not in harmony with the general tone of the magazine, you would be quite at liberty to strike it out if you chose. I always mention this to my editors, as it simplifies matters. I do not, however, think you will meet with any such passage, as you will perceive that the story deals with a world almost isolated from civilization—moreover before beginning it I had resolved to write with a partial view to *Blackwood*.

I shall be greatly pleased if you think well of the story—partly from a personal wish to appear in your pages, & partly, as I before stated, that by changing into another periodical occasionally one acquires new readers for the book when it appears in volumes. Even should you not be disposed to accept it I trust you will not refrain from making any remarks upon it that you may think fit, in the shape of criticism—from which, I am sure, I shall profit.

Believe me, my dear Sir

Yours very faithfully
Thomas Hardy.

We go to London in May—but I suppose I shall hear from
you before then.

Blackwood: John Blackwood (1818–79), publisher of *Blackwood's Magazine*.
new story: *The Return of the Native*, eventually serialized in *Belgravia*.

To Arthur Hopkins

1 Bolingbroke Grove. | London S. W. | Feb. 8. 78

My dear Sir,

I am glad to receive a letter from you, for it is more
satisfactory when artist & author are in correspondence. I
liked your first drawing much: the third I have not yet seen,
but I daresay that it is a good one, from your description.
Strangely enough I myself thought that Thomasin in the
apple-loft would be the best illustration for the fourth number.
It is rather ungenerous to criticise; but since you invite me to
do so I will say that I think Eustacia should have been
represented as more youthful in face, supple in figure, &, in
general, with a little more roundness & softness than have
been given her.

My opinion, & I believe that of most novelists, is that the
writer & illustrator of a story can hardly ever be in thorough
accord unless they live in constant communication during its
progress, & in these days that is almost impossible. However
I trust some day to make your acquaintance, & obtain your
pardon for my remarks.

I leave town to-morrow morning for Salisbury, & return to
Sturminster Newton in about a week, where I shall be happy
to hear from you at any time.

Believe me

Very truly yours
Thomas Hardy.

Perhaps it is well for me to give you the following ideas of the
story as a guide—Thomasin, as you have divined, is the *good*
heroine, & she ultimately marries the reddleman, & lives
happily. Eustacia is the wayward & erring heroine—She

marries Yeobright, the son of Mrs Yeobright, is unhappy, &
dies. The order of importance of the characters is as follows.

1 Clym Yeobright
2 Eustacia
3 Thomasin & the reddleman
4 Wildeve
5 Mrs Yeobright.

Should you, at any time after choosing a subject for illustration, be in doubt about any of the accessories to the scene,
&c. I shall have great pleasure in sending a rough sketch,
done to the best of my power. I mention this because the
scenes are somewhat outlandish, & may be unduly troublesome to you.

Hopkins: Arthur Hopkins (1848–1930), artist, younger brother of Gerard
Manley Hopkins; he illustrated the serial version of *The Return of the Native*.
Bolingbroke Grove: temporary lodgings taken by the Hardys while looking for
a house in south-west London.

To Arthur Hopkins

STURMINSTER NEWTON, | BLANDFORD. | February 20. 1878

My dear Sir,
    I think you have chosen well for the May illustration—
certainly the incident after the mumming, with the mummers
looking on, will be better than the mumming performance
itself. Eustacia in boy's clothes, though pleasant enough to
the imagination, would perhaps be unsafe as a picture. The
sketch of a mummer's dress which I sent was merely intended
to show the general system on which they used to decorate
themselves: the surcoat or tunic was formed of a white
smockfrock rather shorter than usual, tied in round the waist
by a strap—this was almost invariably the groundwork of the
costume: thus.

original smockf^k.   *same tied'in*   *same decorated
                                                       with ribbon*

The figure in these sketches is however too short, except the
third. The helmet was made of pasteboard, & was much like
one of those articles called "tea-cosys" which people use now
a days for keeping the tea-pot warm, with a tuft
at the top. The sword was wood, of course, &

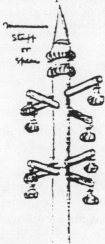

staff
rr
spear

the *staff*, which was never dispensed with,
consisted of a straight stick the size of a
broom handle, 5 or 6 feet long, with small
sticks inserted cross wise at the upper end:
from the end of these small sticks paper
tassels dangled. This was held erect in the
left hand while the sword was brandished
in the right. Father Christmas was a conventional figure—an old man with a hump-
back, & a great club.

    I should prefer to leave Clym's face
entirely to you. A thoughtful young man of
25 is all that can be shown, as the particulars of his appearance given in the story are
too minute to be represented in a small
drawing.

    A mummer or two in the picture would make it very
interesting—but do not be at all hampered by my suggestions
for I may attach an undue importance to the mummers.

Very truly yours
Thomas Hardy.

my suggestions: in fact adopted by Hopkins for his illustration to the May
1878 issue of *Belgravia*.

To Smith, Elder & Co.

1, ARUNDEL TERRACE, | TRINITY ROAD, UPPER TOOTING. S. W. |
                                          Oct 1. 1878

Dear Sirs,

I enclose for your inspection a Sketch of the supposed scene in which the "Return of the Native" is laid—copied from the one I used in writing the story—& my suggestion is that we place an engraving of it as frontispiece to the first volume. Unity of place is so seldom preserved in novels that a map of the scene of action is as a rule impracticable: but since the present story affords an opportunity of doing so I am of opinion that it would be a desirable novelty, likely to increase a reader's interest. I may add that a critic once remarked to me that nothing could give such reality to a tale as a map of this sort: & I myself have often felt the same thing.

The expense of the engraving would not, I imagine, be very great. In the drawing for the book it would be desirable to shade the hills more fully than I have done in the sketch.

Hoping that you will be disposed to give the suggestion a trial, I am, Dear Sirs

Yours faithfully
Thomas Hardy.

Smith, Elder: publishers of the Cornhill and of the three-volume first edition of The Return of the Native; TH's map, roughly corresponding to the heathlands near his birthplace, was used as he here suggests.

[During the early 1880s Hardy's reputation as a successful and productive novelist attracted a degree of public attention that was not always welcome, especially when it touched upon his social and educational background. Sensitive though he was about his provinciality, his lack of a university education, and the recentness of his ascent into the middle class, he also knew that his father's status as an independent master-mason or 'builder' had enabled him to receive the best education locally available, train as an architect, and meet the sons of

Henry Moule, the famous vicar of Fordington, on terms of some equality.]

To the Revd Handley Moule

SAVILE CLUB, | 15, SAVILE ROW. W. | Feb 11. 1880

Dear Mr Moule,

I have just been reading in a Dorset paper a report of your sermon on the death of the Revd H. Moule, & I cannot refrain from sending you a line to tell you how deeply it has affected me, & —what is more to the point—to express my sense of the singular power with which you have brought Mr Moule's life & innermost heart before all readers of that address.

You will, I am sure, believe me when I say that I have been frequently with you & your brothers in spirit during the last few days. Though not, topographically, a parishioner of your father's I virtually stood in that relation to him, & his house generally, during many years of my life, & I always feel precisely as if I had been one. I had many times resolved during the year or two before his death to try to attend a service in the old church in the old way, before he should be gone: But to-morrow, & to-morrow & to-morrow!—I never did.

A day or two ago Matthew Arnold talked a good deal about him to me: he was greatly struck with an imperfect description I gave him (from what I have heard my father say) of the state of Fordington 50 years ago, & its state after the vicar had brought his energies to bear upon the village for a few years. His words "energy is genius" express your father very happily.

Please give my kind remembrances to Mr Chas Moule & your other brothers who have not forgotten me—if they are with you—& believe me

Sincerely yours
Thomas Hardy.

Moule: the Revd Handley Carr Glyn Moule (1841–1920), fellow of Trinity College, Cambridge, became bishop of Durham in 1901. He was the youngest of the 'seven brethren', the sons of the Revd Henry Moule (1801–80), who was vicar of the Dorchester suburb of Fordington from 1829 until his death and became a national figure through his writings and inventions and his exertions during the cholera epidemics of 1849 and 1854. *Savile Club*: TH was elected to membership in June 1878.   *your other brothers*: though closest to Horace, whose suicide had occurred in 1873, TH knew all the Moule brothers well; Charles Walter Moule (1834–1921), later president of Corpus Christi College, Cambridge, was one of those with whom he kept most actively in touch.

To Charles Kegan Paul

Upper Tooting. April 18. 81

My dear Paul,

Owing to a misapprehension that the date of the British Quarterly was the 15th, like that of the other Quarterlies, I only sent for it last week; & then it was out of print for a day or two—so that I have but just now read your article.

Well, what can I say? If I have never yet written a good novel your essay should stimulate me to produce one without delay, & indeed will, in a measure: for nothing tends to draw out a writer's best work like the consciousness of a kindly feeling in his critics: & the worst work I have ever done has been written under the influence of stupidly adverse criticism—not just criticism of the adverse sort, which of course does good when deserved, as it often has been in my case.

What an exhaustive acquaintance with English fiction your article indirectly reveals in the writer. And when I remember that your reading in other literatures is proportionately wide I cannot help wondering how you can have found time in your life to do so many things. I have nothing to say against the few personal remarks you make, as I fancy you expected I should, though I have an opinion that the less people know of a writer's antecedents (till he is dead) the better. By the way I can tell you (privately) what you may be interested in knowing clearly—that my father is one of the last of the old "master-masons" left—anywhere in England, I should think—the modern "builders & contractors" having obliterated them. From time immemorial—I can speak from certain knowledge of four generations—my direct ancestors have all been master-masons, with a set of journeymen masons under them: though they have never risen above this level, they have *never* sunk below it—i.e. they have never been journeymen themselves. Whether they came from Jersey in the 14th century, like the other Dorset Hardys is uncertain—but probable, from the strong family likeness between all.

I go out now for about an hour a day—& am getting on nicely.

With kind regards to all

Believe me

Yours sincerely
Thomas Hardy.

Paul: the Revd Charles Kegan Paul (1828–1902), author and publisher, formerly vicar of Sturminster Marshall, Dorset; his article 'Mr. Hardy's Novels' appeared anonymously in the *British Quarterly Review*, Apr. 1881. *Upper Tooting*: the Hardys lived at 1 Arundel Terrace, Upper Tooting, from Mar. 1878 to June 1881. *getting on nicely*: as he recuperated from the serious illness that had begun in Oct. 1880.

[The Hardys moved several times during the early years of their marriage, torn between the attractions of living in Dorset, close to those regional materials upon which Hardy depended for his best and most characteristic work, and the practical advantages of living in or near London, the great centre of professional literary activity and influence. But the long illness which Hardy suffered while he and Emma were renting a house in Tooting in 1880–1 seemed to constitute final proof that he could not live in London and stay well, and in the summer of 1881 they made yet another move, to the east Dorset market town of Wimborne. Hardy continued to keep in touch with the London literary world, however—not least through his correspondence with his friend Edmund Gosse, one of that world's liveliest and most industrious representatives.]

To John Antell

The Avenue | Wimborne | June 29. [1881]

Dear John,

Your letter only reached me an hour ago, owing to our having come down here for the air, which is considered necessary to my complete restoration.

I am glad to hear that you have decided to have a square head to the stone, as that shape looks much better than an arched one, besides being more correct. Oak leaves would be quite appropriate for the corners, unless you can think of any other plant or tree that he liked or admired. He used to be fond of what grew on the heath, such as ferns, but they would be more difficult to carve than oak leaves—so I think you are right. Ivy also looks well.

The carving as shown in your sketch is too near the margin of the stone, to my eye. The leaves would be, I imagine, in a sunk spandrel, as I have roughly indicated on the other page—their surface being level with the general surface of the stone.

The character of the carving should be somewhat similar to that on the pier capitals from which the arches spring on the north side of the nave, inside church.

With kind regards to all—

Yours truly
T. Hardy.

Antell: John Antell (1848–1935), TH's first cousin; he spent all his life in Puddletown, Dorset, and had a local reputation as a poet.   *The Avenue*: where the Hardys rented a house from June 1881 to June 1883.   *the stone*: the tombstone of John Antell senior (1816–78), Puddletown shoemaker, TH's uncle and father of the addressee; he appears to have been one of the 'models' for Jude Fawley.   *inside church*: St Mary's, Puddletown.

To Alexandra Sutherland Orr

THE AVENUE, | WIMBORNE, DORSET. | December 14. 1881

Dear Mrs Orr,

I wish all my critics were as appreciative as you, & so well able to express their appreciation—though, as this seems rather a selfish wish, I may add that I regret not having you for a reviewer quite as much in thereby missing the opportunity of getting an instructive light upon my work as in losing a kindly notice. I am much pleased to find that you feel De Stancy *might* have proved a very satisfactory husband for Paula, & that poetic justice did not demand Somerset's success too exclusively. That much may be said on both sides is my continual feeling, on real situations as well as on ideal ones in life, & if the story exhibits this feeling I have thus far succeeded in it.

The architectural portion of the novel embodies, as you will have guessed, much of my own experience, which enabled me to write the story with, I think, less effort than others have cost me. If you should ever have time to look into the library form of the book you will find that some crudities in Paula's character &c. (which invariably occur in writing from month to month) have been smoothed out—I hope to her advantage.

I sincerely hope your little working power, as you modestly term it, is not to be suspended or interrupted in any way. Your critical writing seems to me to possess a quality singularly absent from the mass of such writings in these days— the quality of gracefulness—which when I first observed it quite charmed me. This being the case you must in common kindness write as much as you can, & develope your speciality still further.

Your kind inquiry about my health reminds me to tell you that it is quite re-established. The fact is I have lived too much in the country to bear transplanting to town, while curiously enough I seem to see more of London now than when we lived in the suburbs. I very frequently run up, &

enjoy those very commonplaces of town life which used to be a weariness.

With best wishes I am

Yours sincerely

Thomas Hardy.

Orr: Alexandra Sutherland Orr, née Leighton (1828–1903), biographer and critic, author of a long and positive article about TH's work published anonymously in the *New Quarterly Magazine*, Oct. 1879.   *the library form*: i.e. the three-volume first edition of TH's *A Laodicean*, published earlier that same month; the novel had previously been serialized in *Harper's New Monthly Magazine*.

To Edmund Gosse

Wimborne: Dorset | Dec 10. 1882

My dear Gosse,

Do by all means convey my best wishes to W. D. Howells when you are writing to him. I shall be glad to meet him on his return; & I think I shall be staying in town about that time, so there will be no difficulty. We propose to leave Wimborne for good about March: the house we are in lies rather too near the Stour level for health.

Yesterday in talking to the master of the Grammar School I asked him if any record were kept of scholars so long ago as 1820. No, he says, not a name. I told him that by such negligence the school had lost the chance of claiming as its own, at least by written proof, an eminent man, & possibly others. He says that every name now is registered, & regrets that it was not done before.

I get most extraordinary criticisms of T. on a T. Eminent critics write & tell me in private that it is the most original thing I have done—that the affair of the Bishop is a triumph in tragi-comedy, &c, &c, while other eminent critics (I wonder if they are the same) *print* the most cutting rebukes you can conceive—show me (to my amazement) that I am quite an immoral person: till I conclude that we are never

never again to be allowed to laugh & say with Launce—"it is
a wise father that knows his own child."

Sincerely yours
Thomas Hardy.

Gosse: Edmund William Gosse (1849–1928), poet and man of letters,
perhaps best remembered as the author of the autobiographical *Father and
Son* (1907).   *Howells*: William Dean Howells (1837–1920), the American
novelist; TH eventually met him in June 1883.   *eminent man*: Gosse had
written on 8 Dec. to say that his father, the zoologist Philip Henry Gosse
(1810–88), had gone to school in Wimborne 'circa 1820'.   *T. on a T.*:
Two on a Tower, published in three volumes in Oct. 1882; TH had sent
Gosse a copy on 4 Dec.   *Launce*: correctly, Launcelot Gobbo (*Merchant of
Venice*, ii.ii).

To George Manville Fenn

[1882?]

Dear Mr. Fenn,
   An accident has delayed for a day or two my reply to your
letter. Any episode from "A Pair of Blue Eyes" that you think
good enough for your purpose is at your service; the scene
you mention would, I should think, be as good as any. I
should tell you that the one volume edition contains the
finally revised text.
   I am so glad to perceive how successful your "Gleanings"
have been hitherto, particularly, I think, in the country,
where people take them, even if they possess the original
works—to save themselves the trouble of using their own
judgment, I suppose. The world gets indolent in its reading,
and there seems now to be quite a demand for trained minds
as pioneers.
   I was not aware till now that *The Echo* critique was yours,
and I take this late opportunity of expressing my sincere
thanks for it. Indeed, if any fault could be found with your
critiques at that time, it was that you were too kind.

Believe me, yours sincerely,
Thomas Hardy.

P.S. I hope you don't forget the birds in the whirl of your critical writings. I am expecting a big work from you some day embodying those tender essays on the humbler creatures that you seem to have a special gift for writing.

Fenn: George Manville Fenn (1831–1909), novelist and editor; the second volume of his *Gleanings from Popular Authors, Grave and Gay* (1883) includes an extract from the cliff episode in ch. 21 of *A Pair of Blue Eyes*. *The Echo critique*: perhaps the (anonymous) comment of 4 July 1873 on the final serial instalment of *A Pair of Blue Eyes*. *tender essays*: on 2 Sept. 1880 TH had written Fenn an appreciative letter about his 'Nightingale Notes' in the 24 July 1880 issue of the *Graphic*.

To Edmund Gosse

Wimborne 21 Jan. 83

My dear Gosse,

I wish the book had been up to the level of the criticism— I mean your letter of yesterday: indeed, I feel I have been adopting artful means to get valuable information—"wrinkles"—on the construction of romantic fictions.

You are too generous when you only see slightness in the work. The truth is that, though the plan of the story was carefully thought out, the actual writing was lamentably hurried—having been produced month by month, & the MS. dispatched to America, where it was printed without my seeing the proofs. It would have been rewritten for the book form if I had not played truant & gone off to Paris. The odd blunder about Viviettes name arose from her having been originally called Lady Viviette Constantine, daughter of an earl, & wife of *Mr* Constantine. But this of course is no excuse.

I remember no more of Crashaw's Love's Horoscope than that I have seen it. Crashaw's "Whoe'er she be" is more familiar to me. I'll hunt up the other, with a view to a motto for the next edition.

We are literally in an atmosphere of mud down here. Oh you should see Poole now.—But rather be thankful that you don't see Poole, if you have any respect for her.

We were discussing just now the curiously tonic effect (morally) of having to get up by candlelight on a dark morning early for some bustling mean utilitarian purpose. If you have not tried the plan do so the next time you feel in a nervous overdone state. I trust however, & believe, that you never reach any such unhappy condition.

With my warmest thanks for your kind letter, & my wifes best regards, I am

Ever yours sincerely
Thomas Hardy.

the book: *Two on a Tower* (see letter of 10 Dec. 1882), praised by Gosse in a letter of 18 Jan.   *Paris*: revisited by the Hardys during Oct. and early Nov. 1882.   *Viviettes name*: TH had been chastised by reviewers for carrying over his heroine's title from her first marriage (as the wife of Sir Blount Constantine) to her second (as the wife of Bishop Helmsdale); there is, however, no evidence in the manuscript that she was ever intended to be the daughter of an earl, hence permanently entitled to be addressed as 'Lady'.   *motto for the next edition*: TH did indeed introduce an epigraph from Richard Crashaw's poem 'Love's Horoscope' on to the title-page of the Sampson Low one-volume edition of *Two on a Tower*, published Apr. 1883.   *Poole*: where Gosse's father had lived as a child.

To Mary Christie

Wimborne. April 11. 1883

Dear Madam,

I have read with great interest the account of your scheme to encourage a feeling for art in National schools, & if my name be of any service in support of the general proposition I willingly consent to your using it.

As to the details of such a scheme, my views differ somewhat from your own. For instance I think that for children between 9 & 12 or 13—the great mass of those in elementary schools—fairly good engravings, such as those in the Graphic, Illustrated News &c (not the coloured pictures) to be as conducive to the end desired as good photographs or more finished pictures. A child's imagination is powerful, & only requires the idea to set it to work: & hence a dozen suggestions of scenes & persons by as many prints would seem to me to be of more value in the case than the perfect representation of one—while the latter would cost as much as the former. This however is altogether a secondary point, & I daresay that if we were to talk over the subject we should soon be quite at one about it.

With best wishes for your success in the project
I am, dear Madam

Yours truly
Thomas Hardy.

Christie: Mary Elizabeth Christie (1847–1906), author and active supporter of the Art for Schools Association, dedicated to supplying elementary schools with reproductions of good pictures.

To Havelock Ellis

Wimborne. April 29. 1883

My dear Sir,

I have read with great interest your article in the *Westminster*, & can inadequately express by letter my sense of your generous treatment of the subject. I consider the essay a remarkable paper in many ways, & can truly say that the writing itself, with its charm of style, & variety of allusion, occupied my mind when first reading it far more than the fact that my own unmethodical books were its subject-matter. If novelists were a little less in the dark about the appearance of their own works what productions they might bring forth, but they are much in the position of the man inside the hobby-horse at a Christmas masque, & have no consciousness of the absurdity of its trot, at times, in the spectators' eyes.

However, I cannot complain of any invidious remarks thereon in my case. The keen appreciativeness which the article discloses sets me thinking, as I mentioned above, of the writer: it is an appreciativeness which, having the novelists work as a skeleton to build upon, seems in many cases to create the beauties it fancies it perceives in that work. "The prosperity of a jest lies in the ear of him" &c.; & the truism is not a whit less forcible when applied to a novel.

As to certain conditions & peculiarities that you notice in the stories, I may mention that many are the result of temporary accidents connected with the time of their production, rather than of deliberate choice. By-the-by, I think that in speaking of men of the Wilhelm Meister & Daniel Deronda class as being my favourite heroes, you are only saying in another way that these men are the modern man—the type to which the great mass of educated modern men of ordinary capacity are assimilating more or less.

I hope to read some more of your critical writings in the future, & believe I shall discover them without a mark. Trusting that they may be frequent,

I am, my dear Sir

Yours very truly
Thomas Hardy.

Ellis: Henry Havelock Ellis (1859–1939), psychologist and critic; his article 'Thomas Hardy's Novels' appeared in the *Westminster Review* for Apr. 1883.   "*The prosperity . . . him*": *Love's Labour's Lost*, v.ii.861–2. *Meister . . . Deronda*: the central characters of Goethe's *Wilhelm Meisters Lehrjahre* and George Eliot's *Daniel Deronda*.

[Hardy had determined to build himself a house in the familiar surroundings of Dorchester once a suitable plot of land could be obtained, and between June 1883 and June 1885 he and Emma took temporary accommodation in the town until the new house, Max Gate, designed by himself and built by his father, was ready for occupation. His intense interest in Dorset life and history during this period found its main expression in the writing of *The Mayor of Casterbridge* (1886), but he also participated in the activities of such local groups as the Dorset Natural History and Antiquarian Field Club and published a mildly controversial essay on the condition of the Dorset agricultural worker. Although Hardy was a lifelong Liberal, even going so far as to appear on a party platform in Dorchester in the mid-1880s, he sought to avoid overt political engagement in his published writings, fearing that he would thus alienate himself from a portion of his potential audience.]

To Percy Bunting

Dorchester. Nov 5. 1883

My dear Sir,

Since my last letter to you I have been looking into the question of the labourer & his vote, & find it to be such a purely political subject that I must decline to attempt it— much as I appreciate your request for the article. I notice that other pens are already busy with the discussion—& it seems probable that the labourer will be rather a prominent figure in the public eye during the next twelve months or so.

You ask me if I am clear about the labourer's dread of being turned out of his house. There is no doubt that what weighs most heavily upon the *farm*labourer's mind is the general insecurity of his position: this oppresses him much more than the question of so many shillings a week; & the knowledge that his house is a mere tent for his use while working in the fields of any given farmer, is a great portion of this feeling of insecurity. It is obvious that there is no remedy for this growing dis-association with localities—this complete reversal of the old condition of things—but some system by which he could have a personal interest in a particular piece of land. Believe me, dear Sir,

Yours sincerely
Thomas Hardy.

Bunting: Percy William Bunting (1836–1911), social reformer and editor of the *Contemporary Review*, had approached TH for an article following the publication of 'The Dorsetshire Labourer' in *Longman's Magazine* for July 1883. Interested at first, TH seems to have become alarmed by current controversy over the Liberal party's announced intention to give agricultural workers the vote.

To an Unidentified Correspondent

[1883?]

Persevering Sir,

When I have a spare month or six weeks in which to write out the documents you require I will not fail to send them. The autographs are less formidable, & here follows one.

Thomas Hardy,
again—
Thomas Hardy.
again again!
Thomas Hardy.

Unidentified: TH was to be troubled by autograph-hunters for the rest of his life, and there is only minimal evidence for associating this speculatively dated letter with James Greig (d. 1941), art critic of the *Morning Post*.

[Although the triviality and even casualness of many of Hardy's letters to his wife may well be said to reflect the gradual deterioration of their marriage, those of the 1880s and 1890s seem suggestive rather of an easy companionability. It needs to be remembered that Hardy and Emma were rarely apart for more than a few days at a time, so that almost all of their letters would have been written in expectation of an early reunion. It was the Hardys' custom over a long period of years to rent a house or flat in London for two or three months of the spring and early summer (roughly corresponding to the London 'season'), and many of Hardy's letters home are devoted to his annual search for suitable accommodation; others pass on gossipy details that he thought Emma might be interested in—especially those pertaining to the literary and aristocratic circles in which he was now moving.]

To Emma Lavinia Hardy

Eggesford House | Wembworthy | N. Devon. |
Friday March 13. 85

My dearest Em,

I arrived at Eggesford Station a little after 4, & found there Ld P.'s brougham waiting to take me up to the house, so there was no trouble at all. The scenery here is lovely & the house very handsome—not an enormous one—but telling on account of its position, which is on a hill in the park. I have had tea with Lady P. & the ladies—the only members of the family at home—Lord P. not having returned from hunting yet (6 p.m.) The young ladies are very attentive, & interested in what I tell them. Lady P. charges them to take care of me—& goes away to her parish people &c—altogether a delightful household. There are ladies here too, visiting—but of course I have only had a glimpse as yet. They sympathize with you—& Lady P. says you *must* come when you are well. I am now in the library writing this. I shd say that a married daughter, Lady Rosamond Christie, I think she is, who is here, strikes me as a particularly sensible woman. If Lady P's orders are to be carried out my room will be like a furnace—she is so particularly anxious that I shd not take cold &c. The drawing room is lined with oak panels from a monastery. When I arrived the schoolchildren were practising singing in the hall, for Sunday in church. In haste (as you will believe)

Yours ever
Tom.

Hardy: Emma Lavinia Hardy (1840–1912), daughter of John Attersoll Gifford, a Plymouth solicitor.   *Eggesford House*: where TH was visiting Newton Wallop, 5th earl of Portsmouth (1825–91), his wife Eveline, and their numerous daughters—of whom Lady Rosamond, wife of Augustus Langham Christie, was the third.

To Emma Lavinia Hardy

29. Montague St. [16 May 1885]

My dear(est) Emmie,

I went to Lady Carnarvon's last night—& was very well received—indeed they all seemed more friendly than on the first occasion. I rather wish I had known the contents of her note, as she evidently wants the address we are staying or going to stay at—& I did not give it her. If I call Monday, & leave it pencilled on my cards will that be sufficient do you think—or ought I to see her in making such a call? The Portsmouth sisters were there—except Lady Camilla. You were much enquired for—Lady Dorothea, Lady Margaret, Lady Winifred Herbert, & Lady C. herself, all expressing sorrow that you could not come. Lady Portsmouth's daughters are at present staying at their aunt's—Lady P. comes to town to-day or Monday. There were more people—rather more—present than the other Friday, but more of a mixed kind—not quite so select. Among others there was Mrs Oliphant, to whom I was introduced. I don't care a bit for her—& you lose nothing by not knowing her. She is propriety & primness incarnate. Robert Browning was there—& Lady C's mother, to whom she introduced me. Also Mrs Jeune the irrepressible. She was very cool—I think because you have not called—& I could not get to tell her why. However a little delay will do her no harm. Nearly all the ladies were wearing the same dresses as before—Lady Winifred's divine blue looking decidedly crumpled about the neck—the stick-up ruff I mean—not so well as when we saw it in all its new glory. Lady Margaret was in black lace, with gloves between salmon & buff, & a dull red fan—& necklace of brilliants & black ornaments between—dress low—Both the sisters tell me in confidence that they feel shy of meeting so many people having been shut up in the country so long. Lady W. slaved away at the tea-pouring—complaining bitterly of the heaviness of the teapot—which was an enormous one. I forgot to include Murray Smith among those present—he was very warm.

I am going to ask Miss Stokoe today about a sitting room—
but whether we arrange or not will make no difference, as I
am in the bedroom you had—so that you can arrive at any
time. I should think Tuesday wd do. Will you bring the
flexible map of London. I have been confined all the morning
by a dreadful headache—owing to some soup—but it is going
off. Fitzgerald Molloy ("Court Life Below Stairs") met me in
the B. Museum reading room yesterday. He is an impulsive
rather interesting Irishman. Shall we ask him to call? This we
can settle when you come. I am going to write to Weston
now.

Yours affectionately ever
Tom.

—Will you caution the servants about turning on & off the
gas.
—Fill up form at the Post office for letters &c. To be sent on
here.

Lady Carnarvon's: Elisabeth Catharine Herbert, née Howard (d. 1929),
second wife of the 4th earl of Carnarvon.   *Portsmouth sisters*: the daughters
of the earl and countess of Portsmouth; Lady Carnarvon was their mother's
sister.   *Lady Dorothea, Lady Margaret, Lady Winifred Herbert*: daughters of
Lady Carnarvon; for Lady Winifred see letter of 3 Jan. 1886; for Lady
Margaret see letter of 24 Jan. 1891.   *Mrs Oliphant*: Margaret Oliphant
Wilson Oliphant (1828–97), novelist and critic.   *Robert Browning*: the
poet (1812–89), whom TH had first met about five years earlier.   *Lady
C's mother*: Charlotte Caroline Georgiana Howard.   *Mrs Jeune*: Mary
Jeune, wife of Francis Jeune; see letter of 24 Jan. 1891.   *Murray Smith*:
George Murray Smith, publisher, elder son of the George Smith who
founded the *Cornhill Magazine*.   *Miss Stokoe*: proprietor of the Montague
Street lodgings, near the British Museum, from which TH was writing.
Molloy: Joseph Fitzgerald Molloy (1858–1908), author of *Court Life Below
Stairs: or, London Under the First Georges*(1882) and its sequel *London Under the
Last Georges* (1883).   *Weston*: Montague C. Weston, a Dorchester solicitor.

[Hardy's mother had seen to it that he received a strongly
Anglican upbringing, and for many years he had looked
forward to ordination as a long-term goal. By the time that
scheme was abandoned in 1866, along with his hopes of a
university education, his religious commitment had already

suffered erosion, and he experienced over the succeeding years a gradual, undramatic loss of faith that still left him with a profound attachment to the language and ceremonies of the Church of England and a firm belief in its potential as an instrument for social harmony and moral instruction.]

To John Morley

MAX GATE, | NEAR DORCHESTER. | Nov. 20. 1885

Dear Mr Morley,

The articles & letters in the *Times* about disestablishment prompt me to address a line to you—whose speeches on that or any other subject have for me not only the attraction they must always exercise by their intellectual power, but (what delights me still more) that interest of personality by which the image of the speaker is beheld behind the printed words—

Is it not strange that the thinkers—the literary multitude—whose nature it is to cry aloud, are the dumb section of the population in the present discussions? And why is it that the religious wants of these & other thoughtful people who have ceased to believe in supernatural theology are ignored in the public press? The battle of establishment v. disestabt is there fought out as between the old fashioned nonconformist & the ordinary churchman; whilst of the growing masses of people who for conscientious reasons can enter neither church nor chapel (I speak of country places like this) nobody raises up his voice in the schemes for readjustment.

I have sometimes had a dream that the church, instead of being disendowed, could be made to modulate by degrees (say as the present incumbents die out) into an undogmatic, non-theological establishment for the promotion of that virtuous living on which all honest men are agreed—leaving to voluntary bodies the organization of whatever societies they may think best for teaching their various forms of doctrinal religion.

I was to have met you at Mr F. Harrisons one day last summer but much to my regret I could not be there.

Believe me

Ever sincerely yours
Thomas Hardy.

Best wishes in the coming campaign.

Morley: John Morley (1838–1923), later Viscount Morley of Blackburn, statesman and man of letters.   *Max Gate*: the Hardys had moved into their new house, just outside Dorchester, in late June 1885.   *disestablishment*: of the Church of England, a major issue in the general election then in progress.   *F. Harrisons*: Frederic Harrison, the positivist; see letter of 1 Jan. 1892.

To Lady Winifred Herbert

MAX GATE, | NEAR DORCHESTER. | Jan 3. 1886

Dear Lady Winifred Herbert,

You will recollect my promise to introduce "Winifred" as heroine of one of my novels. I am just beginning to write the story, but alas—according to my plot her destiny is a tragic one. Now it seems a cruel return for your friendship to associate your name with tragedy—& I confess that I have not the heart to do it unless you assure me that you would really like it to be done. So will you be so good as to let me know your commands: is my heroine with a sombre destiny to be Winifred, or shall I reserve that excellent name for some future heroine whose career may be of a brighter kind?

I have pleasure in sending Lady Carnarvon a copy of *The Graphic* containing the opening Chapters of "The Mayor of Casterbridge"—a portion of which I read to you from the MS. at Eggesford.

Yours sincerely
Thomas Hardy.

Herbert: Lady Winifred Anne Henrietta Christine Herbert (1864–1933), eldest daughter of Lord and Lady Carnarvon.   *heroine . . . the story*: *The Woodlanders*, whose heroine was eventually called Grace. TH never did use the name in his fiction.   *of Casterbridge"*: serialization had begun in the *Graphic* of 2 Jan.; for Eggesford see letter of 13 Mar. 1885.

[Hardy had friends and correspondents enough among his literary and artistic contemporaries, and he became a familiar presence in the rooms of the Savile Club and at gatherings of the Rabelais Club and other such convivial societies. But he had few relationships of any intimacy with intellectual or creative equals. Meredith was too much his senior, Henry James (whose work he greatly admired) perhaps too obviously his rival, and while his acquaintance with Robert Louis Stevenson remained undeveloped chiefly as a result of the latter's early departure from Britain in search of better health overseas, that with George Gissing foundered on an ultimate lack of either personal or professional sympathy.]

To Robert Louis Stevenson

SAVILE CLUB, | 107, PICCADILLY. W. | 7. 6. 86

My dear Stevenson,

I feel several inches taller at the idea of your thinking of dramatizing the *Mayor*, Yes, by all means. The story, to my surprise, has met with approval from competent critics. The *Saturday* has thrown cold water on it but then the *Saturday* man into whose hands my books are put has always been saying that my stories are dull. We are up here for a time, & are both so very glad to hear that you are better. Curiously enough your name was on my tongue a good many times last night, at the Rabelais dinner—Henry James sat next me on one side, & on the other Cotter Morrison & George Meredith. We were talking of your immense imaginative power—& wished you could have been there. O. Wendell Holmes was the guest. He is not quite used up yet, though I wonder how he stands so much. I have some writing to do whilst in town, & *can't* touch it: it is becoming quite a nightmare. I wish you would write something on the art of criticism. Meredith says somebody who has produced creative work ought to do it— so that the critics may get some rudimentary knowledge of the trade they profess. Believe me, with kind regards

Yours sincerely
Thomas Hardy.

Stevenson: the novelist and poet (1850–94), currently living at Bournemouth; he had called at Max Gate in late Aug. 1885 just before illness forced him to abandon an intended visit to Dartmoor (see letter of 20 May 1917). His proposed dramatization of *The Mayor of Casterbridge* never materialized. *Saturday man*: the anonymous reviewer in the *Saturday Review* of 29 May was probably George Saintsbury (1845–1933), then the assistant editor. *Rabelais dinner*: TH had been a member of the Rabelais Club, a dining club devoted to 'virility in literature', since its inception in 1879.   *Henry James*: the novelist (1843–1916).   *Cotter Morrison*: correctly, James Cotter Morison (1832–88), author and critic.   *George Meredith*: the novelist (1828–1909), whom TH had first met, as one of the readers of *The Poor Man and the Lady*, in 1869.   *Holmes*: Oliver Wendell Holmes (1809–94), the American essayist, poet, and physician, was in Britain to receive honorary degrees from the universities of Cambridge, Edinburgh, and Oxford.

To George Gissing

28 Upper Bedford Place | 1. 7. 86

My dear Sir,

I really feel as if I did not at all deserve the interesting present you have made me. But you may be assured that nobody could value it more than I shall do. As I am in Town only about three weeks longer, & that time will be full of interruptions to anything like quiet reading I probably shall not get through the books till after my return home.

Your working powers must be immense if you have—as you seem to have—written "Isabel Clarendon" since writing "Demos".

I am much afraid that one who has such a keen eye for good work as yourself will be disappointed at my story now running in *Macmillans*, "The Woodlanders". It would have made a beautiful story if I could have carried out my idea of it: but somehow I come so far short of my intention that I fear it will be quite otherwise—unless I pick up towards the end.

It is a great pleasure to me to find from what you say that you are bent upon high artistic aims, & not merely striving for circulating-library popularity.

We shall meet again, no doubt. If you are passing here any afternoon (except next Monday, Tuesday & Wedny) & will call on the chance of finding me in, please do.

Yours very truly
Thomas Hardy.

Gissing: George Robert Gissing (1857–1903), novelist; he had sent TH copies of his *The Unclassed* and *Isabel Clarendon*.   *Upper Bedford Place*: TH's lodgings near the British Museum.   *"Demos"*: in fact written after *Isabel Clarendon*, though published in the same year.

To Edmund Gosse

Max Gate: Tuesday [19 October 1886]

My dear Gosse,

I am glad you liked the account of Barnes: it was written quite as an afterthought, & at MacColl's request, when I had given up all idea of undertaking such a task. Of course I liked your graceful article. I was much struck with your remembrance of characteristic points in our old friend which I had seen but not heeded. I met the Bishop of this diocese (Wordsworth) a day or two ago—& he suggests "a runic cross" on the road near Barnes's as a fitting memorial, with lines on it from his poems.

I accidentally opened the Quarterly at the Museum yesterday and there I saw the article you speak of. Do not, my dear Gosse, let it interfere with your digestion or your sleep for a single day. It seemed terrible at first—but after a while it seemed quite different. Virtuous indignation has an unhappy tendency to appear ludicrous in print, and the writer of the article does not seem to know this. Never did a man show himself more wildly in a rage, & with you *personally*. The literary points in dispute between you & your assailant are quite ousted from the reader's mind by wondering conjectures as to what you have done in private life to offend him so! By the way, surely the great surgical operation is necessary for a critic who implies that a Lecturer must show neither fancy nor humour in his dedicatory lines.

But I do seriously think that the article is a strong argument against anonymous journalism. I have suffered terribly at times from reviews—pecuniarily, & still more mentally, & the crown of my bitterness has been my sense of unfairness in such impersonal means of attack, wh. conveys to an unthinking public the idea of an immense weight of opinion behind,

to which you can only oppose your own little solitary personality: when the truth is that there is only another little solitary
personality against yours all the time. I repeat *don't* take it to
heart—& believe me

Sincerely yours
Thomas Hardy.

Barnes: TH's obituary of his friend and neighbour the Revd William Barnes
(1801–86), philologist and dialect poet, appeared in the *Athenaeum*, edited
by Norman MacColl (1843–1904), on 16 Oct., the same day as Gosse's
tribute in the *Saturday Review*.   *(Wordsworth)*: John Wordsworth
(1843–1911), bishop of Salisbury 1885–1911.   *article you speak of*: 'English
Literature at the Universities', *Quarterly Review*, Oct. 1886, an unsigned
attack by John Churton Collins on Gosse's *From Shakespeare to Pope* (1885).

[The journey which Hardy made to Italy with Emma in the
spring of 1887 was by far the most important of his relatively
few foreign expeditions. He made a point while in Rome of
visiting the graves of Keats and Shelley, two of the poets he
most profoundly admired, and of sending his mother a post-
card (the only piece of correspondence between them that
seems to have survived) that stressed the specifically Christian
aspects of the city's history.]

To Edmund Gosse

Hôtel d'Allemagne | Via dei Condotti 18 | Rome.
[31 March 1887]

My dear Gosse,
   I am so glad to get a letter from you in return for my
miserable post-card: & still more that you like the story—
though I dread your opinion of the last volume. Little Hintock
has more of *Melbury Osmond* in it than of Minterne—the other
places you have spotted with perfect accuracy.
   We have been pottering on from city to city—& have now
been here about a week. I am so overpowered by the presence
of *decay* in Ancient Rome that I feel it like a nightmare in my
sleep. Modern Rome is full of building energy—but how any

community can go on building in the face of the "Vanitas vanitatum" reiterated by the ruins is quite marvellous. For my part if I were going to erect a mere shed I shd say Is it worth while?

From this you will gather that we are mostly confining our attention to the older section of the city. This morning we drove to the English Cemetery, to the graves of Keats & Shelley—I send you a violet or two which I gathered from Keats's—He is covered with violets in full bloom just now, & thousands of daisies stud the grass around. The whole place is indeed quite lovely at this time with the greenery of spring. Believe me

Always yours sincerely
Thomas Hardy.

Minterne: Gosse, reading the copy of *The Woodlanders* sent him by TH, had speculated in a letter of 22 Mar. that Little Hintock was based on the Dorset hamlet of Minterne Parva.   *violet or two*: these still accompany the original letter.

To Jemima Hardy

Hôtel d'Allemagne: Vià dei Condotti | Rome. |
April 1st [1887]

We have been here about a week, and intend to leave to-morrow. We went to-day along the Appian Way towards the Three Taverns, the road by which St Paul came into Rome, as described in the last Chapter of Acts.

T. H.

Hardy: Jemima Hardy, née Hand (1813–1904), TH's mother.

To Lord Lytton

5 Campden Hill Road | July 12. 1887

My dear Lord Lytton,

I can hardly tell you how highly I value your letter containing your impressions of The Woodlanders. Indeed, I have been so much struck with the picture that your imagination has raised of the scene of the story that it seems a new revelation, quite transcending my own imperfect view of sylvan life. It is not often one gets a reader who helps out a conception in this way by his own creative power.

The misfortune of novelists nowadays is that they seldom can learn the opinion of competent judges—still less imaginative ones—printed criticism of light literature being for the most part from the pens of beginners, any of whom are considered good enough to review a novel. I fear too that the same fate usually attends writers of verse: I hope your new volume may not suffer from any such cause.

It is somewhat singular—and if one believed in prevision more might be said—but nearly twenty years ago, or quite, before I knew that Owen Meredith was not a real name, I was much attracted by it, & by the peculiar vein of feeling in the verse, so different from anything I had ever read before. One might remark now that it was a grateful sense of favours to come in the shape of highly suggestive & stimulating criticism of my own work from the pen of that author.

I need not say how much pleasure I shall have in receiving your book, & the fact of its publication seems to imply, as I hope, that you mean to be faithful after all to the old "idle trade."

I should much like to see Knebworth & its surroundings, & I must express my warmest thanks for the opportunity of doing so that you offer me. But I fear I shall have to hold aloof from such temptations this autumn. I have done absolutely nothing since February, & for the remainder of the year I shall be compelled to retire to a cottage in the south of England where I do most of my writing.

I hope your journey will be a pleasant one. I leave town

myself in about a week, when my address will be Max Gate, Dorchester, till after Christmas. From what I have seen of Herts I am inclined to think that the woods there are of a grander type—at any rate the trees themselves—than those in the part of England in which my story is supposed to take place. But I find that in such matters—indeed in any matter—it is not absolute size but the attitude of the observer which makes things great or small. Believe me,

most sincerely yours
Thomas Hardy.

P.S. The poems have arrived since I began writing. Accept my renewed thanks.

Lytton: Edward Robert Bulwer-Lytton, 1st earl of Lytton (1831–91), Viceroy of India 1876–80, published poetry under the pseudonym of 'Owen Meredith'; his 'new volume' was *After Paradise: or, Legends of Exile, with Other Poems* (1887). *Knebworth*: Lytton's country seat in Hertfordshire.

To Edmund Gosse

MAX GATE, | NEAR DORCHESTER. | Aug 30. 1887

My dear Gosse,

I shall be very pleased indeed to hand on the subscription to the Barnes memorial: or your friend can send it direct to the Treasurers Messrs Williams & Co, Dorsetshire Bank Dorchester. You probably know that Mullins has been instructed to go on with the full sized model. The small sketch-model was considered a very good likeness by all the people here who knew Barnes. I wish I could have seen R. L. Stevenson: will he ever come back? I imagine, although you do not say so, that he was in the same high-spirited ardent mood we are accustomed to look upon as his natural state, irrespective of circumstances. As to despondency I have known the very depths of it—you would be quite shocked if I were to tell you how many weeks & months in byegone years I have gone to bed wishing never to see daylight again. This blackest state of mind was however several years ago—&

seldom recurs now. One day I was saying to myself "Why art thou so heavy, O my soul, & why art thou so disquieted within me?" I could not help answering "Because you eat that pastry after a long walk, & would not profit by experience". The stomach is no doubt a main cause, if there is no mental reason: but I totally disagree with those who insist upon blaming the stomach always. In my worst times years ago my digestion was as sound as a labourer's.

Devonshire in September is lovely. It is a county I have a weakness for at all times: but will you not get on to Dartmoor? That's the place to pick you up. But you *must* get a cottage like this one—on the chalk formation—& keep it on. If you demur to the expense remember you can get deal furniture—& it does just as well to knock about as a better kind, while if you shut up your house it does not injure.

My best respects to Teresa—& our kindest regards to Mrs Gosse. If you could show Mrs Gosse the cliffs near Boscastle, Cornwall, (which I attempted to describe in A Pair of Blue Eyes,) she would appreciate them I am sure. It would only be a little further on for you.

Sincerely yours
Thomas Hardy.

Mullins: Edwin Roscoe Mullins (1848–1907), sculptor; he was at work on the statue of William Barnes that now stands in front of St Peter's Church, Dorchester.   *Stevenson*: he never returned to Britain following the departure for New York described by Gosse in his 28 Aug. letter to TH. *"Why . . . within me?"*: a slight misquotation of Ps. 43: 5.   *Teresa*: Emily Teresa (Tessa), Gosse's elder daughter, just approaching her 10th birthday; for Gosse's wife see letter of 12 Dec. 1912.

To Edmund Gosse

Max Gate: Dorchester | 26. 10. 88.

My dear Gosse,
    The article has interested me much. How I wish that I had known your father, & that he had thought it worth while to jot down more. The only remarks that I have to make are unimportant:—

p. 5 "ducks off"—called "cobb on" in the interior of the
county.

p. 6. "Oak-apple day"—this is exotic—"sic-sac day", or
"shic-sac day" being what the peasantry call it.

„ 12. "Ich". This & kindred words—e.g.—"Ich woll", "er
woll", "er war", &c, are still used by old people in N.W.
Dorset & Somerset. (*vide* Grammer Oliver's conversation in
The Woodlanders which is an attempted reproduction.) I heard
"Ich" only last Sunday; but it is dying rapidly. I know nobody
under seventy who speaks so, & those above it use the form
only in impulsive moments when they forget themselves.

I return proof herewith—

Believe me, with kind regards

Yours sincerely
Thomas Hardy.

Thanks for the *Critic* cutting. I shd not have seen [*remainder
missing*]

The article: 'A Country Day-School Seventy Years Ago', an autobiographical
essay by Gosse's father (see letter of 10 Dec. 1882), who had died on 23
Aug. Gosse had asked TH for potentially publishable comments, and
slightly different versions of these remarks accompanied the essay's appearance in *Longman's Magazine*, Mar. 1889.   *only last Sunday*: probably from
one or other of his parents, whom he was accustomed to visit on Sundays.

[Sir George Douglas, Scottish landowner and miscellaneous
writer, first met Hardy in 1881 and remained thereafter one of
his staunchest admirers and correspondents. In responding
politely to his friend's undistinguished verses Hardy seems
also to glance at the survival, and prospective emergence, of
his own poetic ambitions. Of the three female correspondents
represented in the next group of letters, Mrs Linton was a
notable figure of an older generation, the American-born Mrs
Sheridan a greatly valued Dorset friend, and Mrs Tomson a
younger woman with literary pretensions for whom Hardy felt
at least a temporary sexual attraction.]

To Sir George Douglas

MAX GATE, | NEAR DORCHESTER. | 21 Dec 1888

My dear Sir George Douglas,

I have been looking into the poems—for which I thank you very sincerely—& have lighted upon some very happy lines: one couplet, for instance, strikes a genuinely pathetic note—that of the bird

> "Singing—uncared for and unheard—
> A song that's all too hard for me!"

Without venturing to express any opinion as to ultimate results I feel that verse is your more natural form of utterance. It sometimes occurs to me that it is better to fail in poetry than to succeed in prose. At any rate, more mental satisfaction is to be got out of verse—if you have not to cover so many pages a year, like some of us.

Poetry certainly has not had its day. You must remember that the Muses have occasionally to "draw back for a spring"—or, as they themselves would probably express it, *reculer pour mieux sauter*: & they may have been doing so lately.

Your contemplated title is an *excellent* one: it ought almost to sell the book. But of course I am imagining that the contents will, to some extent at least, bear out one's expectations as to the *nature* of the poems. The image it raises is that of a meditative man walking about his fields & hills, & writing down what is suggested by the natural objects before his eyes—their relations to mankind, & the like: a sort of Thomson's Seasons with the added force of all the modern spirit we have acquired since Thomson's day. But this looks like dictating—& it is only my fancy.

My wife sends her best Christmas wishes to you & your house—in which I unite.

Very truly yours
Thomas Hardy.

The short story I sent a day or two ago is for you to read at your leisure—if you care to.

Douglas: George Brisbane Douglas, 5th baronet (1856–1935); the poems
appear to have been those subsequently published in Douglas's *Poems of a
Country Gentleman* (1897).   *Thomson's Seasons*: *The Seasons* (1730) by the
poet James Thomson (1700–48).   *short story*: TH's 'A Tragedy of Two
Ambitions', *Universal Review*, Dec. 1888.

To Eliza Lynn Linton

MAX GATE, | NEAR DORCHESTER. | Dec. 24. 1888

Dear Mrs Lynn Linton,

It was a very great pleasure to me this morning to receive
your kindly letter, & I hope that now the ice has been broken
we shall be able to exchange an occasional word, if only on a
post-card. The little story I sent was not at all worthy of your
critical powers, but it was the only new thing I had written this
Christmas, & I particularly wanted to keep you in mind of my
existence, along with the rest of your friends, at this time. My
wife and I live in comparative solitude in our little house here
for six months of the year & more, & we sometimes think that
though we meet a good many people when we are away, we
secure very few real & permanent friends, people in London
having a habit of looking upon you as dead if you are outside
the 4 mile circle. I now know that there is one, at least, who will
not be of that way of thinking. If ever you come down into these
parts, & I hope you will do so some summer, I shall be able to
show you the exact spot—a green slope in a pasture—on which
I used to sit down & read your renowned articles in the S.R. In
my innocence I never suspected the sex of the writer. I always
thought that the essay which became most celebrated was not
quite so fine & incisive as some of the others that you wrote in
the series: but that's how things go in this world. I am just in
the worrying stage of coming to a decision upon my leading
idea of a long story planned sometime ago; & between my own
conviction of what is truest to life, & what editors & critics will
tolerate as being true to their conventional principles, bless
them! I get an unpleasant time, till the thing is settled. I wish I
could sometimes consult you!

Believe me, dear Mrs Lynn Linton,

Yours always sincerely
Thomas Hardy.

Linton: Eliza Lynn Linton, née Lynn (1822–98), novelist and woman of letters; in 1866–8 she published anonymously in the *Saturday Review* a series of controversial essays on the 'woman question', the best known, 'The Girl of the Period', appearing 14 Mar. 1868.   *little story*: 'A Tragedy of Two Ambitions'.   *long story*: *Tess of the d'Urbervilles*.

To John Addington Symonds

MAX GATE, | NEAR DORCHESTER. | April 14. 1889

Dear Mr Symonds,

I have often thought that I should like to write a line to you—silently doing your good & enduring work in the romantic place in which you live—so that your letter is a greater pleasure to me than you may imagine. Since receiving it I have spread out the map of Switzerland, the better to realize where you are, & it lies before me while I write.

Years before we met I used to read your essays (as correctives to those of M. Arnold, which are in need of the counterpoise that some of yours afford). Thus when I find that anything written by me has in any way met your views it is a great delight, for I get smart raps sometimes from critics who appear to think that to call me a pessimist & a pagan is to say all that is necessary for my condemnation.

The tragical conditions of life imperfectly denoted in The Return of the Native & some other stories of mine I am less & less able to keep out of my work. I often begin a story with the intention of making it brighter & gayer than usual; but the question of conscience soon comes in; & it does not seem right, even in novels, to wilfully belie one's own views. All comedy, is tragedy, if you only look deep enough into it. A question which used to trouble me was whether we ought to write sad stories, considering how much sadness there is in the world already. But of late I have come to the conclusion that, the first step towards cure of, or even relief from, any disease being to understand it, the study of tragedy in fiction may possibly here & there be the means of showing how to escape the worst forms of it, at least, in real life.

I, too, am in a sense exiled. I was obliged to leave Town

after a severe illness some years ago—& the spot on which I
live here is very lonely. However I think that, though one
does get a little rusty by living in remote places, one gains, on
the other hand, freedom from those temporary currents of
opinion by which town people are caught up & distracted out
of their true courses.

I half promised to send you a copy of The Woodlanders. It
is rather a failure towards the end. But I will do so if possible,
if you will accept it.

Believe me, with thanks for your kind letter

Sincerely yours
Thomas Hardy.

Symonds: John Addington Symonds (1840–93), poet and essayist; he was
currently living at Davos Platz, in the Swiss Alps, for the sake of his health,
and had written to TH on 9 Apr. to express his admiration for *The Return of
the Native*.

To Mary Sheridan

(20, Monmouth Road, Bayswater. W.) | 1. 6. 89
Dear Mrs Sheridan,

I am glad to get your note, with its discriminating remarks
upon the book—which are, indeed, a better review of it than
many that have been printed. This run upon theological
novels is quite extraordinary, when we consider that a few
years ago nobody would read them at all.

As to the pictures of the year, they are not very great, I am
sorry to say. Sargent's attract attention, especially his portrait
of Ellen Terry as Lady Macbeth. An exhibition of "impression" pictures by Claude Monet was very interesting—he
being the latest exponent of that school. In looking at them
you could almost feel the heat of the sun depicted in the
painting, & the dazzle of noon-day. Alma Tadema's picture
of the year is exhibited at a private gallery, & I have not yet
been to see it—though I saw it on the easel when it was about
half finished. A few days ago at his house I met a most
interesting man—M. Taine the French critic & historian.

Probably you know him. He told me that one of the first
English books he read was Spenser's "Fairy Queen"—every
word of it: & I was obliged to confess that, in common with
so many English, I had never read it quite through.

I have tried to get Sheridan's "How oft Louisa," as I said I
would do: but it has not yet come to hand—the music I
mean.

My wife sends her kind regards: we shall have much
pleasure in coming to see you when we are again in the
country.

Yours very sincerely
Thomas Hardy.

P.S. Mr Lowell arrived last Tuesday. Mrs Smalley tells me
that he has aged very much. Her husband has gone over to
Paris to help Mr Reed, the new American Minister; who was
ed. of the *Tribune*.

Sheridan: Mary Sheridan (d. 1918) was the daughter of John Lothrop
Motley, the American historian, and the wife of Algernon Thomas Brinsley
Sheridan (1845–1931), descendant of the dramatist, of Frampton Court,
near Dorchester.   *Monmouth Road*: the Hardys rented two floors at this
address for the spring and early summer of 1889.   *the book*: perhaps Mrs
Humphry Ward's *Robert Elsmere* (1888).   *pictures of the year*: at the Royal
Academy's Summer Exhibition.   *Sargent's*: John Singer Sargent
(1856–1925), American painter, whose portrait of Ellen Terry is now at the
National Portrait Gallery (on loan from the Tate Gallery).   *Monet*:
Claude Monet (1840–1926), French painter, twenty of whose pictures were
currently on exhibition at the Goupil Gallery.   *Tadema's*: Lawrence
Alma-Tadema (1836–1912), Dutch-born painter—and Edmund Gosse's
brother-in-law.   *Taine*: Hippolyte Taine (1828–93).   *Louisa'*: a song
from Richard Brinsley Sheridan's *The Duenna*; TH had been shocked to
discover that it was quite unknown to one of Mrs Sheridan's daughters.
Lowell . . . Smalley . . . Reed: James Russell Lowell (1819–91), American
poet and diplomat; Phoebe, wife of George Washburn Smalley (1833–1916),
chief European correspondent of the *New York Tribune*; Whitelaw Reid
(1837–1912), US minister to France 1889–92.

To Rosamund Tomson

Max Gate: Dorchester. | 6. 10. 89.

My dear Mrs Tomson,

We are greatly disappointed to learn that you are not able to include Dorset in your programme. We pictured some of our local scenery hanging on the walls of next year's Academy: & now it probably will have to wait for that honour; unless some enterprising painter should have come secretly this summer, & transfixed some of it. No: I cannot come to Sussex either: but then my conscience does not prick me in saying my negative as yours ought to prick you in saying yours; for, you see—I had never raised anybody's hopes. But I should much have liked to come, & please accept my warm thanks for your suggestion that I should do so. If I go anywhere between now & the year's end it will probably be to Town, on some business errand or other.

How good of you to send the newspaper cutting. I was so glad to see the Daily News leader on the Anthology. I thought you would be sure to meet with it, so did not send it on.

It rains a drizzle here today, so that we cannot see the hills—But the lovers walk two-&-two just the same, under umbrellas—or rather under one umbrella (which makes all the difference).

I see another poem of yours in Quilter's magazine—but I was just leaving the reading-room when I discovered it, so that I have not yet read it. The conversation you overheard was certainly very humorous. You must have fine opportunities at such an old-fashioned inn.

I am sorry to say that my mind is not occupied with any higher subject just now than how to paint or otherwise treat the gable of my house, to keep out a stain of damp inside.

Accept our kindest regards, & believe me,

Always yours sincerely
Thomas Hardy.

Tomson: Rosamund Tomson (1863–1911), poet and writer on art under the pseudonym of 'Graham R. Tomson'; her first marriage, with the painter Arthur Tomson, ended in divorce in 1896, her second was with the novelist

Henry Brereton Marriott Watson.   *Academy*: Arthur Tomson's paintings
of Dorset and Sussex landscapes were regularly exhibited at the Royal
Academy 1883–92).   *Anthology*: Mrs Tomson had presented TH with an
inscribed copy of her *Selections from the Greek Anthology* (1889).   *Quilter's
magazine*: Harry Quilter (1851–1907), art critic and editor of the *Universal
Review* 1888–90; the poem, 'The Story of Marpessa', appeared in the Sept.
1889 issue.

[Although fully engaged in his work as a novelist and short-
story writer, Hardy maintained an active interest in the
theatre and in his original profession of architecture. His
contempt for the artificiality of the theatre and the triteness of
much contemporary drama by no means rendered him
immune to that fascination with theatrical success experienced
by Henry James and other novelists of the day. He had co-
authored a dramatization of *Far from the Madding Crowd* in
1881 and was later to write his own stage versions of *Tess of
the d'Urbervilles* and the short story 'The Three Strangers'; in
the mean time, nothing came either of Stevenson's plan to
make a play out of *The Mayor of Casterbridge* or of the attempt
to find a producer for the dramatization of *The Woodlanders* by
C. W. Jarvis and his better-known colleague Jack T. Grein.
Throughout the period of his literary career Hardy had also
kept occasionally active as an architect, designing his own
house and giving practical assistance to the building business
run by his father and brother, and he was naturally drawn
both by this architectural background and by his concern for
the preservation of local artefacts, traditions, and associations
into the orbit of the Society for the Protection of Ancient
Buildings, founded by William Morris and others in 1877,
largely in outraged response to the destruction being visited
upon so many English churches in the name of 'restoration'.]

To C. W. Jarvis

MAX GATE, | DORCHESTER. | 31 March 1890

Dear Sir,
    I am much obliged for the copy of the Play, which I have
read with great interest & return by this post.

My suggestions are of a minor character—the general outline of the piece being as satisfactory as labour can make it, I think. Melbury's character comes out with unexpected strength.

The first questionable point which struck me was that the audience will hardly realize sufficiently, from the remarks of Creedle, &c. the scene of Fitzpiers letting Suke out of his house in the morning. The interest of the play up to the marriage depends so largely upon the suspense which the aforesaid revelation of Fitzpiers's character engenders, that the incident ought to be driven home at the outset. I don't see how this is to be done, except by dumb-show through a window—or by some unusual means, which, if not admirable in itself, would have some novelty as an opening.

Another point is with regard to the two letters received by Giles, in Act 4. I am rather strongly of opinion that one letter only would be more effective: departing from the details of the novel in this case, wh. are too complicated for the stage. Giles, thinking she will be free, makes love honestly. Then Melbury's "take away that arm" comes as a shock to characters as well as to audience. This love scene, being an emotional climax, might be made longer, & very warm, to add pathos to what follows.

The second Scene of Act 4 strikes one as coming too immediately after Scene I in time. But some days must really have elapsed (as we find later). There is, I suppose, some way of conveying the idea that time has elapsed—by a few words at the beginning of the Scene perhaps.

I do not at all dislike the ending. But could Melbury say finally:

"In two or three years, maybe, you'll bring yourself to live with him again."

These are the only criticisms of the play which occur to me on a first reading. I could correct the speeches of the servants &c here & there, later on, if necessary.

Believe me

Yours truly
Thomas Hardy.

the Play: a dramatization of The Woodlanders by C. W. Jarvis and Jack T. Grein, co-editors of the periodical Weekly Comedy and co-founders (in 1891) of the Independent Theatre; it was never performed.

To Thackeray Turner

MAX GATE, | DORCHESTER. | NOV 29. 1890.

Stratton Church: Dorset

Dear Sir,

I am sorry to learn that the Chancel arch & hagioscopes of this Church are not to be retained in the rebuilding.

They are Early English in style: & are most interesting & characteristic features.

On account of my protest against the obliteration of so much that lends character to the old church I was invited to attend a meeting of the Committee for the rebuilding: & I gathered from the tone of the meeting at its conclusion that my remarks had had the desired effect. As I thought the matter urgent, & as you had no official representative present, I took upon myself to say that I represented the Society—

The meeting was held on Nov. 8, & it seems strange that the Committee should have drifted back to their original views, particularly as I have good reason to believe that the Bishop of the diocese holds the same opinions on the case as the Society & myself.

The 3 points are:—

(1) The aforesaid retention of Chancel arch & hagioscopes (instead of a wide new arch)

(2) The refixing all the old windows in their present positions (the architect proposes to space them out regularly)

(3) The retention of present level of floor, eaves, roofs &c. (wh. the architect proposes to raise, so as to swamp the tower).

I should inform you that the walls are so far decayed that they must be taken down: but almost every stone could be put up again in its old place.

I believe that the architect is moved rather by the wishes of the committee than by his own judgment, & that he would willingly work with the Society in the matter if he could.

The chief subscriber is

The Hon Mrs Ashley
Stratton Manor
Dorchester.

& a line to her from the Society might I think, be of some effect, if it be couched in gentle terms. She does not wish to wilfully destroy anything; but has I think been badly advised.

Yours faithfully
Thomas Hardy.

Turner: Hugh Thackeray Turner (1853–1937), architect and secretary to the Society for the Protection of Ancient Buildings.   *Stratton Church*: the church, in a village just to the north-west of Dorchester, was to be demolished (apart from the tower) and then rebuilt, with the retention of some but by no means all of its original features.   *the Bishop*: John Wordsworth; see letter of 19 Oct. 1886.   *Mrs Ashley*: Jane Frances Ashley (d. 1893), widow of Henry Ashley, third son of the 6th earl of Shaftesbury; TH himself drafted a letter to her on behalf of the Society but it is not clear that it was ever sent.   *of some effect*: the destruction and rebuilding did, however, proceed as planned.

To Emma Lavinia Hardy

SAVILE CLUB, | 107, PICCADILLY. W. | Saturday ¼ to 5
[24 January 1891]

My dearest Em:

I telegraphed at lunch time to tell you I was not coming till Monday: & I hope you have received the message—otherwise you may be alarmed. This morning at breakfast Mrs & Mr J. both pressed me to stay over to-morrow. Irving & Ellen Terry are coming to dine with them to-morrow: & I felt I might as well stay on. I intend to return Monday, either by the 6.13, or an earlier one—probably however the first-mentioned. It rains in torrents here—& the difficulty of getting about without becoming damp is great. To-night is the first night of a comedy at the *Globe*—& I am going with the rest—or rather to meet them there, for I think of dining here.

I have been feeling anxious about your adventures—& wonder if it rained with you last night as it did here: if so it

must have been unpleasant getting to P. Edgcumbe's. I hope
your cold is better: the air is much softer now—so that
probably you have escaped a very bad cold. I called at Miss
Grylls's—the gown was sent off Wedny night—so I paid the
bill. She hopes to do more for you, & to have more time &
opportunity of getting your pattern—she seems anxious to go
on with you. I have seen the usual men here to-day. Gosse
has been attacked in last nights Pall Mall—as you may have
seen. Mrs J. seems to wish we lived in town. It was a great
pleasure to take the children last night—or rather to be taken
by them: Miss Maude Stanley also accompanied us—(the 2
girls, she & I altogether) & as she said, it is not always one
gets taken to theatres by such experienced playgoers—Their
eyes were so bright, & their whisperings incessant, in their
anxiety that we should not miss the points of the performance.
Mrs J. would have gone: but had to attend a Conservative
ball (quite a mixed affair) & cd not.

The rain still pours down—& I have to get back to
Wimpole St (first calling at a shirt-makers for an extra shirt if
I can)—I have declined to dine with them to-night—not
anticipating such weather.

If you have time to write a line to-morrow, will you mention
the number of the house Lady Margaret is going to in
Berkeley Square? (if she mentions it in her letter). Mrs J.
wants to know. Direct to 37 Wimpole St.

The J.s are leaving—yes—really—at Easter—& going into
Harley Street—exactly at the back of present house.

> Ever yours
> Tom

Mrs & Mr J.: TH was staying at the Wimpole Street house of Susan Mary
Elizabeth Jeune, née Stewart-Mackenzie (1845–1931), and her husband
Francis Henry Jeune (1843–1905), a distinguished lawyer and divorce court
judge who was knighted later in 1891 and created Baron St Helier shortly
before his death. Initially famous as a hostess—through whom TH met
such celebrities as the actors Henry Irving and Ellen Terry—Mary Jeune
also possessed a deep social conscience which she expressed through her
writings, her charitable work, and her later service on the London County
Council.   *a comedy*: it was called *All the Comforts of Home*; as TH reported
in his second paragraph, written the next morning, he went with Mary
Jeune's two children by her first marriage, Dorothy and Madeleine Stanley,
and with their father's sister Maude Stanley, daughter of the 2nd Lord

Stanley of Alderley.   *P. Edgcumbe's*: see letter of 23 Apr. 1891.   *Miss Grylls's*: a London dressmaker.   *Gosse . . . attacked*: by William Archer (*Pall Mall Gazette*, 23 Jan. 1891), for his translation of Ibsen's *Hedda Gabler*.   *Lady Margaret*: Lady Gwendolen Margaret Wallop (d. 1943), fifth daughter of the earl and countess of Portsmouth (see letter of 16 May 1885), was to marry Vernon James Watney on 3 Feb.

To Emma Lavinia Hardy

SAVILE CLUB, | 107, PICCADILLY. W. | Saturday.
[11 April 1891]

My dearest Em:

I have received your letter. Nothing has happened here, except that I have called on Osgood; the book is coming out about the first week in May. The weather is so bad here—a cold east wind, with now & then a drizzle, that I am glad you are not in town for your own sake, though not for mine, everything being so dull. A certain lack of energy I feel may be owing to my having hitherto kept to milk & water as a beverage in alternation to tea. I went to the Gaiety theatre last night—some of the burlesque was funny—some of it stupid. "The bogie man" which I went to hear, is not much. "That's how you mesmerize him", another song in the piece, is funnier. I have written two pages of MS. & shall recover energy no doubt next week. I am at the *annexe* of the hotel—a comfortable room—except that the street is noisy at night— all the single rooms are in front. I am going to try Mr Herriot's plan of wool in the ears to-night. I have slept however pretty well—& have had no dyspepsia at all. I lunched with Besant yesterday here; we met by accident. I should not go to the "At home", unless you wish to. Next week I shall look about more—& write again—

Ever your affecte husbd
Tom

Osgood: James Ripley Osgood (1836–92), American publisher, whose London-based firm Osgood, McIlvaine & Co. brought out *A Group of Noble Dames* 30 May 1891.   *Gaiety . . . burlesque*: the current production was *Carmen Up to Data*, featuring Florence St John.   *Mr Herriot's*: George

Herriot (d. 1910), land steward for the Duchy of Cornwall's western district; TH had dealt with him when purchasing the land for the building of Max Gate.   *Besant*: Walter Besant (1836–1901), novelist, man of letters, and founder of the Rabelais Club and the Incorporated Society of Authors.

To Robert Pearce Edgcumbe

SAVILE CLUB, | 107, PICCADILLY. W. | 23 April 1891

Dear Mr Pearce Edgcumbe:

From my previous note on my view of the latter Gladstonian policy you will have gathered my answer to your memorandum. It matters very little, however, for in Dorset my name would carry no political weight.

Moreover the pursuit of what people are pleased to call Art so as to win unbiassed attention to it as such, absolutely forbids political action. This may be unfortunate, but it is true. I therefore never take any, beyond occasionally recording a vote. Even that I should not do just at this time if the candidate were anybody in whose future I had less belief than I have in yours. Even your opponents must feel that hardly ever before has our county had a chance of returning a local man of intellectual rank equal to your own.

Believe me

Yours sincerely

Thomas Hardy

Edgcumbe: Robert Pearce Edgcumbe (1851–1929), banker, politician, and author, then living at Somerleigh Court, Dorchester, and contesting the South Dorset parliamentary constituency as a Gladstonian Liberal; he was narrowly defeated in the by-election held 7 May 1891.   *Gladstonian policy*: in a letter to Edgcumbe of 21 Apr. 1891 TH had confessed that on the central issue of home rule for Ireland 'I can hardly write myself as of either party'.

To H. Rider Haggard

12 Mandeville Place. W. | Monday. [May 1891?]

My dear Haggard:

I called at the Savile a day or two ago, & found Eric awaiting me there. Many thanks for your thoughtful kindness in sending me a copy. My wife, who is with me here, took it as soon as I got home, & has appropriated it ever since. I have, however, read the Introduction, & (I am ashamed to confess) a chapter nearer the end than the beginning—but this was the fault of the artist, not mine, (for I am most conscientious on such matters) in putting such a wild illustration. I shall presently begin & take it straight on.

Please give my kind regards to Mrs Haggard, & tell her how deeply our sympathy was with you both in your bereavement. Though, to be candid, I think the death of a child is never really to be regretted, when one reflects on what he has escaped.

It is miserably cold here still, & you are well to be away— as I believe you are.

Believe me

Yours sincerely
Thomas Hardy.

Haggard: Henry Rider Haggard (1856–1925), novelist. His introduction to *Eric Brighteyes* (1891) discusses the nature of Norse sagas and the way they are used in the novel; the Lancelot Speed illustration which caught TH's attention was probably that opposite p. 286, showing a huge sword impaled between a woman's naked breasts.　*Mandeville Place*: a rented flat near Manchester Square.　*your bereavement*: their son Rider (b. 1881) had died in Feb. 1891.

To Lord Lytton

12 Mandeville Place | W. | 15. 7. 91.

My dear Lord Lytton:

Of all the welcomes that have been accorded to the Noble Dames I value none more highly than that with which you

have honoured them; & when I consider the compeers in real
life that they must have encountered on their arrival at the
brilliant centre whither they were dispatched, & your memories of the same, I feel that considerable good nature must
have tempered your critical eye. I am truly glad however to
know that any pleasure has been given by what is, I fear,
rather a frivolous piece of work, which I took in hand in a
sort of desperation during a fit of low spirits—making use of
some legendary notes I had taken down from the lips of aged
people in a remote part of the country, where traditions of the
local families linger on, & are remembered by the yeomen &
peasantry long after they are forgotten by the families concerned. Some day I must tell you how much truth there is in
some of the tales, & the real names.

I have just been led to think that the true evidence of being
known as a writer is after all the sight of one's works scattered
about bookstalls in ridiculously cheap editions, e.g: I was
walking along that end of the Strand where the discount
booksellers have their shops, when I saw Owen Meredith's
poems in a popular series—nicely bound square little books
published at only a shilling. The numbers of people who buy
these books must be enormous, since the publishers say that
it is only the large sale which enables them to set such a low
price on volumes of so good an appearance. Among the poems
I found some I had not before known—I have often been
struck with the way in which the late Lord Lytton forestalled
recent ideas on this matter of cheapness: at a time when it
was almost risky to sell at a low price he was one of the few
who saw that there lay the secret of the future in wide literary
fame, & abolished prohibitiveness as between himself & the
mass of the thinking public—the poorer class of thinkers—by
consenting to paper covers at 2s/-. Had it not been for this I
for one should never as a boy have wept over his heroines—
living as I did live in a lonely place where borrowing was
impracticable.

The possibilities of the Marchioness of Stonehenge as a
play had not struck me, & I am glad to have your suggestion
on the point. I am outside theatrical life, except very occasionally; but if any opportunity offers of putting the suggestion
in practice I shall not fail to do so.

The air of the coast—if you get the right coast—is the surest restorer of vigour, & I hope that by this time it has not failed you in this respect. I went down to Aldborough, Suffolk, for only three days after influenza & general debility—& the effect was wonderful upon myself. I should like you to give it a trial some day: certainly no seaside place ever had such power in my case before.

But probably you are past all such considerations now, & robust as ever; I trust so.

Yours very truly
Thomas Hardy.

brilliant centre: Paris, where Lytton had been British ambassador since 1887.   *late Lord Lytton*: Lytton's father Edward George Earle Lytton Bulwer-Lytton, 1st Lord Lytton (1803–73), the novelist.   *Marchioness of Stonehenge*: one of the stories in *A Group of Noble Dames*.   *Aldborough*: correctly, Aldeburgh, where TH's friend Edward Clodd had a house; see letter of 20 Jan. 1892.

[The enormous success of *Tess of the d'Urbervilles*, first published in volume form late in 1891, made Hardy genuinely famous for the first time. Because the United States Congress had enacted a new copyright law earlier that same year Hardy was able to profit from the American as well as the British sales of the novel, and thus attain a level of economic security he had not previously known. *Tess* was harshly criticized in some quarters, however, and Hardy was deeply offended by attacks on the morality of a book which he had written with such a strong sense of social purpose.]

To H. W. Massingham

MAX GATE, | DORCHESTER. | 31 Dec. 1891

Dear Sir:

I am greatly obliged to you for sending me the copy of the D.C. containing your generous article on Tess. Owing to the Xmas holidays the usual outlook kept by my publishers, &

myself to some extent, for notices, was hindered, particularly for Dec 26.

For the article itself I thank you warmly. Ever since I began to write—certainly ever since I wrote "Two on a Tower" in 1881—I have felt that the doll of English fiction must be demolished, if England is to have a school of fiction at all: & I think great honour is due to the D: Chronicle for frankly recognizing that the development of a more virile type of novel is not incompatible with sound morality, & to you as one of the voices of that paper.

I take this opportunity of remarking that the lead given lately by the D.C. in making literature as important a topic for a newspaper as, say, the latest farce or burlesque, is a distinct advance in journalism.

Yours very truly
Thomas Hardy.

Massingham: Henry William Massingham (1860–1924), liberal journalist and editor; his *Daily Chronicle* review of *Tess of the d'Urbervilles* was in fact published 28 Dec. 1891.

To Frederic Harrison

MAX GATE, | DORCHESTER. | New Year's Day. | 1892.

Dear Mr Harrison:

I must just send a line to wish you & Mrs Harrison a happy new year, to thank you for your letter, & also for the really valuable New Calendar. What a mass of information!— moreover, though on the most controversial of subjects—the lives of men—given with (so far as I can discover) absolute impartiality. It is a terrible reminder of one's ignorance.

"Tess" has been fairly received so far, but the theological prints have not yet spoken. As to my choice of such a character after such a fall, it has been borne in upon my mind for many years that justice has never been done to such women in fiction. I do not know if the rule is general, but in this county the girls who have made the mistake of Tess almost invariably lead chaste lives thereafter, even under strong temptation.

In the first draft of the story I said much more on religion as apart from theology. But I thought it might do more harm than good, and omitted the arguments, merely retaining the conclusions.

Sincerely yours
Thomas Hardy.

Harrison: Frederic Harrison (1831–1923), positivist thinker and prolific writer on literary, historical, and social subjects; he had edited and partly written the *New Calendar of Great Men: Biographies of the 558 Worthies . . . in the Positivist Calendar of Auguste Comte* (1892). For Harrison's wife see letter of 13 Nov. 1913.

To Edward Clodd

MAX GATE, | DORCHESTER. | 20 Jan. 1892

My dear Clodd:

Your letter is full of excellent criticism of "Tess"—generous, yet incisive at the same time. What you say: "The motive—as a constant—is everything; the deed—as a passing accident—nothing," contains the whole gist of the story, & might stand as its motto, so well have you put it.

To think that *you*, of all people, can't see that "road" in the sentence beginning "The Durbeyfield waggon", is a misprint for "load". I read the proofs twice, & yet that "r" slipped in without my perceiving it—in order to afford that mean paper the S.R. an opportunity of attack. You will be surprised to hear (if you have not seen the review) that they alter my preface, omit the second title of the book, which is absolutely necessary to show its meaning, & indulge in innuendoes of indecent intentions on my part, which never entered my mind. Strangely enough however, the review has quickened the sale—I suppose the *animus* was too apparent. Besant will tell you what he thinks of the morality of that review, if you see him.

Should you meet with the club copy again, or any other

copy, would you be so kind as to delete the *r* & put an *l*? It occurs at p 198, Vol III. 3d line from bottom.

Well: what a couple of days we had down at Aldeburgh!— I shall never forget their bracing effect—mental & physical. When you come here our air & society shall do the same for you. I am going to build on a room to my little house, to be able to accommodate a friend or two.

An image of you as *the skipper*, (your best character on any stage) often rises before my eyes—& that of Barrie with his black nightcap, & Besant with a Rabelaisian gleam now and then.

My wife sends kind regards

Yours sincerely
Thomas Hardy.

I wonder if you think well of the City of London Electric Lighting Co. for an investment? It is recommended to me.

Clodd: Edward Clodd (1840–1930), banker, author, and leading rationalist; he often entertained his friends (including TH) at his house on the seafront at Aldeburgh, Suffolk, and was—as TH's reference to him as *'the skipper'* indicates—an enthusiastic yachtsman.   *S.R. ... attack*: the *Saturday Review* notice, 16 Jan. 1892, may again have been the work of George Saintsbury (see letter of 7 June 1886).   *Barrie ... & Besant*: James M. Barrie (see letter of 19 Dec. 1924) and Walter Besant had both been staying with Clodd at the time of TH's visit to Aldeburgh in June 1891.

To Edward Clodd

MAX GATE, | DORCHESTER. | Feb 4. 1892

My dear Clodd:

Lang's article on "Tess" in the New Review is, of course, Langy. If Andrew, with his knowledge & opportunities, had a heart instead of a hollow place where his heart ought to be, he would by this time have been among the immortals of letters instead of in the sorry position of gnawing his quill over my poor production. Or, if accident forced him to this business, he would have felt the smallness of stooping to pick

out the trivial accidents of a first edn of a book of 140,000
words, and have put his finger on the real and serious faults
of the story, which not one of these gentry has had the wit to
find out.

The only clear objection he makes to the novel is that it is
tragedy; and every word he says against it in this respect tells
with equal force against all the Greek tragic dramatists,
Shakespeare, and the Elizabethans. While his Christian (?)
objection (I suppose it is meant to be Christian) to the words
"President of the Immortals" &c., is evidently factitious—for
I distinctly state that the words are paraphrased from
Æschylus.

You will be glad to know that there is no check to the sale
of the book. Mudie keeps ordering more and more—and
others *pari passu*.

It is odd that nearly every adverse criticism is written by a
fellow-Savilian.

Yours sincerely
Thomas Hardy.

P.S. The supposed error in the baptismal rite is not really an
error. It happened, for one thing. Moreover the refusal to
bury is described as being the result of personal feeling in the
parson, owing to his exclusion from the house. T. H.

Lang's article: Andrew Lang (1844–1912), scholar and man of letters,
discussed *Tess* in his regular 'Literature and the Drama' section of the *New
Review*, Feb. 1892; on the final 'President of the Immortals' passage he had
commented, 'If there be a God, who can seriously think of Him as a
malicious fiend?'   *Mudie*: i.e. the great circulating library founded by
Charles Edward Mudie (1818–90).

To Mary Harrison

MAX GATE, | DORCHESTER. | March 18. 1892

Dear Mrs Harrison:

I find myself the possessor of a novel which I am now glad
I did not buy, though I have had its name on a list for a long
time. You are very generous to send it, & when "Tess" comes

out in one volume, which will be in the late summer, or autumn, I must ask you to let me send you a copy of her. I have read the first chapter of your book already & shall go straight on—without peeping—a trick I particularly detest. I know, of course, that the story is a tragedy.

I know what it is to write in illness. I once had to dictate a novel, or rather half of one, in a reclining position, with my feet higher than my head. But that was when I lived in London.

I have long seen what you say about a woman's disadvantages. And the worst of it is that even when, by accident, she does gain knowledge of matters usually sealed to her sex people will not believe that she knows at first hand. However, you have a counterpoise in other matters: there being many scenes in life—though not so many as in the other case—wherein the knowledge is to the woman only.

I sincerely hope you will feel vigorous again soon. Pain—that is our enemy. Believe me

> Yours very truly
> Thomas Hardy.

═Whenever you want to drive a bargain for a new novel I can recommend you to a man who will get you the best price possible. T.H.

Harrison: Mary St Leger Harrison (1852–1931), daughter of Charles Kingsley, wife of the Revd William Harrison; she had sent TH a copy of *The Wages of Sin* (1891), one of the novels she published under the pseudonym of 'Lucas Malet'.   *write in illness*: Mrs Harrison suffered badly from malarial fever; the novel TH dictated was *A Laodicean*, completed during his illness of 1880–1.   *a man*: the literary agent Alexander Pollock Watt (1834–1914), whom TH had himself employed on one or two occasions.

[Although he was widely read in nineteenth-century philosophy and social thought, Hardy can scarcely be said to have had either the background or the sophistication to justify the many discussions of him as a 'philosophical' writer. He certainly did not claim any philosophical consistency for his work, insisting instead that his ideas were essentially fragmentary, fleeting, and impressionistic, and fiercely rejecting the

popular assumption—and critical assertion—that he was a
systematic pessimist. The track of his reading and thinking
remains well worth following, however, leading as it does to
the centre of such works as *Jude the Obscure*, *The Dynasts*, and
some of the philosophical poems.]

To Roden Noel

MAX GATE, | DORCHESTER. | 3. 4. 92

Dear Mr Noel:

I returned from London last night, & was greeted by your
note. I had hoped to write to you while there on the subjects
opened up by your first letter: but as usual all my energy was
consumed in locomotion. So far from being bored by your
ideas as expressed in that letter I was deeply interested, &
they started me off on a mental journey into the infinite—
whatever that may be. I hope you will not mind my owning
to a mistrust of metaphysic. My shyness arises from my
consciousness of its paternity—that it is a sort of bastard,
begotten of science upon theology—or, in another form, a
halfway house between Deism & Materialism. It ultimately
comes to this—such & such things *may* be. But they will ever
be improbable: & since infinitely other things may also be,
with equal probability, why select any one bundle of supposi-
tions in preference to another? I prefer to relegate such
thoughts to the domain of fancy, & to recognize them as pure
imagination.

Still, there is a fascination in these labyrinths even when
regarded as philosophy.

As to one thing you say: if the body be only sensations *plus*
perceptions & concepts, then to hold that the ego may be
related to many more forms of corporeity than the one our
senses inform us of at present is a gratuitous assumption
without ground. You may call the whole human race a single
ego if you like; & in that view a man's consciousness may be
said to pervade the world; but nothing is gained. Each is, to
all knowledge, limited to his own frame. Or with Spinoza, &
the late W. K. Clifford, you may call all matter mind-stuff (a
very attractive idea this, to me) but you cannot find the link
(at least I can't) of one form of consciousness with another.

What you, & so many more, have called Pessimism, is, after all, to be regarded as such only in respect to a fancy-standard. Pessimism is used arbitrarily of such views, say, as mine: but it is really only a relative term. Suppose the conditions of existence on this earth to change to such a degree that normal life becomes pervaded by a sensation equivalent to what we now call pain, & the pains of that period to be what we now call tortures, our present pessimism will be optimism to those unhappy souls.

I too, believe in Byron—though less in what he says, than in what he struggles to say, yet cannot. He was a clumsy fellow—but I, for one, am always willing to meet him half way.

I am sorry you should have had trouble about placing the article. Most of the reviews have had their say—I forget if Scribner's has. But the American reviews & magazines are so difficult to get at. Believe me

Yours very truly
Thomas Hardy.

Noel: Roden Berkeley Wriothesley Noel (1834–94), poet, fourth son of the 1st earl of Gainsborough.   *Spinoza . . . Clifford*: Benedict (or Baruch) de Spinoza (1632–77), Dutch-born Jewish philosopher; William Kingdon Clifford (1845–79), mathematician and metaphysician.   *the article*: on *Tess*; see letter of 17 May 1892.

To Sir George Douglas

MAX GATE, | DORCHESTER. | 13. 4. 92

My dear Douglas:

Yes—your letter *did* reach me duly; there lies the guilt of your unhappy friend. As I was just starting for London I resolved to delay my answer till I got there, not quite thinking that I should be able to say Yes to your proposal, but having a glimmer of expectation that something might occur to modify the simple "can't," which I should have sent from here. I was intending to go on as far as Oxford, & I was not absolutely sure what I might do next. However last evening I was obliged to return here rather suddenly, giving up Oxford: so that really I kept back my answer for nothing, & much regret that I have to forego the pleasure of stepping northward.

The few days that I spent in town were pleasant enough. I met among many other people "Lucas Malet", Frederic Harrison, Ellen Terry, Lord Randolph, Miss Norris (ballet dancer), Arthur Balfour, &c. &c. For the due improvement of the mind I went with Mr Justice Jeune to hear Lottie Collins in "Ta-ra-ra-boom de-ay" at the Gaiety. It is really a very unusual performance, & not altogether so silly as people say. My companion was spotted by Fred Leslie (who sings a sort of patter song), & he put in (I think *extempore*) a verse about going to the Divorce Court, & the judge saying to him "You have beha-ved nob-ly!" The verse may possibly, however, have been in the original.

I hope your Burns does not drag. It struck me that you would coquet with the pen till you were caught. I should not be surprised if you were to become as perfect a hack as I am before you have done.

Our plans are uncertain just now, owing to my wife's continued weakness, but if she quite recovers her strength we shall go to Town, & hope to meet you there. With best regards to all,

Yours ever
Thomas Hardy.

your proposal: evidently an invitation to stay with Douglas in Scotland; see letter of 8 Oct. 1892.   *Lord Randolph* ... *Balfour*: Lord Randolph Churchill (1849–94), formerly chancellor of the exchequer, and Arthur James Balfour (1848–1930), prime minister 1902–5; Miss Norris has not been confidently identified.   *the Gaiety*: at which Lottie Collins (1866–1910), the music-hall performer, was currently making guest appearances in *Cinder-ellen Up Too Late*; Fred Leslie (1855–92), comic actor, was both co-author of the burlesque and one of its performers.   *your Burns*: *Love-Songs of Robert Burns*, selected and edited by Douglas, appeared later in 1892.

To Millicent Fawcett

Max Gate, | Dorchester. | April 14. 1892

Dear Mrs Fawcett:

I hope you will have guessed that the delay in my reply to your letter has arisen from my being away from home. I recollect quite well the pleasant meeting we had at Lady Portsmouth's—as does also my wife, who wishes to be kindly remembered to you. She has unfortunately been far from well lately, but I think she is now getting stronger.

I am much gratified to learn that so good a critic as yourself has found interest in Tess—a book which, like so many books, comes far short in its execution of what I had hoped beforehand to make it.

With regard to your idea of a short story showing how the trifling with the physical element in love leads to corruption: I do not see that much more can be done by fiction in that direction than has been done already. You may say the treatment hitherto has been vague & general only, which is quite true. Possibly on that account nobody has profited greatly by such works. To do the thing well there should be no mincing of matters, & all details should be clear & directly given. This I fear the British public would not stand just now; though, to be sure, we are educating it by degrees. The other day I read a story entitled "The Wages of Sin" by Lucas Malet, expecting to find something of the sort therein. But the wages are that the young man falls over a cliff, & the young woman dies of consumption—not very consequent, as I told the authoress.

I shall be in Town soon, & if you are likely to be at home any afternoon I will if possible give myself the pleasure of calling. Believe me

Yours sincerely
Thomas Hardy.

Fawcett: Millicent Garrett Fawcett (1847–1929), wife of Henry Fawcett, was a leader of the women's suffrage movement.   *Malet*: see letter of 18 Mar. 1892.

To Roden Noel

MAX GATE, | DORCHESTER. | 17. 5. 92

Dear Mr Noel:

I have just received your letter. The answer of the E.R.
editor is, of course, just what one would expect from such a
quarter. As if it mattered a straw whether I have, or have not,
put too liberal a construction on the word "pure". Reading
over the story after it was finished, the conviction was thrust
upon me, without any straining or wish for it on my own
part—rather, indeed, with some surprise—that the heroine
was essentially pure—purer than many a so-called unsullied
virgin: therefore I called her so. That was my impression of
her—nothing more. But the parochial British understanding
knocks itself against this word like a humblebee against a
wall, not seeing that "paradoxical morality" may have a very
great deal to say for itself, especially in a work of fiction.

Then the literalists who are willing to concede something,
say "She was not pure *at the end*." Well—even granting it, was
Mary Queen of Scots beautiful during the later years of her
life? But she is called the beautiful Q. of Scots. One might
easily argue on in this fashion, if it were worth while.

I may be in Town about the 26th but I am not sure. I will
certainly try to be: & will let you know if I am. As long as
there is any chance of your printing your review perhaps I
ought not to see it? However we can settle that when we meet.

Yours sincerely
Thomas Hardy.

the E.R. editor: Noel reported on 17 May 1892 that the editor of the *Edinburgh
Review* had not only declined his article on *Tess* but rejected the implications
of the novel's subtitle 'A pure woman'.

To Sir George Douglas

Max Gate | 8. 10. 92

My dear Douglas:

I am sorry to hear of the change you propose to make—&
should be still more sorry if I thought such necessities much
affected personal happiness. As you know, or guess, I have
passed through glooms such as I hope you will never see: & I
cannot say they were ever the result of material surroundings.
If you live in or near London there will be at any rate this
advantage for me—that you will be more readily accessible
than in Roxburghshire.

I was in London very little last season—owing to the illness
of my dear father—which ended in death last July. He had
been an invalid for many years, & was seen of nobody but
ourselves in the secluded spot near here in which he lived—
& was born, about 81 years ago.

I may be in London next week, if I get rid of the slight cold
from which I am now suffering. My wife sends her kind
regards.

Ever yours sincerely
Thomas Hardy.

in Roxburghshire: Douglas continued to live, however, at his estate, Spring-
wood Park, just outside Kelso.   *secluded spot*: Higher Bockhampton.

To Clement Shorter

MAX GATE, | DORCHESTER. | March 28. 1893

Dear Mr Shorter:

I have done the best I could do—& send it herewith. Good
measure, I think.

If you don't like the word "bastard" which I have used you
are kindly welcome to *dele* it.

Yours truly
Thomas Hardy.

Shorter: Clement King Shorter (1857–1926), journalist, editor at this date of the *Illustrated London News*; he retained the word 'bastard' when printing TH's story 'Master John Horseleigh, Knight' in the summer number, 1893.

[Visiting Dublin with Emma in May 1893 as the guest of the second Lord Houghton, the current Lord-Lieutenant of Ireland, Hardy met and fell in love with Lord Houghton's sister Florence Henniker, a 'charming, *intuitive* woman' married to a distinguished professional soldier. Florence Henniker had already published three novels, and Hardy hoped that by encouraging her literary ambitions—above all, by collaborating with her in the composition of a short story originally called 'Desire' but eventually published as 'The Spectre of the Real'—he might succeed in extending and deepening a relationship to which his commitment was always much greater than hers. Despite, or perhaps because of, Florence Henniker's coolness—originating, presumably, in the happiness of her marriage as well as in the conventionality of her opinions—Hardy wrote her some of the frankest and liveliest of his surviving letters, especially in the weeks and months immediately following their first meeting but also, at longer intervals, over the years that followed.]

To Florence Henniker

70 Hamilton Terrace | N.W. | June 3. 1893

My dear Mrs Henniker:

I am glad to get your note, as I was beginning to wonder if you would soon be here, and I much desire to go somewhere with you. I will see about Ibsen immediately, & let you know. I don't think the series is finished as yet.

I have already obtained the books—& should have sent them on to you, but that I want to ask you something first. I will accordingly keep them till we meet.

I have nothing to do next week from Monday till Thursday that is of any consequence. But I have a dreadful confession

to make. In a weak moment I have accepted an invitation to
lunch, to meet

John Oliver Hobbes!

She is very pretty, they say; but on my honour that had
nothing to do with it—purely literary reasons only.

My little scrap of a play has taken up so much of my time
this week—more than it is worth. It is to be produced to
night with 4 others—& I prophesy a *fiasco* for such a
heterogeneous collection. If there should be any kind of
success in the performance I will ask you to see it. I have
wished so much that you had been in Town these last few
days so that you might have accompanied me to a rehearsal
and given me your opinion.

Many thanks for the book and the letter, which fortunately
you had posted.

Believe me

Ever yours sincerely
Thomas Hardy.

Henniker: Florence Ellen Hungerford Henniker (1855–1923), daughter of
Richard Monckton Milnes, 1st Lord Houghton (1809–85), and wife of
Arthur Henry Henniker-Major (1855–1912), youngest son of the 4th Lord
Henniker.   *Ibsen*: see letter of 10 June 1893.   *the books*: apparently
copies of some of his own works.   *Hobbes*: the pseudonym of the novelist
Pearl Mary Teresa Craigie (1867–1906).   *scrap of a play*: *The Three
Wayfarers*, TH's dramatization of his story 'The Three Strangers', was being
produced as part of a quintuple bill at Terry's Theatre.

To Florence Henniker

ATHENAEUM CLUB | PALL MALL S.W. | Saturday.
[10 June 1893]

My dear Mrs Henniker:

Herewith the book, which I should have sent yesterday on
receipt of your note if there had been time. Will you please
first impress on your mind the elementary facts of date given
at pp. 19–20—(if you are not already familiar with them)
and after doing this you can go on to the characteristics of

each style. I am sure you will not be a slow scholar: the
danger with you lies rather the other way—if I may be
allowed to be so critical. Indeed I fancy you write your MSS.
a little too rapidly: though "Sir George", which I have just
finished, is a far more promising book than I guessed it was
going to be when I began it, and I should like ten minutes
conversation with you concerning it when you come to
London.

I may possibly run out of Town for a day or two Monday
or Tuesday next week, or merely for the day—but this is
uncertain.

I think "Merely Mary Ann" very good up to the point at
which she comes into the dollars. After that I don't care for
it.

I wonder if you like my little story in *Scribner*. I see in to-
day's papers that a lady-critic is going to drag me over the
coals in next month's *Century* for the way in which I spoilt
"Tess". She is an unmarried lady, and I shall be much
interested to see how she handles the subject.

The evening of yesterday I spent in what I fear you will
call a frivolous manner—indeed, during the time, my mind
reverted to our Ibsen experience; and I could not help being
regretfully struck by the contrast—although I honestly was
amused. Barrie had arranged to take us & Maarten Martens
to see B's play of "Walker London", and lunching yesterday
with the Milmans at the Tower we asked Miss Milman to be
of the party. Mr Toole heard we had come, and invited us
behind the scenes. We accordingly went, and sat with him in
his dressing-room, where he entertained us with hock and
champagne, he meanwhile in his paint, wig, & blazer, as he
had come off the stage, amusing us with the drollest of stories
about a visit he and a friend paid to the Tower some years
ago: how he amazed the custodian by entreating the loan of
the crown jewels for an amateur dramatic performance for a
charitable purpose, offering to deposit 30s/- as a guarantee
that he would return them—&c &c &c. We were rather late
home, as you may suppose.

Several lords spiritual are near me as I write this letter,
which I would rather be penning than one of their sermons. I
have, by the way, had a sermon sent me about Tess, of which

I will if possible get a copy for you. Forgive this disjointed epistle from

Ever yours sincerely
Thomas Hardy

P.S. I am afraid my chronicle is mere "frivel", or a great part of it: but having made a serious business of un-serious things I must follow on for the present, to redress by any possible means the one-sidedness I spoke of, of which I am still keenly conscious.

I sincerely hope to number you all my life among the most valued of my friends.

I rush back to Hamilton Tce where Miss Milman comes to tea—this afternoon—Miss Preston's (The old maids) article is out in the Century.

Athenaeum Club: to which TH had recently been elected.   *the book*: on architecture, which TH was urging Florence Henniker to study under his personal guidance.   "*Sir George*": a novel (1891) by Florence Henniker. "*Merely Mary Ann*": a novel (1893) by Israel Zangwill (see letter of 16 Nov. 1903).   *my little story*: 'The Fiddler of the Reels', *Scribner's Magazine*, May 1893.   *lady-critic*: Harriet W. Preston (1836–1911), whose 'Thomas Hardy' appeared in the *Century*, July 1893; she had visited TH at Max Gate in 1886.   *Ibsen experience*: TH and Florence Henniker had seen Ibsen's *The Master Builder* together a day or two earlier.   *Barrie . . . the scenes*: for J. M. Barrie see letter of 19 Dec. 1924; his play *Walker, London* was being performed at Toole's Theatre, with John Lawrence Toole (1830–1906) in the role of Jasper Phipps. Maarten Maartens was the pseudonym of the Dutch novelist Joost van der Poorten Schwartz (1858–1915); for the Milmans see letter of 17 July 1893.   *Hamilton Tce*: the Hardys had rented 70 Hamilton Terrace, in St John's Wood, for the London season.

To Florence Henniker

ATHENAEUM CLUB | PALL MALL S.W. | Thursday.
[29 June 1893]

My dear Mrs Henniker:

It is such a privilege to write to you that I avail myself of it at the earliest opportunity. Yesterday was very dreary—the most dreary and melancholy day I have known in London for

a long time—the rain having come at last—though only
fitfully. I sat down in the morning and tried to write a little—
then gave it up; & read your novel "Foiled". It is really a
clever book—quite above what I had been led to expect from
the reviews. I don't like some of the men in it—though they
are truly drawn: and speaking generally I may say that as a
transcript from human nature it ranks far above some novels
that have received much more praise: e.g. The Heavenly
Twins. If ever I were to consult any woman on a point in my
own novels I should let that woman be yourself—my belief in
your insight and your sympathies being strong, and
increasing.

I said I would chronicle my doings: and I must therefore in
honesty tell you that I *have* entered on my scheme—the plan
I spoke of—little pleasure as it has given me, as you will well
imagine. Whether I can keep it up is another matter, though
I have lunched today with a lot of people, dine at Lady
Shrewsbury's to-night, & lunch tomorrow at the Jeunes to
meet a party including Miss Ada Rehan—whom I really do
wish to meet—She is a genius, as you would have said if you
had been present Tuesday night. Her reception was tremendous. It is so provoking that you are not here; as Lady J.,
who was at the theatre, asked if you could also come to meet
Miss R.

After the theatre we went on to the Academy crush—
where, of course, we met a great many vain people we knew.
One amusing thing occurred to me. A well known woman in
society, who is one of those despicable creatures a flirt, said
to me when I was talking to her: "Don't look at me so!" I said,
"Why?—because you feel I can see *too much of you?*" (she was
excessively *décolletée*). "Good heavens!" said she. "I am not
coming to pieces, am I?" and clutching her bodice she was quite
overcome. When next I met her she said bitterly: "You have
spoilt my evening: and it was too cruel of you!" However I don't
think it was, for she deserved it. She was not H. B. by the way,
though one of that sort, and an acquaintance of hers.

Saturday night is the date of the Lord Mayor's dinner to
literature. I accepted in an inconsiderate moment; it is usually
a lively, dyspeptic entertainment: and I hear it will be very
crowded.

I wish so much you could see Miss Rehan as The Shrew, if you have not already. Could you fix any evening next week, for certain? I could get stalls if you will go—my reason for wishing you to see the play being purely an artistic one.

Yours very sincerely

T. H.

"Foiled": published earlier in 1893, as was *The Heavenly Twins*, by 'Sarah Grand', pseudonym of Mrs Frances Elizabeth MacFall (1862–1943). *Lady Shrewsbury's*: Theresa, dowager countess of Shrewsbury, widow of the 19th earl.   *Ada Rehan*: American actress (1860–1916); TH had seen her at the opening night of *The Taming of the Shrew* (and of Daly's Theatre) on 27 June.   *Lady J.*: Mary Jeune.   *Academy crush*: the Royal Academy's summer soirée.   *H. B.*: perhaps Lady Hilda Brodrick, daughter of the 10th earl of Wemyss and March, and wife of St John Brodrick, a prominent politician.

To Florence Henniker

MAX GATE, | DORCHESTER. | Sunday. July 16. 1893

It is so good of you, my dear Mrs Henniker, to send the book of ballads, that I must thank you at once. Also for the promised copy of Lord Houghton's poems, which I really covet as a gift from you. It lends such a continuity to one's life.

The notes I put to "Tess" cost me no trouble; and with a map of Dorset you might now trace her journeyings exactly, if you cared to.

As to my beginning to write again Heaven only knows when I shall do it.—I feel much more inclined to fly off to foreign scenes or plunge into wild dissipation. Next week in London may bring some change of mood. And though at Lady J's dinner I may be able to fill your place at table with some new female acquaintance she will certainly not remove my disappointment at your absence.

I will religiously obey orders about the architectural lessons. You shall hold the copyright in them. Is not that promise very handsome of me?

I too have been reading "Epipsychidion"—indeed by

mutual influence we must have been reading it simultaneously. I had a regret in reading it at thinking that one who is pre-eminently the child of the Shelleyean tradition— whom one would have expected to be an ardent disciple of his school and views—should have allowed herself to be enfeebled to a belief in ritualistic ecclesiasticism. My impression is that you do not know your own views. You feel the need of emotional expression of some sort, and being surrounded by the conventional society form of such expression you have mechanically adopted it. Is this the daughter of the man who went from Cambridge to Oxford on the now historic errand! Depend upon it there are other values for feeling than the ordinances of Mother Church—my Mother Church no less than yours.

I am writing too much as the mentor, and you may ask me for my licence. Well; forgive me, and I will follow Tennyson's advice in future, ("Leave thou thy sister . . .") and trust to imagination only for an enfranchised woman. I thought I had found one some years ago—(I told you of her)—and it is somewhat singular that she contributes some of the best pieces to the volume of *ballades* you send. Her desire, however, was to use your correspondent as a means of gratifying her vanity by exhibiting him as her admirer, the discovery of which promptly ended the friendship, with considerable disgust on his side.

Tell me if your cold is better.

Ever sincerely yours
T. H.

book of ballads: Florence Henniker had sent an inscribed copy of *Ballades and Rondeaus, Chants Royal, Sestinas, Villanelles, &c.*, ed. Gleeson White (1887); the two-volume edition (1876) of her father's poems, *The Poetical Works of (Richard Monckton Milnes) Lord Houghton*, followed two months later. *historic errand*: in Dec. 1829 Monckton Milnes, Arthur Hallam, and another speaker from Cambridge had argued in the Oxford Union that Shelley was superior to Byron as a poet.   *Tennyson's advice*: in section xxxiii of *In Memoriam*.   *I thought . . . years ago*: the reference is to Rosamund Tomson, twelve of whose poems appear in *Ballades and Rondeaus*.

To Lena Milman

MAX GATE, | DORCHESTER. | July 17. 1893

Dear Miss Milman:

I promised myself the pleasure of answering your letter on Spencer, &c. as soon as I could get into a quiet corner of the world, which I have at last done. I am glad to find that you are interested in "First Principles"—a book which acts, or used to act, upon me as a sort of patent expander when I had been particularly narrowed down by the events of life. Whether the theories are true or false, their effect upon the imagination is unquestionable, and I think beneficial. You will soon get hold of the phraseology, for which he has been ridiculed by some critics; the fact being that it is a style of writing from which he could hardly escape in handling such subjects.

I have been looking into Sir T. Browne's "Urn Burial"— which has a kindred effect upon one to Spencer—though different, too: the *coup d'œil* being limited to the human race gives the feeling of a clipped canvas after "First Principles"; but the literary rank of the work is immeasurably higher than Spencer's.

I shall be in London after Wednesday next for a few days, and will drop in on you for a cup of tea if I can one day. Have you any afternoon? I shall be staying at Lady Jeune's 79 Harley St., or The Athenaeum Club will always find me.

My wife sends kind remembrances, and I am

Yours always sincerely
Thomas Hardy.

Milman: Angelena (Lena) Frances Milman (d. 1914), daughter of Lieutenant-General George Bryan Milman, commander of the Tower of London; she was active in the 1890s as a translator and critic.   *"First Principles"*: Herbert Spencer's *A System of Synthetic Philosophy: First Principles*, originally published as *First Principles* (1862).

To Florence Henniker

MAX GATE, | NEAR DORCHESTER. | Saturday. Sept. 16. 1893

To day I send you, my dear Mrs Henniker, "The Woodlanders" & "Desperate Remedies"—which you thought worth having, though I hardly think so. You will be amused to read my first venture. Would that I could write all my books over again: I might make them worth reading.

I write this with ink from your pretty present; & I have already jotted down a few notes for the next long story— which I hope may be big as well as long.

Since you are nice, & a *little* candid in your last, I will be *quite* so, & tell you that I was a trifle chilled by your letters from Dublin & your first from Crewe, & much regretted having sent the effusive ones to which they were in answer, especially as you read parts of them aloud. Feeling that something was influencing you adversely, & destroying the charm of your letters & personality, I lost confidence in you somewhat. I know, of course, that there is nothing in my epistles which it matters in the least about all the world knowing, but I have always a feeling that such publicity destroys the pleasure of a friendly correspondence.

My wife has gone on horseback to a place miles away, near Weymouth, on the strength of my opinion that it would not rain. It has now come on heavily, & I fear she will get drenched to the skin.

Up-Cerne is only about a mile from "Cross in Hand" where D'urberville swore never to molest Tess again. This is the actual name of the spot, which is exactly as I describe it.

I thought you might know that Capt. Henniker & I had corresponded.

We are much exercised here about enlarging the house. We have hardly room to do anything as things are, although I have given up my original writing-room for a temporary little one. Yet we hate the idea of the discomfort that alterations will cause. (I have written this so stupidly that it seems as if we *were* altering, which of course we are not.) Yes: I *do* sigh a little; over your position less than over your conventional

views. I do not mind its results upon the present little story
(which please alter as you like)—but upon your future literary
career. If you mean to make the world listen to you, you must
say now what they will all be thinking & saying five & twenty
years hence: & if you do that you must offend your conventional friends. "Sarah Grand," who has not, to my mind, such
a sympathetic & intuitive knowledge of human nature as you,
has yet an immense advantage over you in this respect—in
the fact of having decided to offend her friends (so she told
me)—& now that they are all alienated she can write boldly,
& get listened to. "Fellow Townsmen" is one I thought rather
good myself; but it is a story to write *after* you have drawn
attention to your work, rather than to draw it with. But, my
dear friend, don't let this disturb you.

The photograph, if good, of course! As to my having
"contempt" as you suggest, for your rendering of the "Desire",
you know I *never* can have that for *anything* you do.

Always your friend
T. H.

your pretty present: a silver inkstand; it now stands on TH's desk in the
reconstructed study in the Dorset County Museum.   *next long story*: *Jude
the Obscure*.   *Henniker . . . corresponded*: the occasion of this correspondence
is not known, but TH later described Florence Henniker's husband as
'really a very good fellow'.   *"Fellow Townsmen"*: first published 1880,
collected in *Wessex Tales* (1888).   *the 'Desire'*: the working title of the
story, eventually published as 'The Spectre of the Real', on which TH and
Florence Henniker were collaborating.

To Florence Henniker

MAX GATE, | DORCHESTER. | Friday 6. 10. 93

How thoughtful & nice of you to give me these beautiful large
photographs!—which have come to me here. Many many
thanks. The one with the sweetest expression is, I think, that
with the bird-cage; but perhaps Chancellor's recall what is
best in your *nature*. I prize them all highly, though they
represent only the outward form of my most charming

friend!—which reminds me of Bacon's words: "The best part
of beauty is that which a picture cannot express."

I enclose with this a letter I wrote at Arlington, having
kept it back on the chance of your sending a more specific
address. Of the three you have given me I will select Lady
Ashburton's, I think—which perhaps you meant me to do?—
If not unavoidable, this vagueness is rather wicked of you! Or
perhaps you are so engrossed with millionaire sportsmen that
you take small thought of a mere scribbler who would not kill
a fly!

I did not at all *mean* my last note to be unkind, & am sorry
that it seemed so, & hurt you about the MS. The fact is that
letters have grown trollish again of late; therefore I propose
to drop the subjects we drifted into, which we can explain
when we meet. Never would I give *you* pain!

I have several things to ask you on our literary partnership,
but I cannot enter into them till a distinct postal communication is re-established between us—or, still better, a meeting
is feasible. I wish as much as ever to carry out the joint story.
It is unfortunate that just when this scheme rendered it
necessary for us to communicate freely & easily you shd have
rushed off to such outlandish latitudes: otherwise we should
almost have been in print by this time.

If I think of a still better story than The "Desire"—since I
cannot consult you on the arrangement of that—& put back
the Desire for the present, would you mind the trouble of
writing it out?

We had a delightful picnic to Savernake Forest from
Arlington—a party of about 10—Lady J. cooked the lunch-
eon at the picnic-house with the dexterity of a *chef*. One
evening she played & sang at least a dozen Scotch ballads to
me—so kindly—& will she says, at any time that I wish her
to. She thinks you may stay with her aunt for some time.—
Mrs C. being a R.C., & I being a Pagan, we were obliged to
go for a walk in the woods on Sunday when the others went
to church. Lewis Morris, who was also amongst the guests,
wrote off-hand a charming little poem to one of the girls.

There is a remark about Zola & myself in The World this
week, wh. perhaps you may have seen.

So far from my not forgiving you anything, & not feeling as

friendly as ever, I can say that if we are not to be the *thorough*
friends in future that we hitherto have been, life will have lost
a very very great attraction for one who is above all things

Ever sincerely yours

T. H.

Chancellor's: Chancellor was a professional photographer in Dublin; the
Bacon quotation is from his essay 'Of Beauty'.   *Arlington*: Arlington
Manor, near Newbury, the country house of Sir Francis and Lady Jeune.
Mrs C.: Pearl Craigie.   *Morris*: Lewis Morris (1833–1907), poet and
educationist; the 'girls' were Lady Jeune's daughters Dorothy and
Madeleine.   *Zola & myself*: the *World* of 4 Oct., noting TH's absence
from the Authors' Club dinner of 28 Sept. in honour of Émile Zola
(1840–1902), the French novelist, complained that he 'thus deprived his
fellow-writers of a fine opportunity of mentally comparing the author of
Tess with the author of *Nana*'.

To Florence Henniker

MAX GATE, | DORCHESTER. | Saturday. 28. 10. 93

You will say, "What, another letter so soon!" And perhaps
you may add "Yes—& so prosy too!" Our correspondence of
late might indeed almost have been cut from the pages of
"The Author" (which you ought to take in, by the way).

However, I must let you know that the story is finished
virtually, & that the MS. was sent early this morning to Miss
Tigan. I have told her to return me the original (in case I
should want to insert a little more detail from it) & to send to
you direct the type-written copy. Will you please read it from
the beginning (*without* glancing first at the end!) so as to get
the intended effect, & judge of its strength or weakness. It is,
as you wished, very tragic; a modified form of Ending II—
which I think better than any we have thought of before. If
anything in it is what you don't like please tell me quite
freely,—& it shall be modified. As I said last time, all the
wickedness (if it has any) will be laid on my unfortunate
head, while all the tender & proper parts will be attributed to
you. Without wishing to make you promise, I suggest that we
keep it a secret to our two selves which is my work & which

yours. We may be amusingly bothered by friends & others to confess.

In reading it over, particularly the bride's doings in the morning from dawn till the wedding-hour, please insert in pencil any details that I have omitted, & that would only be known to a woman. I may not be quite correct in what I have hastily written, never having had the pleasure of being a bride-elect myself. If you will then send me the copy I will go through it for final corrections, & send it off.

The ending, good or bad, has the merit of being in exact keeping with Lord P.'s character.

Yesterday's photograph was a charming little surprise: many thanks for your thoughtfulness, dear friend. It is the best, I think, of Lafayettes: & is very good as a specimen of his art. Now I suppose it will sound like heresy to say that the profile by Chancellor still *beats all of them* as yet. It has the quality of *charm* in the expression of the face, which Lafayette's have in a far less degree. It is a very mysterious thing that photographers should differ in this point. Chancellor is incomparably the truer *artist*, to my mind. He lets you take a more natural pose, too. When you are in Dublin again *please* have another by Chancellor. If you do decide to put the portrait at the beginning of the volume take my advice & have the profile one—(the first you sent me.) Perhaps you won't however, since you won't adopt the "Milnes" as part of your literary name. If you *don't* have the Chancellor profile the one you now send is next best: the features are sculpturesque.

I will send you back the pages of detail omitted, if you wd like to have them, as they may be useful. You will *quite* understand that they were not omitted because they weren't good; but because the scale of the story was too small to admit them without injury to the proportion of the whole. I refer particularly to the description of the pool, & the bird tracks; which I *much* wished to retain.

I did not mean to flow over into another sheet with literary affairs, but there are one or two things more to say under that head. One is the title. Our old title was in itself rather good, but as it does not quite apply, I have provisionally substituted "The Spectre of the Real".—"The Looming of the Real" is perhaps almost better. I have also thought of "A passion &

after"; "To-day's kiss & yesterday's."— "Husband's corpse
& husband's kiss", "A shattering of Ideals". When you have
read the modifications you will be able to choose; or suggest.

This question also arises: shall we print the story in
America &c. simultaneously. It will cause a delay of a few
weeks perhaps (not so long possibly). On the other hand if
we sacrifice America for the sake of being sooner out here, we
may lose, say, £20 or £25.

Ever yours sincerely
Tom H.

Blathwayt is on tour, lecturing about "Celebrities" he has
met & interviewed. I wonder what he says about you & me.

Lady Jeune is writing an article on "Conversation," for wh.
she is promised £10 she says.

Would you like me to send *The Two Lancrofts*? Also your
Swinburne, which I have by me. T. H.

another letter so soon!": TH had last written on 25 Oct.   *"The Author"*: the
journal of the Incorporated Society of Authors.   *the MS.*: of 'The Spectre
of the Real'; Miss Tigan was evidently a professional typist.   *Lord P.'s*:
Lord Parkhurst, who commits suicide at the end of the story.   *Lafayettes*:
Lafayette was, like Chancellor, a Dublin photographer.   *Blathwayt*:
Raymond Blathwayt (1855–1935), journalist; his interview with TH
appeared in 1892, that with Florence Henniker in 1895.   *article on
"Conversation"*: it appeared, as 'Conversation in Society', in the *English
Illustrated Magazine*, July 1894.   *"The Two Lancrofts"*: a novel (1893) by
Charles F. Keary.   *your Swinburne*: TH and Florence Henniker had been
marking and annotating each other's copies of Swinburne's *Poems and
Ballads*.

To Florence Henniker

MAX GATE, | DORCHESTER. | January 15. 1894

I have just received your yesterday's note, and am glad to
hear that you are taking more rest, for I fear you have been
feeling less well than in your kindness you let me know of. I
hope not?

My neuralgia has quite gone—it is not what I often get.
Thank you for telling me of the remedy.

I think more cruelties are perpetrated on animals by butchers, drovers, & cab-people, than by vivisectors. I wish you & I could work together some day for the prevention of such barbarities.

I have met Henry Harland at the Savile Club, I think, but I may be mistaken. I have found out no more about Mrs Clairmont, but if I go to stay with the Jeunes, as they want me to do soon, I may possibly hear something of her, though I am not greatly curious.

I hope the bequest of your uncle will not cause you to desert literature & break up our comradeship in that pursuit, just now when you are getting so nicely into notice? But perhaps it will.

I am creeping on a little with the long story, & am beginning to get interested in my heroine as she takes shape & reality: though she is very nebulous at present. Life's Little Ironies comes out at the end of the month. Don't order it, of course.

I have been thinking that the sort of friend one wants most is a friend with whom mutual confessions can be made of weaknesses without fear of reproach or contempt. What an indescribable luxury! Do you want such an one for yourself?—I wonder if I shall ever find one.

Ever sincerely yours
Tom H.

Harland: Henry Harland (1861–1905), American novelist, literary editor of the *Yellow Book*.   *Mrs Clairmont*: Mary Chavelita Clairmonte (1859?–1945), Australian-born novelist using the pseudonym 'George Egerton'; her short-story collection *Keynotes* (1893) had provoked controversy by its treatment of relations between the sexes.   *your uncle*: her mother's brother, Lord Crewe, had died on 3 Jan.   *my heroine*: Sue Bridehead.

To Edward Clodd

MAX GATE, | DORCHESTER. | April 1. 1894

My dear Clodd:

I have just returned from London to find your letter.

Certainly, all that about the "miller's-soul" is, or was till lately, an actual belief down here. It was told me years ago by an old woman. I may say, once for all, that every superstition, custom, &c., described in my novels may be depended on as true records of the same (whatever merit in folklorists eyes they may have as such)—& not inventions of mine.

Many thanks for the pages on Fitzgerald. I am glad you like the "Ironies".

Sincerely yours
Thomas Hardy.

"*miller's-soul*": a reference to 'The Superstitious Man's Story' in *Life's Little Ironies*, published Feb. 1894; the 'old woman' was almost certainly TH's mother.   *pages on Fitzgerald*: Clodd's article 'Edward Fitzgerald' in the *English Illustrated Magazine*, Feb. 1894.

To Emma Lavinia Hardy

Athenaeum Club Pall Mall | Wedny. 1.0 pm [8 May 1895]

My dear Em:

I wired to you just now to say that I had taken a place at last—90 Ashley Gardens. It was the best thing I cd do, I thought. We cd not have 16 Pelham C. Mrs Fyler being too unwell to leave for a fortnight. My choice lay between the Flat taken & a delightful house between Hyde Park Gardens & Sussex Gardens, on the North side of the Park. Had it not been for getting to the Athenaeum Club, I shd have taken the house, wh. was beautifully furnished. But I thought convenience above everything—& Ashley G. being near Victoria Station you will be able to get to yr Club by a Royal Blue easily—and we shall be *close* to the Army & Navy stores—

near the abbey—&c—as you will see if you look at the map.
I have not yet seen what kind of china &c they have at the
Flat. If you write a list of a few things I must look for it will
help you perhaps to know what to bring up.

They don't leave their servants behind, so you must bring
a parlour maid. As we enter Tuesday I do not see any use in
your coming till then—Do you think I need come home to
come up with you? I hardly see the necessity—& I am
overwhelmed with neglected proofs wh. I want to get at.

What I shd require you to bring for me wd be my big
portmanteau & in it all the things on the enclosed list. I may
write again today, or at any moment, as things come into my
head. I do not *think* any rugs are necessary—but I will look,
& let you know.

One advantage of the Flat is that Mrs Patrick Campbell
lives in an adjoining block—& if the play goes on that may
be convenient for the work.

There is a nice entrance hall to the Flat—I mean our own
flat—*inside* our door on the landing.

Ever yrs
Tom.

Will you tell Henry when he is to begin paying John &c. Also
leave say 10/- with John for paying little charges.

16 Pelham C.: the Hardys had rented this Pelham Crescent house in the
spring of 1894.   *Royal Blue*: a horse-drawn omnibus.   *neglected proofs*:
of the early volumes of the Osgood, McIlvaine 'Wessex Novels' edition of
TH's works.   *Campbell*: Beatrice Stella Campbell (1865–1940), usually
known as Mrs Patrick Campbell, actress. She and Johnston Forbes-
Robertson (1853–1937), the actor-manager, were showing an eager (though
temporary) interest in a possible production of TH's dramatization of
Tess.   *Henry*: TH's brother Henry Hardy had evidently agreed to keep
an eye on Max Gate during the Hardys' absence. The surname of John,
the Max Gate 'man', has not been discovered.

To Emma Lavinia Hardy

THE ATHENAEUM, | PALL MALL. S.W. | Wedny night. |
July 24. [1895]

My dear Em:

I have just received your note & enclosures. George Curzon's dinner I will accept, as I am all alone, & the evenings
are dismal. I will send a cheque to Barker's—& another
when the other bill comes. One letter you enclosed was from
Miss Shirley about her grate. There has been no rain here in
the *day*time. I think I shd accept the Thorntons invitation—
for both—& if I am not at home you can go alone.

I am going to meet Mr Forbes Robertson at his house to-
morrow morning about the play—if all goes well I shall have
to see solicitor, &c.—so that I shall be some days before
anything is settled I suppose. It is not altogether cheerful to
be here now that we have no foothold—& the season seems
over. I *live* almost entirely at this Club or at the Savile. I am
going to see Lady Fitzgd & Mrs H. on Friday—& will tell
the latter about the neuralgia remedy—They are leaving
London in a few days I think.

I *think* that before I come back I will go & stay at the
Jeunes' for a day or two—if they can have me. I wish we had
a permanent place here—it wd be so much nicer. But I don't
see how to afford £200 a year for flat. Mr. Spencer Smith
happens to be in Town *en garçon* like me—& we meet here.
You will have seen that Birrell has got in—whom I know a
little—that Conybeare is out—& that Sir W. Harcourt has
been elected for W. Monmouth after his overthrow at
Derby—I have been reading here—Max Nordaus "Conventional Lies" this afternoon. I went to the city this morning, &
got the hinges for the spare room.

Ever affly
Tom

Curzon's: George Nathaniel Curzon (1859–1925), Viceroy of India
1899–1905.   *Barker's*: the London department store.   *Miss Shirley*:
tenant of the house TH then owned in High West Street, Dorchester; the
banker Reginald Douglas Thornton (d. 1915) and his wife lived at Birkin

House, just outside Dorchester.   *Robertson*: see notes to letter of 8 May
1895.   *Lady Fitzgd & Mrs H.*: Amicia, née Milnes, wife of Sir Gerald
Fitzgerald, accountant-general of the Navy, and her sister Florence Henniker.   *Spencer Smith*: the Revd Spencer Compton Hamilton-Spencer-Smith
(1842–1911), vicar of Kingston, Dorset.   *Birrell has got in*: the 1895
general election had resulted in the re-election of Augustine Birrell
(1850–1933), author and statesman, the defeat of Charles Conybeare
(1853–1919), barrister and politician, and the re-election (though in a
different constituency) of Sir William Harcourt (1827–1904), former chancellor of the exchequer.   *"Conventional Lies"*: *Conventional Lies of Our
Civilization* (1895), translated from the German of Max Simon Nordau.

To Florence Henniker

MAX GATE, | DORCHESTER. | Monday. Aug 12. 1895

My dear friend: you will have reached Marienbad about the
time this letter gets there, I am thinking, though I don't like
to reckon much upon your movements since I found myself
wrong in supposing you on the Rhine when you were still in
London. I am recovered of my attack, though I feel a little
weak still. Perhaps however that is no great disadvantage, for
I have no wish to go out much, & so have more time for my
clerical drudgery—for what I am doing is hardly literary
work. In addition to the proofs of the monthly volumes I am
restoring the MS. of the Harper story to its original state.
Fortunately I wrote the alterations & abridgments in blue
ink—which makes it easy to recover the first form. Curiously
enough I am more interested in this Sue story than in any I
have written.

I am so glad to hear that you meant to stop at Nuremburg.
If you adhere to your programme you are there at this
moment probably. How I shd like to explain the quaint
architecture to you! But that's all over, I suppose.

We had a man staying here one night last week—Mr F.
Wedmore, the critic—who remembered you as a girl when he
visited yr father at Fryston. It was pleasant to hear him recall
his recollections of the "bright lively girl."

I have only promised to go to two places this autumn—the

Jeunes, & the Pitt-Rivers's. I dont mean to stay anywhere long—till next year, when I hope to have plenty of leisure.

I seem to see nothing in many modern writers but *form*—good form, certainly. I am led to say this by having tried to discover a great poet in Robert Bridges.—But he hands the torch on no further than the rest of them do.

When am I to hear that zither?

Tell me how you find Marienbad. Numbers of people seem to be drifting to German baths this year. You have set the fashion perhaps.

A good book for carrying on a long journey is the G. Treasury—as it contains so much in a small compass. I have been looking for a motto for the title page of the "Woodlrs" & not being able to find one, composed it.

Believe me always,

yr affectte friend,
Tom H.

"The way they loved at Grimpat" was sent me by the author. I will look it up.

---

the Harper story: *Jude the Obscure*, originally serialized in *Harper's New Monthly Magazine*, was now being prepared for publication as one of the 'monthly volumes' of the 'Wessex Novels' edition.   *Wedmore*: Frederick Wedmore (1844–1921), art critic; Fryston was Monckton Milnes's house in Yorkshire.   *Pitt-Rivers's*: see letter of 11 Sept. 1895.   *Bridges*: Robert Seymour Bridges (1844–1930), appointed Poet Laureate in 1913. *zither*: an instrument on which Florence Henniker had played at the time of TH's first meeting with her in Dublin.   *G. Treasury*: Francis Turner Palgrave's famous anthology *The Golden Treasury of the Best Songs and Lyrical Poems in the English Language* (1861).   *at Grimpat"*: Erminda Rentoul Esler's *The Way They Loved at Grimpat: Village Idylls* (1894).

To Florence Henniker

MAX GATE, | DORCHESTER. | Sept 11. 1895

My dear friend:

This time your letter travelled to me at a decent pace—arriving by the Monday afternoon post—a two days' transit. I do not think Marienbad would suit me just now—heat, &

particularly hot baths, pulling me down terribly. Where I was last week, on the top of the high Wilts downs, suited me eminently, & I felt quite languid on coming back here nearer the coast. (Rushmore is very high up—near Shaftesbury, described as "Shaston" in Jude) It was a pleasant visit, (notwithstanding the trying temper of the hostess)—the most romantic time I have had since I visited you at Dublin.

How we waste our labours in reading without system—or even with system. I have been led to think again of this by looking over some notes of reading that I took years ago, & finding I had forgotten them entirely. To stick to a few books & read these over & over again is the only way—introducing some really valuable new book as a sauce now & then.

I am going to get Mill's Subjection of Women—which I do not remember ever reading.

I fear that after the Vicar I cannot be of much service in saying anything that would commend your stories to an editor or publisher. But I do remember thinking that "In the Infirmary" was a striking little sketch, which had in it much of the actuality of life itself.

The "God in the Car" has been lent me. I am not so struck with it as I expected to be. My taste inclines less & less towards smart writing.

I am gradually working my way through the proofs. Do you go to Kiedrich this time? How restored you will be when you come back! By the way Miss Dowie (Mrs Norman) author of "Gallia" the "Girl in the Carpathians" &c—has come to Shaftesbury on my recommendation of the bracing air. I think it will become a health resort some day.

Ever yours
T. H.

Rushmore: the home of General Augustus Henry Lane Fox Pitt-Rivers (1827–1900), anthropologist and archaeologist, and his wife Alice, a daughter of the 2nd Lord Stanley of Alderley.   *of Women*: John Stuart Mill's *On the Subjection of Women* (1869), which Florence Henniker had recently been reading.   *after the Vicar*: TH's recommendation to Clement Shorter of Florence Henniker's 'A Page from a Vicar's History' had led to the embarrassing revelation that he had himself written the story's conclusion.   *in the Car"*: *The God in the Car* (1894), a novel by 'Anthony Hope'; see letter of 4 Mar. 1902.   *the proofs*: of the 'Wessex Novels' volumes.   *Kiedrich*: one of the

German spas Florence Henniker was visiting.   *Miss Dowie*: Ménie Muriel
Dowie (1867–1945), novelist; *Gallia* (1895), her first novel, was preceded by
A Girl in the Karpathians (1891), a travel narrative.

[What made Hardy's visit to Rushmore especially memorable
was his having met there, and danced with, the Pitt-Riverses'
daughter Agnes Grove—who became Lady Grove when her
husband succeeded to a baronetcy in 1897. She was beautiful,
intelligent, and very much aware of Hardy's literary distinction, and since she also had literary ambitions of her own,
Hardy slipped quickly, happily, and more than a little roman-
tically into another teacher–pupil relationship. Unlike Florence Henniker, however, Agnes Grove was interested in the
writing of social commentaries, of both a serious and semi-
humorous kind, and she was one of the few women to whom
Hardy felt it appropriate to send a copy of his most socially
conscious and, as it proved, controversial novel, *Jude the
Obscure*, published in volume form on 1 November 1895. The
attack on *Jude*, and especially on its treatment of the 'marriage-
question', came from many different quarters, but Hardy—as
his letters to Clodd, Gosse, and Lady Jeune clearly show—
remained vigorous in its defence.]

To Agnes Grove

MAX GATE, | DORCHESTER. | Nov. 3. 1895.

Dear Mrs Grove:

I have read your "Reply" with much interest, as you might
have guessed that I should do. I think it a spirited & sincerely
written article, & quite worth sending to the Review on the
chance of getting it inserted.

I do not know how freely I am to criticize it, & whether I
may suggest any modifications? Assuming that I can be of
more use to you by speaking frankly than by mere compliment
I will say this much: that before sending it I should rewrite it.
(I do not think the question of a little delay of any great
importance). Here & there the work bears evidence of inex-
perience, as is natural enough, & there is a tendency to

redundance which you can correct by rewriting. If you like, I will mark the places which I consider faulty, & send it back to you to revise & get recopied. If you then cared to return it to me I could despatch it.

Editors, as you are aware, consider their own convenience & advantage solely, in accepting contributions. You must therefore not feel hurt if he returns it, & must take such refusal as implying no opinion as to the merit of your essay, but simply that he is overstocked, or wishes to drop the subject.

I have often thought of the pleasant conversation we had at the Larmer, & shall hope to renew it some day.

I am sending, as I promised, a copy of my new book "Jude the Obscure" for your acceptance. You are, I know, sufficiently broad of view to estimate without bias a tragedy of very unconventional lives.

Ever sincerely yours
Thomas Hardy.

Grove: Agnes Geraldine Grove, née Pitt-Rivers (1863–1926), author, wife of Walter John Grove; TH's reference in his fourth paragraph to the 'Larmer' Tree in the Rushmore pleasure-grounds recalls their meeting two months earlier.   "*Reply*": Agnes Grove had drafted a response to an article, 'Why Women Do Not Want the Ballot', by the bishop of Albany, NY, in the Sept. 1895 issue of the *North American Review*.

To Edward Clodd

MAX GATE, | DORCHESTER. | Nov 10. 1895

My dear Clodd:

Your thoughtful letter gives one much matter for meditation. What you say is pertinent & true of the modern views of marriage are a survival from the custom of capture & purchase, propped up by a theological superstition.

The story of Jude, however, makes only an objective use of marriage & its superstitions as one, & only one, of the antagonistic forces in the tragedy. You are right in assuming that I have no suggestion or guidance to offer. I can only state (most imperfectly, alas!) cases in which natural & human laws create tragic dramas. The philanthropists must do the rest.

Owing, I suppose, to the accident of its appearance just after the sheaf of purpose-novels we have had lately on the marriage question,—though written long before them—some of the papers class mine with them—though the case of my people is one of temperamental unfitness for the contract, peculiar to the family of the parties.

I hope you did not feel any ill effects from that really rash jump you took in the dark on the heath?

Ever sincerely yours,
T. H.

marriage are a survival: TH seems to have intended something like, 'marriage—that they are a survival'.

To Edmund Gosse

MAX GATE, | DORCHESTER. | Nov 10. 1895

My dear Gosse:

Your review is the most discriminating that has yet appeared. It required an artist to see that the plot is almost geometrically constructed—I ought not to say *constructed*, for, beyond a certain point, the characters necessitated it, & I simply let it come. As for the story itself, it is really sent out to those into whose souls the iron has entered, & has entered deeply, at some time of their lives. But one cannot choose one's readers.

It is curious that some of the papers should look upon the novel as a manifesto on "the marriage question" (although of course, it involves it)—seeing that it is concerned first with the labours of a poor student to get a University degree, & secondly with the tragic issues of two bad marriages, owing in the main to a doom or curse of hereditary temperament peculiar to the family of the parties. The only remarks which can be said to bear on the *general* marriage question occur in dialogue, & comprise no more than half a dozen pages in a book of five hundred. And of these remarks I state (p. 362) that my own views are not expressed therein. I suppose the attitude of these critics is to be accounted for by the accident that, during the serial publication of my story, a sheaf of "purpose" novels on the matter appeared.

You have hardly an idea how poor & feeble the book seems to me, as executed, beside the idea of it that I had formed in prospect.

I have received some interesting letters about it already— yours not the least so. Swinburne writes, too enthusiastically for me to quote with modesty. Believe me, with sincere thanks for your review,

Ever yrs
T. H.

P.S. One thing I did not answer. The "grimy" features of the story go to show the contrast between the ideal life a man wished to lead, & the squalid real life he was fated to lead. The throwing of the pizzle, at the supreme moment of his young dream, is to sharply initiate this contrast. But I must have lamentably failed, as I feel I have, if this requires explanation & is not self evident. The idea was meant to run all through the novel. It is, in fact to be discovered in *every* body's life—though it lies less on the surface perhaps than it does in my poor puppet's. T.H.

Your review: Gosse's first review of *Jude* appeared in the *St. James's Gazette*, 8 Nov. 1895; though essentially favourable, it did open with the sentence to which TH alludes in his postscript, 'It is a very gloomy, it is even a grimy, story that Mr. Hardy has at last presented to his admirers.'   *Swinburne*: see letter of 1 Apr. 1897; writing to TH on 5 Nov. he had spoken of *Jude* as a tragedy 'equally beautiful and terrible in its pathos'.

To Lady Jeune

MAX GATE, | DORCHESTER. | 17. 11. 95

Dear Lady Jeune:
I have had such a bad cold that I have been unable to get

to London. Otherwise I would at least have come to see you.
Thanks for your kind note.

You will have seen how "Jude" has been attacked in two or
three quarters. I am much surprised at the *nature* of the
attack—the book having been announced as for men &
women: & my only fear having been that it was too much a
book of moral teaching—the inculcation of *Mercy*, to youths
& girls who have made a bad marriage, & to animals who
have to be butchered. The chapter on the pig-killing is going
to be reprinted by the Society for the Protection of Animals.

As to the "marriage question" I wonder they do not see
that my own opinions are nowhere given: indeed, I felt that
by the heroine's recantation of all her views, at the end of the
story, & becoming a penance-seeking Christian, I was almost
too High-Churchy.

Believe me

Ever yours
Thomas Hardy.

A. throwing the offal was, of course, intended to symbolize
the conflict of animalism with spiritualism.

for men & women: TH's preface to the first edition spoke of *Jude* as 'a novel
addressed by a man to men and women of full age'.   *reprinted* . . .
Animals: it appeared, under the title 'A Merciful Man', in the Dec. 1895
issue of the Society's journal, the *Animals' Friend*.   *A.*: Arabella, in the
novel's sixth chapter.

To Edmund Gosse

MAX GATE, | DORCHESTER. | 20. 11. 95

My dear Gosse:

I am keen about the new magazine. How interesting that
you shd be writing this review for it! I wish the book were
more worthy of such notice & place.

You are quite right: there is nothing perverted or depraved
in Sue's nature. The abnormalism consists in disproportion:
not in inversion, her sexual instinct being healthy so far as it
goes, but unusually weak & fastidious; her sensibilities remain

painfully alert notwithstanding, (as they do in nature with such women). One point illustrating this I cd not dwell upon: that, though she has children, her intimacies with Jude have never been more than occasional, even while they were living together (I mention that they occupy separate rooms, except towards the end), & one of her reasons for fearing the marriage ceremony is that she fears it wd be breaking faith with Jude to withhold herself at pleasure, or altogether, after it; though while uncontracted she feels at liberty to yield herself as seldom as she chooses. This has tended to keep his passion as hot at the end as at the beginning, & helps to break his heart. He has never really possessed her as freely as he desired.

Sue is a type of woman which has always had an attraction for me—but the difficulty of drawing the type has kept me from attempting it till now.

Of couse the book is all contrasts—or was meant to be in its original conception. Alas, what a miserable accomplishment it is, when I compare it with what I meant to make it!—e.g., Sue & her heathen gods set against Jude's reading the Greek Testt; Christminster academical, Chr in the slums; Jude the saint, Jude the sinner; Sue the Pagan, Sue the saint; marriage, no marriage; &c. &c.

As to the "coarse" scenes with Arabella, the battle in the school room, &c., the newspaper critics might, I thought, have sneered at them for their Fielding-ism rather than for their Zolaism. But your everyday critic knows nothing of Fielding. I am read in Zola very little, but have felt akin locally to Fielding, so many of his scenes having been laid down this way, & his home near.

Did I tell you I feared I shd seem too High-Churchy at the end of the book, where Sue recants? You can imagine my surprise at some of the reviews.

What a self-occupied letter!

Ever sincerely
T. H.

---

new magazine . . . review: Gosse published his second review of *Jude* in the first issue of *Cosmopolis*, Jan. 1896.   *Fielding*: Henry Fielding (1707–54), the novelist, was born at East Stour, Dorset; for Zola see letter of 6 Oct. 1893.

To Harper & Brothers

MAX GATE, | NEAR DORCHESTER. | Dec 24. 1895

Dear Sirs:

I have just received the form of agreement forwarded by you. As some of its clauses are new to me, our previous agreements having been brief ones by letter, I will consider it a little before returning it.

I write for the moment on another question respecting *Jude*. I am much surprised, & I may say distressed, by the nature of the attack on it in the N.Y. *World*, which has just come into my hands. This is the only American notice of the novel I have yet seen, except Mr Howells's in the *Weekly*. I do not know how far the *World* is representative of American feeling & opinion. But it is so much against my wish to offend the tastes of the American public, or to thrust any book of mine upon readers there, that if it should be in your own judgment advisable, please withdraw the novel.

You will probably know that it has been received here with about equal voices for & against—somewhat as Tess was received. All sensible readers here see at least that the intention of the book is honest & good. I myself thought it was somewhat overburdened with the interests of morality.

I have also received the application for the production of the play of *Tess* in America. I fear I may not be able to give an answer so soon as asked for, but I will let you know as early as possible. Though if *Jude* is much assailed over there it would perhaps be better to let the play question rest awhile.

Yours faithfully
Thomas Hardy

Messrs Harper & Bros.

Harper & Brothers: the American publishers; they had just sent TH a contract for publication of the American edition of *Jude*.   *World*: the review, in the issue of 8 Dec., was signed by Jeannette Gilder (see letter of 16 July 1896); William Dean Howells (1837–1920) noticed *Jude* in his regular 'Life and Letters' section of *Harper's Weekly*, 7 Dec. 1895. *withdraw the novel*: no such action was taken.   *Tess in America*: a version of

the play was produced in New York in Mar. 1897 with Minnie Maddern
Fiske as Tess.

To Florence Henniker

16 PELHAM CRESCENT, | SOUTH KENSINGTON. | June 1. 1896

My dear friend:

I am glad to get your little note. I was just thinking of
sending out one on a voyage of discovery, not knowing where
you were.

I returned from Dorset last Wedny, & before leaving
packed up & sent off a few books for the Crewe bazaar, which
you will find awaiting you at Sloane Gdns. You will say they
are the sweepings of my study.—I much wish I could have
sent some copies of the new edition.

I think I may say I am now quite well—the two or three
days at Max Gate, where the air is extraordinarily dry,
effected a cure which Brighton failed in. It would set you up
when you are languid, I am sure, & we hope you will try it
some day—though there wd be not a soul for you to speak to
except ourselves.

I fancy it was the same malignant quality in the air of
London that pulled down both Major Henniker & myself. I
am very sorry that his illness shd have been so serious as it
evidently was.

We are going out this week, for the first time in the evening
for nearly 2 months, to one or two places. I met Lady Fitzgd
at a little party at Lady Queensberry's one afternoon.

I congratulate you on getting "A Brand of Discord"
accepted. The title is rather good. Shorter, Clodd, G. Douglas,
& 2 or 3 other Bohemians are coming here to tea to-morrow.
I wish you could also. Can you come on the afternoon of the
11th—next Thursday week?—try to if you can. Lionel Johnson, Douglas, a great American authoress who is a total
stranger to us, &c., are coming then. You will perceive how
very small are the functions we attempt this season.

The unexpected result of *Jude* is that I am overwhelmed
with requests for stories to an extent that I have never before

experienced—though I imagined before publishing it that it
wd considerably lower my commercial value. By the way, I
have been offended with you for some time, though I have
forgotten to say so, for what you said—that I was an advocate
for "free love". I hold no theory whatever on the subject,
except by way of experimental remarks at tea parties, &
seriously I don't see any possible scheme for the union of the
sexes that wd be satisfactory.

I have been asked to stand as Liberal Candidate for the
Lord Rectorship of Glasgow University: they have asked me
twice, but I have declined. I will come to see you Sunday.
But perhaps you will let me know that you have really
returned, or are returning.

Ever sincerely yrs
Tho H.

Remembrances to Miss Thornhills.
P.S. I don't think much of Platt, from what I have seen of his
writing: mere sexuality without any counterpoise. I am now
reading the Life of J. A. Symonds—There is a feeble attack
on *Jude* in this month's Fortnightly. How much better I cd
cut it up myself! T. H.

Pelham Crescent: the Hardys were renting for the 'season' the house they had
had in 1894 but failed to get in 1895.   *Crewe bazaar*: evidently a
charitable event at Crewe Hall, Cheshire, the seat of her brother (now earl
of Crewe); Florence Henniker herself was living at 39 Sloane Gardens.
new edition: the 'Wessex Novels' edition.   *Brighton*: where the Hardys had
recently spent a few days.   *Lady Queensberry's*: Sybil (1845–1935),
divorced wife of the 8th marquess of Queensberry; Lady Fitzgerald was
Florence Henniker's sister (see letter of 24 July 1895).   *of Discord"*:
published in the *English Illustrated Magazine*, Christmas number, 1896.
Johnson: Lionel Pigot Johnson (1867–1902), poet and critic, author of *The
Art of Thomas Hardy* (1894), one of the earliest studies of TH's work; the
American visitor was Constance Cary Harrison (1843–1920), novelist and
short-story writer.   *Miss Thornhills*: Constance Emily and Mary Cecilia
Thornhill, sisters of Sir Thomas Thornhill, Bt., formerly MP for West
Suffolk.   *Platt . . . Fortnightly*: William Platt was the author of *Women,
Love, and Life* (1895), Horatio Brown of *John Addington Symonds: A Biography*
(1895), and R. Y. Tyrrell of the *Jude* review.

To Jeannette Gilder

SAVILE CLUB, | 107, PICCADILLY. W. | July 16. 1896

My dear Madam:

I have to inform you in answer to your letter that ever since the publication of "Jude the Obscure" I have declined to be interviewed on the subject of that book; & you must make allowance for human nature when I tell you that I do not feel disposed to depart from this rule in favour of the author of the review of the novel in the New York *World*.

I am aware that the outcry against it in America was only an echo of its misrepresentation here by one or two scurrilous papers which got the start of the more sober press, & that dumb public opinion was never with these writers. But the fact remains that such a meeting would be painful to me &, I think, a disappointment to you.

Moreover, my respect for my own writings & reputation is so very slight that I care little about what happens to either, so that the rectification of judgments, &c., & the way in which my books are interpreted, do not much interest me. Those readers who, like yourself, could not see that "Jude" (though a book quite without a "purpose", as it is called) makes for morality more than any other book I have written, are not likely to be made to do so by a newspaper article, even from your attractive pen.

At the same time I cannot but be touched by your kindly wish to set right any misapprehension you may have caused about the story. Such a wish will always be cherished in my recollection, & it removes from my vision of you some obviously unjust characteristics I had given it in my mind. This is, at any rate on my part, a pleasant gain from your letter, whilst I am

> ". . . never the worse for a touch or two
> On my speckled hide"

as the consequence of your review.

Believe me, dear Madam,

Yours sincerely
Thomas Hardy.

Miss Jeannette Gilder.

Gilder: Jeannette Leonard Gilder (1849–1916), American journalist and editor; see letter of 24 Dec. 1895 for TH's response to her review of *Jude* in the New York *World*.   *speckled hide*": from Browning's 'The Worst of It'.

To Florence Henniker

Hôtel Mohren | Liège | Belgium | Sept 24. 1896

My dear little friend:

I have been wandering about over here since I last wrote, & have not stayed at any one place long enough to give it as an address. After crossing to Ostend, where we stayed observing its frivolities a few days, we went on to Bruges—a bygone, melancholy interesting town, as you probably know from experience,—& thence to Brussels & Dinant, on the Meuse. There I made the acquaintance of a veritable gambler—who was staying at our hotel—& for the first time really perceived what it is to be possessed of the gaming fever. He won largely at the tables yesterday before dinner, & at dinner time I persuaded him to leave off; but he would not, & returned to the rooms in the evening. I saw him this morning looking wild, & he said he had lost everything, except enough to pay his fare to England. The curious thing is that he fully believes in his ultimate success by means of a system, & is going to Monte Carlo in November to retrieve all his losses!

The "Grasshopper" (bicycle), which has accompanied us, has been the source of extraordinary alarms, (& expenses!—) It disappears unexpectedly on the railway journeys, & turns up again just as unexpectedly—its discoverer exclaiming "V'la le *veloze* de Madame!"

I should so much have liked to go through with you some of the churches &c., that I have seen. I have mostly kept away from the fashionable hotels—life is so much easier among the natives than where the English & Americans are.

Much admiration has been expressed for the mediæval brick architecture of Belgium, but after Bruges I craved the sight of a *stone* building again.

This city is a sort of Belgian Sheffield, &, though picturesque, is entirely given over to manufacture. In a day or two

I shall reach Brussels again, where my address (till about a
week hence, or more,) will be,

> Hôtel de la Poste
> Rue Fossé aux Loups 28,

(If you shd write put *Mr.*)

E.s shoulder, where the bicyclist ran into her, is practically
well, though she occasionally feels twinges. There is a man
staying at this hotel just like Ld Salisbury. I hope the sea has
made you strong & well—& that you are not killing yourself
with literary labour. It is 20 years since I was last in this part
of Europe, & the reflection is rather saddening. I ask myself,
why am I here again, & not underground!

The chimes are playing 10 o'c.

> Ever yrs
> Tom H.

"*Grasshopper*": Emma Hardy's bicycle was painted green.   *Ld Salisbury*:
Robert Arthur Talbot Gascoyne-Cecil, 3rd marquess of Salisbury
(1830–1903), the prime minister.   *in this part of Europe*: the Hardys had
visited Holland and the Rhine in May–June 1876.

To Edward Clodd

MAX GATE, | DORCHESTER. | Jan 17. 1897

My dear Clodd:

I am delighted with your book as far as I have got, & thank
you sincerely for your generous gift of it. Of course, not being
a scientific man's, my opinion may not be worth much, but I
must tell you that I think this book shows a breadth of grasp,
& a power of condensing the stupendous ideas scattered over
Time in fragments, which you have never before equalled. It
is just as when one sees a landscape of miles length reproduced in a charming miniature picture inside a camera.
Knowing what you have had to sift & reject, I can see that
the labour of producing such a book must have been
enormous.

What seems to me the most striking idea dwelt upon is that

of the arrest of light & reason by theology for 16,00 years.
The older one gets, the more deplorable seems the effect of
that terrible, dogmatic ecclesiasticism—Christianity so called
(but really Paulinism *plus* idolatry)—on morals & true religion: a dogma with which the real teaching of Christ has
hardly anything in common.

Prepare yourself to be burnt by some bigot, as I was last
year, (theology and burning have been kindred always). But
if you are I hope it may be by the head of a really dignified
bishoprick, or an archbishop outright, not by a miserable
second class prelate like him under whom I ignominiously
suffered.

I am glad to see what due honour you give to that glorious
Double-man—poet & scientist—Lucretius. I see you refer to
Munro's translation. I do not know it, but it seems an
extraordinarily close one, to judge from the few passages
quoted in your book, which I have tested.

With kind regards

Sincerely yrs
Thomas Hardy.

your book: *Pioneers of Evolution from Thales to Huxley* (1897). *second class
prelate*: it was William Walsham How (1823–97), bishop of Wakefield, who
claimed in June 1896 that he had burned his copy of *Jude the Obscure*.
Munro's translation: Hugh Andrew Johnstone Munro's translation (1864) of
the *De rerum natura* of Lucretius.

[The last of Hardy's novels to be published in volume form,
The Well-Beloved had in fact been serialized as early as 1892.
Although he had gone far beyond the 'correction' referred to
in a letter to Florence Henniker, subjecting the serial version
to a radical revision and toning down or cutting out much of
its original hostility towards marriage as an institution, Hardy
still encountered in some quarters the kind of savage and even
personal attack that had been such a distressing feature of the
reception of *Jude*.]

To Florence Henniker

MAX GATE, | DORCHESTER. | Sunday, Jan 24. '97

My dear friend:

I have to-day finished the correction of the little sketch or story of The Well Beloved (which is to come out I believe next month, & might come out now but for America): & I must now answer your nice last letter. I am so sorry the weather has given you the toothache. I *wish* I could suggest some remedy: but I am such a hopeless doctor. During this very cold time I have been free from aches (our air is so dry & fogless—*you* ought to live down this way 6 months out of the 12). I hate the frost nevertheless—it makes my fingers slippery as glass, so that I can hardly hold a pen firmly. I believe you have had much snow; We have had only the merest sprinkle which soon disappeared.

I am glad that you enjoyed yr visit to Ld Winchester's. I don't know the present Digbys, though I knew the late Lady D. & know her daughter Lady Ashburton. She was a nice neighbour while living near here a short while. But the ordinary Dorset landowners only tolerate an author; they do not associate with him (especially when he is such a fearful wild fowl as this misunderstood man is supposed to be). Writing this recalls to my mind Lady Waldegrave's answer to Browning, when he proposed to her. "We dine our poets, Mr Browning, but we do not marry them." *Mutatis mutandis*, that's the spirit down here—much intensified of course.

I do remember taking in Lady Evelyn Ewart to dinner somewhere—possibly at Lady Wimborne's house in London.

I am going to read Mrs Steel's novel, &, in fact, lots of books soon. The Byrons seem to object to the publication of more of Lord Byron's letters: just as if any possible revelation could affect his character at this time of day!

I have been thinking that of all men dead whom I should like to meet in the Elysian fields I would choose Shelley, not only for his unearthly, weird, wild appearance & genius, but for his genuineness, earnestness, & enthusiasms on behalf of the oppressed.

Ever yrs affly
Tho H.

Ld Winchester's: the 15th marquess of Winchester (1858–99) was, like Florence Henniker's husband, an officer in the Coldstream Guards. *Digbys*: of Minterne House, Dorset; Lady Theresa Digby (d. 1874), wife of the 9th Lord Digby, was a daughter of the 3rd earl of Ilchester; her daughter Leonora (d. 1930) was the wife (at this date the widow) of the 4th Lord Ashburton.   *Lady Waldegrave's answer*: the anecdote is perhaps to be associated rather with the rejection of Browning by Louisa, Lady Ashburton, widow of the 2nd Lord Ashburton.   *Ewart*: Lady Evelyn Clementina Ewart (1864–1924), wife of General Sir Henry Ewart and daughter of the 1st earl of Ancaster; TH had met Lady Wimborne (d. 1927), wife of the 1st Lord Wimborne and daughter of the 7th duke of Marlborough, when living in Wimborne in the early 1880s.   *Mrs Steel's novel*: Flora Annie Steel, *On the Face of the Waters* (1897).

To Lewis Hind

MAX GATE, | DORCHESTER. | March 27. 1897

My dear Sir,
No: I do not intend to answer the article on "The Well Beloved", in the paper which shall be nameless. Personal abuse best answers itself. What struck me, next to its ferocious malice, was its maladroitness—as if the writer were blinded by rage; & the curious thing is that I was not aware till now that a soul on the staff of the paper wished to do me any wrong.

A dozen charges might plausibly have been brought against the tale except the particular one he brings. Upon those who have read the book the review must have produced the amazed risibility we used to experience in our youth at Wildings assertions in Foote's comedy of "The Liar". The young woman in Dickens, who never sang, was considered a nightingale by her imaginative father; Mr Wemmick, too, called his house an island; but I can defy any sane person to see immorality or impropriety in an applied Platonic Idea—

a phantasmal narrative of the adventures of a Visionary Artist in pursuit of the unattainable Perfect in female form— a man repeatedly stated to be singularly free from animalism. Why, there is more fleshliness in The Loves of the Triangles.

To be sure, there is one explanation which should not be overlooked—a reviewer *himself* afflicted with "sex-mania" might write so—a thing terrible to think of. If there are such people in the world, it wd explain what has seemed inexplicable in some reviews of my writings.

I know nothing of editing, but it strikes me as odd that an editor should go out of his way to fool his subscribers by statements whose absurdity can be proved by a five minutes' glance at the book.

Yours truly
Thomas Hardy.

Hind: Charles Lewis Hind (1862–1927), editor of the *Academy* 1896–1903, had invited TH to reply in the *Academy* to a hostile review of *The Well-Beloved* in the London *World* of 24 Mar.; on 29 Mar. TH sent for publication (on 3 Apr.) a letter which ignored the *World*'s accusation of sexual obsession but expanded upon some comments made in the favourable review published in the *Academy* itself on 27 Mar.   *Wildings . . . Liar*": Young Wilding is the extragavant liar in *The Liar*, a play by Samuel Foote (1720–77).   *Dickens*: the 'imaginative father' is presumably Mr Pecksniff, in the second chapter of *Martin Chuzzlewit*; Wemmick appears in *Great Expectations*.   *of the Triangles*: an anonymous parody of Erasmus Darwin's *The Loves of the Plants*, first published in the *Anti-Jacobin* (1798).   "*sex-mania*": according to the *World* reviewer, 'Of all forms of sex-mania in fiction we have no hesitation in pronouncing the most unpleasant to be the Wessex-mania of Mr. Thomas Hardy'.

To Edmund Gosse

MAX GATE, | DORCHESTER. | 31. 3. 97

My dear Gosse:

Thanks for your note. Since you last wrote I have read in The World that extraordinary stab in the back of my poor innocent little tale. At first I took the charge of immorality as a grotesque blunder of the reviewer or editor, not seeing the full meaning of the article, but now that I better realize the scope of it I am rather depressed by the thought that some people who have not read the book may believe him.

I wonder if you know that the tale was sketched many years ago, when I was virtually a young man, & interested in the Platonic Idea. I afterwards developed & modified it to what you now see. This will account for its coming as such a contrast to the novels of my later years. You will judge my amazement at the article when I tell you that one of the reasons why I consented to the reprinting of such a bygone, wildly romantic fancy was that it would please Mrs Grundy & her young Person, & her respected husband, by its absolutely "harmless" quality.

The attack must have been dictated by personal malignity, since nobody could honestly read such ideas into a book containing repeated demonstrations & statements that the Visionary hero's craze for the Ideal woman was innocent.

I had a walk yesterday with a Cambridge Don, of 40 years experience of every kind of young man; he had read the story through twice, without the least sense of anything but its obvious meaning, or want of meaning.

Ever yours
T.H.

The World: see preceding letter.   *Mrs Grundy . . . Person*: T.H. has conflated Mrs Grundy (originating in Thomas Morton's play *Speed the Plough*) with Mr Podsnap's 'young person' (from Charles Dickens's *Our Mutual Friend*) into a generalized image of repressive propriety.   *Cambridge Don*: Charles Walter Moule.

To Algernon Charles Swinburne

MAX GATE, | DORCHESTER. | April 1. 1897

Dear Mr Swinburne:

I must thank you for your kind note about my fantastic little tale which, if it can make, in its better parts, any faint claim to imaginative feeling, will owe something of such feeling to you, for I often thought of lines of yours during the writing; & indeed, was not able to resist the quotation of your words now & then.

And this reminds me that one day, when examining several English imitations of a well-known fragment of Sappho, I interested myself in trying to strike out a better equivalent for it than the commonplace "Thou, too, shalt die" &c. which all the translators had used during the last hundred years. I then stumbled upon your "Thee, too, the years shall cover", & all my spirit for poetic pains died out of me. Those few words present, I think, the finest *drama* of Death & Oblivion, so to speak, in our tongue. Having rediscovered this phrase, it carried me back to the buoyant time of 30 years ago, when I used to read your early works walking along the crowded London streets, to my imminent risk of being knocked down.

Believe me to be

Yours very sincerely
Thomas Hardy.

P.S. I should have added that "The Well Beloved" is a fanciful exhibition of the artistic nature, & has, I think, some little foundation in fact. I have been much surprised, & even grieved, by a ferocious review attributing an immoral quality to the tale. The writer's meaning is beyond me. T.H.

Swinburne: Algernon Charles Swinburne (1837–1909), poet, whose work TH had profoundly admired since the publication of *Poems and Ballads* in 1866; he wrote in praise of *The Well-Beloved* on 28 Mar.   *Sappho*: the allusions are to no. 68 in Henry Thornton Wharton's *Sappho* (the edition TH owned) and to Swinburne's 'Anactoria'.

To Florence Henniker

GD HÔTEL DE LA PAIX GENÈVE | 3 June [July] 1897

My dear friend:

I have received your nice letter, & am inclined to think you *rather* good, for very few women so busy, & unwell too, wd have so promptly replied to my dull note. We have gone hither & thither, to the top of the Wengern Alp facing the Jungfrau, among other places, also to Interlaken, Zermatt, Thun, &c

&c & have not felt inconvenienced greatly by the heat till
within the last 2 or 3 days. Here it is like a melon-frame, &
we shall soon clear out to move homeward. At Zermatt I saw
the exact place where the tragedy occurred on the Matterhorn
in wh. Whymper was the only Englishmn saved. Yet it is only
myself who am pulled down a little, Em being in excellent
health & vigour. I think you, too, wd be well here now, since
you, like her, enjoy warmth by the water side.

It is ten years since we were in Switzerland last, &, strange
reverse of what is customary, I have been much more
impressed this time than I was then. The windows here
command a full view of the Lake, & the haunts of the poets;
also of the "arrowy Rhone" (Byron is literally true in what he
says of "Lake Leman" (Geneva) in Childe Harold). Yet what
is the use of coming to such places for association's sake?
Those who wrote rapturously about them from Rousseau
onwards care nothing about them *now*.

I am so sorry to hear that Lady Grove has been so ill. I
have not seen her since you & she were at our house last
year, & thought she had only had a slight illness—some time
ago.

I have no book ready or in hand: of course I should have
told *you* if I had.

We think of getting home by the middle of next week. I
shall be delighted to read the Chapman's & Cassell's stories
you have written. Not only is it untrue that I have a novel
ready, but also that I have changed my style, am in doubt
about a title, &c. &c. Indeed I have not given a single
thought to novels of my own or other peoples since I finished
the corrections of the W.B.

I wonder if I ever told you that the plot of that story was
suggested to me by the remark of a sculptor that he had often
pursued a beautiful ear, nose, chin, &c, about London in
omnibuses & on foot?

I don't think it can be true that Lady J. writes Belles
Letters in that horrid "World". She told me some time ago
that the woman who then wrote them came to her party one
evening, & pointed out her description of it. She told me also
the lady's name, but I have forgotten it. She also wrote to me
expressing her indignation at the libel of my last book in The

World: as did also Lady Londonderry—the latter expressing her contempt for the paper.

Please let me hear from you soon after I get home, & tell me where you are.

I thought of going this afternoon to try to find the cottage in which Shelley & Mary lived, a little way below Byron's "Campagne Diodati" (*vide* Dowden's Shelley) but I doubt if I shall.

Ever yours sincerely
Tom H.

E. is actually thinking of hiring a bicycle: I don't feel up to it!

Genève: this visit of the Hardys to Switzerland was to prove their last continental holiday.   *Whymper*: Edward Whymper (1840–1911), alpinist; TH had recently met him at Clodd's house in Aldeburgh.   *in Switzerland last*: the Hardys had passed through the country by train on their return from Italy in Apr. 1887.   *"arrowy Rhone"*: from Byron's *Childe Harold's Pilgrimage*, III. lxxi.   *stories you have written*: Florence Henniker published 'Mrs. Livesey' in *Chapman's Magazine*, July 1897, and 'The Man Who Waited' in *Cassell's Family Magazine*, Nov. 1897.   *Letters*: correctly, 'Belle's Letters', an anonymous gossip column.   *Lady Londonderry*: Lady Theresa (d. 1919), wife of the 6th marquess; she was a daughter of the 19th earl of Shrewsbury.   *Dowden's Shelley*: Edward Dowden, *The Life of Percy Bysshe Shelley* (1886), ii.14–15.

[Although few of Hardy's letters to members of his own family seem to have survived, he always remained on the closest and most affectionate terms not only with his father, mother, and elder sister but also with the two younger children, Henry, who had taken over the family building business, and Katharine, who had spent two unhappy years at the Salisbury training college for teachers and subsequently joined Mary on the staff of a Dorchester elementary school. Mary and Katharine had in fact just resigned their teaching positions, partly for health reasons, partly to enable them to devote more time to the care of their mother—still living in the Bockhampton cottage—but chiefly because Hardy's greater affluence and continuing family loyalty made it possible for them to abandon a profession in which neither of them had been especially comfortable.]

To Katharine Hardy

Crown Hotel | Salisbury | 7. 8. 97

My dear Katharine:

I have just come in from a walk round the Two Harnhams (as they call it)—a walk I expect you know well as I think you said you used to often go that way. The sun was setting over the meadows, & the scene was altogether very beautiful (though Sir A. Blomfield's scaffolding rather disfigures the Cathedral spire just now).

I write to ask if you will run up for a day—say next Monday or Tuesday? You could come by the 10.29 SWR & go back by the last train having lunch & tea here. I would meet you, & you could have a good long day. The weather is so fine that it wd be worth while.

I went to the Cathl service this afternoon. "Kings House" appears to be emptied for the holidays, so you wd have no unpleasant reminders.

This inn is not far from the Close Gate, & the result of my coming is that I am more interested in Sarum than I used to be. It is so improved & altogether more picturesque than it was.

I heard a story of Mr Richardson the late organist to day (tell Mary). The new organ so distracted him that he could not play it, & went out of his mind, & was obliged to leave. Last night I went into the Close by moonlight—the moon was going down a little to the left of the T.S. where there was one lamp at the corner—& the place was very peaceful. Bats were flying around the gates of the Bishop's Palace. I am writing this nearly in the dark, & don't know how you will read it.

Yr affte br
T.

Hardy: Katharine [Kate] Hardy (1856–1940), TH's younger sister.   *Two Harnhams*: the villages of West and East Harnham, just to the south of Salisbury; King's House, situated in the cathedral close, was part of the teachers' training school ('T.S.'), or college, which both Kate and Mary Hardy had attended.   *Blomfield's*: TH's former employer.   *Richardson*: J. E. Richardson was the cathedral organist when Mary Hardy was in Salisbury in the early 1860s.

To Lady Grove

MAX GATE, | DORCHESTER. | April 18. 1898
My dear Lady Grove:

I return by book post the copy of yr story, which I should have sent a day or two sooner if I had not met with a slight accident to my right hand, wh. makes it difficult to do anything just now. A sash window came down upon my thumb & finger, & though the wounds are small the joints are stiffened for the present. Fortunately no bone was broken.

I have re-read parts of the tale since my first reading. The incident on the house is good in itself & most picturesque, but it shd have been *indispensable* to the *ending* of the story that it shd be told in detail to make it artistically good. (For instance, if he had jumped off & killed himself.) You are right about the wife's convn with the Doctor being necessary. I tell you this quite frankly, as I am sure you wd not wish me to do otherwise, nothing being so harmful to a young writer as deceiving him or her by uncritical commendation. But you must understand that thousands of novels are published, & popular, which have the same defect, & to a worse degree.

The same remark applies to the conversation between the lovers near the beginning: something more should come of it since it is given at length. But this less so.

I had a conviction that some madman *had* used such expressions when I said no madman would—as it always happens or nearly always, that the unbelievable parts of a story are real incidents. You however have, as I gather from your letter, rightly judged why fiction must be more probable than history.

I thought of Temple Bar because it is a magazine of respectable standing, & with no prejudice against women writers, as is the case with some. I do not however know anybody connected with it now old Mr Bentley is dead. You might of course try any other such as the Woman at Home, Chapman's Magazine, &c.

I return the new written page. Upon the whole I prefer the old as it stands—(as far as that particular is concerned). It is

I think less hackneyed to leave the reader in ignorance on whether Berkley did so & so & what they thought of it. But use your own judgment on this. You have anticipated criticism by perceiving that the pathetic might appear grotesque here & there. I shd therefore prevent that if possible.

I am afraid I shall appear a wretched caviller by so coldly vivisecting your performance. One day a man well known in the magazines sent me the MS. of a long story to express my candid opinion on, wh. he *much* desired. I did not like it (the tale) & told him so—& he replied by a withering letter of satire—almost insult—though it had been a trouble to me to oblige him, who was a total stranger. I hope your little boy has arrived safely, & that you are all well. Believe me

Always yrs sincerely
Thomas Hardy.

yr story: the story by Lady Grove (as she now was) remains unidentified and was perhaps never published; TH had suggested in a letter of 9 Apr. that it might be submitted to *Temple Bar*—of which George Bentley (1828–95) had long been the editor—and he himself later sent it, unsuccessfully, to *Chapman's Magazine*.   *no madman would*: in that earlier letter TH had declared, 'Such phrases as "Avaunt, fiend!" "Speak woman", &c., would not be used by any modern human being, even were he as mad as ten hatters.'

To Katharine Hardy

9 Wynnstay Gardens | Kensington. W. | Sunday eveg
[8 May 1898]

My dear Kitty:

The letters arrived by the last post last night, thanks. I hope you did not inconvenience yourself by going to D. very early to post them. It wd be well to ask at the P.O. the latest time at which to post for delivery in Kensington the same evening.

When you are at Max G. again please ask Sarah Ann if she wants anything—if she has enough coals, potatoes, &c.

This is a snug little flat that we are in, & so far all seems comfortable. Our luggage was drenched coming, but not ourselves. Friday & Saturday were cloudless. Wet again to-day.

The young people seem to cycle about the streets here more than ever. I asked an omnibus conductor if the young women (who ride recklessly into the midst of the traffic) did not meet with accidents. He said "Oh, nao; their sex pertects them. We dares not drive over them, wotever they do; & they do jist wot they likes. 'Tis their sex, yer see; & its wot I coll takin' a mean adventege. No man dares to go where they go."

I hope you will be accomplished on yours by the time I return.

Yours affecty
Tom.

Thumb nearly well, but stiff, which makes writing awkward.

D.: Dorchester; Sarah Ann (surname unknown) was the servant left in charge at Max Gate while the Hardys again moved into rented London accommodation for the 'season'.   *cycle about the streets*: TH and Emma had themselves taken up the new sport of cycling about three years earlier. *Thumb*: see previous letter.

To Katharine Hardy

9 Wynnstay Gns | Thursday night [26 May 1898]

My dear Kitty:

I learn with much satisfaction that you have cycled to W. I thought such news would come soon. The cycling here makes it dangerous to cross the streets.

Tell Henry I inquired at the C.S. Stores about the picture-glass, & they hunted up all particulars. If he paid the enclosed amount, it did not include glass: if more, the clerk did not enter it. In the latter case perhaps he can send up the bill.

Open anything you have any doubt about sending on. No books required—unless you find a note or anything inside which seems to make it imperative to forward them or it. I shall be sending home some in parcels in a few days, to lessen the weight & bulk of luggage.

We were shocked to hear of Mrs Hayne's death. She was such a kind neighbour.

I went to see Gladstone "lying in state" this morning—
though it can hardly be called in state—so plain, even to
bareness was the whole scene—a plain oak coffin on a kind of
altar covered with a black cloth, a tall candle at each corner,
a cross, & "requiescat in pace" embroidered on the *white* pall
under the coffin. Two carpenters in front of me said "a rough
job—¾ panels, & 1¼ framing" referring to the coffin, which
was made by the village carpenter at Hawarden. The scene
however, was impressive, as being in Westminster Hall, &
close to where his voice had echoed for 50 years.

Tell S.A. we are much obliged to her for sending on the
Telegram.

Your affectte br
Tom.

to W.: to Weymouth, a distance of about 8 miles.   *C.S. Stores*: Civil
Service Stores, London.   *Mrs Hayne's*: Mary Ann Hayne, wife of Robert
Hayne, JP, died in Fordington (Dorchester) on 6 May, aged 73.
Gladstone: William Ewart Gladstone (1809–98), statesman and author; he
died at Hawarden, his Scottish home, on 19 May.   *S.A.*: Sarah Ann; see
preceding letter.

To Edmund Gosse

MAX GATE, | DORCHESTER. | 8. 9. 98

My dear Gosse:
As you ask for comments I will tell you exactly how the
Essay strikes me. First, what you say seems but a mere
picking from what you could say if you chose. This, of course,
is as it should be; but I for one wish you had said a little
more.

"Between F. & all his contemps there rose a wall of
imperfect sympathy" &c. (p.xxx.) This paragraph is full of
suggestiveness, & might be made longer if you wished. It is a
key to the obstructiveness which retarded, say, a man so
different from Fielding as Shelley; & the ready acceptance
which so materially assisted Scott was precisely the reverse
fact—i.e. "He [*was*] as they were; his ideals were [*not*]
different."

You just allude to F.'s "aristocratic temper". This temper of his always strikes me forcibly—more than it does most people I imagine: especially in his attitude towards Molly. His date has, no doubt, something to do with it: but I can never forgive him (as a youth, even, I never could) for regarding her as a grotesque creature, a slut, &c.—& my impression is that the shadowy original (or originals) of Molly were town girls with whom F. came into sensual contact, dressed up in peasant clothes; & no cottager. It would be too long to say why I have come to this conclusion; but I feel certain that F. never knew thoroughly the seduced rustic girl; or that, if he did, the "aristocratic temper" you mention & the prejudices of his time, absolutely blinded him to her true character.

It is curious that such a woman of the people as George Eliot shd have carried on the prejudice to some extent in her treatment of Hetty, whom she wd not have us regard as possessing equal rights with Donnithorne. If I think of anything more I will write again.

Ever yrs
T.H.

I have omitted to say how conscious I am of the honour (undeserved) you have done me by what you write.

the Essay: Gosse's introduction to the forthcoming Library Edition of Henry Fielding's novels; though greatly interested in Fielding, TH had earlier declined an invitation to write the introduction himself.   Molly: Molly Seagrim, in Fielding's Tom Jones.   Hetty . . . Donnithorne: characters in Eliot's Adam Bede.   honour . . . done me: Gosse had referred to TH as that 'son of [Fielding's] who is our living glory'.

[The publication of Wessex Poems in December 1898 marked a major shift in Hardy's career, one that his readers only gradually learned to accept as permanent. The peculiarly hostile nature of some of the attacks levelled against his last three novels undoubtedly played a part in this decision, but (as he insists in a letter to Gosse) he had always wished and hoped to become a poet, and had long looked forward to the

moment when he would feel secure enough financially to take
the risk of abandoning fiction for poetry.]

To William Archer

MAX GATE, | DORCHESTER. | Nov 24. 1898

Dear Archer:

Your good opinion of a book is quite enough to make me
wish to read it. So that I shall accept the novel with pleasure.

As to a novel from me, I don't incline to one. There is no
enlightened literary opinion sufficiently audible to tempt an
author, who knows that in the nature of things he must always
come short of real excellence. I mean that the little sound &
just opinion we get is swamped by the flood of ignorant &
venal opinion, & is as if it were not uttered at all. And zest is
quenched by the knowledge that by printing a novel which
attempts to deal honestly & artistically with the facts of life
one stands up to be abused by any scamp who thinks he can
advance the sale of his paper by lying about one.

At the beginning of Dec. I am going to send & ask you to
accept a copy of my volume of verses, which will come out
about then. I have been going to publish it for years. But
please don't expect to find much in them.

Yours sincerely
Thomas Hardy.

Yes: The Well Beloved was published many years earlier as a
serial, & reprinted. T.H.

Archer: William Archer (1856–1924), critic, translator, and journalist; the
novel he had offered to send TH remains unidentified.   *volume of verses*:
Wessex Poems and Other Verses (1898), subsequently reviewed by Archer for
the *Daily Chronicle*.

To Edmund Gosse

MAX GATE, | DORCHESTER. | 27. 12. 98

My dear Gosse:

Many thanks for your kind letter. Our good wishes also to you & Mrs Gosse for 1899.

Well: the poems were lying about, & I did not quite know what to do with them. Considering that the Britisher resents a change of utterance, instrument, even of note, I do not expect a particularly gracious reception of them. It is difficult to let people who think I have made a fresh start know that to indulge in rhymes was my original weakness, & the prose only an afterthought. Besides, in the full tide of a fashion which seems to view poetry as the art of saying nothing with mellifluous preciosity, the principle of regarding form as second to content is not likely to be popular.

When your letter came I had just put back to my bookshelf your two compact & teeming volumes "Firdausi" & "On Viol": & I had been looking also into the second Golden Treasury of Palgrave. The conjunction of the three books in my mind led me to think of the absolutely arbitrary character of these anthologies. Here (in P.) we find included a dozen of Tennyson Turner's & many other such, while poems like "Two points of view", "Wind of Provence", & "The lemon petals gently fall" are omitted. But your poems lack the supreme quality of their author being dead, or what might suffice, starving in a garret. However they will keep.

I am not going to Crewe, or anywhere for this new year, unless I run across to the Jeunes at Arlington for a few days.

I will send a copy of the lines with pleasure.

Ever sincerely yrs
Thomas Hardy.

your kind letter: Gosse had written to thank TH for his Christmas gift of *Wessex Poems*.   *your two . . . volumes*: Gosse's *Firdausi in Exile and Other Poems* (1885) and *On Viol and Flute* (1890); the individual poems mentioned later in the paragraph are all by Gosse.   *second Golden Treasury*: i.e. the Second Series, published in 1897 and edited, like the first, by Francis Turner Palgrave.   *Turner's*: Charles Tennyson Turner (1808–79), poet;

he was Alfred Tennyson's elder brother.   *to Crewe*: Gosse, invited to Crewe Hall (see letter of 1 June 1896) in Jan., had asked if TH would be there at the same time.   *the lines*: Gosse had asked TH if he would copy out in his own hand the poem 'I Look into My Glass'.

To Sir George Douglas

MAX GATE, | DORCHESTER. | Jan 13. 1899

My dear Douglas:

It is good news that you think of being in London during the coming season. I suppose we shall go, but we have not really decided yet on the matter. Anyhow I shall be there I hope; off & on, if not continuously.

For the present I stay here, so unfortunately shall not see you when you are up there next week. January in London usually gives me influenza, even if I don't get wet: & I should not have the genial influence of a wedding festivity to drive it away, as you will.

I am glad to hear that the County history is finished. It is an interesting sort of work (if one has any local interest) & the pleasure of doing it has to be its reward, for the public fight shy of works that are painstaking & of permanent value as records. I have brought out, as you may have seen, those Wessex Poems I may have mentioned to you at some time or another; & they have probably as your history may have, an unspoken disqualification in being "local"—as if humanity could not be sampled as readily in a western county as in, say, a Fleet Street office.

The Ettrick shepherd's poems are known to me, though they have never impressed me sufficiently to give me any great familiarity with them. I will take those I have down from my shelf, & revive my memories of them.

The winter here has been extraordinarily mild: not one flake of snow. Yesterday we had a great gale & rain, & I walked about mumbling those fine lines in Pericles Prince of Tyre: "Thou God of this great Vast, rebuke these surges, Which wash both Heaven & Hell!"—(though they did not quite apply to the case). My wife is quite well, & sends her best remembrances.

Always yrs sincerely
T. Hardy.

the County history: Douglas's *A History of the Border Counties* (1899). *The Ettrick shepherd's*: James Hogg (1770–1835), poet and novelist. *& Hell!"*: *Pericles*, III. i. 1–2.

To Florence Henniker

MAX GATE, | DORCHESTER. | 15. 2. 99

My dear friend:
I did not hurry to tell you what I thought of the Corporals—which I read *immediately*—being under the impression that you were busy with social affairs, to the displacement of literary. Had you been a "woman-writer" struggling with a pen in a Grub street garret, it might have quickened me. Well: I am glad to say, sincerely, that this tale is the best thing you have done, in my opinion. Strikingly picturesque, it seizes hold of one immediately, & I never felt more disappointment in the reading of a tale than when I turned over the leaf & found there was no more. The pity of it lies in that: you have cut if off ruthlessly, when you might have raised a large design on your foundation. To speak of it as a story to *sell*—if you were to carry it on, without letting the gipsy die, & reintroduce that girl of the shooting gallery (who arrests the attention from the first moment of her appearance) it wd make a good one-vol. story.

But, as a transcript from life the case is different. The sense that you have recklessly thrown away a fine opening upon a mere sketch is absent now you tell me it is mostly true: or even if it is a study of human nature with no aim at story, but at the inconsequence of life. And this leads me to suggest that you write a series of *true* stories of soldier-life—announcing them as such. You are in a position to come across a great many. I do not recollect that anything of the kind has been

done of late years. I shd limit the chief actors to privates &
N. C. officers.

I must have given a wrong impression of the criticisms on
the W. Poems. I shd have said that the reviews were all that
cd be wished (except a few spiteful ones, quite minor,) as
friendliness, but that the complaints of pessimism were
absurdly conventional, & of the nature of cant.—Did I tell
you that I have had an application for leave to set "At an
Inn" to music? You have never noticed that one, by the way.

You know I shd *not* be sarcastic if I were to drop in &
criticize yr work! Will you go to see the Rembrandts with me
if I come to London? Again congratulating you on The 3 C.'s
I am

ever yrs
Tho H.

P.S. I have never met Ld Rosebery's daughters, so far as I
recollect, though I know him. What a nice time you must
have had at Crewe.

the Corporals: her story 'Three Corporals', published in the *Idler*, Feb. 1899.
N.C.: non-commissioned. *"At an Inn"*: the poem, in the recently
published *Wessex Poems*, relates to a visit which TH and Florence Henniker
made to Winchester together one day in 1893. *the Rembrandts*: in the
current Royal Academy Winter Exhibition. *Ld Rosebery's daughters*: Lord
Rosebery's second daughter Lady Peggy Primrose married Florence Henniker's brother Lord Crewe in Apr. 1899.

To Edmund Gosse

MAX GATE, | DORCHESTER. 6. 3. 99

My dear Gosse:

I was, as you will have guessed, much interested in reading
your leader; & have no small pride in your thinking the
Poems worth making the text of an article so teeming with
ideas in every line. As you rise to higher instances than the
humble one you start with, innumerable thoughts are suggested: one in particular—by your phrase "Browning is a
curious specimen of genius", &c. The longer I live the more

does B.'s character seem *the* literary puzzle of the 19th century. How could smug Christian optimism worthy of a dissenting grocer find a place inside a man who was so vast a seer & feeler when on neutral ground? You, from your intimacy with Browning, could probably answer all that, if any living man can: & don't think me officious if I say that you ought to give an explanation to the world. One day I had a theory which you will call horrible—that perceiving he wd obtain in a stupid nation no hearing as a poet if he gave himself in his entirety, he professed a certain mass of commonplace opinion as a bait to get the rest of him taken. Well "The Riddle of Browning" is what I want to read from your pen.

  Believe me

Always yours
Thomas Hardy.

your leader: Gosse had made *Wessex Poems* the occasion of an unsigned leading article, 'Form in Poetry', in the 4 Mar. issue of *Literature*.

To Florence Henniker

MAX GATE, | DORCHESTER. | July 25. 99

My dear friend:
  I have been here ever since leaving London, not having felt vigour enough to do anything or go anywhere. But the eye is practically well, though a little weaker than the other as yet. Thank you for remembering about the lotion.
  I wonder if you have gone or are going to Westgate. We fortunately left London before the great heat set in; but you like a high temperature I know.
  I am starting to-morrow if all goes well for a 2 or 3 days bicycle tour in the New Forest—just to make a beginning, for I want to go further later on. I miss the music one can get in London, & the chief objection to a country life is that difficulty of hearing good music when one wishes to—though to be sure at this time of the year there is little enough anywhere. I have just read Tolstoi's "What is Art?"—a suggestive book, in which are a good many true things, & many more that

hover round the truth but just miss it—at least as I judge. Two short stories of mine have been appearing in Paris in the *Journal des Débats*—translated by Mlle Rolland. Which of your stories is the play to be based on? And are you filling your inkbottle to set about adapting it? There is room for a good play anywhere just now—the specimens of dramatic art that we see upon the English stage being mediocre to a degree. I find far more interesting forms of art at the music halls. May your name soon appear on the omnibuses beside that of Mrs Allen the Hair-restorer & the Little Liver Pill genius!

Tell me if the galvanism does good: I think the seaside wd do more.

Ever yours
Tho. H.

Westgate: a seaside resort in Kent.   *"What is Art?"*: TH read Aylmer Maude's English translation (1899), marking the pages quite extensively as he did so.   *short stories . . . Rolland*: 'A Tragedy of Two Ambitions' and 'Tony Kytes, the Arch-Deceiver'; Madeleine Rolland, sister of the novelist Romain Rolland, became a friend of TH's as a result of her translation of *Tess*, completed by this date but not published until 1901.   *the play*: Florence Henniker had spoken earlier of dramatizing one of her stories. *galvanism*: she received many electrical treatments over the years.

To Edmund Gosse

MAX GATE, | DORCHESTER. | Oct 1. 1899

My dear Gosse:

I am much interested in your undertaking, & charmed by your way of telling me about it. But the question of my doing the essay devoted to Zola is disposed of without disturbing the belief I hope you cherish of my willingness to render you any personal service that lies in my power. On account of what I already have in hand, & am pledged to, I cannot possibly give the necessary time to the labour of such an essay—even if short—a labour which would be a serious one to me—absolutely inexperienced in criticism, & constitutionally uncritical. Indeed I question if I could do it, even if I had the time, & overcame my strong opinion that one novelist should not write on another except in eulogy—a tone I could not adopt towards Zola as a novelist—believing him no artist, but at bottom a man of affairs, who would just as soon have written twenty volumes of, say, the statistics of crime, or commerce, as of fiction—a passionate reformer, who has latterly found his vocation.

However, as I say, I am spared these considerations by the circumstances I am in. And as years increase, things to be done which used to seem small loom large.

So much for myself. To turn to you: I cannot conceive why you should ask anybody at all to do that particular essay. From what I know of your familiarity with Zola & French fiction generally you could sit down, without giving a single hour to preparation, & write off the article *currente calamo*.

I can think of half a dozen men who would do it *well enough*, but I am strongly of opinion that you ought to do it yourself.

I hope you enjoyed your journey to the North Pole—or somewhere in that direction—which you told me you were intending to take. I have been suffering from several unimportant ailments, one after another, since returning from London, which have prevented my doing much, either by way of holiday or of work.

Sincerely yours
Thomas Hardy.

your undertaking: Gosse had become general editor of a series of translations to be published by Heinemann under the title 'A Century of French Romance'; TH's refusal to write an introduction to a volume by Zola apparently led to Zola's being omitted from the series altogether.   *found his vocation*: the allusion is to the Dreyfus affair and to Zola's publication of 'J'accuse' in Jan. 1898.   *North Pole*: Gosse spent six weeks in Norway in the summer of 1899.

[As the South African War approached in the autumn of 1899 Hardy knew himself well enough to recognize that his instinctive and intellectual opposition to the crude imperialism, jingoism, and war fever of the day would not prevent him from becoming caught up in the excitement of the military operations themselves. Florence Henniker's husband—whom Hardy had met and liked—was sent to South Africa at an early stage of the war, and Hardy kept close track both of his career and of the overall fortunes of the war, managing to combine a critical attitude towards the policies of the British government with an active sympathy for those on both sides who were caught up in the fighting itself. Not surprisingly, given his passionate sensitivity to the sufferings of animals, his deepest concern was for the miserable fate of horses in battlefield conditions.]

To Florence Henniker

MAX GATE, | DORCHESTER. | Oct 11. 1899.

I imagine you to be back in town by this time, dear friend, in all the excitement & interest, &, I should add, regret, which the sense of war in the near future always awakens, even amongst people less closely connected with the army than you are. I constantly deplore the fact that "civilized" nations have not learnt some more excellent & apostolic way of settling disputes than the old & barbarous one, after all these centuries; but when I feel that it must be, few persons are more martial than I, or like better to write of war in prose & rhyme.

Such a position appears to have been now reached; & the sooner we get at it, & get it done, the better, I think. You refer to the sufferings of the horses in war, & unfortunately the Boer horses seem to be already undergoing much hardship from exposure.

Since returning from Arlington I have been using the fine weather in taking little day excursions to places in this neighbourhood. Are you any better for your visit to the north? I hope you have nothing that you want to publish just now, for I fancy books will be neglected for newspapers awhile. Is it the opinion in military circles that the S. Africa business will soon be over?

Swinburne's sonnet in to-day's *Times* disappoints me, but probably it was dashed off in a hurry. I was about to send a few rhymed lines to some paper, on Game Birds, but shall

probably keep them by me now, for other slaughter will fill
people's minds for some time to come.

Ever sincerely yours
Tho. H.

from Arlington: the Jeunes' house near Newbury.   *Swinburne's sonnet*: 'The
Transvaal: October 9, 1899'; its final sentence, 'Strike, England, and strike
home', typifies the martial tone sustained throughout.   *on Game Birds*:
TH's poem 'The Puzzled Game-Birds' first appeared in his 1902 volume
Poems of the Past and the Present.

To Florence Henniker

MAX GATE, | DORCHESTER. | Dec 19. 1899

My dear friend:

"The hand of Midian prevails against Israel". I wonder
how you have been bearing the tension of the last week or
two? As I do not see that you were present at the memorial
service to Ld Winchester yesterday it has occurred to me that
you may be ailing, & unable to go out? What a Christmas for
us this will be: I do not remember such another. I have not
run up to London after all, this month; but I have written a
little poem, of 2 stanzas only, on the scene at the War Office
after a battle, which, though I have not witnessed it, I can
imagine with painful realism. Our Dorset regiment has gone
out, as perhaps you saw, & of the Artillery & Infantry in our
two barracks here as a rule we have only *2 men* left at present.
Col. Long of the Horse Artillery, who has lost the guns at the
Tugela, & is dangerously wounded, is well known here, where
he was lying with his battery down to 2 or 3 yrs ago. But of
course you know an immense number of the names we get
sent home. I am so sorry for Buller, as possibly the reverse he
has met with might have occurred to a Napoleon in the
circumstances. Speaking generally however, I think our generals are deficient in strategic instincts, though they have a
superabundance of courage. This Imperial idea is, I fear,
leading us into strange waters. Personally I was not so
sanguine of success at the beginning as most people were, &

I am not now so disconcerted at the want of it as they. I always imagined the business wd take us 3 years, rather than 3 months, & I still adhere to my opinion. Write soon, & do send my remembrances & hopes & wishes when you are writing to Africa.

Ever yrs sincerely, with sympathy
Tho H.

I can send you the W.O. poem, if you wd like.

against Israel": an adaptation of Judg. 6: 2.　　*Ld Winchester*: see letter of 24 Jan. 1897; he was killed in action in South Africa while serving with Major Henniker's battalion of the Coldstream Guards.　　*little poem*: 'At the War Office After a Bloody Battle', published in the *Sphere*, 27 Jan. 1900, and later retitled 'At the War Office, London'; TH's postscript refers to it as 'the W.O. poem'.　　*at the Tugela*: the battle at the river Tugela, reported in that day's newspapers, in which Colonel Charles J. Long was wounded and the British forces commanded by General Sir Redvers Buller (1839–1908) suffered a serious reverse. TH had met Buller in 1894.

To Florence Henniker

MAX GATE, | DORCHESTER. | Feb 25. 1900

My dear friend:

I was glad to get your letter, & to hear that you are fairly well. But I fear that London is not a likely place to make you strong, even though it may be the headquarters of good advice. Probably Bournemouth for a fortnight would give you a good start for the spring? If you do think of it, remember you are to come on here.

Possibly you know by this time the result of the attack on Cronje, which I do not. How horrible it all is: they say that his wife & other women are in that riverbed with his unfortunate army: & the mangled animals too, who must have terror superadded to their physical sufferings. I take a keen pleasure in war strategy & tactics, following it as if it were a game of chess; but all the while I am obliged to blind myself to the human side of the matter: directly I think of that, the romance looks somewhat tawdry, & worse. I do not, of course, refer to this particular war, & the precise shade of blame or otherwise which attaches to us. I met a religious man on Friday (by the way, he is son of the old parson whose portrait I partially drew in Angel Clare's father), & I said, We the civilized world have given Christianity a fair trial for nearly 2000 years, & it has not yet taught countries the rudimentary virtue of keeping peace: so why not throw it over, & try, say, Buddhism? (I may have said the same thing to you). It shocked him, for he could only see the unchristianity of Kruger.

I wonder if you have had a cablegram from Major Henniker lately? He must be in Kimberley by this time, must he not? I wonder if he suffers much from the heat. But I think he likes hot weather. Lady Grove was in Dorchester a week or two ago, & she came out to see us—bringing a friend in khaki (young Ivor Guest, Lady Wimborne's son) who is leaving next week for S. Africa. She has just heard from Lady Wynford, who is at Cimiez: but is coming back soon.

I have read no recent books: when I get to London I am going to read them up. I should like to be in town for a day or two just now; but a miserable sick headache, with pain at the back of the head, has been almost chronic with me for the last month, though I eat scarcely anything in endeavours to prevent it. I fear I must see a doctor.

Always yours
Tho. H.

Poor Mr Bunbury: I met him at your house I think. It must be grievous to you knowing so many.

Cronje: Piet Arnoldus Cronje (1835?–1911), a Boer general.   *religious man*: probably the Revd Handley Moule; see letter of 11 Feb. 1880 for him and for his father, the Revd Henry Moule, the 'original' of parson Clare in *Tess*.   *Kruger*: Stephanus Johannes Paulus Krüger (1825–1904), the Boer leader.   *Guest*: Ivor Churchill Guest (1873–1939), later the 1st Viscount Wimborne, was currently an officer in the Dorset Imperial Yeomanry.   *Lady Wynford*: Edith, wife of the 5th Lord Wynford; Cimiez is on the French Riviera.   *Bunbury*: William McLintock-Bunbury, eldest son of the 2nd Lord Rathdonnell, had died of wounds while serving in South Africa with the Scots Greys.

[The Hardys had fallen temporarily into a quasi-parental role in relation to Emma's nephew and niece Gordon and Lilian Gifford. Gordon made Max Gate his home while he was attending the Dorset County School, on the outskirts of Dorchester, and Lilian also stayed there for extended periods, both at this time and later on. Hardy, who regretted the childlessness of his marriage, was deeply attached to both of them. He gave Gordon a basic introduction to architecture—having kept his own skills alive by doing occasional design-work for his brother Henry—and then, early in 1900, arranged for him to go to London and receive more advanced training in the office of a professional architect.]

To Emma Lavinia Hardy

SAVILE CLUB, | 107, PICCADILLY. W. | Thursday.
[17 May 1900?]

Dear Em:

I think of returning to-morrow by train arriving about 6.15—as I have toothache, headache &c. I am coming up again the middle of next week for a day or two if possible—or longer. That, I think, will finish London for me this season. I don't see why you cannot stay at the Alexandra Club this year, it being a particularly dull one, & London not full—though I strongly advise you not to come till the cold weather leaves us. Lilian has earache &c: everybody has aches in fact. I meant to take her to the Academy, but as she is not well it will be better for you to take her when you come. Gordon is, if he can, coming to lunch here with me to-day, & going on with me to the S. Kensington Art Library: I thought I had better show him how to get out books &c—so as to start him there. He is looking thin in the face, but says he is well. I want also to go through the Architecture in the Academy with him, but am not sure if I shall be up to it—A crowd of Americans & Colonials are coming to London, on their way to Paris Exhn but they will be disappointed at its dulness.

T.H.

If I cannot come tomorrow I will telegraph. Keep an eye on the parcel's box, as I am sending home things.

Alexandra Club: a women's club in London of which Emma was a member. *Lilian . . . Gordon*: the children of Emma's brother Walter Edwin Gifford (see letter of 18 Sept. 1874); Gordon (1877–1952) was subsequently employed as an architect by the London County Council.   *the Architecture*: the architectural section of the Royal Academy's Summer Exhibition. *its dulness*: i.e. the dulness of London, not of the 1900 Paris Exhibition, which TH did not visit.

To Florence Henniker

MAX GATE, | DORCHESTER. | Oct 22. 1900

My dear friend:

I remember that it is a year ago that we were in the excitement of sending off the army to the Cape. I spoke to some of the men at Southampton, who expected that they would be home in three months. Well, twelve have passed, & they have not yet returned. Have you heard from Col. Henniker lately, & are you expecting him soon? I should imagine that he must be nearly tired of the campaign by this time, & all of them. It is sad, or not, as you look at it, to think that 40,000 will have found their rest there. Could we ask them if they wish to wake up again, would they say Yes, do you think?

However, I was not meaning to write like that, & you must forgive me. What have you yourself been doing? Things theatrical, or more exclusively literary? Mrs Pat has written to ask me for a play: but though I try I cannot kindle enough interest in myself in the British stage to care to write for it. By the way, the Stage Society is going to give (in Nov.) two performances of that casual little thing of mine "The Three Wayfarers", which you once wanted to see.

I am puzzled what to do with some poems, written at various dates, a few lately, some long ago. If I print them I know exactly what will be said about them: "You hold opinions which we don't hold: therefore shut up." Not that there are any opinions in the verses; but English reviewers go behind the book & review the man. I am of opinion that the present condition of the English novel is due to the paralysing effect of English criticism upon those who would have developed it—possibly in a wrong direction in many cases, but ultimately towards excellence.

I read Lord Crewe's letter in Saturday's *Times*, & thought it well argued, &, of course, of a far higher literary quality than most letters to the *Times*. Still, the external policy of the Tories is mostly *smarter*, (Heaven forbid that I should say *better*, in a moral sense,) I think, than that of the Liberals. That seems to me to be the *crux* in politics; external or foreign policy. You must play that game as other nations play it, & they will not play it humanely. At home you may give your humanity free play. To educate Europe is such a big thing!

6.30. Since writing the above I have been out on a little cycle tour with our niece, who is staying here—to Upwey, where there is a wishing-well. We duly wished, & what will result remains to be seen. I sometimes go, too, to Cerne Abbas, where there are the ruins of the old abbey (on land belonging to Lady Grove's brother): & I have been endeavouring to make out where the buildings stood. It is an interesting & difficult problem, to waste time upon, owing to the meagreness of the remains.

If I come to London this autumn I shall let you know.

Always yrs
Tho H.

I have just been correcting (at the request of the author) the life of William Barnes in the Dic. of Natl Biography. Have you read T.E.B.'s poems? It is a pity he was a parson, as it compelled him to write parsonically—as it did Barnes also.

T.H.

at Southampton: on 20 Oct. 1899 TH had cycled to Southampton to watch the departure of some of the ships carrying British troops to the South African war.   *Mrs Pat*: Mrs Patrick Campbell.   *Lord Crewe's letter*: printed under the heading 'British Parties and Disintegration', *The Times*, 20 Oct. 1900.   *our niece*: Lilian Gifford.   *the author*: Thomas Seccombe (1866–1923).   *T.E.B.'s poems*: Thomas Edward Brown (1830–97), the Manx dialect poet; his *Collected Poems* had just been published.

To Emma Lavinia Hardy

Tuesday. Nov 6. 1900

Dear Em:

I am fresh from parting Tip & Croppy—whom we cannot get to agree anyhow. Croppy defies us, & goes for Tip again & again when scolded & driven away. I keep Tip mostly in the study to avoid these quarrels, but they occur now & then.

It is continually raining here, but though I have a troublesome neuralgia in the teeth (not serious) left by the cold, I went to Dorchester this afternoon. There I heard that Arthur Lock died suddenly this morning—apoplexy, owing to an effusion of blood on the brain they say, possibly connected with the operation he underwent. Case, who told me, also told me that his daughters had bought a milliner's business in Wigmore St, (near Debenham & Freebody's therefore) & had gone there to carry it on—in the old name, that of Wright. So I suppose you will deal with them, though I do not know what booksellers can do with bonnets.

At the assizes last week, one of the sons of Dairyman Kingman, whom you knew when he was alive, was sentenced to 5 years penal servitde for nearly killing his wife. He is supposed to be wrong in his head by the family—owing to the kick of a horse in the temple—but the judge did not know this as he ought to have.

I am dreadfully afraid you will break down; & cannot tell why you shd have so much to do. Lilian is longing for you to come back—less, I tell her, from a wish to see you than from a desire to escape her penal servitude here. Since seeing Fisher she has been livelier: what she wants is more exercise; but I cannot get her to take it.

We did not go to the Sheridans after all—It rained heavily off & on, & as we could not bicycle, & my cold was bad just then I wired to Mrs S. that we could not come. My thumb is well.

I like the mild weather in spite of the rain, & hope it will last till Christmas. L. says you may mean that you are coming *this* week; but I do not think so.

Yours affly

T.

I only received yr Sunday letter *this* morning.

Tip & Croppy: two of the Max Gate cats.   *Lock*: Arthur Henry Lock (1845–1900), TH's solicitor.   *Case*: Dorchester bookseller and stationer. *the assizes*: although TH, as a county magistrate, sometimes served on the Grand Jury at the Dorset assizes, he seems not to have done so on this occasion; the man sentenced was Francis Kingman, aged 38.   *break down*: Emma was in Lee-on-Solent, Hampshire, attending the sick-bed of her sister Helen Holder, who died in Dec. 1900.   *Fisher*: Frederick Bazley Fisher, the Hardys' doctor.   *Sheridans*: see letter of 1 June 1889.

To Florence Henniker

MAX GATE, | DORCHESTER. | Christmas Eve: 1900

This is my Christmas card, my dear friend; all written by myself. I wonder whether you are in London, or have run down to Crewe Hall or elsewhere? If in town, it is, I fear, rather depressing to you to think that this is the second winter you have spent there alone, in spite of our expectation & hope that the war would be over long before now. I said, if you recollect, that it would be three years before all was settled & quiet, & I don't think I shall be far wrong. War resembles a snow storm in one respect: it is grand & romantic at the first, but dreary & tedious in its disappearance.

I am sorry indeed to hear that you have been feeling tired again. I always think Bournemouth would be a good place for you to winter in. You mention Lady D. Nevill. She was down here in the summer, & amused me much as usual. It was just at the time that "harvesters" are so troublesome if one gets among the grass, &c. & we were all suggesting remedies for their sting: one used ammonia, another vinegar, &c.; she said "Well, for my part, I scratch."

I was induced by a review to buy Q. Couch's Oxford book of Verse the other day; & was much disappointed: the selected names are a good & fairly exhaustive list, but the specimens chosen show a narrow judgment & a bias in favour of particular views of life which make the book second-rate of its class. "An Englishwoman's Loveletters" turns out to be a novel: it was suggested, I suppose, by the Browning Loveletters, which made such an excellent novel, & a true one.

My Soldiers' Wives' Song finishes up my war effusions, of which I am happy to say that not a single one is Jingo or Imperial—a fatal defect according to the judgment of the British majority at present, I dare say. The *Cornhill* editor has asked me for another, but I cannot rise to war any more. With best wishes from

Your affectte friend
Tho H.

I sent the Harpers with the soldier story.

Nevill: Lady Dorothy Nevill (d. 1913), widow of Reginald Henry Nevill and daughter of the 3rd earl of Orford; she spent much of her childhood in Puddletown, Dorset.   *Q. Couch's* . . . *Verse*: Arthur Thomas Quiller-Couch (1863–1944), man of letters, editor of *The Oxford Book of Engish Verse 1250–1900* (1900).   *Loveletters*": Laurence Housman's anonymously published *An Englishwoman's Love-Letters* (1900); *The Letters of Robert Browning and Elizabeth Barrett Barrett, 1845–1846* appeared in two volumes in 1899. *Soldiers' Wives' Song*: TH's 'Song of the Soldiers' Wives', *Morning Post*, 30 Nov. 1900.   *soldier story*: TH's 'Enter a Dragoon', *Harper's Monthly Magazine*, Dec. 1900.

To Florence Henniker

MAX GATE, | DORCHESTER. | Feb 15. 1901

My dear friend:

We seem to have entered on a new tract of time since we last communicated (as a lawyer down here used to say) with each other—Here we are in a new reign, & with a general sense of the unknown lying round us, which in itself is a novelty. Not that such changes affect me greatly, if at all. But what French editors call "Le God save" has to be sung somewhat differently by me when I feel musical, & my money all looks old-fashioned pending the new coinage; so that I feel there *is* a change.

But I ought not to begin with "frivol"—(the Right Reverend inventor of that dignified word has also passed away), since you may be unwell, or depressed on account of the tedious dreary length of the war: in which case I ask you to forgive me. That I should for one moment write anyhow but gravely is a marvel, for I have been unwell & sad enough myself in the interval—feeling that I could not write a letter or do anything. I have felt much better—indeed quite well—during the last week.

I wonder if you saw some lines I wrote about the Queen, that were printed in the Times? I did not send them to you (or anybody) for they were really not worth calling your attention to. I wrote them during a bad headache, & posted them immediately & they came out the next day—so that they have all the crudeness of an unrevised performance.

Wm Archer—whom you know—came here about a week ago. He experimented on me in a new kind of interviewing: knowing him well I did not mind it at the time, but I have felt some misgivings since, & suppose I shall be thought to have prompted the production when it is printed. It is, however, only a discussion of abstract subjects: & the second person might have been anybody for that matter.

Please let me know what news you have had from S. Africa, & if anything to cause you anxiety. As to your hope that the horses & mules will receive compensation somewhere for their sufferings, I, too, hope the same, though according to modern philosophies they, like ourselves, will pass into nothing, & have to be *re-willed* into existence as other horses & mules before they have a chance of such compensation.

Have you seen many people lately?—many more than I have, of course. I had thought of taking a little flat in London this year again; but Emma seems averse to the trouble of doing it: so that I cannot say what our plans are. My being unwell prevented my going to see William Watson. I hope he is well by this time. Believe me

Ever yrs sincerely
Tho. H.

new reign: Queen Victoria had died on 22 Jan.; the following day the prince of Wales was proclaimed King Edward VII.   *"frivol" . . . inventor*: the obituary of Mandell Creighton, bishop of London, in *The Times* of 15 Jan. 1901 had mentioned his love of fun and added, 'he must have invented the verb "to frivol" for himself'.   *about the Queen*: 'V.R. 1819–1901', *The Times*, 29 Jan. 1901.   *Wm Archer*: the interview appeared under the series title of 'Real Conversations' in the *Pall Mall Magazine*, Apr. 1901. *Watson*: William Watson (1858–1935), poet.

To Sir George Douglas

Max Gate | 3 April: 1901

My dear Douglas:

I am so glad to hear that you are going to continue faithful to Thurloe Square, as I like to think of you there, even if I myself am not much in Town. My wife thinks again this year that a flat, & still more a house, would be burdensome, which is perfectly true for her, though for me either is more comfortable than an hotel or lodging—& as cheap. Anyhow I suppose I shall be in London by the third week or so of this month, for a short time or longer—

I am not without misgivings that the reperusal of my books may have shown you more of their weaknesses, as it certainly does to myself.

A gloom has been cast over us here since yesterday by the loss of a favourite cat, which was mutilated by the mail-train the night before last. The violent death of dumb creature always makes me revile the contingencies of a world in which animals are in the best of cases pitiable for their limitations.

As you have been re-reading my books I shall ask you when I see you what you think of my opinion that "Her Death & After," & "The Dance at the Phoenix" (both in Poems) are two as good stories as I have ever told? I shall also want to know what you have been doing on your own account.

Always sincerely yrs
Thomas Hardy.

Thurloe Square: Douglas's address when staying in London.   *Poems*: i.e. *Wessex Poems*, the only volume of verse TH had as yet published.

To Edward Clodd

MAX GATE, | DORCHESTER. | Feb 27. 1902

My dear Clodd:

I have finished reading every word of your "Huxley", & must thank you for being so good as to send me such an interesting volume. Part IV—"The controversialist"—kept me up last night in spite of the inconveniences of a weak eye, caused by a cold. I may say at once that I do not think the work could have been done better by any one, in the space at your command.

What is forced upon one again, after reading such a life as Huxley's, is the sad fact of the extent to which Theological lumber is still allowed to discredit religion, in spite of such devoted attempts as his to shake it off. If the doctrines of the supernatural were quietly abandoned to-morrow by the Church, & "reverence & love for an ethical ideal" alone retained, not one in ten thousand would object to the read-justment, while the enormous bulk of thinkers excluded by the old teaching would be brought into the fold, & our venerable old churches & cathedrals would become the centres of emotional life that they once were.

Well: what we gain by science is, after all, sadness, as the Preacher saith. The more we know of the laws & nature of the Universe the more ghastly a business we perceive it all to be—& the non-necessity of it. As some philosopher says, if nothing at all existed, it would be a completely natural thing; but that the world exists is a fact absolutely logicless & senseless.

I hope you have kept free of colds this winter, & am

Always yrs sincerely
Thomas Hardy.

your "Huxley": Clodd's *Thomas Henry Huxley* (1902); it was the source (p. 150) of the quotation from Huxley's 'Agnosticism' essay of 1889 in TH's second paragraph.   *as the Preacher saith*: an allusion to Eccles. 1: 18.

[Because he felt that he had been left without a London publisher as a result of Harper & Brothers' absorption of its English subsidiary Osgood, McIlvaine & Co., Hardy sought to transfer all his books to the house of Macmillan, which had published *The Woodlanders* and *Wessex Tales* in the 1880s. When Osgood, McIlvaine objected to this defection, Hardy sought support and reassurance from the Incorporated Society of Authors, an organization devoted to protecting the rights and interests of professional writers. Once the new arrangements were in place Frederick Macmillan rapidly became one of the most trusted and frequently consulted of Hardy's friends and advisers, the letters included in this volume representing only a small proportion of those Hardy addressed to him over the succeeding years.]

To G. Herbert Thring

(Copy) <u>Private</u>   March 4. 1902

My dear Sir:

I suppose I am at liberty to consult the Society on the following matter—though it is not exactly a legal one.

My contracts with my present publishers, (the firm trading as Harper Brothers) expire shortly, as far as England is concerned, & I have concluded that it will be better that I transfer my publishing on this side of the Atlantic to an English house, leaving Harper & Bros as before to act for me in America. My justification in making the change is among other things that the firm was not Harper Brothers when the contracts were entered into, but a young firm, Messrs Osgood & McIlvaine, who though personally Americans had started as a London house only. This firm merged in Harpers during the run of the contracts,—&, I may add, later on the Harpers themselves, owing to commercial difficulties, dropped out of the firm. Thus I have been carried by currents, & against my intentions, into the position of having only a subsidiary branch of an American house as my English publishers.

Now it is obvious,(as it seems to me) that seeing that I am getting older & less enterprizing than I was, I should desire to have as my London publishers a house whose head office is in London & not New York.

On the other hand, "Harper Bros."—who are really a gentleman named Harvey now, I believe, of New York, represented here by Mr McIlvaine, who has a share in the business,—have always dealt fairly with me, & moreover I lost nothing by the financial troubles of the old firm.

Well: on informing Mr McIlvaine that I do not think of renewing the contracts, he says it will be a stigma on his firm, that other authors wd be deterred from coming to them: loss of prestige: in short, a great injury will be done. But surely that is not the case? I naturally do not want to do anything that is unfair; but, bearing in mind the unexpected transmutations in the firm, & in view of possible contingencies which might make it awkward that my publishers should have their headquarters in America, is not my proposed change an obvious & defensible one, even though there has been no particular fault to find with anybody?

Yours trly
T.H.

P.S. Shd my friend Mr Ant. H. Hawkins be at hand I shd not at all mind his knowing the contents of this letter, & should of course, value his views on the case in addition to yours. T.H.

G. Herbt Thring Esq. Sec. Society of Authors

Thring: George Herbert Thring (1859-1941), from 1892 to 1930 secretary of the Incorporated Society of Authors, Playwrights, and Composers; he wrote on 5 Mar. to assure TH that his position, as set out in this letter, was perfectly justified.   *Osgood & McIlvaine*: Osgood (see letter of 11 Apr. 1891) was dead, but the other partner, Clarence Walworth McIlvaine (1865–1912), also American-born, had stayed on in London as the representative of Harper & Brothers.   *the Harpers themselves*: i.e. the members of the Harper family.   *Harvey*: George Brinton McClellan Harvey (1864–1928), American editor and political journalist, was president of the reorganized Harper firm.   *Hawkins*: Anthony Hope Hawkins (1863–1933), author of *The Prisoner of Zenda* and other novels under the pseudonym of 'Anthony Hope'; he had long been a member and officer of the Society of Authors and wrote on 7 Mar. to assure TH that his position was correct.

To Frederick Macmillan

Dear Mr Macmillan:

The term of years for which I entrusted the publication of my books to Messrs Osgood McIlvaine & Co—now the Messrs Harper—expires on April 4 next—(except as to one novel & the poems, which have a little longer to run).

The unexpected vicissitudes of the firm, owing to which it befalls that my publisher here has become only a subordinate member of a New York house, make it necessary—from obvious considerations of convenience—that I transfer the English edition of the books to a publisher whose head-quarters are London.

As you already publish the Colonial edn, & in view of my long personal acquaintance with the members of your firm, I write to you first on the matter, to inquire if you would be willing to take up the books, when they fall into my hands.

The Messrs Harper, I ought to say, have dealt quite fairly with me since I have been with them, & though they complain of "loss of prestige" by my withdrawal, (which is an error, theirs being the American view, & London differing from New York in that respect) they perceive my natural reasons for the step, & we part amicably enough. Out of consideration for them I have allowed them six months for selling off the stock on hand, which brings the actual end of the term to Oct. 4. next.

I have stipulated that the plates shall be on offer at that date at half cost.

You may perhaps like to know that there have been no systematic cheap editions of the novels (the cheapest uniform edn having been 6s/-) so that the course is open for such; & that I have had some offers for the publication of a large limited edn; but this too has been left in abeyance. The curious accident of a topographical interest having arisen in "Wessex" also helps the vitality of the volumes.

However, I will not go into details now; & indeed, I did not intend to open communications with new publishers just yet, till it occurred to me that it might be for their convenience to do so. I should add that Mr McIlvaine asks me not to let it be publicly known that I am leaving his firm.

Yours very truly
Thomas Hardy.

Frederick Macmillan Esq.

Macmillan: Frederick Orridge Macmillan (1851–1936), son of Daniel Macmillan, co-founder of the Macmillan publishing house; following the death of Alexander Macmillan, the other founder, the firm had become a limited company, with Frederick as its chairman.   *no systematic cheap editions*: although Sampson, Low had brought out several of the novels in cheap formats in the 1880s and early 1890s.

To Frederick Macmillan

MAX GATE, | DORCHESTER. | March 31. 1902

Dear Mr Macmillan:

I have examined the draft, & have marked on it all that occurs to me as requisite, which are mainly a few words I find in old agreements.

I transferred the phrase about the new novel to a clause by itself merely because, as it stood, it seemed to say that if, for any reason, you did not wish to publish any such new book, I could not get it published anywhere.

As you surmise, I have no financial interest in "Under the Greenwood Tree", & I suppose that any arrangement for including it in the series would have to be made between Messrs Chatto & yourselves, as was done by Osgood. I believe Chatto likes to keep the copyright because he thinks the book helps his list; but he may part with it.

I find that in my agreements with the New York firm of Harpers for the American edns, they have "control of the Canadian Market" for the three or four novels which are copyright in the United States. What this means I do not know, but if it has any importance I presume we shd except Canada from our agreement.

The clause pencilled at the end of the draft is a sort of

memorandum which I thought it would be well to put on record. So many books seem to be coming out concerning "the Wessex of the novels & poems" (the fourth, I see is just announced) that I fancy I shall be compelled, in self defence as it were, to publish an annotated edn giving a really trustworthy account of real places, scenery, &c (somewhat as Scott did): since it does not seem to be quite fair that capital shd be made out of my materials to such an extent as promises to be done. These matters wd then be embodied in my own books. An "Annotated edition", wd perhaps be in demand, as I cd make the notes very interesting. If you think so I can begin to collect matter. Please consider this idea as a private one.

Yours very truly
Thomas Hardy.

draft: of a Memorandum of Agreement covering the transfer of fifteen of TH's books from Harper & Brothers to Macmillan & Co. as of 4 Oct. 1902. *Greenwood Tree"*: the copyright in this novel, sold outright by TH early in his career, was now the property of the publishing house of Chatto & Windus.   *the fourth*: Bertram Windle's *The Wessex of Thomas Hardy* (1902). *as Scott did*: in the introductions and notes to the 'magnum opus' edition of 1829–33.

To E. W. Kerr

MAX GATE, | DORCHESTER. | April 6. 1902

Dear Sir:

I am glad to hear that a guide book to Dorchester is contemplated: I have often thought it desirable. I hope it will contain a clear *map* of the Town; for, needless as it may seem to us, strangers often complain of the difficulty of finding their way about.

I do not feel able to assist in the work by writing an introduction; all I have to say about the town being said already, in another form. I think too—& your Committee may agree with me when it is put to them—that it would hardly be good policy for me to have an overt hand in the preparation of a guide, such visitors as are attracted to the Town by anything I have written being moved by a feeling that they are penetrating a disguise which (as is quite true) I had no wish for them to penetrate. An impression that I have any practical object in popularizing the town would I think undo what little I may have unconsciously done towards it in the past.

Therefore I believe that I could render more assistance by, say, guiding the editor to some passages in my books that bear upon the subject, than in any other way.

I have been intending to write to the Town Council on a kindred matter; but perhaps an informal communication through you will have the same effect. Strangers who come here complain that the old names of streets & spots are not to be found. An American Professor in one of the Universities said bitterly the other day that he would not have come so many miles to see Dorchester had he known what awaited him in this respect. Now there are some points which I should like to urge upon the Council in this connection, & if your Committee would like, I could meet them at any time—(or what would be more easy for me, I would receive them here any afternoon)—& offer them some suggestions on some inexpensive trifles that might be seen to, to enable the town to retain, in some measure, its historic & romantic interest under the changes which are taking place.

Yours very truly
Thomas Hardy.

E. W. Kerr Esq. M.D. | Chairman of Committee

Kerr: Elias William Kerr (1849–1920), physician; he was mayor of Dorchester in 1903.   *an introduction*: TH did, however, supply a brief preface to the guidebook, *Dorchester (Dorset), and Its Surroundings* by F. R. and Sidney Heath, when it was eventually published in 1905.   *old names of streets*: see letter of 28 Apr. 1902; the 'American Professor' has not been identified.

To the Town Clerk of Dorchester

Max Gate, | Dorchester. | April 28. 1902

Dear Sir:

Guide to Dorchester, &c

Herewith I send as promised a few suggestions to the Corporation Committee as to the Guide, & some place-naming which is naturally involved in the matter.

I may say that I have been led to make these suggestions by the remarks & requests of visitors & correspondents English & American.

Yours truly
Thomas Hardy

The Town Clerk, Dorchester.

The Suggestions referred to—

—That, a clear map of the town be given in the proposed *Guide*.

—That the said Guide there contain an itinerary through the town, showing the order in which the various features of the place may most conveniently be taken by a visitor.

—That to this end, several historic spots, not now readily discoverable in the town, should be marked *in loco*, namely,

—That the curved S.E. wall of St Peters Churchyard be inscribed "*The Bow*" (Its old name. This would be a convenience for the inhabitants generally, as the place is one difficult to designate)

—That the name "*Bull Stake*" be preserved—either by calling North Square "*Bull-Stake square*", or (if the occupiers object) by calling the passage into North Square "*Bull Stake passage*"; Failing that, a stone shd be fixed somewhere in North Square, bearing the words "*The Bull Stake stood near this spot*".

—That "*Town-Pump: in use till 1860*" (?) be cut on the present structure.

—That "*The Old Theatre: Edmund Kean acted here*" (see life of Kean) be affixed to the side wall of Mr Godwins shop.

—That "*The old Gallows stood near this spot*" be inscribed on a stone let into the gravel of South-walks at the end nearest

Gallows Hill; & a similar inscription fixed by the Amphi-
theatre on the side where the gallows stood.
—That *"Site of the Romano-British Burial Ground"* be inscribed
on a stone on Fordington Hill.
—That *"Site of the Franciscan Friary"* be marked by Friary Hill.
—That *"On the hill within stood Dorchester Castle"* be marked
near the Gaol Entrance.
—That "Swan Bridge" be so designated.
—That *"To Maiden Castle 1½ mile"* & *"To the Ampheatre ¼
mile"* be inscribed at the bottom of South Street, with an
index.

T.H.

these suggestions: the guidebook (see previous letter) did have the two features
TH specified in this letter, but the only other suggestion which seems to
have been adopted was the renaming of 'The Bow'.   *Kean*: it was while
performing in Dorchester (in a theatre subsequently converted into the
china-shop owned by John Thomas Godwin) that Edmund Kean
(1787–1833), the actor, was 'discovered' by the manager of the Drury Lane
theatre; TH wrote three letters on this topic to the *Dorset County Chronicle* in
May and June 1902.   *Ampheatre*: so spelled by TH; the text of these
'Suggestions' is taken from a rough and heavily corrected draft.

To Sir George Douglas

MAX GATE, | DORCHESTER. | 2: 12: 1902

My dear Douglas:
   I quite entertained the notion of going to London before
Christmas; but last week a wretched face-ache, including
tooth & ear as occasional chorus, came on, & though it is not
so bad this week it makes me shy of going out of doors just
yet.
   What a painful malady it is that you have been undergoing.
Yes, a "felon" is a mild variety of whitlow. They pronounce it
"vellon" here, & I suppose I ought to have spelt it that way.
   About a month ago we were staying in Bath. I newly
discovered the place, as it were, after an absence of 20 years;
&, deducting sad memories of people dead, I enjoyed revisit-
ing it. I wish you would try it for a few days. A map is

published there now which shows at a glance the houses that have been occupied by well-known people. I found some omissions, but on the whole it is useful, & is free from gossip about the personages, which one does not want on a stroll. I stayed close to where Pitt was living when he received the news of Austerlitz that is said to have killed him, & looking out of window in the small hours I could in fancy see his emaciated form.

I see that the National Review for this month contains an article by Leslie Stephen on "Browning's Casuistry". I have not yet read the article, but I hope to. For it so happens that it is a matter I have often reflected on: indeed, I once went so far as to think I would write about it, but my intention ended in my suggesting the subject to somebody else (not L.S.) who did not carry it out. You will meet with the essay in London: let me know how it impresses you.

It is a mark of courageous fidelity in you to lecture about my writings to 1500 people—Edinburgh ones too. I might make them worth your lecturing about it if I could write them over again with less ephemeral intention!

My wife has had bronchitis, but is improving.

Always sincerely yrs
Thomas Hardy.

spelt it that way: in ch. 33 of *Far from the Madding Crowd*.   *Austerlitz*: William Pitt's reception of the news of Napoleon's victory over the combined Russian and Austrian armies at the battle of Austerlitz (1805) was dramatized in the sixth act of *The Dynasts*, Part First, published at the beginning of 1904.   *often reflected on*: see e.g. the letter of 6 Mar. 1899.

To Mary and Katharine Hardy

[24 December 1902]

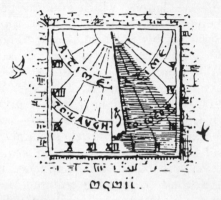

CRISTES MÆSSE

WITH·BEST·WISHES   FROM T.H.

CRISTES MAESSE: TH's Christmas card to his sisters, drawn and sent on a postcard, reflects the fascination with sundials also shown in his illustration to 'The Temporary the All' in *Wessex Poems*; the sundial fixed to the front of Max Gate was made in Dorchester to his design but not put in place until after his death.

To Florence Henniker

MAX GATE, | DORCHESTER. | March 17. 1903

My dear friend:

Your last letter found me disabled by rheumatism, which stuck about me a long while, & left a lassitude that I have only now got over. I think I caught the complaint by standing out of doors in the rain superintending the lopping of some trees. I had been thinking about a week before that I had not for years had an attack, & possibly never might again. We were going to stay for a day or two with Lady Grove at Sedgehill, but had to put her off on two occasions on account of it. In fact I have been scarcely out of the house (except just to Dorchester, &c) since I was in London.

I hope Brighton did you some permanent good, but the London season seems to be so early this year that doubtless you have had some trying functions from which humble people are sheltered.

R. L. Stevenson's letters, which you say you have been reading, are very attractive, particularly to those who knew him. The very fact of his not being quite "Thorough", as a man & as an author (i.e. critic of life), makes the letters, perhaps, all the more pleasant reading. In my enforced idleness I have been reading H. James's "Wings of the Dove"—the first of his that I have looked into for years & years. I read it with a fair amount of care—as much as one would wish to expend on any novel, certainly, seeing what there is to read besides novels—& so did Em; but we have been arguing ever since about what happened to the people, & find we have wholly conflicting opinions thereon. At the same time James is almost the only living novelist I can read, & taken in small doses I like him exceedingly, being as he is a real man of letters.

If we come to London this year we shall probably go into quite miniature lodgings of a Dickensian cast, finding the smallest house or flat a burden, & of course saving something—though not much, because the servants have to be kept on here, & may therefore just as well be taken up to town & made use of. But why shd I bore you with this! Did you go to the Winter Exhibition at the Academy? I liked it much. I saw that Col. Hr was at the Levée the other day. Believe me

Ever aff (!) sincerely yours
Tho H.

Stevenson's letters: *The Letters of Robert Louis Stevenson to his Family and Friends*, ed. Sidney Colvin, published in two volumes in 1899. *"Wings of the Dove"*: published in Aug. 1902. *at the Academy*: the Royal Academy's Winter Exhibition of Old Masters. *the Levée*: Florence Henniker's husband, now a colonel, had been presented to the king on his return from active service in South Africa to command the 2nd battalion of the Coldstream Guards.

To Emma Lavinia Hardy

THE ATHENAEUM, | PALL MALL. S.W. | Sunday [24 May 1903?]

My dear Em:

On thinking the matter over again I feel that I should like to avoid the racket of going home & coming up to London again this season: so that I am planning to stay on till you come (if you do). The only difficulty is (unless you really want me for anything at home) about that lost illustration, the original of which must be in the printers' hands before July 10. I will therefore try to explain to you how to find it.

The second of the two keys that you separated when you sent me the smaller one the other day, fits the left hand front drawer of the large table. In that drawer you will find a bunch of miscellaneous keys. One of these opens the cupboard under the smaller of the two bookcases that *face* the window. I *think* the drawings for "Wessex Poems" are in a flat packet of brown paper in that cupboard—one of these, "Leipzig", is the one wanted. They are all stitched together I think, & you must cut the string & separate that one. If you cannot identify it please refer to Wessex Poems in the glazed bookcase, & see the illustration to the "Leipzig" poem, which will enable you to do so.

In the middle cupbaord of the *glazed* bookcase you will find plenty of stiff cardboard to pack it in. Send by parcel post to me at this address. Please pack it safely, as, should that also be lost, there will be no means of replacing the lost illustration.

If you cannot find it in the cupboard I mention search in the cupbd with its back to your stairs. (Another key of the bunch unlocks that). If it is not there look in the bottom drawer of the oak chest of drawers. If not there, try the *back* drawers of the large table that are unfastened. (The fastened one I have the key of, & only cheque books, &c., are there.)

If not found yet, unlock the cupd under the bookcase on right hand of fireplace. If not yet I must leave you to exercise your own conjectures, for I cannot think further.

It will save me a journey if you do find it.

Ever yrs

lost illustration: TH had included a number of his own drawings as illustrations to *Wessex Poems*, first published by Harper in 1898; Macmillan, preparing to reissue the volume, found that the reproduction plate for the illustration to 'Leipzig' was missing and asked TH to send the original.

To Elizabeth Churchill

THE ATHENAEUM, | PALL MALL. S.W. | June 4. 1903

Dear Bessie,

You did quite right in sending the telegram with the letters, & if another comes send it in the same way, but post it immediately. Should any package come by railway requiring payment of carriage you may as well pay it, & if much, write & tell me what it amounts to, & I will send the amount; if trifling, I will settle with you when I return.

I think some potatoes were left in the cellar. Will you examine them & get the gardener to chimp them if they are worth keeping till we come back. Any green stuff in the garden that will spoil you had better use. Write & tell me how the vegetable marrows are getting on, & if they are kept watered. Also if the slugs eat the french beans. At dusk in the evening is the time to find them.

I hope you are well.

Yours truly
T. Hardy.

Churchill: the Max Gate parlourmaid, left in charge there during the period of the Hardys' annual London visit; to 'chimp' is, in Dorset dialect, to remove the shoots from sprouting potatoes.

To James Murray

MAX GATE, | DORCHESTER. | July 9: 1903

Dear Sir:

I have vaguely understood that the term "pair-royal" may be used of dice as well as of cards when three of the same value occur together; as was intended in the passage from "The Return of the Native" to which you draw my attention, where three dice were supposed to be thrown (as will be seen by reading on into the next Chapter).

The only instance I can lay my hands on of the application of the words to dice in print, except by myself, is the following: *Rees's Chambers's Cyclopaedia*, or *Universal Dictionary of the Arts & Sciences*, in 4 vols, 1786. Vol 4. Art. "Raffling":—

"Raffling, a sort of game with three dice, wherein he who throws the greatest pair, or pair royal, in three casts, wins the prize or stake".

Possibly an example may also be found in Steinmitz on Gambling. But of this I am not sure, as I have no copy by me.

My own experience of raffling was, curiously enough, not unlike yours. It was at the age of 10 or so, that I joined a raffle at a cottage for a live hen, at 2d a head. Being but a child, & the rest adults, I was made to throw first (the first thrower being deemed least likely to win). But to the consternation of all I threw a "pair royal", & won the bird—to my great inconvenience as I did not know what to do with it. The event was considered such a direct attempt of the devil to lead one of tender years to ruin that I was forbidden to gamble any more—& as a matter of fact, never did.

I am sorry that owing to my having left London there should be a delay in my reply.

Very truly yours
Thomas Hardy.

Murray: James Augustus Henry Murray (1837–1915), principal editor until his death of the *Oxford English Dictionary*; part of the passage from bk. III, ch. 7, of *The Return of the Native* is cited in the entry for 'pair-royal'.

Steinmitz: correctly, Andrew Steinmetz, whose *The Gaming Table: Its Votaries and Victims* was published in two volumes in 1870.

To Florence Henniker

MAX GATE, | DORCHESTER. | Sept 13. 1903

My dear friend:

I had a sort of spiritual intimation that you were wandering about, & not at Stratford Place. I cannot imagine you taking part in an agricultural Exhibition this year without also imagining you wet through. Our yearly one took place in deluges of rain, & I did not go near it. I have not yet really *read* the Shambles of Science, but everybody who comes into this room, where it lies on my table, dips into it, &, I hope, profits something. For my part, the world is so greatly out of joint that the question of vivisection looms rather small beside the *general* cruelty of man to the "lower" animals. I hear them complaining in the railway trucks sometimes, & think what an unfortunate result it was that *our* race acquired the upper hand, & not a more kindly one, in the development of species. If, say, lions had, they wd have been less cruel by this time.

I do recollect that story you speak of, & can conceive that it would make the *beginning* of a play. Walter Besant used to say that his method of dramatizing was (you know that he wrote plays with *some* success) to take a story, up to a certain point; then strike out with no regard to the story at all. This is an excellent plan when the story is not well known.

I am sorry about the manoeuvres—& hope your Colonel won't catch cold. As you are a military lady (one of our cats has jumped up here) I vent the following small grievance to you, in the hope that you will hand it on "to the proper quarter" as they say. Our Dorset regiment has been known from time immemorial as the "Green Linnets"—the facings having always been green. Of late the facings have been white, for no known reason, since some other regiments of the line still retain their green facings. As we fought under Clive at Plassy, & all through the Peninsular War in green (I suppose), this change is a petty annoyance which I resent, though I am not aware that the regt itself does.

The usual rank & file of summer tourists have called here, & I have given mortal offence to some by not seeing them in the morning at any hour. I send down a message that they must come after 4 o'clock, & they seem to go off in dudgeon. I was tourist myself last week, & as such was shown over Montacute House, Somerset (a show mansion of great interest). The amusing thing was that the residents sat like statues, reading in their library, & without speaking a word, whilst I was inspecting it, as if they, too, were part of the architecture. They are a very ancient family, I admit.

Let me hear again soon please.

Ever yr affecte friend
Tho H.

Stratford Place: Florence Henniker's London address at this period.   *of Science*: Lizzy Lind-af-Hageby and Leisa K. Schartau, *The Shambles of Science: Extracts from Two Students of Physiology* (1903).   *story . . . play*: Florence Henniker had returned (see letter of 25 July 1899) to the idea of dramatizing one of her own stories.   *jumped up here*: there is an ink smear on the page at this point.   *ancient family*: the Phelips family of Montacute (now owned by the National Trust) traced its ancestry back to the 14th century.

[Although Horace Moule, who committed suicide in 1873, had been far closer to him than any of the other sons of the Revd Henry Moule, Hardy later became extremely friendly with Horace's eldest brother Henry Joseph Moule, who was appointed the first curator of the new Dorset County Museum in 1883 and shared Hardy's own fascination with all aspects of local history and folklore. The Revd Arthur Moule, a missionary in China, was yet another of the Moule brothers with whom Hardy remained—despite all their differences in matters of belief—on the friendliest terms, and in writing to him of Henry's illness he was led on to speak of his own mother with a naturalness and directness that are still more marked in the intensely personal letter about Henry's death and funeral which he found himself addressing to the same correspondent less than six months later.]

To the Revd Arthur Moule

MAX GATE, | DORCHESTER. | October 19. 1903

Dear Mr Moule:

After setting here in the west you seem to have rearisen in the East with surprising rapidity. I could hardly have supposed that you would get settled down to work over there in so short a time.—In one respect you were fortunate in the date of your leaving England; we have had the wettest of weather here, particularly this year: & your stay in Dorset roughly corresponded with a dry cycle of summers. They say we are to have many more wet ones before the dry ones begin again.

I am so glad that your brother's short occupation of our house was of real benefit to his health. I wish he could have stayed longer. It was really as much a convenience to us as to him, for we dislike leaving the house in the custody of strangers when we go away. I have not seen him very lately, though my wife has. He is still keeping up to his ordinary level of activity. Some watercolours of his are at present on exhibition, with those of other painters, at a sort of art gallery in the town—on the premises formerly Bascombe's shop—which have been taken by a newcomer, a music seller, who intends to wake up the town in art & music. May he succeed.

Your remark that, if China were to range herself with England & Japan, peace would be secured for the East, brings impressively to mind the enormous specific gravity of China amongst the nations of the earth, & how easily she, with her vast population, could act as a buffer to Russia if she chose. Here in the west the activity of Russia leads us to forget the ponderousness of China by comparison. Western ideas will, I suppose, make their way there by degrees. But you, as a man continually accustomed to encounter beliefs & opinions differing from your own, will not, I am sure, mind my saying that I think the ideas that will make way there— even at the hands of missionaries—will not be largely of a doctrinal kind, but rather those bearing on the material arts, &, in morals, those of humanity & kindness to the lower animals, & the weak generally. It seems to me that the peoples of the East are so much older in religion than we of the west, that they must view our teaching thereon with something of the amused surprise of elders towards children's news & theories. This, of course, is a question of mental attitude, which has nothing to do with the question of whether they are wrongheaded in so doing, & perverse, to their own loss.

Your amusing discovery that I was wrong in making a character in "Under the Greenwood Tree" see the *rising* new moon in the evening has been anticipated by other correspondents. I should have said "setting" of course: I have meant to correct it for years, but have always forgotten when a new edition has been required.

Your knowledge of Chinese gives you an almost unique position among English writers—I mean, the knowledge of the tongue which enables you to write in it, & print a book in it. If you were not engaged in missionary work such a gift would be of great value in many ways for making the Chinese acquainted with what we westerns think. No doubt they make you acquainted with what they think freely enough—or it may be reservedly.

My mother has been unwell, but is recovering. She was 90 last month, but is unchanged mentally, & speaks of & recollects you & yours the same as ever. My wife sends her kindest regards, & I am,

Sincerely yours
Thomas Hardy.

I have also written some lines on a thrush, but they are too long to quote. T.H.

Moule: the Revd Arthur Evans Moule (1836–1918), sixth son of the Revd Henry Moule; he had recently returned to missionary work in China after four years as rector of a Dorset parish.   *your brother's*: Henry Joseph Moule (1825–1904), eldest of the Moule brothers, spent two or three weeks at Max Gate in the early summer of 1903 but never fully recovered from his illness (see letter of 20 Mar. 1904).   *correct it*: the change from 'rising' to 'setting' in *Under the Greenwood Tree* (Part II, ch. 3, third paragraph) was first made in the Wessex Edition of 1912.   *My mother*: Moule's letter (from China) of 29 Aug. 1903 had concluded with 'loving memories of Upper Bockhampton hamlet & its apples—& your dear mother there'.

lines on a thrush: 'The Darkling Thrush', first published (as 'By the Century's Deathbed') in the *Graphic*, 29 Dec. 1900.

To Emma Lavinia Hardy

Max Gate | Monday, 12 o'clock [16 November 1903]

Dear E:

Bessie wrote last night enclosing a note—nothing else here worth sending on. I received your card of Saturday, with the enclosures, this morning—there having been no afternoon post yesterday.

I am paying baker, washing, & milkman as directed. Poor Marky is not home even yet—but will come probably at the end of the week. Bessie says she is happy enough, in a large cage with straw &c—It seems that there was danger of gangrene if her foot had not been dressed every day—The others are well, & friendly with each other, but they are all learning to get inside the fender on the warm bricks.

The great event of this morning here has been the shifting of a large apple-tree from the old fruit garden to the new orchard. It took two men to lift, but I think it will grow: the other trees were preventing it bearing in its original place.

I went to the Hall on Saturday, a local case which has caused some excitement having come before us. Mr Duke's ricks at Woodsford were all burnt one night—eight or ten large corn stacks—the whole produce of his farm this year having been destroyed—value £1000—enough corn wasted to have fed 100 families through the winter. There is no proof that the man did it who has been apprehended, though he probably did.We committed him to the Assizes, when I fancy he may get off.

I don't think we can go to the Zangwill wedding. When you come back will be soon enough to reply, if you come this week: if not I will write. You have probably replied to Mrs Rowland Hill—so I will not.

I do not know if Paris may not give you colds this time of the year. You remember we were once there in November, & what a cold I had—but you must use your own judgment. I shall have finished the proofs this week—& should like to go away for a few days, but do not put yourself out on that account, as I may not care to go after all—Mother is much better, & will probably come downstairs for a little while today.

That ballad of mine—"A Trampwoman's Tragedy" is out in this month's North American Review—Gosse writes enthusiastically about it. I shall get this posted before 2 o'clock, in the hope that you may get it by the morning. I am glad to hear that Lilian likes being there—Shall be glad to see her again whenever fate ordains.

Yours
T.

Pretor's pictures china, &c. are come—he says he is quite brilliant now in his surroundings, & calls his lodgings the New Jerusalem.

Bessie . . . worth sending: Elizabeth Churchill and TH were sharing the domestic duties at Max Gate in the absence of Emma, who had taken Lilian Gifford with her on a somewhat unseasonable trip to Dover and thence on an apparently unpremeditated Channel crossing to Calais. *Marky*: one of the Max Gate cats, sent to a veterinary surgeon for treatment.   *come before us*: i.e. before TH and the other magistrates at the County Petty Sessions; the man accused of arson was indeed acquitted at the January assizes.   *Zangwill wedding*: Israel Zangwill (1864–1926), author and Zionist, was married to Edith Ayrton on 26 Nov. 1903. *Mrs Rowland Hill*: wife of the rector of Holy Trinity, Dorchester.   *the proofs*: of *The Dynasts*, Part First.   *Pretor*: Alfred Pretor (1840–1908), classical scholar and short-story writer; he had recently gone to live at Wyke Regis, near Weymouth.

To Emma Lavinia Hardy

Max Gate. | Saturday 11. a.m. [21 November 1903]

Dear Em:

I received your card last night, by calling at the P.O., otherwise it would have been delivered here this morng. The event of the morning is that Charles has fetched Markie, who is now wandering about the house gradually recalling

the place. She wants to be friendly with Snowdove, &
remembers him perfectly, but he does not remember her—at
least spits at her—as also does Pixie: but Comfy is indifferent.
I may want to go to London for one night next week, but I do
not like to be away longer. I finished the proofs last night.—
In returning you will have to be ruled by weather: it is now
practically winter, with all its treacheries. Our two or three
hard frosts have passed, & it is getting windy, but is not
cold.

You must be mistaken in thinking we stayed at the hotel
you are in—as we have never put up in Calais to my
recollection, though we have passed through. I fancy you are
thinking of the Hôtel Christol, at Boulogne, where we did
stay once. I wonder if you have looked for the celebrated
Hôtel Dessein of Sterne's Sentimental Journey? The guide
book says that the present Hôtel Dessein is not the old one,
which is now turned into Baths, Museum, &c. Calais, as you
know, belonged to us for 200 years down to Mary's reign. It
has always had the reputation of a place where the English
are fleeced, but that was before railways.—I see in Shelley's
Life that when he & Mary landed after crossing in the boat
on the day of their flight, they "walked over the sands to the
inn", but the name of the inn is not given: it was there that
Mrs Godwin overtook them, & vainly requested Mary to
return with her. The inn seems, anyhow, to have been near
the sands.

Abbot writes this morning from London. He goes to St
Paul's every day. He says nothing about returning yet. I am
going to post this before 2, in the hope that you may get it to-
morrow morning. But for the circumstance of Markie's arrival
& demand of attention I should have posted before 11.
Mention the *town* when you give yr address as I am not sure
sometimes. Also leave yr address when you come away, in
case a late letter arrives, but the best plan is to stay to the
day you say you are going to leave on. Wherever you go (if
you go anywhere else) it will be best to keep near the sea, as
you may get a cold inland, particularly at Paris.

I posted a card to you at the "Poste Restante"—so if you
have called you will have received it. The Miss Shirley's have
called, & I have just finished reading Mr Faulkner's new

novel—an interesting romance of the old fashioned sort. Love to Lilian: & a pleasant crossing.

Yrs
T.

Remember not to overrun money in hand, as I cannot send cheque to be quickly cashed, as in London. It would take some days to get into your hands.

Charles: one of the Max Gate servants; Markie (or Marky), Snowdove, Pixie, and Comfy were Max Gate cats.   *Shelley's Life*: see letter of 3 July 1897.   *Abbot*: TH's friend Reymond Abbott; see letter of 5 Nov. 1915. *Miss Shirley's*: former tenants of TH's; see letter of 24 July 1895.   *Mr Faulkner's*: John Meade Falkner (see letter of 17 Dec. 1911) had just published *The Nebuly Coat*.

[Hardy published the first of the three parts of *The Dynasts* in January 1904. The work, originally conceived more than thirty years earlier, now brought him before the public in yet another unfamiliar guise, and its initial reception, though respectful, was distinctly cautious. When all three parts had been published—and given additional relevance by Britain's involvement in the First World War—it became critical orthodoxy to regard *The Dynasts* as its author's single most impressive achievement. Later in the twentieth century, however, it has tended to be criticized for the relative inertness of its verse and assigned a much lower place in the Hardy canon.]

To Florence Henniker

Max Gate: | 23: 12: 03

My dear friend:

I must make a prosy letter do duty for a Xmas card, for I cannot match in this latitude the pretty one you have sent me. I had hoped to be able by this time to send you an early copy of the drama I mentioned to you in the summer (I think) as having in my head to publish, though I have said very little about it owing to my doubts on the question, the play being, in fact, only one-third the proposed whole, & until the last moment before sending up the MS. to the publishers I did not decide to print now, but thought of keeping the MS. till the thing was complete, which would have meant a year or two's delay. However it will be out at the beginning of Jan., & you will know what to think of it, though whether it will interest you at all, or anybody, I am in heathen ignorance, never having attempted the kind of performance before.

I was in London for a few days at the end of last month, but I did not stay over Sunday, as the rainy days gave me a cold in the head. You were, I believe, at Aldershot at the time. Em spent a month partly at Dover, partly at Calais, the air there having an invigorating effect upon her, but I did not go on to her as I had intended.

You must miss the battalion very much. I suppose colonels when they retire frequent the Service Clubs, & look at maps, & fight their battles over again? at least I think I should if *I* were one. I have been dipping into an amusing book, The Creevy Papers, which I think you will like if you have not already met with it. The Waterloo part reads like additional chapters of Vanity Fair, the Creevys being people quite of the Thackeray pattern.

If I should run up to Town again this winter I shall try to see you. I find that after three days a cold developes, so that I must see London in snatches in winter, or not at all. It seems to have the same effect on most people who rush there out of fresh air, but not on the Londoners themselves. We shall have a lively political time next year, I fancy—do not you? A Tory lady calmly admits to me that they have no statesmanship on their side to speak of (omitting J.): I wonder if the Liberals have, outside the few whom we can all readily think of.

A happy Christmas & new year.

Ever yr friend
Tho H.

Creevy Papers: correctly *The Creevey Papers: A Selection from the Correspondence & Diaries of the Late Thomas Creevey, M.P.*, edited in two volumes by Sir Herbert Maxwell, Bt. (1903).   *omitting J.*: an apparent reference to Joseph Chamberlain (1836–1914), who had recently resigned as Colonial Secretary; the 'Tory lady' was probably Lady Jeune.

To Edmund Gosse

MAX GATE, | DORCHESTER. | 31: 1: 04

My dear Gosse:

I have delayed sending an answer to your kind & stimulating letter till I had finished the Jeremy Taylor, a personage who is now far more interesting to me than ever he was before. The only works of his that I am really acquainted with are, of course, the "Living", & "Dying", & those, I fear, I have read mostly for their style, keeping to the "Living" by preference (though that is the less rich in imagery) because of what you excellently call the "mortuary" odour of the other in places.—The most brilliant chapter of your work is, I think, the last, though the Orinda chapter is also fine. The blue-stocking's headaches too, are inimitably hit off, though you only allot them a dozen words or so. But the book everywhere testifies to the marvellous fulness of your vocabulary & the swing of your general style, which leaves upon the mind the torrent-like impression that Macaulay's used to leave, with the substitution of striking verbal felicities for his comparatively commonplace diction.

But the chapter that I like best is—which do you think?—the one which probable cost you no trouble at all—the description of the deserted Portmore scene. It takes a sad & curious hold upon the imagination—not unlike that of Childe Roland's Dark Tower. It sent me to the map to hunt up the exact contours of the district. Very few descriptions do that nowadays.

However, I have to reply to your inquiries about The Dynasts. As for the title, it was the best & shortest inclusive one I could think of to express the rulers of Europe in their desperate struggle to maintain their dynasties rather than to benefit their peoples.

The Spirits do, indeed (owing perhaps to the evil example set by scientists & philosophers) seem to prefer words from the Greek to simpler ones; though they have some trying things to say to a respectable Philistine world. Whenever I have ventured to open the book since its publication I have been appalled at some of the oversights in this direction. I had meant to keep it by me longer, but a sudden feeling last autumn that I should never finish it, & that I would get rid of what was done, caused me to rush it out incontinently.

As for your general estimate of the performance I know that, as usual, you

"Piece out my imperfections with your thoughts"

but if I ever do go on with the production it will be largely owing to your cheerful views about it.

Believe me

Always yrs sincerely
Thomas Hardy.

Taylor: Gosse's *Jeremy Taylor* (1903); TH owned Taylor's most famous works in a single volume, *Holy Living and Dying*. Orinda was the pseudonym of Taylor's friend Katherine Philips (1631–64), poet.   *Macaulay's*: Thomas Babington Macaulay, 1st Baron Macaulay (1800–59), historian and essayist.   *Portmore*: a village near Lisburn, Co. Antrim, where Taylor lived for two years.   *Dark Tower*: an allusion to Browning's 'Childe Roland to the Dark Tower Came'.   *your thoughts"*: from the Prologue to *Henry V*.

[Hardy's hatred of cruelty to animals made him a passionate proponent of such causes as slaughterhouse reform and an active supporter of animal welfare organizations and movements for the abolition of fox-hunting, stag-hunting, hare-coursing, and other field sports. In the letter of 2 March 1904 his indignation found ironic expression of an almost Swiftian kind, although his vision of the world quite seriously enabled him to believe that it was a happy fate to die young (see letter of May 1891), or not to be born at all.]

To the Revd S. Whittell Key

March 2. 1904

Dear Sir:

I am not sufficiently acquainted with the many varieties of sport to pronounce which is, quantitatively, the most cruel.

I can only say generally that the prevalence of those sports that consist in the pleasure of watching a fellow-creature, weaker & less favoured than ourselves, in its struggles to escape the death-agony we mean to inflict by a treacherous contrivance, seems to me one of the many convincing proofs that we have not yet emerged from barbarism.

In the present state of affairs there would appear to be no reason why the children, say, of overcrowded families should not be used for sporting purposes. There would be no difference in principle: moreover these children would often escape lives intrinsically less happy than those of wild birds & animals.

Yours truly
Thomas Hardy.

Revd S. Whittell Key, M.A.

Key: the Revd Samuel Whittell Key (1874–1948), clergyman and author; he had apparently asked TH for his views on the degree of cruelty involved in different blood-sports, perhaps intending to publish several such solicited responses in book or pamphlet form.

To Henry Newbolt

MAX GATE, | DORCHESTER. | March 13. 1904

Dear Mr Newbolt:

I read the kind review of The Dynasts in the *Monthly* ten days or more ago, & I should have written sooner to thank you for it if I had not at that time had a troublesome face & ear-ache which prevented my doing much.

I think you yourself must be the writer, & the review is interesting to me (apart from its good opinion, which always makes a review interesting to the subject of it!) because you approach the book from the right side, which so few critics have done. Instead of saying to themselves, "Here is a performance hugely defective: is there anything in it notwithstanding the huge defects?" they have mostly contented themselves with picking out bad lines, which any child could do, there being myriads of them, as I knew too well before they said so.

I have, indeed, had some odd experiences of criticism in respect of this book. For one thing, I find that my reviewers have largely been women, especially in America. Surely Editors ought to know that such a subject could hardly be expected to appeal to women.

Your pertinent remarks on the word "Will" also interest me very much. You say truly, that, in its ordinary sense, it is not quite accurately used in the drama. But the difficulty was to find another, fit for poetry, which would express an idea as yet novel in poetry—that condition of energy between attentive & inattentive effort which the scientific call "reflex", "instinctive", "involuntary", action; "unconscious formative activity", &c. "Urgence" occurred to me, & I think I used it once, but it seemed scarcely naturalized enough. Just as the Original Cause did not (apparently) foresee the pitch of intelligence to which humanity would arrive in the course of the ages, & therefore did not prepare a world adequate to it, so the makers of language did not foresee the uses to which poor poets would wish to put words, & stinted the supply.

Your generous remarks make me feel that you have met me halfway: "Pieced out my imperfections with your thoughts" (a line which often occurs to me in these cases)—as indeed, was to be expected from the writer.

Yours sincerely
Thomas Hardy.

Newbolt: Henry John Newbolt (1862–1938), poet and man of letters; he was both editor of the *Monthly Review* and author of the anonymous review of *The Dynasts*, Part First, in the Mar. 1904 issue.   *your thoughts"*: see letter of 31 Jan. 1904.

To the Revd Arthur Moule

Max Gate | Dorchester | March 20. 1904

Dear Mr. Moule,

Long before these lines reach you, you will have learnt of the loss of your dear brother Henry, & my dear friend. His friendship with me reaches, of course, much further back than that of any person now alive, & it was of that staunch, undemonstrative kind which survives all differences of opinion, all contrasting conduct, & all separations. This really is the only true friendship, to my mind; which "many waters cannot quench, nor the floods drown".

You will have learnt particulars of his illness & death from other quarters, & therefore I need not dwell upon them. What you possibly may not hear of so clearly are the scene & circumstances of his funeral at that pleasant corner of F. Churchyard that you know so well. The day was absolutely cloudless—a marvellous day, indeed, for March, & the sun lit up the view over the meadows, Grey's bridge, & the river, to a gleaming brilliancy. Mr Boulter took the part of the service inside the church, & Mr Metcalfe the Committal. A person standing on Grey's bridge might virtually have taken part in the service, so calm was the air, & so clear. The grave was lined (as they possibly have told you) with moss & violets. A great many wreaths were sent—one by my mother from Bockhampton, now in her 91st year. She has known him more than 60 years—longer, I suppose, than any living person outside his family. She is now lying on a sickbed, from which I fear, she may never rise, & has been so much distressed at yr brother's death that we are compelled to change the subject as soon as we can. She used always to say to him, when they compared ages— "You are a mere boy to me."—& yet, you see, he has gone first. The wreath she sent was made on the premises of the old fashioned flowers up there (which he had often admired), & charmingly contrasted with the other more usual ones. At 8 in the evening before, there was found to be not quite enough green to finish it, & she sent out my sister with a lantern for more, fearing it might not reach the house in time, if left till the morning. I should have mentioned that after the last words of the funeral service, in the few moments of silence, an old navvy, evidently a friend of yr brother's, said in a low, yet distinct voice, "that's a good man gone!" It aptly summed up everybody's feeling.

It may interest you to know of a conversation I had with my mother this very afternoon. She told me, as well as she could in her feeble voice, of her first sight of your father (about the year 1830, as I gather—what a time ago!) She was visiting her brother in Dorchester, who obtained for her by some means a view of the barrack-service, which was held between 9 & 10 on Sundays, in the riding-school. She describes your father as "a fine, noble-looking young man": he preached at the drum-head, the congregation of soldiers standing in the saw-dust: a guinea lay on the drum-head all through the service, at the end of which the preacher took it up & hastened away to his parish service at the Church. How hard he worked!—& what a picture it gives of old Dorchester rough-&-ready life.

My letter is full of trivial detail, yet to you it may not be unwelcome. I certainly should not send it to any other person in the world, except possibly to either of yr brothers. I have left myself no room to reply at length on the subjects of yr last letter. I do not remember thrushes singing as you say. Your stanzas were very good indeed, I thought. Do you recollect writing when you were young (or was it yr br?) some verses beginning "Roll on noble Frome, through Grey's gleaming arches!" which appeared in the Dorset Chronicle? I admired them much as a boy. But one *can* admire much when one is so far from the sere & yellow leaf as we were then!

I hope you continue in good health. We have got through the winter so far, fairly well.

Believe me

Always sincerely yrs
Thomas Hardy.

floods drown": Song of Solomon 8: 7.   *F. Churchyard*: the churchyard of Fordington St George, Dorchester, in which many members of the Moule family, including Horace Moule, are buried.   *Boulter . . . Metcalfe*: local clergy.   *barrack-service*: the Dorchester barracks fell until 1847 within the parish of Fordington St George, and the Revd Henry Moule was appointed official chaplain in 1829.   *Dorset Chronicle*: in the issue of 7 Jan. 1858; they were in fact written by Horace Moule and began, 'Flow gently, sweet Frome, under Gray's gleaming arches'.   *sere & yellow leaf: Macbeth*, v.iii.23.

To Edward Clodd

Max Gate | 22: 3: '04

My dear Clodd:

I did not quite think that "The Dynasts" would suit your scientific mind, or shall I say the scientific side of your mind, so that I am much pleased to hear that you have really got pleasure out of it.

As to my having said nothing or little (I think I did just allude to it a long while ago) about having it in hand, the explanation is simple enough—I did not mean to publish Part I by itself until quite a few days before I sent it up to the publishers: & to be engaged in a desultory way on a MS. which may be finished in 5 years (the date at which I thought I might print it, complete) does not lead one to say much about it. On my return here from London I had a sudden feeling that I should never carry the thing any further, so off it went. But now I am rather inclined to go on with it. Though I rather wish I had kept back thc Parts till the whole could be launched, as I at first intended.

What you say about the "Will" is true enough, if you take the word in its ordinary sense. But in the lack of another word to express precisely what is meant, a secondary sense has gradually arisen, that of effort exercised in a reflex or unconscious manner. Another word would have been better if one could have had it, though "Power" would not do, as power can be suspended or withheld, & the forces of nature cannot. However, there are inconsistencies in the Phantoms, no doubt. But that was a point to which I was somewhat indifferent, since they are not supposed to be more than the best human intelligence of their time in a sort of quintessential form. I speak of the "Years". The "Pities" are, of course, merely Humanity, with all its weaknesses.

You speak of Meredith. I am sorry to learn that he has been so seriously ill. Leslie Stephen gone, too! They are thinning out ahead of us. I have just lost an old friend down here, of 47 years standing: a man whose opinions differed almost entirely from my own on most subjects: & yet he was a good & sincere friend—the brother of the present Bp. of Durham, & like him in old fashioned views of the Evangelical school.

I hope Aldeburgh keeps you blooming, & am

Sincerely yours
Thomas Hardy.

Meredith: he had suffered severe heart attacks in the summer and autumn of 1903; Stephen died on 22 Feb. 1904.   *an old friend*: see preceding letter; Handley Moule had recently been installed as bishop of Durham.

To Edward Clodd

MAX GATE, | DORCHESTER. | 12 April 1904

My dear Clodd:

My real thanks for your kind letter. Although my mother was 90, & what the papers call an "aged lady", & had been, owing to deafness & other infirmities, shut out from much intercourse with her kind of late years, she did not seem to me to be old, since she was mentally just as she had been from my earliest recollection. I shall miss her in many ways— her powers in humorous remark, for instance, which were immediate. It took me hours to be able to think & express what she had at the tip of her tongue.

She knew of you, of course, & thought it so very good of you to ask me (always, in her mind, her rather delicate "boy") to Aldeburgh for change of air that time I had been so unwell, if you remember.

The gap you speak of is wide, & not to be filled. I suppose if one had a family of children one would be less sensible of it.

However, she suffered latterly, & wished to go, so that there is really nothing for commonsense to regret. Yet one does regret.

Sincerely yrs
Thomas Hardy.

my mother: Jemima Hardy died at Higher Bockhampton, 3 Apr. 1904.

To William Archer

MAX GATE, | DORCHESTER. | Nov. 1. 1904

My dear Archer:

I have read the Blue Book so far as is necessary for understanding the general principles of the Scheme; & I can say, as you wish, that it seems to me to be a desirable one in its main points.

On details I will express no opinion, except to remark cursorily that the bodies proposed for nominating the Board of Trustees, &c., do not seem divergent enough in character, & may produce a net result of Philistinism. Indeed, it is in this direction that the *crux* will be found to lie: Where are you to get in England people with ideas detached enough to form, or nominate, the working committee. "Quis custodiet ipsos custodes?"

But this *may* be got over; & I must say that it is most praiseworthy devotion in you to theatrical art to labour so sincerely in its cause.

To my mind a humorous feature in the movement has been the earnestness in supporting it of those living English dramatists who, by writing bad plays, are piling up vast fortunes through the absence of such a theatre. They are like smugglers who should earnestly entreat the Government to establish a more efficient system of Coastguarding. Believe me

Yours sincerely
Thomas Hardy.

P.S. I will return the book.

Blue Book: not, in fact, a government document but the detailed proposal for the establishment and operation of a national theatre which Archer had prepared in collaboration with Harley Granville Barker (1877–1946), the producer, dramatist, and critic.   "*Quis . . . custodes?*": 'Who is to guard the guards themselves?' (Juvenal, *Satires*, vi.347).   *living English dramatists*: those endorsing the scheme included J. M. Barrie, Henry Arthur Jones, and Arthur Wing Pinero.

To Hermann Lea

MAX GATE, | DORCHESTER. | 9 Nov. 1904

Dear Mr Lea:

In case you should be thinking of giving a view of spots in Upper Bockhampton as scenes in "Under the G. Tree" (or for any other purpose) I think I ought to let you know that there are reasons against it—not the least being the nuisance occasioned to those who live there by trippers with Kodaks looking over hedges, & other undesirable visitors, which would be increased by the publication of such views. Moreover much of the detail of 60 years ago, as given in the book, is now changed by pulling down, or entirely imaginary.

Yours truly
T. Hardy.

Lea: the photographer Hermann Lea (1869–1952), who became friendly with TH while gathering information and illustrations for his *Handbook to the Wessex Country of Thomas Hardy's Novels and Poems* (1905) and the much more comprehensive *Thomas Hardy's Wessex* (London, 1913).   *trippers with Kodaks*: writing again to Lea two days later TH explained that he had himself been surreptitiously 'Kodaked' on his way to the Higher Bockhampton cottage by 'some young men who were on the watch'.

To Edward Garnett

MAX GATE, | DORCHESTER. | 21: 11: 1904

Dear Sir:

I have finished reading the book that you have been kind enough to send me. I had not seen it before, though I recollected the title, & I should probably never have read a line of it but for this presentation of yours.

It is a very thorough study, on a large scale, of a farmer & his family, & would have made a good first book of a novel as long as Tom Jones or Clarissa. I like it exceedingly.

The question that you raise in your preface, of the relative virtues, as fiction, of studies or sketches of character & scenery like the present, & the same when connected by a rounded plot, or drama, that (if perfectly constructed) is like an animal organism, & does not contain a line which fails to help on the development—is one of interest. I understand you to hold that it is greater to succeed in the first kind, without attempting the more subtle second, than to attempt the second & succeed but indifferently therein outside the qualities of the first, (assuming these to be equal in both cases.) Some might answer that this is despising in the story with a cohering plot all that you have valued in the other, & the higher aim in addition. Nevertheless it is the attitude of English critics in general not to value the artistic aspect of a composition as a whole, so that you are not singular in your doctrine.

I should add that I have not for many years looked into the novel of mine that you name, & have no opinion for or against it.

With thanks for the book, I am

Yours truly
Thomas Hardy.

Garnett: Edward Garnett (1868–1937), author and editor; in his introduction to the new reprint of Richard Jefferies' *Amaryllis at the Fair* (first published 1887), on which he was seeking TH's opinion, he had argued that the spontaneity and 'naturalness' of the loosely structured *Amaryllis* made it superior to a novel such as Hardy's *The Mayor of Casterbridge* in which the heaviness of the plotting made the reader too conscious of the author's controlling presence.

To Henry Symonds

MAX GATE, | DORCHESTER. | Feb 24. 1905

Dear Mr Symonds:

I must thank you for your interesting letter on my remark about the charm of the Middle Ages in their religious aspect, which was printed in the "Interview". Its weight, as an expression of opinion, will be much lessened for you when I tell you that I had no idea that what I was saying was being taken down, the person who did so having, inexcusably, called on another errand, so that I dropped the words as a fancy rather than as a deliberate conclusion, & they would require some qualifying to make them the latter.

The questions to which you lead up from it are large ones, & could not profitably be discussed without certain definitions being understood—the meaning of the words "religion", "faith" &c. One argument used by Catholic friends of mine (at least *professing* catholics, if not inherently such) I always consider to have weight: the wisdom of accepting certain formulae without question, & of assuming them to be true, for the sake of the calm such a process affords; or, to put it brutally, (which of course they do not), a fool's paradise is better than none. This position is intelligible, & its advantages can be recognized. There is little doubt that to know the truth in some matters lessens happiness. But the fact of a thing being unpleasant does not make it untrue, even if scepticism in transcendental matters should be one of these things. I should say that, upon the whole, whatever may be true, is best known, & not disguised.

Yours sincerely
Thomas Hardy

Symonds: Henry Symonds, solicitor, formerly town clerk of Dorchester; a recent convert to Catholicism, he had enquired about an interview in the *Daily Chronicle* of 8 Feb. in which TH was quoted as wishing that he 'had lived in the Middle Ages, when the Church was supreme and unquestioned. Life must have been very sweet and beautiful then, before doubts had arisen.'

[Hardy's correspondence with his publishers is marked throughout by an attractive combination of personal courtesy and professional good sense. The letter of 16 July 1905 is, however, something of an exception. Hardy seems to have had only one meeting with Violet Nicolson, who wrote *The Garden of Karma* and other volumes of verse under the pseudonym of 'Laurence Hope', but he admired both her and her work and was greatly moved in October 1904 by the news of her 'romantic' suicide following the death of her husband, a general in the Bengal Army many years her senior. Hardy

wrote an obituary of her for the *Athenaeum* and agreed to
supply a preface to a posthumous volume of her poems, but
when it transpired that his preface had not been used his
irritation found vent in a letter of quite uncharacteristic
sharpness.]

To William Heinemann

MAX GATE, | DORCHESTER. | 16: 7: 1905

Dear Mr Heinemann:
Will you kindly return to me the MS. of the Preface to
Laurence Hope's last poems (which I was particularly pressed
to write) & let me know as a mere matter of civility, why you
did not print it?—seeing that, though worthless in itself, it
would have helped the sale, if the prices paid me for a few
lines of fugitive writing be any criterion, & was gratuitously
contributed.

Yours truly
Thomas Hardy.

To avoid misapprehension I hereby withdraw all right to its
publication, in another impression of the poems or elsewhere.
T. H.

Heinemann: William Heinemann (1863–1920), publisher of *Indian Love* (1905)
by 'Laurence Hope', the pseudonym of Violet Nicolson (1865–1904), wife
of Lieutenant-General Malcolm Hassels Nicolson (1843–1904). It is possible that he had found TH's preface to be insufficiently enthusiastic.
pressed to write: by Blanche Crackanthorpe (see letter of 13 May 1910), at
whose house TH and Violet Nicolson had met.

To Arthur Symons

MAX GATE, | DORCHESTER. | Oct 20. 1905

My dear Symons:
Many thanks for the "Spiritual Adventures", which I have
read not only with the interest which any book of yours would

have for me, but with a deep interest begotten by its contents without regard to the author.

"Seaward Lackland", "Peter Waydelin", & "Harry Luxulian" attract me most; but I know, of course, that the others (& to some extent the last of these) end blankly—are in fact, not tales, but slices of life solely—of your set purpose, & that each is a mental study, in which the rounding it off into a tale with an upshot, or result, is considered superfluous. (Anyhow I believe I am not wrong in supposing this.)

Now a very wide question is here opened up: should *fiction* ever be anything but an organic piece of construction like "S. Lackland"—? which I consider an almost perfect bit of narrative art. Should not studies of the other sort—which end nowhere, like an "Autumn City," be confined to actual beings? This is what I have been thinking after escaping from the immediate fascination of reading the book.

There used to be only one school of fiction—that of the rounded story of which "S.L" is so excellent a specimen. There are now two schools—the second being the slice-of-life school or impressionist as I suppose it would be called; & I know that the men of the more modern school are looked upon as the advanced set. I do not think, however, that they will wholly, or even partially, displace the school of long standing because that is founded on something outside literary rules—the eternal instinct of human nature to remember & to re-tell & muse over a tale with an ending, & to forget the more numerous incidents of life which come to nothing. Had, for instance, some striking result been caused by the character of the boy in "A Prelude to Life," which could have resulted to a boy of no other character, the principle of construction would have been carried out which I call the organic—as in "S. Lackland":—the consequence would have led the cause to be remembered & recorded, if fact. From the beginning one sees that this has been the rule, & one does not see how it can be largely superseded.

Many of Henry James's stories are of the other sort (your last study, by the way, reminds me a little of him) & it remains to be seen whether they will stand as art,—the *selecting reason* being absent, that of difference from other cases in which no issue results from the person's qualities.

I infer from your book containing specimens of both kinds that you have not as yet come to any conclusion on this point.

Another thing is suggested to me by these experiments of yours, (as I may call them?) You have shown in one or two places that you have unusual power in the *weird*. The music dancing like a snake over the piano, the scar on the lady's face, &c, &c., show very plainly that if you cared to write popular fiction—or, not to use the horrid word popular, fiction absorbing to the man in his slippers over the fire late at night—you could easily do it. I have a weakness for reading such! But possibly you will say you want to do something more realistic & less exceptional: & that you can do such you show.

If I have been too stringent in this hasty criticism, forgive me. You asked me to be frank. Moreover there was room for frankness, as the studies are miles above what we get in that kind year by year.

Sincerely yours
Thomas Hardy.

Symons: Arthur William Symons (1865–1945), poet, critic, and editor; his *Spiritual Adventures* (1905), dedicated to TH, included the stories entitled 'Seaward Lackland', 'The Death of Peter Weydelin', 'An Autumn City', 'A Prelude to Life', and 'Extracts from the Journal of Henry Luxulyan' (also referred to by TH as 'your last study').

To Edmund Gosse

MAX GATE, | DORCHESTER. | 7: 11: 1905

My dear Gosse:

I am glad to learn that you have got back safely from the South, after your adventures on the railways there. Beyond your welcome post card with its vague address the only sound I caught of you was your letter in *The Times*, where I duly noticed the Italian consternation it caused. Well done: one to us poor scribblers, who always get pushed about.—We were there in March & April (18 years ago!)—a time of year when one has more elbow-room than in the autumn—though the country scenes are not so beautiful, being too suggestive of market-gardens in the levels, & not of "Bacchus & his crew" as at the vintage. The old market was still standing in Florence when I was there, &, of course, some human friends who are now horizontal.

I was so sorry to hear of Meredith's accident. His bad angel might just as well have left his legs alone, seeing what little use they were to him already. It was, indeed, slaying the slain. I hope he will get over this soon. I, too, hear that he is quite cheerful about it. It is curious (& very good of him) that he was concerned for my pessimism, for I was afraid after leaving that I had shaken his optimism, & G. M. converted to pessimism by me is too terrible a catastrophe to think of. It would lead to my speedy "removal" by the young Meredithians.

Why people make the mistake of supposing pessimists, or what are called such, incurably melancholy, I do not know. The very fact of their having touched bottom gives them a substantial cheerfulness in the consciousness that they have nothing to lose.

Personally, however, I am oppressed just now by a practical gloom. I am correcting the proofs of Pt II of The Dynasts; & I know it will be abused right & left, both for badnesses which deserve severity, & undeservedly for the hidden reason that the author's views are not palateable to the smug & conventional. Nevertheless I shall send you a copy.

I may be in town at the end of this month for a day or so, but I am not sure.

Always sincerely yours
Thomas Hardy.

letter in The Times: published in the issue of 5 Oct., its complaints about unpunctuality and overcrowding on the Italian railways appeared to be echoed by reports of protests originating from within Italy itself. concerned for my pessimism: George Meredith (who had recently broken an ankle) was said by Gosse to have been 'grieved' by TH's pessimism when they last met.

To Arthur Symons

MAX GATE, | DORCHESTER. | 2: 3: '06

My dear Symons;

It is really very kind of you to read & think over The Dynasts II, as you have evidently done, & to write such a generous & suggestive letter about it.

I do not myself know at all how it looks to other people, or what it is worth. I shall simply go on with it & finish it now, if I can. I felt, as I have felt for 20 years, that I must do it; & the unfortunate thing is that I did not begin sooner, so as to have more time over the blank & other verse, which has been rushed out rather, & could have been much improved in places, no doubt.

Your theory that verse should be confined to emotional expression is one that I used to hold, & was very uncomfortable under. (I believe that a good many hold it now besides yourself). What settled it for me was a superimposed theory, or view; viz, the theory of contiguity, if I may use such a word for it: by which I mean that unemotional writing which has no claim of itself to verse-form may properly be attracted into verse-form by its nearness to emotional verse in the same piece. Leave alone plays, some of our best lyrics are not lyrical every moment throughout, but the neutral lines are warmed by the remainder. This justifies, e.g. those blank verse passages in Shakespeare's histories which are mere transcripts from chronicles. I would even hold that one of Pope's coldest Essays in verse would be legitimate as such, if it were a section of a large emotional poem & not an independent piece. But I cannot discuss this fully in a letter.

Do certainly ask Mr & Mrs Hutton to let us know when they come to Dorchester. We shall be glad to see them.

I have received quite anonymously the French publication you speak of. I will read it more attentively.

Sincerely yours
Thomas Hardy.

Dynasts II: Symons, responding to TH's gift of an inscribed copy of *The Dynasts*, Part Second (published 9 Feb. 1906), had expressed the view that verse should not be used 'for ordinary conversation (apart from emotion)'. *Hutton*: Edward Hutton (1875–1969), traveller and author, and his wife Charlotte.   *French publication: Milieu d'art*, a privately printed pamphlet by Charles Bonnier, professor of French at the University of Liverpool.

To J. McT. E. McTaggart

23rd May, 1906

Dear Sir,

Quite by chance I took up from the table here a day or two ago your recent work *Some Dogmas of Religion* (to which I was attracted by seeing on its back a name I have been familiar with in the pages of *Mind*, etc.) and I think I ought to write and tell you what a very great pleasure the reading of the book has given me, though this is a thing I very seldom do. The clearness, acuteness and vigour of the thinking throughout, its entire freedom from sophisms and the indubitable moral good to be derived from a perusal of it are cheering to others whose minds have run more or less in the same groove but have rather despaired of seeing harmful conventions shaken—in this country at least—by lucid argument and, what is more, human emotions.

My own personal connection with the subject is merely that in a book of which I have published a portion, *The Dynasts*, I have vaguely sketched a philosophic basis for the drama, or poem, or whatever it may be called, which is not far from what you suggest by your negative conclusions.

With many thanks for the book, I am,

Yours truly,
Thomas Hardy.

McTaggart: John McTaggart Ellis McTaggart (1866–1925), philosopher. Although the printed source of this letter does not reproduce its address, it seems clear that TH was in London and had come across *Some Dogmas of Religion* (1906) in the library of the Athenaeum.   *Mind*: *Mind: A Quarterly Review of Psychology and Philosophy*.

To the Secretary of the Society for the Prevention of Cruelty to Animals

THE ATHENAEUM, | PALL MALL. S.W. | 19: 6: 06

Dear Sir:

I venture to draw your attention to a conjuring performance now going on at the Alhambra Theatre, which, as it appears to me, is cruelty to the animals made use of by the conjurors. The creatures—rabbits, pigeons, barn-fowls, ducks, &c.— may possibly be drugged or blinded to make them passive— though I cannot definitely state anything about their treatment, having witnessed the scene only from a distance.

At any rate you may think it well to let one of your inspectors visit the place & see for himself.

Your obedient servant
Thomas Hardy.

The Secretary, | Soc: for Prevention of Cruelty to Animals

Alhambra Theatre: in Leicester Square; it specialized in music-hall and ballet performances. Since advertisements for the Alhambra at this period mention only a series of ballets it seems likely that TH is referring to an entr'acte.

To Edmund Gosse

MAX GATE, | DORCHESTER. | 25: 7: 1906

My dear Gosse:

The illustrator of Far from the Madding Crowd began as a charming young lady, Miss Helen Paterson, & ended as a married woman,—charms unknown—wife of Allingham the poet. I have never set eyes on her since she was the former & I met her & corresponded with her about the pictures to the story. She was the best illustrator I ever had. She & I were married about the same time in the progress of our mutual work, but not to each other, which I fear rather spoils the information. Though I have never thought of her for the last

20 years your inquiry makes me feel "quite romantical" about her (as they say here), & as she is a London artist, well known as Mrs A. you might hunt her up, & tell me what she looks like as an elderly widow woman. If you do, please give her my kind regards; but you must not add that those two almost simultaneous weddings would have been one but for a stupid blunder of God Almighty.

Why did you go wasting your money on that first edition! I could have sent you the last edition, much more correct, the first not having been corrected by me, but hurriedly set up from the magazine by the publishers.

I am trying to enter into Part III of the Dynasts. I am so sorry to learn that Mrs Gosse is a prisoner still. Do you think that if you could get her to the sea she would recover?

All I have heard more about Mrs S. is what F. Macmillan told me the day before I left town. He said that the story (like that of the death of Mark Twain) had been much exaggerated. The pair have for some time been unable to get on well together (her fault, I should say) & she has therefore taken a flat in London as a bachelor woman, which she comes up to for the week, going down to Leatherhead, their home, from Sat. to Mon. The "Italian Count" has vanished from the narrative. I hope I may see you some time in the Autumn.

Sincerely yours
Thomas Hardy.

Paterson: Gosse had recently purchased a first edition of *Far from the Madding Crowd* and found there the illustrations originally drawn for the *Cornhill* serialization by Helen Paterson (1848–1926), subsequently the wife of William Allingham (1824–89).   *Mrs Gosse*: see letter of 12 Dec. 1912. *Mrs S.*: apparently George Meredith's daughter Mary (Riette) Sturgis, the wife of Henry Parkman Sturgis.

To Florence Henniker

MAX GATE, | DORCHESTER. | 12: 9: 1906

My dear friend:

I am glad you liked my paper on Ancient Churches, though I really wrote it only after repeated requests. Evidently we shall never agree about all things connected therewith, e.g., the high old Georgian pews, which I love.

I hope your stay in Hayling has added still more to your strength as it was when you wrote. As you note, the French have been saying good things about me lately. Perhaps you saw the long article in the Revue des deux Mondes for July 1? If you did not, I can lend it to you at any time you would like to read it.

Last Monday—apparently the last day of summer—I bicycled with my younger sister to Yeovil by a route which affords beautiful views over the Vale of Blackmore. I wish you could come down to the seaside near here, & drive out that way. I am sure that Lulworth Cove would suit you, & all the trippers are gone now. The people there let delightful cottages & lodgings.

You knew by postcard of my visit to Lincoln Cathl. I also went to Ely, Cambridge, & Canterbury.

It is so provoking that where you are, or were, is so difficult of access from this side. To get to Lincoln is less tedious than the train to Hayling.

Were you not struck by the unexpected news of poor Pearl Craigie's end? We met her, for the only time this summer, at the only evening party I went to in London—one at Stafford House—& she was looking better & fuller in the face than when she called here in the Spring. I fear she broke down through attempting too much. To keep three plates spinning, literature, fashion, & the Holy Catholic religion, is more than ordinary strength can stand. Perhaps it is rather unkind to put it that way, but you will take me rightly.

The author of "A Man of Property" sent me the book, & I

began it, but found the people too materialistic & sordid to be interesting.

Always affectly yrs

Tho H.

my paper: TH's lecture 'Memories of Church Restoration', read in his absence at the 20 June General Meeting of the Society for the Protection of Ancient Buildings and published both in the Society's *Proceedings* and (where Florence Henniker probably saw it) in the *Cornhill* of Aug. 1906. *Hayling*: Hayling Island, a Hampshire seaside resort.   *long article*: 'Thomas Hardy', by Firmin Roz.   *Craigie's end*: she died of heart failure in Aug. 1906; Stafford House was the home of the duke and duchess of Sutherland.   *of Property*": correctly, *The Man of Property*; John Galsworthy sent TH a copy in Apr. 1906.

[Frederic Harrison was the leading British exponent of Positivism, the fundamentally optimistic system of conduct and belief advocated by the French philosopher Auguste Comte. Hardy had read Comte in his earlier years and been attracted to some of his theories, but long friendship with Harrison had not prevented him from becoming increasingly sceptical of any such sanguine visions of human amelioration. It is characteristic that in writing to Millicent Garrett Fawcett, the women's suffrage leader, he should have grounded his essential support for the principle of votes for women in so bleak a conception of current social evils and of the radical actions needed to confront them.]

To Frederic Harrison

MAX GATE, | DORCHESTER. | 17: 10: 1906

My dear Harrison:

I was delighted to receive "Memories & Thoughts" that you so kindly send, & I have been reading it with great interest at intervals, till I remember that I have never written a line of thanks to you for it.

In going from article to article I am struck with the exceptional many-sidedness of your active mind: indeed I don't know anybody else who at all rivals you in that respect.

In most of what you say & feel I am quite with you, e.g., on Sport, Tobacco, Church-restoration, & endless other things.

I, too, call myself a "meliorist", but then, I find myself unable to be in such good spirits as you are at the prospect. In regard of Sport for instance, will ever the great body of human beings, of whom the commonplace & denegerate breed most, ever see its immorality? Worse than that, supposing they do, when will the still more numerous terrestrial animals—our kin, having the same ancestry—learn to be merciful? The fact is that when you get to the bottom of things you find no bed-rock of righteousness to rest on—nature is *un*moral—& our puny efforts are those of people who try to keep their leaky house dry by wiping off the waterdrops from the ceiling.

The question, indeed, of the treatment of animals is a tremendous one. As long as Christian & other theologies were really credited, & the non-human animal was regarded as a creature distinct from man, there was a consistency in treating "brutes" brutally. "Arise Peter, kill & eat," was a natural command to a man with a soul concerning animals without one. But now that this view of difference is exploded, a tremendous responsibility is thrust upon us—an impossibility almost, of doing right according to our new lights: & this, as I say, prevents my taking such a hopeful look forward as you do.

This, however is only one of the crowd of thoughts that your varied volume gives rise to. I am interested in the brief—too brief—autobiography at the beginning, & am going to read it over again. (By the way, I wish you had put your portrait as a frontispiece.)

I am trying to do something down here after my idleness in London during the summer. I hope Mrs Harrison is well, & send her my kind regards.

Always sincerely yours
Thomas Hardy.

& Thoughts": Harrison's *Memories and Thoughts: Men—Books—Cities—Art* (1906).   *& eat*,": Acts 10: 13.

To Millicent Fawcett

MAX GATE, | DORCHESTER. | Nov. 30. 1906

Dear Mrs Fawcett:

I have been suffering from neuralgia in the face, which I often get in winter, or I would have replied to your inquiry sooner.

I have for a long time been in favour of woman-suffrage. I fear I shall spoil the effect of this information (if it has any) in my next sentence by giving you my reasons. I am in favour of it because I think the tendency of the woman's vote will be to break up the present pernicious conventions in respect of manners, customs, religion, illegitimacy, the stereotyped household (that it must be the unit of society), the father of a woman's child (that it is anybody's business but the woman's own, except in cases of disease or insanity), sport (that so-called educated men should be encouraged to harass & kill for pleasure feeble creatures by mean strategems), slaughter-houses (that they should be dark dens of cruelty), & other matters which I got into hot water for touching on many years ago.

I do not mean that I think all women, or even a majority, will actively press some or any of the first mentioned of such points, but that their being able to assert themselves will loosen the tongues of men who have not liked to speak out on such subjects while women have been their helpless dependents.

You may disapprove of many of these reasons for woman-suffrage, or think them mistaken, but I am sure you will forgive my stating them.

Always sincerely yours
Thomas Hardy.

your inquiry: Millicent Fawcett was planning to publish a pamphlet devoted to the views of eminent men on the issue of women's suffrage; she later told TH that she could not use his letter because she feared 'John Bull is not ripe for it at present'.

[Florence Emily Dugdale, the second of the five daughters of an Enfield schoolmaster and his wife, was in her late twenties at this date and struggling to make an independent career for herself as a journalist and writer of children's stories. Although it is not entirely clear how she and Hardy first met, she seems to have sought an interview with him in the late summer of 1905 and called at Max Gate shortly afterwards. Moved by Florence's situation and attracted by her gentle seriousness, Hardy employed her to do occasional research for the last part of *The Dynasts*, on which he was then working, and there gradually grew up between them the mutual affection and dependence which led, after Emma's death, to Hardy's second marriage.]

To Florence Dugdale

MAX GATE, | DORCHESTER. | 21: 3: 1907

My dear Miss Dugdale:

I am so sorry to hear that you have had such a severe cold—why were you so careless as not to change when damp! I daresay it has been even worse than you say. What I want to say particularly is, that you are not to go & search in the B. Museum for me if you are not *quite* well. The reading room is just the place for you to catch a new influenza of somebody or other, & I should never forgive myself if you were to get it on my account.

I hope you have not agreed to write that 21,000 words of Children's stories for £8. The *lowest* you should agree to is 21 guineas—a guinea a thousand words. It is poor pay at that. If you mention that sum as the lowest he will probably agree to it—& if he does not you will have lost nothing worth having.

You have read about the Keats–Shelley exhibition in the papers, no doubt. I could not go, but I should much have liked to.

Forgive a hasty note. It has been a beautiful spring day here—for March.

Sincerely yours
T.H.

Dugdale: Florence Emily Dugdale (1879–1937); she became TH's second wife in 1914.   *B. Museum*: the British Museum.   *poor pay at that*: she was apparently negotiating with Collins, the publishers, the terms for *Country Life* (1908), her next volume of stories for children.   *exhibition*: held at Stafford House (see letter of 12 Sept. 1906) on 20 Mar. in aid of the Keats–Shelley Memorial Fund.

To H. W. Massingham

1 Hyde Park Mansions | 1: 7: '07

Dear Mr Massingham:

All I meant was that I should not agree to Mr Evans printing anything in the form of an interview.

As to my view of tendencies in literature, I think there may be a great reaction in favour of poetry before very long.

The reason that suggests itself is this: about a dozen years ago the English novel (&, I may add, the English drama) was developing on sound lines in the direction of a real grasp of life, which would I think have resulted in the formation of a school unequalled in any other literature, though there were naturally mistakes, cross-currents, & failures in the course of this development, as there always are in pioneering-work. However, the English & American press set itself with a will to stamp out the torch, on the grounds of morality (some of the examples were bizarre enough unquestionably) & the result was that English fiction was paralyzed into feeble imitations of Dumas *père* &c., resulting in what we now see— the field being left almost entirely to women at the present time.

It is curious that a track once lost in this way is never regained; but, as human emotion cannot be dammed up indefinitely, the checked tendency in prose may, as I said, approximately be resumed in verse; so "somehow good may be the future goal of ill."

But don't think that I am altogether optimistic thereon. Anyhow, the statements one sees in the papers on the taste for poetry being dead is the absurdest among the many absurd conclusions reached by the young critics of our time.

What has always been a part of human nature will remain a part of it as long as human nature remains.

I wonder if this is what Mr Evans wanted to ask me. I should of course tell him the same thing by word of mouth, in a more diffuse form.

Very truly yours
T. Hardy.

Massingham: he was currently editor of the *Nation*.   *Evans*: perhaps Caradoc Evans, Welsh writer and dramatist, who was working as a journalist in London at this period; an unsigned article, 'The Pessimism of Thomas Hardy', appeared in the *Nation* of 27 July.   *goal of ill."*: a slight misquotation of Tennyson, *In Memoriam*, section liv.

To Clement Shorter

MAX GATE, | DORCHESTER. | 3: 8: 1907

My dear Shorter:

Thanks for what you send. I endeavour to profit from the opinions of those wonderful youths & maidens, my reviewers, & am laying to heart a few infallible truths taught by them: e.g.,—

That T.H's verse is his only claim to notice.

That T.H's prose is his only real work.

That T.H's early novels are best.

That T.H's later novels are best.

That T.H's novels are good in plot & bad in character.

That T.H's novels are bad in plot, & good in charr.

That T.H's philosophy is all that matters.

That T.H's writings are good in spite of their bad philosophy.

This is as far as I have got at present, but I struggle gallantly on.

Yours truly
T. Hardy.

what you send: probably the unsigned article on TH in the *New York Times Saturday Review of Books*, 20 July 1907.

To Lady Grove

MAX GATE, | DORCHESTER. | 16: 8: 1907

My dear Lady Grove:

As it is a question of expression merely (the sentiments expressed being entirely your own, I am charmed to think) there is no reason why I should not make suggestions about it. It seems to me, then, that what comes most nearly to your feeling would be the words "and in memory of old and enduring friendship"—the absence of the article before the adjective would also give more finish to the phrase in my opinion; while, on my side, it expresses exactly the truth. I have never ceased to bless the day on which we met at Rushmore, do you remember?—now receding so far into the past—& that dance on the green at the Larmer Tree by moonlight.

But though at this point I have a strong temptation to grow "romantical" (delightful old form of the word, which the old people formerly used down here) I am not going to, being long past all such sentiments.

Certainly send along the proofs. After detecting appalling faults in my own work for two or three hours it will be a nice change to look for them in another's! I am writing this in a hurry, to catch the morning post, having missed yesterday's owing to a Parisian visitor we had yesterday, whose excellent English made me wish I were half as good at French.

Ever yours
Thomas Hardy

question of expression: TH had accepted the dedication of Lady Grove's *The Social Fetich* (1907)—a partly serious, partly humorous critique of contemporary social conventions—and was now being consulted as to its wording; he later gave a close reading to the proofs of the book, suggesting numerous changes both in its style and its content.   *in my own work*: TH was making final revisions to *The Dynasts*, Part Third.   *Parisian visitor*: Madeleine Rolland.

To John Moule

MAX GATE, | DORCHESTER. | Sept 21. 1907

Dear Mr Moule:

I was glad to hear that you are well & enjoying a successful domestic life with children growing up around you. I have never visited Canada, & suppose that I shall never do so now, but the spectacle of a Continent (including the United States) developed by people from this side of the Atlantic in such an amazing degree, & within such a comparatively short time, is one that would be deeply interesting to a visitor who should have the leisure to examine it. You, however, having settled down to your share of the development, have probably not much time for general observation.

You ask me a question which I should have answered a few days sooner but for interruptions—one of the worst being influenza—which has got hold of me rather early in the season. I am honoured by your thinking of me as a godparent for your little boy, & I should have said yes in a moment if I had been a normal Churchman. But I have a conscientious objection to that & many other ceremonies, & though you may say the sponsorial rite means nothing I feel that I must maintain my objection in practice as well as in theory, although it happens to occur in relation to a family of whom I have known so many members & have such pleasant memories. It is a comfort to think that this will do no harm to the baby himself! You must tell him when he is old enough that I had not the slightest personal objection to him, but objected only to the form. Perhaps he may like me all the better when I am dead & gone for respecting my own views.

It is satisfactory to find that you have lighted on a farm that suits; & with kind regards to Mrs Moule believe me

Very truly yours
T. Hardy.

Moule: John Frederick Moule (1870–1958), second son of TH's deceased friend Henry Joseph Moule, had written from rural New Brunswick to ask if TH would become the godfather of his son Henry John Moule, born earlier in the year; Moule did not prosper as a farmer, however, and subsequently moved with his family to Toronto.

To Florence Henniker

MAX GATE, | DORCHESTER. | 29: 9: '07

My dear friend:

I thought I would not write to thank you for your kind gift of "Our Fatal Shadows" till I had read it, which I have now done (finishing it late last night).

In point of workmanship it shows I think a great advance upon your previous novels, & it is, in truth, a really literary production by a facile pen, which cannot be said of many novels nowadays. It is absolutely convincing—nothing in it *made up* to produce a melodramatic effect (my taste was depraved enough to make me wish there had been towards the end, to confess the truth; but please excuse me, it was late at night, when one can swallow anything.) It is quite Trollopian, indeed, in its limitation within certain strict lines of naturalness. When one thinks that flirtations of that pattern are going on by the hundred every season it shows your power that you should make us interested, unflaggingly, in that particular instance, as if it were quite exceptional. Of course *I* should not have kept her respectable, & made a nice, decorous, dull woman of her at the end, but shd have let her go to the d—— for the man, my theory being that an exceptional career alone justifies a history (i.e. novel) being written about a person. But gentle F. H. naturally had not the heart to do that. The only thing I don't care much about is her marrying the Duke's son—whom she did not love; an action quite as immoral, from my point of view, & more so even, than running off with a married man whom she did love would have been. But convention rules still in these things of course.

There is really no reason why you should not go on writing scores of popular novels & making a fortune beyond the dreams of avarice, as poor Walter Besant used to say.

Perhaps you have got back to London by this time, so I

send this to Stratford Place. I have broken the back of "The Dynasts" at last, but have not quite finished it.

Yrs Affly Ever,
Tho H.

I forgot to say that the situation before the story begins, that of the heroine having been engaged to Aurora's *first* husband before she flirted with her second, is very good, & might have made a long novel of the *whole* story. T.H.

Fatal Shadows": published 1907.

To Edmund Gosse

MAX GATE, | DORCHESTER. | 3: 11: 1907

My dear Gosse:

If anybody had asked me last week what was the most unlikely book that I should be reading this week, & had suggested your spiritual autobiography, I should have said that such a book could not be beaten for unlikelihood; but here I am doing it. This is only a clumsy way of saying that your volume took me completely by surprise. And yet, after reading so far as I have got—not nearly through—I ask why should you not have written it; & can find no answer.

I knew, of course, from cursory remarks of yours that you had had some experiences of the sort, but I did not know how extraordinary they really had been. I wonder what finally decided your printing them? Their intrinsic interest was reason enough; possibly also (though I am not sure) you had the feeling that such a clear statement would prevent misrepresentation when you would be no longer able to correct it. It has become a serious question what people ought to do now-a-days in respect of the flood of fictitious gossip that gets into the snippety press about them. I myself, who lead such an obscure private life, have been compelled often to put into handbooks &c. personal details that I detest printing, solely to give this gossip the lie.

However, to return to spiritual things; I am not at all sure that the reign of narrowness in dogma is over as you seem to assume: if it does not exist in an Evangelical direction it goes on in others—in that of conventional morality for instance, where artificial, clumsy, & ineffectual laws are regarded as sacred.

These are only a few jottings of what occurs to me as I read.

Well, your life is a very bright one now—exceptionally bright, to my thinking. I, alas, have been mentally travelling in regions of inspissated gloom—not that I am habitually gloomy, as you can testify.

Best thanks for the book & believe me,

Always yours
Thomas Hardy.

spiritual autobiography: Gosse had arranged for TH to be sent a copy of his anonymously published *Father and Son: A Study of Two Temperaments* (1907). *inspissated gloom*: a phrase of Dr Johnson's, quoted (16 Oct. 1769) in Boswell's *Life of Johnson*.

To Edmund Gosse

FROM THOS. HARDY, | MAX GATE, | DORCHESTER. | 14: 11: 07

Finished. Very striking & unique; & beautifully told. I want the second volume.

T.H.

the second volume: i.e. a sequel to *Father and Son*.

To A. M. Broadley

MAX GATE, | DORCHESTER. | 31: 12: 1907

Dear Mr Broadley:

I did not realize from your remark on sending me your book about Napoleon that I was to receive two such handsome volumes as those you have been generous enough to present to me. I thought it was only one volume, & I fancied it smaller. My poor little reprint of the Trumpet Major, even when supplemented by Part III. of The Dynasts (which I shall send as soon as it comes out) will form but a sorry return for these two. I hope you do not always get the worst of it, as you will in this case.

That the T. M. should have any accuracy, or any value nowadays, is a wonder; for it was written 30 years ago, from hand to mouth as it were, for a periodical merely, & I used documents in a much more haphazard way then than I do now. However, it was the writing of that book which led to The Dynasts, the matter I collected being 5 times as much as I required for the T. M., including what is now very valuable to me (in writing The D.)—oral information on those times from people who lived in them, which now could not be got: e.g., the arrival of the regiments at camp, at the beginning of the story, which was described to me by eyewitnesses. Perhaps you know that the marks of the encampment are still visible on the hills. An odd coincidence is that the grandfather of a friend of mine, who was never in Dorset in his life till lately, was an officer in the York Hussars when they camped there, so he tells me.

I have known for a long time about Knapp the Wareham composer. I have also the tunes of another man born in or near Dorset—S. Wakely. But beyond these two I cannot get. Possibly they exhaust Dorset's musical powers.

Mr Pouncy called here yesterday. I think he can get (as he wants to do) a very good scene out of the T. M. for acting, as a finale to your lecture when you deliver it here.

My thanks for your New Year's wishes. I need not say that I reciprocate them. Also renewed thanks for the books & their flattering inscription.

Yours sincerely
T. Hardy.

Broadley: Alexander Meyrick Broadley (1847–1916), lawyer, author, collector, and authority on the Napoleonic period; he had sent TH the two volumes of *Napoleon and the Invasion of England: The Story of the Great Terror* (1908), by H. F. B. Wheeler and himself. *friend of mine*: probably Reymond Abbott. *Knapp . . . Wakely*: Broadley had mentioned William Knapp (1698–1768), parish clerk of Poole, in response to TH's earlier expression of interest in Dorset composers of psalm-tunes (see next letter); Samuel Wakely, of Bridport, appears to have flourished at the beginning of the 19th century, when TH's grandfather subscribed to two volumes of church-music by him.   *Pouncy*: Harry Pouncy (see letter of 3 Sept. 1911); his dramatization of the party at Overcombe Mill (chs. 4 and 5 of *The Trumpet-Major*) was performed in Dorchester on 4 Feb. 1908 at the conclusion of Broadley's lecture on 'Napoleon and the Invasion of England'.

[Although he now enjoyed a high reputation and had long ago given up writing controversial novels, Hardy found that he could still encounter moral censorship—in the shape of editorial refusals to publish his poems 'A Trampwoman's Tragedy' and 'A Sunday Morning Tragedy'—and gross misunderstanding of his ideas—in the form of an article in which he was characterized by A. G. Gardiner, editor of the *Daily News*, as a writer whose 'pilgrimage' had been ever downward, ending 'in despair'. His letter to Gardiner suggests, and later correspondence tends to confirm, that Hardy's sensitivity to hostile criticism increased rather than abated with the years, and it is certainly true that not even his habitual dislike of letter-writing deterred him from speaking in his own defence.]

To Florence Henniker

MAX GATE, | DORCHESTER. | New Year's Eve 1907

I must just write a few lines, my dear, to thank you for that pretty Christmas Card, & to wish you a happy New Year. It was a relief to me to see your figure standing, apparently hale & strong, in the view of your front door, for I was really getting anxious about you, not having heard from you lately, & forgetting that, strictly, it was my turn to write to you. I hope you are as well as you look?

It is dreadfully dull here just now: raw, a little snow on the ground, & descending from the sky something neither rain, snow, nor hail, but what the almanack makers call "downfall". It does not seem to me, however, that we are going to have a very severe winter. I may be quite wrong, however.

I have almost finished the proofs of Dynasts III, & the book will appear, I suppose, some time in Jan. I feel like an

old Campaigner—just as if I had been present at the Peninsular battles & Waterloo (as they say Geo. IV imagined of
himself). It is a good thing to have nearly got rid of it, though
I shall miss the work.

I have had a ballad—what I consider rather a strong one—
refused by the *Fortnightly* & the *Nation* (though they both
wanted something of me) on the ground that those periodicals
"are read in families"—The poem turns upon a tragedy that
"families" read about in the newspapers every week. But I
expected that it would be declined, so was not surprised to
see it come back. Yet people complain nowadays that the
authors of England have no strength like those of Elizabethan
days. If they had it they could not show it!

I am just hunting up old psalm tunes for the Society of
Dorset Men in London—who, much against my wish, have
elected me as their President. I am about the worst they could
possibly have chosen.

Where have you been lately, & where are you going to, if
anywhere? Lady St Helier writes from her new house near
Newbury. Is it not extraordinary that she should have had
the energy to build it after her troubles.

What did you think about Kipling being the Nobel prizeman this year? It is odd to associate him with "peace".

I repeat my wish for the New Year, both as to yourself &
to Gen. Henniker, & am,

Your affecte & rather gloomy friend
Tho H.

a ballad: 'A Sunday Morning Tragedy'.   *Lady St Helier*: the former Mary
Jeune, whose husband had been created Lord St Helier shortly before his
death in 1905; their only child, aged 22, had died in 1904.   *Nobel
prizeman*: the award to Rudyard Kipling (1865–1936) of the Nobel Prize for
Literature had been announced three weeks previously. TH was evidently
thinking of it in the context of the prize for the promotion of peace, the
most remarkable of those endowed by Alfred Bernhard Nobel (1833–96),
inventor and manufacturer of dynamite.

To A. G. Gardiner

MAX GATE, | DORCHESTER. | 19: 3: 1908

My dear Sir:

I am now glad that I sent you a line (which I did very reluctantly, to please others) since it has drawn such an interesting letter from you.

You will scarcely be able to believe, perhaps, that I have become so case-hardened, or soul-hardened, by the rough handling I have received from the press in the past—rougher, I suppose, than any living writer, except perhaps my friend Mr Swinburne—that I read all criticism of myself as if it concerned a third person. And so I read your Article. It was really over-generous in its appreciativeness in one direction, even though in respect of the passages I quoted I thought you were unconsciously caricaturing the philosophy shadowed forth in my later books (if I may give my crude thoughts such a high title as a philosophy). This was what I meant by lack of humour, ridiculous &c,—not your personal self, of course. By speaking of it as "downward, ever downward", "a journey towards despair" &c., you, & all optimists, seem to imply that everybody who does not hold your own views of life must be very miserable, which strikes people who think as I do as having something comic about it. "Pessimism"—as the optimists nickname what is really only a reasoned view of effects & probable causes, deduced from facts unflinchingly observed—leads to a mental quietude that tends rather upwards than downwards, I consider. As for professional optimists, one is always sceptical about them: they wear too much the strained look of the smile on a skull.

So far as my experience goes, conclusions about the universe do not affect the spirits, which are a result of temperament. What does often depress me is the sight of so much pain in the world, constant pain; & it did just as much when I was an orthodox Churchman as now; for no future happiness can remove from the past sufferings that have been endured.

But I am preaching a sermon at you, & you certainly do

not deserve that for the slight error of vision, as you may
allow me to call it, that I think I see in one or two paragraphs
of your article. To criticize it as I have done is rather
ungracious, I fear, & I truly would thank you for your kind
sense of my being worth an article of any sort.

Yours sincerely
Thomas Hardy.

Gardiner: Alfred George Gardiner (1865–1946), author and journalist, editor
of the *Daily News* 1902–19; TH had written on 17 Mar. to protest against
Gardiner's characterization of him in 'Thomas Hardy: A Character Study',
Daily News, 14 Mar. 1908.

To Ford Madox Hueffer

MAX GATE, | DORCHESTER. | Sept. 9. 1908

Dear Mr Hueffer:
    I have been away from here for 3 or 4 days, & so could not
get at the poem to which you allude till now. Since you write
so appreciatively I send it on. But please do not feel yourself
under any obligation to print it: if you have the slightest
doubt or dislike of it return it, & I shall not feel hurt, as it is
my intention to open a volume of poems with it when I issue
another.
    The Editor of the review, who returned it, merely said that
he would have personally liked to print it, but that his review
circulated amongst young people. Of course, with a larger
morality, the guardians of young people would see that it is
the very thing they ought to read, for nobody can say that the
treatment is other than moral, & the crime is one of growing
prevalence, as you probably know, & the false shame which
leads to it is produced by the hypocrisy of the age.

Yours very truly
Thomas Hardy.

P.S. I ought to let you have it gratuitously, but I feel that, as
others are concerned, I must ask some price. Would £8 or £10
be fair for its use in the Review? T.H.

I could let you have a short poem of an ordinary & quite safe kind, if you do not take this. T.H.

Hueffer: Ford Madox Hueffer, later Ford Madox Ford (1873–1939), novelist and critic. TH's poem 'A Sunday Morning Tragedy' had been refused by W. L. Courtney, editor of the *Fortnightly Review*, in Oct. 1907; Hueffer, hearing of this, sought and was given permission to include it in the first (Dec. 1908) number of the *English Review*, of which he was editor. TH did not in fact place the poem first in *Time's Laughingstocks* (1909), presumably because the intended polemical gesture no longer seemed necessary.   *the crime*: abortion, to prevent the birth of an illegitimate child; in the poem a young pregnant but unmarried woman is killed by a folk remedy administered by her mother.

[In the autumn of 1908 extensive building work was put in hand at Max Gate in order to provide Emma with a larger and pleasanter attic-room in which she could have her own 'retreat' for writing, painting, sewing, and simple escape, a kind of counterpart to Hardy's study. As Henry Hardy's men arrived Emma suddenly slipped off again to Calais—cancelling at short notice a garden party to which the guests had already been invited—and while Hardy's letters are amiable enough, full of cat news and good advice, it is noticeable that they do not urge her early return.]

To Emma Lavinia Hardy

Max Gate | 15: 9: '08

My dear E:

I received your letter yesterday afternoon (4 o'c. post) & sent on The Times last night. I will send another if it shd contain anything important. I enclose all the letters that have come. I am glad you are comfortable in Calais. 6 francs a day inclusive is, I should think, as cheap as if you were in lodgings & provided for yourself.

I have not been anywhere yet, as I do not like to leave till the window, &c, is in hand, at any rate. They are making it at the shop, & will come about the end of this week to begin putting it in. It will be rather a troublesome job, as the slope of the roof has to be moved back, to enlarge the room over the W.C. It will I think be a good bedroom when it is done. All we fear is rain while the slates are off, but H. is going to put a tarpaulin over the hole if he can fix it. We have taken up your carpet & cleared everything away.

It is very dull here, & I am glad of it, as it wd be awkward if people were to come now. I have put some boards into the man's room to spread the apples on, but it rains this morning, & I cannot get in some of the riper, as I had intended.

Marky is getting quieter, & as the weather is chillier she & the other two live all together in the kitchen mostly. The excitement of the morning has been Kitsey's conduct: she is looking for a bed for her kittens, & has been up to Jane's room, & torn her Sunday hat in rents, so that she cannot wear it any more. She says it cost 4s/11d, so I have given her 5s/- to buy another, & she is quite content. Kitsey looks on unconcerned.

I could, of course, run over to Calais if I should have to be in London for anything, but it does not seem worth while to go all the way from here. Calais was called in the time of James the first "sluttish & monstrous dear"—& the guide book says that the description still holds good, in the opinion of some. (This was, however, written 30 years ago.) I daresay you know that the principal gate, leading from the sea side into the town, is the one painted by Hogarth.

You must mind not to be too friendly with strangers, as you don't know who's who in a town through which the worst (& no doubt best) of the earth pass on their way out of our country when it gets too hot for them.

Yours,
T.

To-days Times says that Bosworth Smith yesterday underwent "successfully a serious operation in London, & the doctors are so far thoroughly satisfied with his condition".

Jane's: one of the Max Gate servants; Marky and Kitsey were cats. *painted by Hogarth*: William Hogarth's *Calais Gate: O the Roast Beef of Old England*, now in the Tate Gallery.   *satisfied with his condition*": TH's old friend (see letter of 6 Jan. 1874) died a month later, however (see letter of 19 Oct. 1908).

To Emma Lavinia Hardy

Max Gate | Wedny eveng. | 30 Sept. [1908]

Dear E:

Instead of sending on your dividend warrant, which came this morning, I asked the Bank to-day (my bank, the Wilts & Dorset) to send you ten pounds; they said two £5 B. of England notes would be the easiest way of sending it, & quite safe in an official envelope. So it will arrive with, or before, this letter. If they will not take the notes at the hotel there are English banks in Calais, where you can change them. But mind to go to a respectable place, where they will not take you in. You can get English sovereigns, or for *each* £5 note 6 napoleons & about 6 francs, if you want it in French money. To make up the £17 there will be £7 left, which I think will be enough for housekeeping here, as it is on a very small scale. Let me know if the notes arrive safely.

The heat here today, after the rain of Sunday &c, has been tropical: not a cloud: they say it has been the hottest day of the year. I hope it may continue, as we have the roof open now, & the dormer in full progress. It is troublesome, but worth doing. I am glad you are not here in the mess & hammering, though no dirt or dust comes down into the house.

We had a great fright on Monday night about Marky. She slipped out of the dining room about 7 o'clock, & absolutely disappeared. The servants & I wandered about the garden with lanterns till nearly 12; I came down at 1, & at 4, but cd not find her. When they got up at 7 she calmly walked down out of the stable loft. The reason of her affront was that Kitsy thought she wanted to get away her kitten, & flew at her. The kitten (the last one) is now drowned—such a pretty one—white, with black streaks on its back. Marky is now quite happy, & lives mostly in the dining room. I have given all your messages to Jane: she quite understands, & has gone this afternoon to pay some of the bills. Daisy nurses Kitsy now as a part of her work, till she gets over the loss of her kittens. Mrs Kinden's son at the cottage was buried to-day—

16. They sent over to tell you when he died, as they said you had inquired how he was. Mrs Huxtable called to see you: I do not remember anybody else, but I am keeping the cards. Oh, yes—the Faulkners came yesterday: they are staying at Weymouth, leaving on Sunday. You need not hurry, as order reigns. Miss May Sinclair says she is coming to see me, but she has not been yet.

Yrs

T.

Daisy: another of the Max Gate servants. *Mrs Kinden's son*: William Kinden and his wife lived at the old toll-gate cottage opposite Max Gate; their son Charles had died on 25 Sept. *Mrs Huxtable*: wife of Henry Anthony Huxtable, Dorchester solicitor and town clerk of Weymouth. *the Faulkners*: see letter of 17 Dec. 1911. *Sinclair*: see letter of 7 Nov. 1910.

To the Revd Cyril Wix

MAX GATE, | DORCHESTER. | Oct 16: 1908

Dear Mr Wix:

I have read with interest the architect's report on Stinsford Church that you have been kind enough to send me; & I return it herewith.

If I possibly can I will attend the Vestry meeting on Oct 22, but I do not like to promise positively. The architect in his report divines with much accuracy points in the history of the church that I happen to know for facts. The oak pewing he admires, as I do also, is the remnant of the original pewing removed about 1840, & eked out with deal in the rearrangement we see now. Before that date the entrance was in the north wall, beside the Grey monument. The piers on the north side of the nave were bricked round at the same date: inside the brickwork the column & shafts remain, (I have always been told) & are like those on the south side.

The modern Gothic windows were inserted at the second restoration between 1860–1870: before that they were debased classic (in the north aisle & chancel.)

At the third restoration—possibly about 1880, but I am not sure—the fine old waggon roof of the nave was removed (being decayed) & the present deal one unfortunately substituted, the ridge of the roof being raised, & the tower dwarfed thereby—a lamentable proceeding altogether.

Possibly the architect did not see the remains of the old font, or he would have suggested its repair & re-erection (not necessarily for use). Nor did he, apparently, see the chevron mouldings from the original church.

Yours very truly
Thomas Hardy.

Wix: The Revd. Cyril Poynder Wix, vicar of Stinsford 1907–10; Stinsford Church, familiar to TH since earliest childhood, had recently been inspected by Charles Edwin Ponting, the diocesan architect. TH later made his own recommendations as to the work that needed to be done on the church: see letter of 25 April 1909.

To Emma Lavinia Hardy

Max Gate | Monday. [19 October 1908]

Dear E:

We are getting on here much as usual: a hammering all day: front door closed up, so that people have to come to the side door, even the most aristocratic (they do not mind at all, but seem rather to like it), & a general messiness outside, but nothing inside at all. The plastering *will not* get dry in your room, owing to the damp air: otherwise it could be finished. I do not suppose that it really will till next week. Would the first week in November be a good time for you to return? On the 18th the day of the play, a Times man, to whom I have offered a bed, will be sleeping here. I have told him of the alterations, but he will not mind.

You will be shocked to hear that Bosworth Smith died last Saturday evening, two hours after he had been brought home to Melcombe from London. He longed to be at home, but the doctors would not let him be moved till there was no hope: he wd have died on the journey if the nurses had not injected strychnine. I suppose it was well to gratify his wish, but he must have suffered greatly by the way. He is to be buried on Thursday at Stafford.

Sir Elliott Lees died also last week—at the Royal Hotel, Weymouth, where he was taken ill on a speech-making tour. It was strange that *at last* we went to one of their parties, was it not: & how polite he was to you. Poor old Mrs Lees who was so fond of him: how she must suffer.

I miss the psalm & chant tunes very much on Sundays, never hearing a note of music now. Mr Coutts the poet, & a grandson of Coleridge, came to see me yesterday, & I went in to the Antelope to dinner with them. It rained in torrents. The cats are well, except Comfy, who has lost the use of one leg, & eats very little: I fancy he may not live much longer. But he is not unhappy, & purrs just the same as ever when stroked. Mrs Baskett of Evershot wrote to ask us to lunch; she was not sure whether you were come back, so wrote to me. I think of going (to-morrow) as it is very dull staying here alone.

I send on all that has come, except circulars &c.

Yours
T.

Jane asks me to tell you that she is attending to the plants. There is going to be a change of proprietorship at the Broad Mayne baker's, & we think it unadvisable to do anything till you come: moreover Virgin is appointed baker of the stone-ground flour which Prideaux & others have laboured to re-introduce; & I want to try it.

play ... Times man: see next letter.   *Melcombe*: Bingham's Melcombe, the Dorset manor-house Smith had purchased in 1895; West Stafford was the village of his birth.   *Lees*: Sir Elliott Lees, Bt. (1860–1908), a former MP, of Lytchett Minster, Dorset; Mrs Lees was his mother.   *Mr Coutts ... Coleridge*: Francis Burdett Thomas Money-Coutts (1852–1923), poet, was accompanied by Ernest Hartley Coleridge (1846–1920), editor of his grandfather's poetical works.   *Mrs Baskett*: wife of Samuel Russell Baskett, solicitor.   *Virgin ... Prideaux*: James T. Virgin was a local baker, Charles Sydney Prideaux (d. 1934) a Dorchester dentist and antiquarian.

[The popular success of the scene from *The Trumpet-Major* performed on the occasion of A. M. Broadley's Napoleon lecture in February 1908 had prompted the Dorchester Debating and Dramatic Society to undertake a stage version of the entire novel. Although it was an amateur production—the first of an extended series of such dramatizations by the group later calling itself the Hardy Players—the national interest in Hardy was such that several of the London newspapers chose to review it. Harold Child, sent to Dorchester by *The Times*, became friendly with Hardy and later wrote a short book about his work and career.]

To Harold Child

MAX GATE, | DORCHESTER. | Monday [16 November 1908]
Dear Mr Child:

I had no sooner dispatched my letter to you (which has crossed with yours) than a slight cold I have had for a few days developed into furious influenza, & I am writing this in bed. I may be well enough to go to the play on Wedny night, but it is uncertain, & in the circumstances I think it will be wiser that you should not put up here—as this is now an infected house & you might get the horrid malady if you slept here. So that your suggestion to stay at the Antelope I accept reluctantly. The landlord (Mr Dunn) knows me very well, & if you think it worth while to tell him you are a friend of mine he would do all he could I am sure. Or if you telegraph to me I will get the room for you.

I am much disappointed at this clash of events, as is my wife also. But I will consider your visit as postponed only, for I should like you to come some day.

I do not know how the band of amateurs are getting on with their rehearsals. What would be likely to interest London people in the performance is not the technique—which will be of an artless kind—something like the intentional artlessness of the *Theatre Libre*, I imagine—but the special attributes of the production: e.g. that the great grandparents of the actors (many of them) were the real actors more or less in the scenes depicted—that they all know the events traditionally— & of course, are themselves continuators of the dialect, humours, &c., of the personages. An amusing thing is that the Mayor of Dorchester plays Cripplestraw, the Mayor's sister Matilda Johnson, a former Mayor's son is the trumpet major himself, & Anne is a former Mayor's daughter: & the real pikes, firelocks, &c. of the events are to be used I am told.

I shall probably be downstairs by tea-time on Wednesday, & if you come & see us as you say it will be pleasant.

This is all the more provoking in that we have 2 or 3 spare rooms.

Yours sincerely
Thomas Hardy.

Child: Harold Hannyngton Child (1869–1945), author and critic. *Theatre Libre*: TH had earlier supported, in the pages of the *Weekly Comedy* (30 Nov. 1889), a proposal for the foundation of a British 'Free Stage' along the lines of a 'Théâtre libre' recently established in France.

To Lady Grove

MAX GATE, | DORCHESTER. | 13: 1: 1909

My dear Lady Grove:

Now here is a misunderstanding. I read your cogent arguments, & had no other idea than that I was to digest them, & when I had digested them, & become quite convinced that you were right, I was to reply like a lamb. I felt sure that you did not want me to write & say merely that I was not convinced. But evidently I was wrong.

I will not attempt to answer all your arguments even now. I never, as you know, take any active part in politics, having only just sufficient energy to do one sort of work in one little groove. And I have thought that it would be really injuring the women's cause if I were to make known exactly what I think may be result of their success—a result I don't object to, but which one half your supporters certainly would; & hence might withdraw their support.

So we must let this question rest, as between us, for the present.

They have just made me a Governor of our Grammar School here, founded by "Thomas Hardye" in 1569; (I suppose an ancestor of mine) & what has struck me in looking up its history of 350 years, & that of all the many other Grammar Schools of that age & standing, is that it never occurred to any of the pious & practical founders to establish a single Grammar School for women. Every one of these excellent institutions has been for males only. Now there's a point for you.

Ever your affectionate friend
Thomas Hardy.

your cogent arguments: Agnes Grove had presumably sent a draft or proof of her preface to T. W. Berry's *Professions for Girls* (1909).   *ancestor of mine*: the Elizabethan Thomas Hardy (d. 1599)—almost certainly unconnected to TH—was an important early benefactor of the Dorchester Grammar School rather than its 'founder'.

To Henry Newbolt

MAX GATE, | DORCHESTER. | 16: 1: 1909

My dear Newbolt:

I was delighted, as you may imagine, to get your letter informing me of the honour done to "The Dynasts" by a review in The Quarterly from no less eminent a hand than yours. The Quarterly itself came about the same time, & I have read the article.

A review from a practising poet—if I may use such a terribly professional epithet—is worth hundreds of pages from a mere critic, & hence, in reading what you say, a brief passing remark has so much meaning in it for anybody who has been treading, however uncertainly, the same paths as yourself. So that I can read into your article heaps of thoughts which I know passed through your mind though you did not express them.

You put things in such a way that I can read your criticisms as if they were of a drama that I had never heard of: e.g. "Mr H. having decided on a chronicle play had to provide for it a theatre under his own management," which is an inimitable (& startlingly new) way of expressing what is perfectly true. As for the diction, to which you allude, a great deal of it is as good as I could make it; but I had periodic frights lest I should never live to finish the book—when, alas, I rattled along too hurriedly.

I am afraid I am one of those you allude to as undervaluing "In Memoriam", though I did my duty in adoring it in years past. While the details of its expression are perfect, the form as a whole is defective, & much of the content has grown commonplace nowadays. As to the form, why Tennyson, who knew so much, should not have seen the awful anticlimax of finishing off such a poem with a highly respectable middle class wedding, is a mystery, when it ought to have ended with something like an earthquake.

I want to put on the titlepage of a new edition of The Dynasts something more explicit than the words "A Drama", which mislead the public into thinking it is not for reading. I have thought of

> A mental drama
> A vision-drama
> A closet-drama
> An epical drama, &c

or "A chronicle poem of the Napc wars, under the similitude of a drama", but I cannot decide.

I am deeply sensible of the generous view you take of the whole performance: your own imagination does half the work for me, & more. The greatest pleasure I have gained from doing it has been the discovery that you & one or two others have been interested in it. I am getting on now to a time of life when I do not *much* care what happens to my work, though I endeavour to resist this indifference, & nothing helps me to do so more than such articles as the one you have written.

I hope however (though I ought not to say it, in my own interest) that you do not give *too* much time to criticism, when you can do the far better things that we know of. Happily one can afford to dismiss the fear of writing ones self out, which we used to hear so much of. No man ever writes himself out if he goes on living as he lived when he began to write. It is the other thing, the social consequence of his first works, that does the mischief,—if he lets it.

Believe me

Sincerely yours
Thomas Hardy.

P.S. I had nearly forgotten to say that I am sending you my little selection from William Barnes, if you will please me by accepting it. As a Wessex man you will feel a little akin to him. T.H.

a review: Newbolt's 'A New Departure in English Poetry', *Quarterly Review*, Jan. 1909.   *I cannot decide*: the subtitle TH in fact chose for the one-volume complete edition of 1910 was 'An Epic-Drama'.   *William Barnes: Select Poems of William Barnes*, ed. TH (1908).

[Hardy was deeply affected by the deaths of Algernon Charles Swinburne and George Meredith in the spring of 1909. He had never forgotten his intoxication with Swinburne's early verse in the mid-1860s, when he was making his own first abortive efforts towards a poetic career, nor had he lost any of his intense sympathy with Swinburne as a poet who had suffered vilification in the cause of his art. The death of Meredith—whom he had liked and admired as a man even while remaining exasperated by him as a writer—meant less to Hardy in personal terms, but it left him in the position of being the most distinguished of living English novelists and the virtually undisputed 'head' of English letters. His new status was promptly reflected in the request of the Incorporated Society of Authors that he become its president in succession to Meredith—who had himself been the successor to Tennyson—and in his appointment, a year later, to the extreme exclusivity of the Order of Merit.]

To Florence Dugdale

Max Gate, April 12 [19?], 1909.
For several reasons I could not bring myself to write on
Swinburne immediately I heard that, to use his own words,
"Fate had undone the bondage of the gods" for him. . . .

No doubt the press will say some good words about him
now he is dead and does not care whether it says them or no.
Well, I remember what it said in 1866, when he did care,
though you do not remember it, and how it made the blood
of some of us young men boil.

Was there ever such a country—looking back at the life,
work, and death of Swinburne—is there any other country in
Europe whose attitude towards a deceased poet of his rank
would have been so ignoring and almost contemptuous? I
except *The Times*, which has the fairest estimate I have yet
seen. But read the *Academy* and the *Nation*.

The kindly cowardice of many papers is overwhelming him
with such toleration, such theological judgements, hypocriti-
cal sympathy, and misdirected eulogy that, to use his own
words again, "it makes one sick in a corner"—or as we say
down here in Wessex, "it is enough to make every little dog
run to mixen".

However, we are getting on in our appreciativeness of
poets. One thinks of those other two lyricists, Burns and
Shelley, at this time, for obvious reasons, and of how much
harder it was with them. We know how Burns was treated at
Dumfries, but by the time that Swinburne was a young man
Burns had advanced so far to be regarded as no worse than
"the glory and the shame of literature" (in the words of a
critic of that date). As for Shelley, he was not tolerated at all
in his lifetime. But Swinburne has been tolerated—at any
rate since he has not written anything to speak of. And a few
months ago, when old and enfeebled, he was honoured by a
rumour that he had been offered a complimentary degree at
Oxford. And Shelley too, in these latter days of our memory,
has been favoured so far as to be considered no lower than an
ineffectual angel beating his luminous wings in vain. . . .

I was so late in getting my poetical barge under way, and he was so early with his flotilla—besides my being between three and four years younger, and being nominally an architect (an awful imposter at that, really)—that though I read him as he came out I did not personally know him till many years after the *Poems and Ballads* year. . . .

T.H.

April 12 [19?]: this letter survives only in an incomplete printed text, where—Swinburne having died on 10 Apr.—it appears to have been dated a week too early.   *the gods"*: adapted from Swinburne's 'Anactoria'. *in 1866*: the year of publication of Swinburne's much-vilified *Poems and Ballads*.   *The Times . . . Nation*: the *Times* obituary appeared on 12 Apr., the other two on 17 Apr.   *run to mixen"*: the source of the Swinburne quotation has not been identified (it was perhaps spoken rather than printed), but TH assigns the 'Wessex' saying to the Spirit Ironic in *The Dynasts*, Part First, I. iii.   *of literature"*: quoted from the introduction by the Revd Robert Aris Willmott to *The Poetical Works of Robert Burns* (1863); Willmott may also have been TH's source for the information that Burns was 'cut' by the Dumfries gentry while spending his last years as an exciseman in that city.   *wings in vain*: adapted from Matthew Arnold's 'Byron' essay (1881).

To the Stinsford Church Restoration Committee

NOTES ON STINSFORD CHURCH

Athenaeum Club, Pall Mall, | [25] April, 1909.

Dear Sirs,

I have been asked to look at this Church and express an opinion on what should be done to preserve it. Any good church-Architect will, I think, agree with the suggestions below.

Speaking generally of what is called "Church restoration", it should be borne in mind that the only legitimate principle for guidance is to limit all renewals to *repairs for preservation*, and never to indulge in alterations.

Applying this principle—the only one now recognized by the best ecclesiastical societies and authorities—to the present building, it is perceived that repair is, in fact, the one thing positively demanded; though a few removals and obliterations within living memory might be reinstated or uncovered. It is an interesting building, and one very easy to injure beyond remedy.

The actual repairs required are rather a question for a practical man than for myself, but I would advise that procedure should be somewhat as follows:

Insert new floor-joists and floor-boards where ever the present are rotten.

Most of the seating, wainscoting, &c., that is decayed and loose seems to be the parts made of deal that were inserted at the disastrous restoration about 1840, when the excellent old oak pews of Caroline or early Georgian date were swept away, some re-arranged portions of them being replaced, the entrance by a north door having been changed to west at the same time.

This modern deal-work should be renewed where necessary, and all the re-arranged seventeenth or eighteenth century oak pews that remain, which are mostly undecayed still, should be left where they are, much that is in them having not only antiquarian interest, but the interest of association— so valuable in a parish church.

The seats as they stand give sufficient space—averaging from two feet eight inches to nearly three feet from back to back, which, I believe, almost coincides with present regulations for new churches.

The north aisle is being ruined by damp, which soaks down through the parapet. This, I am reliably assured, can be completely cured by removing the coping and resetting it on lead, as in the annexed sketch.

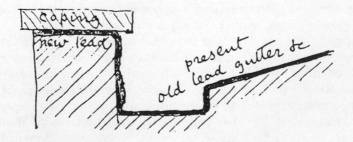

More injury has been done to the ancient stonework inside during the last thirty years by driving nails for decoration than was done during five hundred years of the church's previous existence. Nails should be prohibited.

The interesting Transition arches of the nave show no original columns on the north side. The respond (rather than the pier) of one of these might be examined to discover if the stone shafts are within the brickwork (erected also about 1840); since tradition persistently reports that they are. If so, it would be a question of construction whether the brick casing could be safely taken away. One who assisted at the casing informed me many years ago that it was done because the piers were getting weak.

When the present imitation Early English nave roof was erected about 1870 (by a Dorchester builder, as I have been informed, under no architectural advice) in place of the good old sixteenth century waggon roof with bosses, which had become decayed, the proportions between the tower and the nave were altered. I fear this is beyond remedy. No corbels existed till then, and to put in one of them the Cholmondeley monument was destroyed.

The old font now in fragments might be erected on a plain square base in the south west corner of the nave nearly opposite the present one as a relic, but not for use—the present marble font—date 1700–1750—having seen 150 to 200 years of christenings, and acquired a prescriptive right to remain.

If an Organ be really required I should say, speaking for myself alone, that the old west gallery should be re-erected for it. Its reconstruction would be inexpensive. Such west galleries, which were unadvisedly destroyed in the last century are now getting replaced in some churches, there being no point in the edifice which so completely controls the singing of the congregation as a west gallery. There are three bells in the tower—The first bell, cracked by being hammered at a wedding, should be re-cast if cutting out will not suffice. Care should be taken to employ a respectable founder, that base metal may not be substituted for the old, which is of high quality. If the other bells are rehung the cannons should on no account be cut off, as is the modern reprehensible practice, which can be avoided by giving more camber to the stock.

Outside, the north aisle coping should be removed and replaced as above-mentioned, the gutter between the vestry roof and the aisle-wall treated in the same way, the south parapet repaired, the tower pointed—stack-pipes being put to the aisles, and one to the tower, as the torrents of water that pour down by the present heating apparatus are doing mischief.

I should not advise much interference with the lead of the chancel roof.

I regret that my survey was rather hasty, but having known the church for many years I believe the aforesaid recommendations to be proper ones.

Yours very truly
Thomas Hardy.

To the Restoration Committee.

"Church restoration": TH had expressed his views on this subject in his paper 'Memories of Church Restoration' (see letter of 12 Sept. 1906).   *One who assisted*: probably TH's father, who was often employed to do building work on the church.   *Cholmondeley monument*: a marble tablet to Marcia Cholmondeley, née Pitt, buried in the Pitt family vault.   *of christenings*: including TH's own; for the fonts see letter of 15 Jan. 1914.   *cannons . . . stock*: the stock is the block of wood from which the bell is hung, the cannon the part of the bell by which it is hung.

To Florence Henniker

MAX GATE, | DORCHESTER. | 24: 5: 1909

My dear friend:

How strange—I was thinking of either writing or calling to see if you were in London (where I was last week) when your nice letter came. It was purely by accident that I was up there when Meredith died: I turned the corner at the top of St James's Street that morning, & saw the announcement on a placard before me. It was a sad shock, for he sent to ask if I would run down & see him some time ago, & I was intending to this summer. I send a few lines of verse I was moved to write about him, in case you did not see them in the Times.

I am not surprised that you got stuck in The Egoist. It is awkward for me, of course, to criticise the work of a man I liked & admired so much, but I may say that the difficulty of reading—or at least enjoying—some of his books arises entirely (as I think) from his errors of method. Why he was so perverse as to infringe the first rules of narrative art I cannot tell, when what he had to say was of the very highest, & what he discerned in life was more than almost any novelist had discerned before. A child could almost have told him that to indulge in psychological analysis of the most ingenious kind in the crisis of an emotional scene is fatal—high emotion demanding simplicity of expression above all things,—yet this was what Meredith constantly did. Wordsworth knew better: & so I believe Meredith did, only he would not practise what he knew because he was so exasperated by bad criticism.

This is what makes Swinburne the greater writer, though he is much the smaller thinker: he knew so well how to appeal.

I, also, read that novel "Maurice Guest", the author having sent me a copy. Yes the characters are rather a bad lot, but the woman is well done (utterly unattractive to me person-ally:—there are scores of them about; but attractive as a drawing, because of its accuracy).

I knew John Davidson very slightly. I think he might have rubbed on, if he had had a little more ballast. I am not doing much just now, & think of going to Aldeburgh for Whitsun-tide. It is announced that "Tess" is to be produced at Covent Garden this season as an Italian opera: I gave permission some time ago, & it has already been done in Milan, Venice, Naples, &c, with much success. Let me hear from you again.

Your affectte friend
Tho H.

in the Times: TH's poem 'G.M.' was published on 22 May 1909.   *The Egoist*: Meredith's novel, published in 1879.   *the author*: the Australian novelist Ethel Florence Lindesay Richardson (1870–1946), who wrote under the pseudonym of 'Henry Handel Richardson'.   *Davidson*: John

Davidson (1857–1909), poet, committed suicide in Mar. 1909.   *as an*
Italian opera: *Tess*, composed by Baron Frédéric d'Erlanger, was first
performed at Covent Garden on 14 July 1909.

To Edward Clodd

Max Gate | Friday night. [28 May 1909]

My dear Clodd:

I am prompted to write a line or two, having thought
frequently of you & your guests this evening, & pictured the
trip: the bustle at Liverpool Street, the lively conversation in
the carriage, the gradual sense of the nearing sea & its cool
salt air as you get on to the branch line, the real taste of it on
arrival, & the jolly dinner after. But, as the poet says, O the
difference to me!

The talk, I feel almost sure, is largely about Meredith. I
daresay you read in The Times to-day that letter about him
& the Abbey. The line of defence is a weak one: a doubt if M.
was a big enough man for the place is absurd after Irving &
others. The true line of defence for the refusal to have him
there, or at least the adroit line, would have been that, as
Huxley put it, the Abbey is a Christian Temple & not a
Pantheon for men of all beliefs, & that it contains the ashes of
a few only of our great writers. The absence of such recent
illustrious ones as Meredith, Swinburne, Spencer, &c, will do
good in serving to remove the erroneous modern impression.
If such people are wanted there by the country a heathen
annexe should be built. It is a pity that M. did not leave a
special injunction that he was to be buried at Dorking, so that
the question might not have arisen.

I am getting on by degrees, but am husky & sniffy yet, &
have to keep indoors, till dry-eyed.

Sincerely yours
T.H.

---

the difference to me: from Wordsworth's 'She dwelt among th'untrodden
ways'; a heavy cold had prevented TH from joining Clodd's weekend
house-party at Aldeburgh.   *& the Abbey*: the refusal to allow Meredith's

ashes to be buried in Westminster Abbey had aroused considerable controversy; the letter in *The Times* was attributed to 'A Man of Letters'. *Irving*: Sir Henry Irving (1838–1905), the actor.   *as Huxley put it*: writing on 27 Dec. 1880 to the philosopher Herbert Spencer (1820–1903), who was urging an Abbey burial for George Eliot, Thomas Henry Huxley had declared, 'However much I may regret the circumstances, Westminster Abbey is a Christian Church and not a Pantheon'.   *Dorking*: where Meredith's ashes had in fact been laid.

To Maurice Hewlett

THE ATHENAEUM, | PALL MALL. S.W. | 11: 6: 1909

My dear Hewlett:

I have just received your note of yesterday. There was, in fact, one other reason at the back of my mind which made me feel that in the Society's interests it ought not to elect me; & though I did not mention it at first I will quite frankly do so now. The President (in addition to what I said before) should be a man on the tendency of whose writings there is no difference of opinion: whatever their power, their moral & social teaching should be of the correct & accepted pattern. This was the case with both Tennyson & Meredith. But there is, right up to the present moment, a bitter divergence of view as to such in my case. One of my last poems was called blasphemous by the Guardian, & the Spectator has shaken its head over another. I have had a book burnt by a bishop & the fact announced in the papers. No recent English writer has been so roundly abused by the press as I have been in past times, with the single exception of Swinburne, & he is dead.

Perhaps this would not matter so much if it were all over. But I could not undertake never to kick over the traces again, for on one point I am determined—to exhibit what I feel ought to be exhibited about life to show that what we call immorality, irreligion, &c, are often true morality, true religion, &c, quite freely to the end.

Will you then, as the good friend that I know you to be

both to the Society & to myself, put this aspect of the matter
strongly before the Council?

Always yours sincerely,
Thomas Hardy.

Hewlett: Maurice Henry Hewlett (1861–1923), novelist and poet, had
written on behalf of the Council of the Incorporated Society of Authors,
Playwrights, and Composers to invite TH to succeed Meredith as the
Society's president. TH's initial refusal, on the grounds that the Society
needed more active leadership than he could provide, had been countered
by Hewlett's insistence that no duties were assigned to the president in the
Society's constitution. Hewlett now responded that TH was universally
acknowledged as 'the head of our profession', and TH eventually accepted
the presidency, serving until his death in 1928.   *One of my last . . . papers*:
the *Guardian* reference has not been traced, but the *Spectator* (5 Dec. 1908)
had criticized 'A Sunday Morning Tragedy' for the 'extreme unpleasant-
ness' of its subject (see letter of 9 Sept. 1908); for the burning of *Jude* see
letter of 17 Jan. 1897.

To Edward Clodd

Max Gate | 22: 7: '09

My dear Clodd:

I left London last Saturday, & have not been in the best of
health & spirits since, though I am rapidly picking up.

Your kindly opinion of my young friend & assistant pleases
me much (& her, too, whom I told of it). I have known her
for several years, & am very anxious about her health &
welfare; & am determined to get her away to the seaside if I
can, or she will break down quite. Your timely hint that I
might bring her to Aldeburgh is really charming. After a few
days there I could send or bring her to Weymouth.

What date would be quite convenient? Would Bank holi-
day-week suit, or would you prefer a later time?

If you would fix a date I will suggest it to her, & should it
suit (as it is almost sure to) you could write directly to her, or
through me.

If we do come there will be such a clicking of the typewriter
as never was in your house before (she is not really what is

called "a typist", but as she learns anything she has learnt that, though as I told you she writes original things, is a splendid proof-reader, & a fine critic, her taste in poetry being unerring—only doing my typewriting as a fancy).

I hope you will have another good week-end. I was so glad you liked the Opera. D'Erlanger tells me they have not had such a first night for years.

Always sincerely
Thomas Hardy.

friend & assistant: Florence Dugdale, whom Clodd, at TH's request, had escorted to a performance of the *Tess* opera.

[Hardy's subtly enhanced prestige following Meredith's death did not diminish his old caution—learned painfully but perhaps too well—as to the promulgation of work likely to attract hostility or even censorship on moral or religious grounds. His poem 'Panthera', based on the legend of the Roman centurion who believes the crucified Christ to be his own lost son, had received a mixed reception when read out to the distinguished group gathered together at one of Edward Clodd's genial weekend house-parties, and he therefore sought clearer advice as to its publishability from Frederick Macmillan, for whose practical wisdom in all such matters he had come to have the highest possible respect. Macmillan quickly declared the poem unobjectionable and it appeared for the first time in *Time's Laughingstocks* in December 1909.]

To Frederick Macmillan

Private.   MAX GATE, | DORCHESTER. | 18: 9: '09

My dear Macmillan:

I was going to include in the new volume among the rest of the poems the legendary one I enclose. It has been read by Professor Bury of King's, Cambridge, who says by all means print it—in which opinion a lady of light & leading in University Circles also coincides. Another literary friend—a Rationalist reviewer—says include it; but two others (one a reviewer) advise me not to print it, though they, like the rest, call it a poem of great interest.

I had a good mind to ask another friend, Prothero, Ed. of the Quarterly, but he may not be in London just now.

My own feeling was that, as there are some poems in the collection quite of an opposite kind—quite "churchy" in fact, this would contrast well with them, & excite no bad feeling.

But I should like you or your cousin, or any trusty reader at hand for subjects of this kind, to decide whether to include it or not. To divines of the Higher Criticism, Dr Cheyne for instance, there is, of course, no harm in it at all, the legend being well-known to such scholars—but I do not want to provoke acrimony amongst well-meaning but narrower minded people for the sake of one poem, good or bad.

On the other hand I do not want to leave out a piece which may be liked by advanced readers, & may possibly start a good wholesome controversy: poetry, as you know, is sadly in need of some stimulus to set it going.

You understand these practical matters better than I, so will you say frankly what you think. It comes near the end of the book, so there is time to settle the question before the printers get to it.

Sincerely yours
Thomas Hardy.

P.S. I have omitted to mention the rather important detail that since the objectors read it I have rewritten the poem, & made the events a possibly erroneous fantasy of the narrator—which I think removes all objection. However, you decide. T.H.

Bury: J. B. Bury the historian (see letter of 3 June 1911) was among those who heard TH read 'Panthera' at Aldeburgh; the 'lady of light & leading' was the classical scholar Jane Ellen Harrison (1850–1928), the 'Rationalist reviewer' Clodd himself; of the 'two others' one was Clodd's friend the Revd Robert Frew and the second ('a reviewer') probably William Archer.   *Prothero*: George Walter Prothero (1848–1922), editor of the *Quarterly Review* 1899–1922.   *Dr Cheyne*: Thomas Kelly Cheyne (1841–1915), Old Testament scholar.

To Edmund Gosse

MAX GATE, | DORCHESTER. | 3: 12: 1909.

My dear Gosse:

I agree with every word of your letter to *The Times* on the possibility that the, no doubt well-intentioned censorship proposed by the librarians may degenerate into a grave danger to literary liberty, & I congratulate you on your courage in writing the letter. I am rather surprised at the meekness of the publishers in their response, for it may mean a very serious thing for them. It is a remedy which may turn out to be worse than the disease.

It is curious that the very book you mention, Darwin's Origin of Species, immediately came into my own head yesterday as one that would have been banned. I also wondered at the fate of some of Swinburne's books. Not to mention Poems & Ballads, Atalanta would probably have been suppressed for one line which, I remember, scandalized just the class whose complaints have led to this declaration: i.e. "The supreme evil, God." Yet Mudie circulated it.

The question is, where is the discriminator between the bad & worthless, & the startling & enlightening, to be found—not, I fear, always in the ranks of busy librarians, however much they might wish to do no harm to what is really valuable in literature.

Always sincerely yours
Thomas Hardy.

P.S. I sent off a book to you to-day. T.H.

your letter: Gosse's letter in *The Times* of 3 Dec. had criticized the announced intention of the Circulating Libraries' Association to set up a committee with the power to determine the suitability for circulation of books suspected of being 'personally scandalous, libellous, immoral, or otherwise disagreeable'. The Publishers' Association, on the other hand, had expressed 'sympathetic approval' of the proposal and suggested that the two associations should consult with the Society of Authors as to the best means of preventing the circulation of 'obnoxious literature'. *Atalanta*: Swinburne's *Atalanta in Calydon*, published in 1865, the year before *Poems and Ballads*. *Mudie*: i.e. Mudie's library; see letter of 4 Feb. 1892. *a book*: an inscribed copy of *Time's Laughingstocks*, published that day.

To Lady Grove

MAX GATE, | DORCHESTER. | 29: 12: 1909

My dear Lady Grove:

I was most pleased to get your review—as I may call it—of "T.L.S." But although I call it that by reason of its ability, I should really have known who was the author of such generous appreciativeness if it had appeared in print anonymously.

I have been reticent about the book, for I fancied it might not be considered quite one to push into friends' hands at Christmas time, both because it is preponderantly tragic & for other reasons. In fact a friend of mine says of some of the poems that certain people would hold them to be of a sort which a wise daughter would hesitate to put into her mother's hands.

Some good judges agree with you in liking "Let me enjoy". I fear I am not clear on the precise mental state of the singer of that lyric. In "The Husband's View" to which you also allude, the husband's state of mind is preeminently a sane one, if you reflect on it. In fact he is the man of the future, though it did not strike me that he was till now. If our endeavours shd be directed to the good of humanity at large, & eugenic principles shd prevail, the husband of a century hence will say to his wife, "Pray don't consider my feelings, if you shd meet with a healthier or more intellectual man than I am. The race is the thing."

What a pretty picture your card is—the very prettiest we have had. And the portrait is just like you.

I am just recovering (I hope) from an illness of between 2 & 3 weeks—an obstinate sore throat, that has been very depressing, keeping me in bed part of the time. I have had to take the most horrid medicine you can imagine. Your letter was quite a godsend, as I have been able to see nobody but the doctor all the Christmas.

Best wishes for the new year from your always affectionate friend

Thomas Hardy.

"T.L.S.": *Time's Laughingstocks*; Lady Grove's remarks were contained in a letter.

To Thackeray Turner

Max Gate | Dorchester | 7 Feb. '10
Puddletown Church: Dorset

Dear Sir:

Since the receipt of your letter I have inquired about the size of the congregation usually at the services, & I am told by two persons who frequently attend that the building is never full, & seldom half-full.

The church is the only one I know in the county that has not been tampered with, & I agree with you in deploring the contemplated enlargement. It is not pretended (so far as I gather) that sitting room is required, but that the chancel ought artistically or ecclesiastically, to be longer. It is said that old foundations of a longer chancel have been discovered, but I am sceptical about these foundations. I have not closely examined the present chancel of late years, but the roof is, if I remember, the ordinary waggon roof of the 15–16th cent. The 17th cent. fittings of the chancel are extremely interesting. These I suppose will be swept away.

I went over the church some years ago with the late Sir Arthur Blomfield, & he, though a restorer, emphatically stated that this particular church was one which ought not to be touched.

It is rumoured, I know not with what truth, that an old manor house remaining in the village is to be pulled down to furnish stone for the enlargement.

I am not personally acquainted with the present owner of the estate & parish, who is the brother of the late owner, & who, till he succeeded to the property, was the incumbent of a parish near. The deceased owner assured me that the church should not be altered in his lifetime, & he kept his word.

I enclose a guide book, which you may not have seen, but

if you have it please return it. It is drawn up by a painstaking inhabitant who was organist till recently.

I think this is a case in which the Society should exert itself. I may add that curiously enough, the church happens to be the village church of the novel "Far from the Madding Crowd," which brings many visitors to it every year, particularly Americans. I may say privately, that I cannot help feeling that, if expostulation fail, & as soon as the Society feels sure of its ground, a letter from it to the Times on the matter, adding the fact that it is the church of this well-known novel, might be effective. You will quite understand that in my own view an imaginary story of mine makes no difference to the case, but as some of the public think otherwise, it would be well to enlist their sympathy even though we suppose it bestowed for foolish reasons.

I will reply on any other question if necessary, but I think the church should be visited by an officer of the Society if it has not been already.

Yours very truly
Thomas Hardy.

Thackeray Turner Esq. | Society for the Protection of Ancient Bdgs

your letter: Turner had asked TH to enquire whether the proposed lengthening of the chancel of Puddletown Church was justified by the size of the congregation.   *Blomfield*: TH's old employer had been knighted in 1889, ten years before his death.   *present owner*: the Revd John George Brymer had inherited the family estates from his brother Lieutenant-Colonel William Ernest Brymer, MP, in 1909.   *guide book*: written by William Gover (1853–1914), Puddletown grocer and local historian.   *to the Times*: a letter from Turner which appeared in *The Times* of 24 Feb. 1910 repeated many of the points made here by TH. Despite such protests, however, the 'restoration' went ahead and a new chancel was added.

To Lady Grove

Max Gate. | 18: 4: '10

Dear Lady Grove:

I gather from your letter that my remark that some of your essays "approached literature" has caused you more concern than such superficial words were entitled to cause. The truth is that nobody can pronounce offhand on the first reading of a new book what its ultimate value may be, & I did not mean to pass a judgment on yours. Moreover "literature" is a vague term which requires a good deal of defining before it can be used for classifying purposes.

All the articles are charming (I have finished the book since I wrote) & surely to write charming essays is a triumph, apart from what they may or may not be besides.

The latter ones have amused me most—"Past Rules", "Decorum", & "Clubs". "Quelle surprise pour Papa!" is a lovely story which I had never seen before.

I do not at all see why you should not go on writing if you *like* doing it. That is everything, for upon the whole there is rather more distinction in not writing than in writing in these times, & I sometimes wish I had never penned a line.

A very good test rule is, would you rather lose money & opportunities by writing than gain them by not writing? If you can honestly say yes, I think you are called by nature to do it. I remember testing myself by that query when I stood at the parting of the ways.

I am leaving here in a day or two for London.

Ever your affly
Thomas Hardy.

E. has just come back from looking for a flat in London— quite prostrated.·T.H.

my remark: writing to Lady Grove on 13 Apr. about her new book *On Fads*, TH had praised three of its constituent essays as 'the most successful & the nearest to literature'.

To Lady Grove

4 Blomfield Court, | Maida Vale, | London. N.W. |
13: 5: 1910

My dear Lady Grove:

So far as I see there is not much the matter with such an expression as "prefers you when you are" so & so "to when you are" something else. It is merely an ellipsis for "to [you] when you are", &c. I don't care for ellipses myself; but they are not wrong. Women use them much more frequently than men do.

The second instance you give—that of "and who", or "and which"—I was always taught to avoid, & I believe always have avoided using; but I really don't quite know why, unless because the second who or which is unnecessary, since you may just as well say "who failed to do so & so, & roused" &c., as "& who roused"; & one should never forget to express one's self in the fewest possible words.

"She started to remember" means the same thing as "she started at remembering", which is what I should have written myself, as being less ambiguous, though they are both correct.

"A joke that will not only pass muster but perhaps cause. . . ." is right or wrong according to your meaning. If it must cause [a laugh] to pass muster, the sentence is obviously confused, but if it can pass muster without causing [the laugh], & that is regarded as something additional, the sentence is of course correct enough.

I imagine that critics who object to these & other sentences in your writing object to them in point of style rather than of grammar. A sentence may often be strictly correct in grammar, but wretched in style.

But remember that I am no authority. I have written heaps of ungrammatical sentences I dare say, for I got at my grammar by a species of general reasoning rather than by rules.

I am glad to find, from the extracts you send from Fredk H.'s letter, that I do not disagree with what he says. He speaks of the content or substance of your book; & I spoke merely of its literary form, or rather of sentences in some of the essays, in my first letter. Moreover I rather exaggerate your faults of style in criticizing you, to make you persistently careful, for you are, you know, rather inclined to let your pen run away with you at times!

We have taken this flat till the middle of July. If you are coming to town the way to it is straight up the Edgware Road: I hope you are. I saw Mrs Lowndes at Mrs Crackanthorpe's tea at the Caxton Hall on the occasion of Mr C's lecture on Eugenics.

The King's death will, I suppose, make little difference in public affairs, though some in private. I fear the new court will not be much more intellectual than the old. I am inclined to go away on the day of the funeral, to avoid the frightful crush.

Ever yr affectte friend
Thomas Hardy.

Blomfield Court: the Hardys had taken a flat in Maida Vale for the 'season'. *"to [you] when*: all the square brackets in this letter are TH's; Lady Grove had consulted him about criticisms of her writing in *On Fads*.　　*Fredk H.'s*: presumably (despite the 'k') Frederic Harrison.　　*Lowndes . . . Crackanthorpe's*: Marie Adelaide Belloc Lowndes (1868–1947), author chiefly of mystery stories; Blanche Alethea Crackanthorpe (1846–1928), literary hostess; her husband ('Mr C's') was Montague Crackanthorpe (1832–1913), barrister and writer on social, political, and legal topics. *King's death*: Edward VII died during the night of 6 May 1910.

To Emma Lavinia Hardy

THE ATHENAEUM, │ PALL MALL. S.W. │ Friday. 15: 7: 1910

Dear E:

I am glad to hear that you got home safely, and are not, at any rate, any worse. If your cough does not disappear in a few days perhaps the sea-side would send it away; but I would not go far, & certainly would not come back to London.

I manage very well at the flat now, though at first it seemed awkward. I go out to breakfast at the adjoining restaurant, & while I am out Mrs Smith the porter's wife (a gentle nice woman) comes & does my room, cleans boots, &c. I have all

my other meals at the Club or elsewhere. I had to go to the
city this morning, so I breakfasted on my way at one of
Lyons's places opposite the Marble Arch. It was very pleasant—the view down Park Lane, the cool morning air blowing
in, &c. The only time that is depressing is when I come home
at 10 or ½ past, & go into the dark silent flat, full of the
ghosts of all those who have visited us there. I do not think
you would be able to stay at the flat during the few days I
remain, as you wd not have sufficient conveniences, & cd
hardly go out to breakfast, do without hot water, &c: & I am
away nearly all day.

If I can get off on Tuesday afternoon I think I will run
down to the sea somewhere for a day or two before coming
home. So do not send on anything after *Monday evening*'s post.
Keep the Westmr Bank letter till I return, & any other bank
or divd letters.

Henry sends a post card saying that he *saw* Rolls the aviator
killed at Bournemouth! Put "O.M." *only*, on the envelope
after my name.

T.

Lady St. H. wires to me to dine with her to-night: so I shall.

Westmr . . . divd: abbreviations for 'Westminster' and 'dividend'.   *Rolls
the aviator*: Charles Stewart Rolls (1877–1910), founder of Rolls-Royce,
crashed while participating in a flying competition at Bournemouth on 12
July, thus becoming the first British victim of an aviation accident.
"O.M.": Order of Merit, to which TH had been appointed in June 1910.

To Sir Frederick Macmillan

MAX GATE, | DORCHESTER. | 22 Sept 1910

Dear Sir Frederick Macmillan:

As the large edition of the novels is less correct than the
3/6 edn, & I have none of the latter by me, I shall be obliged
if you will let me have a set for the County Library.

What the librarian & Council want is a complete set of all
my writings—not for lending, but for reference. They say that
the chief literary institution in the County ought not to be

without them, & I don't quite like to say that they ought to buy them. Now this involves 6 vols. more than the novels—3 Dynasts & 3 poems. But if this seems rather a big request I am willing to make them wait for the poetry till it is all in 1 volume; though certainly the advantage of their having it in 6 vols. would be that they would all be uniform, & that we should get rid of the job at once. I will let you settle this question of the poetry.

As to other matters: I quite agree that as long as Time's Laughingstocks sells in its present form it would be a pity to stop it by the 1 vol. of collected verse, & that this, therefore, should be held over for a time.

The editors of periodicals frequently ask me for verses, so that new ones slowly accumulate, & there is not much doubt that, if all goes well, I shall have enough in the future to make up another volume. Tragic narrative poems, like the Tramp-woman's Tragedy, seem to be liked most, & I can do them with ease.

An idea has occurred to me which I mention for what it may be worth. As the 3 parts of The Dynasts are in type for the collected edition, could the interim between now & its publication be filled by issuing The Dynasts by itself in one vol.—say at 7/6? There would be nothing to do to the type except change the paging. People, I think, rather shy at paying 13/6 for one book.

Whichever of you has taken his holidays late this year is fortunate. I bicycled 24 miles over the hills yesterday, & the views were splendid.

Sincerely yours
Thomas Hardy.

Macmillan: he had been knighted in Dec. 1909 for his work in charitable causes.   *large edition*: the 'Wessex Novels' edition, as originally published by Osgood, McIlvaine and subsequently transferred, first to Harper & Brothers and then to Macmillan & Co.; TH made corrections to some volumes in that edition before it was reissued as the '3s/6d' or 'Uniform' edition, in a cheaper and slightly smaller format, following his move to Macmillan & Co. in 1902.   *Council*: Dorset County Council.   *The Dynasts . . . in one vol.*: Macmillan accepted this suggestion and a one-volume complete edition of *The Dynasts* appeared in Nov. 1910.

To May Sinclair

MAX GATE, | DORCHESTER. | 7: 11: 1910

My dear Miss Sinclair:

I must thank you much for so kindly remembering to send me The Creators. I am in the middle of it, having obediently started again at the very beginning, as you suggested, although as I told you I had read four numbers in the magazine. I have enjoyed doing this, having thereby picked up threads that I had missed before.

I am much interested in learning from the female characters the things that go on at the back of women's minds—the invisible rays of their thought (as is said of the spectrum) which are beyond the direct sight or intuition of man. I recollect Leslie Stephen once saying to me that he liked women's novels for that reason: they opened to him qualities of observation which could not be got from the ablest of novels by men.

Poor Rose: I have arrived at a critical point in her career. I have not peeped (I would scorn the action) so I don't know at all what is going to happen.

Sincerely yours,
Thomas Hardy.

Sinclair: Mary (May) Amelia St Clair Sinclair (1863–1946), novelist and campaigner for women's suffrage; her new novel *The Creators: A Comedy* (1910), previously serialized in the *Century Magazine*, centred upon a character named Rose Eldred.

[George Moore and Thomas Hardy had little in common beyond their profession as novelists and a mutual dislike that must have been based—despite the infrequency with which they met—on something more than the 'rivalry' between *Esther Waters* and *Tess of the d'Urbervilles*. Their disagreement in this instance was over the propriety—defended by Moore but questioned by Hardy—of John Lane's having published Hermann Sudermann's *The Song of Songs*, currently under

attack on grounds of obscenity, and it would appear that
Hardy was answering Moore only because the latter had
approached him in his new role as president of the Incorporated Society of Authors.]

To George Moore

MAX GATE, | DORCHESTER. | 26: 12: 1910

Dear Mr Moore:

In writing to Mr Lane I did not enter into the question
whether the book was or was not an immoral one, but merely
told him what I personally should do in the practical circumstances in which he found himself.

I understand you to argue that harmfulness in real literature is as bad as harmfulness in sham literature, but that this
book (assuming it to be sham literature) can do no harm,
either because it is weak or because it has nothing in it which
would justify its suppression as an obscene libel.

I differ from you somewhat in the latter respect. I think it
stands on the doubtful line: it may possibly not do harm, but
possibly may. It is not obscene, as they say, but to my mind
is sensual, & though obscenity is innocuous, sensuality is not
quite the same. Therefore it was not worth while to defend a
position in morals which was doubtful, especially as there
would be no gain to literature in the event of success. If a
protest against interference has to be made, it would be a
wiser policy to do it in connection with some safer book.

Yours sincerely

Thomas Hardy.

Moore: George Augustus Moore (1852–1933), novelist.   *Lane . . . the book*:
on 15 Dec. 1910 TH had advised John Lane, the publisher (see letter of 10
Dec. 1913), to withdraw *The Song of Songs*, a translation of Sudermann's
novel *Das hohe Lied*, on the grounds that the poor quality of the translation
made it difficult to defend as a work of literary merit.

To Sir Frederick Macmillan

MAX GATE, | DORCHESTER. | Jan 17: 1911

Dear Sir Frederick:

The Map of Wessex in the novels was first published in 1895, & is an extension of an idea I first used in The Return of the Native (1st edn 1878) to which was prefixed a map of Egdon Heath, the scene of the story.

As to the map being an authorized picture of where the localities really are, it is not precisely so, for though I certainly drew it, it was rather unwillingly done, owing to the constant inquiries of readers for the actual places. But I stated, I think in one of the Prefaces at the time it was published, that the scenes of the stories were not guaranteed to be solidly standing where shown on the map, but were only suggested more or less by places that stood there, & fully existed nowhere but in the novels themselves.

Believe me

Very truly yours
Thomas Hardy.

P.S. I find that in the only two prefaces I have looked at—to *Tess* & the *Madding Crowd* I do not clearly state as above, but adopt a non-committal tone. However I have said it somewhere in print more than once. A Handbook, "The Wessex Country of T.H" (Rowbottom: Bournemouth. 1s/-) is fairly correct on this point. I think you ought to have a copy of it in the office. T.H.

in the novels: i.e. in the successive volumes of the Osgood, McIlvaine 'Wessex Novels' edition.   *non-committal tone*: none of the 'Wessex Novels' prefaces is altogether explicit on this point, but the issue is certainly addressed in Hermann Lea's 'Handbook' (see letter of 9 Nov. 1904)—and in words which TH himself supplied.

To Florence Henniker

MAX GATE, | DORCHESTER. | May 26: 1911

My dear friend:

I have read your brief story with much interest. It is just long enough for what it tells, & might be made one of a series entitled "Unfulfilled intentions". I think some other of your short ones would go into such a series. The man is just like a politician, or I suppose I ought to say statesman,—a sort of Ld Haldane one fancies? The girl, though so slightly sketched, is very distinct—the modern intelligent, mentally emancipated young woman of cities, for whom the married life you kindly provide for her would ultimately prove no great charm—by far the most interesting type of femininity the world provides for man's eyes at the present day. In fact, between ourselves, I don't quite believe she did marry that other man.

I could not call, for I found I was getting a slight cold in London & felt, too, rather fagged; so I came back Thursday. I return the story.

Yr affectte friend,
Tho H.

brief story: unidentified, and perhaps unpublished.   Haldane: Richard Burdon Haldane (1856–1928), statesman and philosopher.

To J. B. Bury

Max Gate | 3: 6: 11

Dear Professor Bury:

I have read the Romances of Chivalry that you kindly send. The idea of lovers meeting in a dream before they know each other, & awaiting their meeting in life, has been used I think in a modern story by a writer who probably little dreamt of its antiquity. Truly there is nothing new under the sun.

Whether belief in dealings with the Evil One by means of

magic, as in the supposed case of Fitzpiers, still survives in this county I am not quite aware, but belief in witchcraft—another form of it—still flourishes here in nooks & corners. Quite recently a man would not let his newly married son & daughter-in-law go into a cottage lately occupied by an old woman, on the ground that she had been a witch, & that her malign influence lingering in the house would injure them.

However it is not necessary to go very far afield for belief in, or assurance of, the Evil One's existence. Not long ago I was at a fashionable London church, & the sermon went entirely to show that there was undoubtedly a personal devil—with hoofs & horns as I understood—& that the Power of Evil was no abstraction as many people erroneously supposed.

Ever sincerely yours
Thomas Hardy.

P.S. It is very doubtful if I shall be in Suffolk again this year. If so I must try to get to Southwold. Many thanks for reminding me. T.H.

Bury: John Bagnell Bury (1861–1927), Regius Professor of Modern History at Cambridge, had sent TH a copy of his Romanes Lecture *Romances of Chivalry on Greek Soil* (1911). The 'modern story' was presumably Rudyard Kipling's 'The Brushwood Boy' (1895); Fitzpiers is a character in TH's *The Woodlanders* (1887).   *in Suffolk*: i.e. at Clodd's house in Aldeburgh, where TH and Bury had first met; Bury had a summer cottage at nearby Southwold.

[Rufus H. Hinkley, an American publisher, was proposing to collaborate with the house of Macmillan in an *édition de luxe* of Hardy's works. When this scheme fell through Sir Frederick Macmillan promptly suggested that Hardy's textual revisions and specially written prefaces be incorporated instead into a new Macmillan collected edition—handsomely produced but with no limitation as to the number of copies that might be printed and sold. The Wessex Edition, as it was called, had 'definitive' status in Hardy's eyes, and while most of the volumes appeared in 1912 and 1913 each of the later titles—

up to and including the posthumously published *Winter Words*—was duly added to it.]

To Sir Frederick Macmillan

MAX GATE, | DORCHESTER. | 24 June 1911

Dear Sir Frederick:

I have just received your letter of the 16th—Yesterday week I started on a tour in the north to escape the glories of the Coronation, for though I was honoured by an invitation I thought I should never get to the Abbey. At starting I ventured to direct that no letters should be forwarded. Hence my silence, the cause of which I hope you may have approximately guessed.

I am much obliged to you for carrying out the arrangements with Mr Hinkley that I agreed to leave in your hands. I am, further, quite willing to sign the 50 copies on Japanese paper on which he offers to pay the extra fee. The proposal to have a portrait & pictures of the locality in the volumes is no doubt a good one for the books, & I will do what I can to enable him to carry it out.

I believe I shall be staying on here for the greater part of July, with the possible exception of a day or two occasionally in London or elsewhere, & if Mr Hinkley comes down he can be accommodated here if he has sufficient time at his disposal to stay over a day. Or if he would prefer I can meet him in London without trouble.

The books for correction have arrived. My idea for a long time has been to divide the novels into two groups, putting into the second group 4 or 5 of the more superficial & experimental ones, written just for the moment, critics having a way of pitching upon one or other of these lighter ones as typical of the whole. It will make no difference except in the order of numbering & not much in that. I will however write again on any detail of this kind.

Yours very truly
Thomas Hardy.

a tour: although he had received an official invitation to be present at the coronation of King George V, TH preferred to visit the Lake District in the company of his brother Henry, Florence Dugdale, and the latter's father and sister.   *Mr Hinkley*: Rufus H. Hinkley (d. 1942), American publisher.   *into two groups*: the scheme finally adopted for the Wessex Edition involved three divisions, 'Novels of Character and Environment', 'Romances and Fantasies', and 'Novels of Ingenuity'; a fourth division, 'Mixed Novels', was later introduced to allow for the addition of the volume entitled *A Changed Man*.

To John Galsworthy

MAX GATE, | DORCHESTER. | June 26: 1911

Dear Mr Galsworthy:

I have been away in the north for eight days, no letters being forwarded; & yours came just after I had started.

I write a hasty line now to say that I will consider the draft protest you send about flying & war. Of course I quite agree that these machines, if they are ever effectively constructed (which they are not at present) will make war worse than ever. But does not the appeal tacitly admit that war in other ways will have to go on? Now I am one of the extremists about this, & think it an insanity that people in the 20th Century should suppose force to be a moral argument.

Perhaps the addition after the first sentence of some words about "adding a new hideousness to the present hideousness of war", might remove that objection.

However, of late years I have almost despaired of civilization making any big step forward. Possibly in the year 4000 we shall be nearly as barbarous as we are now in belligerency, marriage, treatment of animals, &c.

I suppose I never told you how highly I thought of your novel "The Man of Property". It seems to have been the parent of many that have appeared since & made more noise.

Sincerely yours
Thomas Hardy.

P.S. I hope you live in Devon, & are not merely visiting there. T.H.

Galsworthy: John Galsworthy (1867–1933), the novelist and playwright, had sent TH a copy of *The Man of Property* (see letter of 12 Sept. 1906) and was now seeking support for an international protest against the use of aircraft in wartime.   *in Devon*: the Galsworthys regularly spent the summer in the Devonshire village of Manaton.

To Florence Henniker

MAX GATE, | DORCHESTER. | 22 Aug. 1911

My dear friend:

I don't quite know where you are just now, but no doubt this missive will find you out. I was most interested in your success in seeing the Coronation show by land & sea. Really your enterprise is becoming almost American. I felt myself a poor creature, for I went off to the Lakes to be away from the millions—who did not come to Town after all.

The only thing worth mentioning that I have done since then has been a little trip I took with my sister Kitty (the younger one) about a fortnight ago to the north coast of Somerset & Devon: to Minehead, across Exmoor by coach (a cruel climb for the horses—1400 ft, six being necessary) to Lynmouth (where Shelley & Harriet stayed) Lynton, Ilfracombe by steam boat, Exeter Cathedral, &c. No sooner had we got back than the railway strike began.

I have found an unexpected ally in the slaughter-house reform work—Lady Hoare, of Stour Head, Wilts. She, too, is getting the instruments sent about. She motors over here to tea sometimes, & knowing you are interested in the same causes, would like to make your acquaintance some day.

Steps are being taken to publish an *édition de luxe* of all my books—(the publishers mark their letters on the subject "private", so I suppose I must ask you to treat it as such). I did not feel altogether elated at the proposal, though it will be in some respects a good thing; for it involves re-reading old books of mine, written when my spirits were brisker than they are now, & full of artistic errors which cannot be altered.

I will inquire if the butchers, &c, will use the pig-killer hereabout. I ought to have done so before, but I have had no energy at all.

Will you be in London in the autumn, I wonder? I will try

to see you if you are. It occurred to me the other day that this year completes the eighteenth of our friendship. That is rather good as between man & woman, wh. is usually so brittle.

Ever affectly
Tho H.

by land & sea: Florence Henniker had evidently seen the naval review at Spithead on 24 June as well as the coronation itself in London on 22 June.   *Shelley & Harriet*: Percy Bysshe Shelley and his first wife Harriet spent the summer of 1812 in Lynmouth, Devon.   *Hoare*: see letter of 7 Jan. 1915.

To Harry Pouncy

MAX GATE, | DORCHESTER. | 3: 9: 1911

Dear Mr Pouncy:

I think that little good can be done by our seeing an ox killed. I have been so distressed in past times by such sights that I have vowed I would not witness another, unless for some strong reason.

I *rather* doubt the assurance that the pole-axe is the more merciful implement. In skilful hands it may be almost as sure as the other; but (as in surgical operations) it is the bungler one has to reckon with, & I fear that the majority of slaughtermen are not experts—in the country. I will put this to my London friend when she returns from abroad.

I have read the verses with great pleasure, & like the first piece, The Pulpit Rock, very much. It is, in fact, good enough to print *anywhere*. But alas, editors are quite obdurate when poetry is mentioned. They say that, whatever its merits, it does not benefit a magazine one bit. The literary letter in this week's *Sphere* makes some pertinent remarks on this. I return the verses in case you want to cast them on the waters of journalism, & am,

Very truly yrs
T. Hardy.

Pouncy: Harry Pouncy (1870–1925), Dorchester journalist and lecturer; his poem 'The Pulpit Rock' appeared in the *Society of Dorset Men in London*:

Year-Book, 1911–12.   *distressed . . . by such sights*: as seems clearly to be reflected in the pig-killing episode in *Jude*.   *the other*: evidently some kind of 'painless killer' (see next letter).   *my London friend*: Florence Henniker. *remarks on this*: Clement Shorter's 'A Literary Letter' in the *Sphere*, 2 Sept. 1911, is in fact concerned with the difficulty of selling volumes of poetry.

To Florence Henniker

Max Gate 3: 10: 1911

My dear friend:

At last I know where you are, which I have lately been in some doubt about. Mr Stewart, the Secretary of the Council of Justice, writing to inquire if I would have a "painless killer" (at your suggestion) seemed to imply that you had returned from abroad. What with Harzburg & Scotland I shall expect to find you in rude health when we meet—which I trust may be at no distant date.

I am much interested in "G. Worlingworth" & all his works, & certainly don't mind receiving letters for him, or his MS. which shall be duly posted on. But I really think your own name would have accelerated the reading of a play rather than otherwise.—Whether there is a prejudice against a woman-dramatist I don't know: I should hardly have thought so.

I was *much* interested in your criticisms of "The New Machievelli", & have been saving up power & shot for replying to your arguments, or rather the assumptions involved in your queries. I have not read Wells carefully enough to discern his exact theories on the marriage question (if he has any), but you know what I have thought for many years: that marriage should not thwart nature, & that when it does thwart nature it is no real marriage, & the legal contract should therefore be as speedily cancelled as possible. Half the misery of human life would I think disappear if this were made easy: where there were no children at the wish of both or either: where there were children after an examination of the case by a court, & an order for certain provisions to be made. There would, of course, be difficulties, as you point out, but they would not be insuperable. Every kind of reform is met with the objection that it would be impossible, would have monstrous results, &c., yet the reform takes place, & the impossibility vanishes. However, as I said, I am not sure what it is Wells advocates in this book, & I may really not be answering you. Anyhow we will discuss the question when we are together. But I know beforehand that I shall not move you to sympathize with my views any more than you do with Mr Wells's.

It is so kind of you to have Florence Dugdale sometimes, & she likes coming very much. She has just gone to Weymouth for a week or two's change: I am going to run down this afternoon to see how she is getting on.

I hope you will not find Scotland too cold, but I really should think it must be almost, judging from the weather here. Why don't you come to Bournemouth sometimes: I am sure it would suit you.

I think that another ballad of mine will appear in print in a month or two—this time in the Fortnightly. I *fancy* you may like it—though it is tragic. I will let you know about it in due time.

If I read another novel in the immediate future I think it shall be "Hilda Lessways"—the continuation of "Clayhanger" by Bennett.

Affectionately yours
Tho H.

The Dorchester Dramatic Society is going to do another play from my novels on Nov 16 & 17.

Stewart: Robert Stewart; TH, at Florence Henniker's urging, had agreed to serve on the executive committee of the Council of Justice to Animals. "G. Worlingworth": the pseudonym Florence Henniker had adopted for her dramatic writings.   New Machievelli": correctly, The New Machiavelli, by H. G. Wells (1911).   another ballad: TH's 'The Sacrilege', Fortnightly Review, Nov. 1911.   Bennett: Arnold Bennett (see letter of 8 Sept. 1918); TH had recently read his Clayhanger (1910).   another play: an adaptation of TH's story 'The Distracted Preacher' was presented together with TH's own play The Three Wayfarers.

[Sydney Carlyle Cockerell, director of the Fitzwilliam Museum, Cambridge, visited Max Gate for the first time in late September 1911 and promptly persuaded Hardy that he should distribute his literary manuscripts to selected libraries in Britain and the United States—*Tess* and *The Dynasts* to the British Museum, for example, *Poems of the Past and the Present* to the Bodleian, *A Group of Noble Dames* to the Library of Congress, and (Cockerell's shrewdly chosen reward for his 'trouble') *Jude* and *Time's Laughingstocks* to the Fitzwilliam. In the years that followed Cockerell continued to make himself serviceable in a variety of ways—from reading proofs to facilitating Hardy's honorary doctorate from Cambridge in 1913—and Hardy eventually named him as one of his literary executors.]

To Sydney Cockerell

MAX GATE, | DORCHESTER. | 11: 10: 1911

Dear Mr Cockerell:

I am sending off to you the MSS. other than those forwarded to the British Museum—some in a box by rail, & two by parcel post—to distribute as you think fit. "The Imaginative Woman" (which you allotted to Aberdeen) I have kept back, in the hope of finding something better, or a page or two of verse to accompany it. This shall reach you anon.

I quite agree to "Wessex Poems" going to Birmingham Museum if you think they ought to. In that case, would it not be better for the Fitzwilliam to have "Time's Laughingstocks", & the Bodleian "Poems of the P. & Present"—as the former is said to be the best of my work in verse. But you must decide. "Life's L. Ironies" will do well for Manchester, if that city really cares to have it.

The Library of Congress at Washington certainly for America.

I am rather appalled at the temerity of presenting these old MSS., & I should much like it to appear on each record or label in some way either that they were presented through you, at your wish or suggestion, or presented to you to distribute as you should choose. Or if you would not wish this, could it be stated that they were given by desire of the several directors or librarians? It would, I feel, not be quite becoming for a writer to send his MSS. to a museum on his own judgment, & I do not know what would have happened to mine if you had not appeared.

Yours sincerely
Thomas Hardy.

Cockerell: Sydney Carlyle Cockerell (1867–1962), director of the Fitzwilliam Museum 1908–37, formerly secretary to William Morris and the Kelmscott Press. The manuscript of 'An Imaginative Woman' did finally go to Aberdeen University, as he had suggested, and the other dispositions were all carried out, although only three of the *Life's Little Ironies* manuscripts went to Manchester, and to different libraries.

To the Revd Henry Hardy

MAX GATE, | DORCHESTER. | NOV 2: 1911

Dear Henry:

I am sorry not to have answered your inquiry sooner, but I really know very little about the Hardy ancestry. It is said that the family came from Jersey—(indeed, there are Thomas le Hardys living there still)—& settled in Dorset, & that ours is one of its numerous branches in this country, which, as we have been here for centuries, it no doubt is.

But it would require years of register-searchings to ascertain the exact ramifications.

The Scottish Hardys seem to be a different family. The arms of the Dorset Hardys are, "Sable, on a chevron between three escallops, or, three wyvern's heads erased of the field"— though we don't use them.

I am sorry to hear of your mother's affliction. I keep fairly well.

Yours very truly
Thomas Hardy.

The Revd H. Hardy.

Hardy: the Revd Henry Hardy (1864–1933), rector of St Serf, Bruntisland, Fifeshire, was a son of TH's first cousin Augustus Hardy.   *of the field*":

TH was quoting from the 'Pedigree of Hardy of Toller Welme and Wolcomb-Matravers' in his copy of the third edition of John Hutchins's *The History and Antiquities of the County of Dorset* (4 vols., 1861–73), iv. 433.

To John Meade Falkner

MAX GATE, | DORCHESTER. | Dec 17: 1911.

My dear Mr Falkner:

You may be sure that I did not find your letter too long, nor should I have done so if it had extended to five times as many pages. To get letters that can really be called such in the old sense is a pleasure I seldom experience nowadays—& other people could say the same, I imagine.

I am afraid you let your imagination exaggerate my habits of perseverance—seeing how limited my direct efforts have ever been towards achieving anything because it has value, in the ordinary sense, or for that matter in any sense. Indeed all my doings have been tendencies merely—just what I could not help doing even if they had brought poverty & ruin. And even as things are I have sacrificed thousands of pounds— tens of thousands I may say—in following them. No motors, no palatial hotels, no valuable collections of curios & objects of art for the scribbler of the sort of stuff that I write. But as Seneca said: It is all one not to desire & to have.

To make what you say true about pessimists—that a convinced pessimist could not feel any desire for literary activity, you must assume that he reckons by consequences & works for results. But there is such a thing as creative efforts in prose or verse becoming, or being innately, an irresistible propensity—such as smoking, drinking, gambling, etc., which is indulged for the pleasure of the indulgence itself. And the worst pessimist goes on writing with such an idiosyncrasy.

However, this is enough about myself. I am most sorry to hear that you have been suffering from insomnia. I think it must be caused by external affairs & is not inherent in you physically. Relax the strain, as you can readily do, come down to Weymouth, be absolutely idle in mind & body, & you will soon get rid of it, surely.

"Time's Laughingstocks" is, as you will have perceived after honouring me by reading it so carefully, a very mixed collection of utterances—written in all sorts of moods & circumstances, & at widely differing dates. I am glad that the volume appealed to you. Upon the whole I suppose from what people say that it contains a larger proportion of my best work—or at any rate characteristic work—than any other book I have published.

Yes: the vanity of life—the *cui bono?* is overwhelmingly borne in upon us with years. Yet I am rather surprised that such an active man as you should have become conscious of it yet. I was reading Ecclesiastes only this morning. What an extraordinary pronouncement it is! The latest of the decadents of our day (as people are pleased to term such) is not more advanced, more modern, than the writer of that book was.

I am pleased to hear that Nature appeals to you more & more. I fancy, though I am not sure, that I have lost some of my zest for it under the sense of the apparent undesireableness of the universe. True, its existence may not really be undesirable, but we can only judge with our means for judging.

The press-cutting you enclose is amusing—as if human qualities could be measured by units, as it were, like the power of a steam-engine! Trusting I may see you soon

I am, sincerely yours
Thomas Hardy.

Falkner: John Meade Falkner (1858–1932), author and antiquary; his letter of 8 Dec. mingled general reflections upon life with admiring comments upon TH's work.   *Seneca*: the allusion is apparently to *Epistulae ad Lucilium*, no. 123. 3.   *cui bono?*: 'to whose profit?'; from Cicero, *Pro Milone*, XII. xxxii.

To Florence Dugdale

MAX GATE, | DORCHESTER. | Dec. 1911.

With best wishes for Christmas and the New Year.
"Ye have been called unto liberty".—Gal. V. 13.

T.H.

Gal. V. 13: the complete verse reads, 'For, brethren, ye have been called unto liberty; only use not liberty for an occasion to the flesh, but by love serve one another.'

To William Rothenstein

MAX GATE, | DORCHESTER. | 11: 3: 1912

Dear Mr Rothenstein:

I have read with much interest a good deal of the book you kindly sent me. With details of the last peasant revolt I have, of course, been familiar from childhood, though it occurred earlier than my actual recollection carries me. My father knew a man who was hanged for saying to a farmer "It will be a light night"—(his ricks being set fire to before the morning). As a child I personally knew a boy who was starved to death in the "hungry forties" during my absence in London with my mother. He used to keep sheep near our house. However, those times are happily over, & things are a little the other way now, for the farm-labourers are very comfortable, & better off than the London poor—

Yours sincerely

Thomas Hardy.

Rothenstein: the painter William Rothenstein (1872–1945), who did several portrait drawings of TH at various dates, had sent a copy of *The Village Labourer, 1760–1832* (1911) by J. L. Hammond and Barbara Hammond, drawing TH's attention to the two chapters on 'The Last Labourers' Revolt'. *absence in London*: in fact, TH and his mother only passed through London when on their way to and from Hatfield, Hertfordshire, in the autumn of 1849.

To Florence Henniker

MAX GATE, | DORCHESTER. | Sunday: 21: 4: '12

My dear friend:

I must seem a bad and neglectful person in not having written to acknowledge your kind gift of your new novel, & to answer your letter. But I have had a chill which though it only kept me in bed two or three days pulled me down rather much, & took away all my energy—even that for reading. All this time there were heaps of proofs waiting for me to correct (of a new definitive edition—*édition de luxe* some call it—of all my awfully imperfect books, that you may have seen announced).

At last I feel about as usual, & have tackled most of the proofs, & yesterday & to-day have given myself the holiday of reading "Second Fiddle".

It is one of your best novels, I think, with more matured insight & thought in it than were in your earlier ones. The character drawing is firm and distinct, and the action unforced. Florence Dugdale told me before I began it that she thought it a very good story, but though she is a good judge I would not be influenced, & formed my own opinion.

I notice that you are quite up to date in the mode of constructing your narrative. I had left off writing novels before the mode came in—or rather was revived—& should not in any case adopt it: I mean, the making the story a chronicle covering a good many years—so many yards cut off the roll of life, without any attempt to make an organic whole of the piece, as in a drama. Your method has the attractive swiftness of movement which stories preserving the unities do not possess, & so leads one on skippingly; though it has, on the other hand, the defects of its qualities, unavoidably.

George is *excellently* portrayed. Women's men are usually such unreal duffers that is rather remarkable you should have drawn such a real man. Elizabeth is, also, vivid; but of course you could draw her. Yet I don't see why she should have been so upset by that telegram, as it did not distinctly convey information of the relations between Mrs Vance & her husband—whatever those relations may have been, which you leave rather vague. However I admit that you know best in that matter.

I am rather sceptical about that wonderful garden of Uncle Charles's—in the dust & smoke of London. To me London gardens *always* seem faded & dirty.

How ungrateful of me to be so carping, when you do me the honour of quoting some of my verses. But you would not,

I know, have cared for me to write about the book except just as I felt.

The motor-car, by the way, "as large as a drawing room" is nicely descriptive. Those huge fashionable structures come to our door sometimes & fill us with awe as they superciliously encounter the difficulties of our narrow drive.

I hope you feel more settled & cheerful now? I was thinking—the immediate cause of the thought being the disaster to the Titanic, in which I have lost two acquaint-ances—that we feel it such a blow when friends go off before us, as if we were never going ourselves at all: when the same journey is only postponed for us by a few years.

Believe me

Ever your affectte friend

Tho H.

definitive edition: the 'Wessex Edition', of which the first volume, *Tess of the d'Urbervilles*, was published by Macmillan on 30 Apr. 1912.   *some of my verses*: two stanzas of TH's poem 'The Division' are quoted, without attribution, on p. 259 of Henniker's *Second Fiddle* (1912).   *cheerful now?*: Florence Henniker's husband died in Feb. 1912.   *Titanic . . . acquaintances*: TH had known William Thomas Stead, the crusading journalist, lost in the sinking of the *Titanic*, 15 Apr. 1912.

To Florence Dugdale

[22 April 1912]

. . . I am now on to p. 140 of *The Woodlanders* (in *copy* I mean, not in proofs, of course). That is vol. vi. Some of the later ones will be shorter. I read ten hours yesterday—finishing the *proofs* of the *Native* (wh. I have thus got rid of). I got to like the character of Clym before I had done with him. I think he is the nicest of all my heroes, and *not a bit* like me.

On taking up the Woodlanders & reading it after many years I think I like it, *as a story*, the best of all. Perhaps that is owing to the locality and scenery of the action, a part I am very fond of. It seems a more quaint and fresh story than the "Native", & the characters are very distinctly drawn. . . .

. . . .

Seven o'clock p.m. It has come on to rain a little: a blackbird is singing outside. I have read on to p. 185 of the Woodlanders since the early part of my letter.

... *I am now*: Florence Hardy (as she then was) destroyed this letter after TH's death, first transcribing these two extracts from it. TH was keeping one step ahead of the printers, revising the text of *The Woodlanders*, the sixth volume of the Wessex Edition, even as he was correcting the proofs of *The Return of the Native*, the fourth.

To Sydney Cockerell

MAX GATE, | DORCHESTER. | 15: 5: 1912

Dear Mr Cockerell:

You will have guessed that I have been away for a week-end. I did not dream that there would be this beautiful reproduction of yours awaiting my return. Many & best thanks. I wish I had something worthy to send you back for it.

The point mentioned by Mr Perrins in his introductory note to the volume is what has struck me so often in relation to mediaeval art—the anonymity of its creators. They seem in those days to have had no personal ambition; & thinking of this last year I was led to write a poem bearing on it. It will, I believe, soon be printed in a magazine, & if so I shall send you a copy. The editor has had it for some time.

The copy of the memorial you send is essentially as much to me as the degree itself, & quite contents me. I really don't want anything more. When *Jude* comes out at the end of this month in the new series & you read the Preface & Postscript you will say to yourself (as I did to myself when I passed the proof for press) "How very natural, & even commendable, it is for old-fashioned cautious people to shy at a man who could write that!"

You are quite right in thinking that "form" is, strictly, used only of a hare. I used it somewhere (I fancy) for the nest of a rabbit because I knew no other name that a reader would understand, since a "stop", which is what they call it here, is dialect I suppose, & that is the only specific name I know, as applied to a rabbit. I wish I had sent "stop" to Murray for his dictionary—but perhaps he will have it all the same.

I am so sorry to hear that Verrall is ill: I like what he says about the Greeks: indeed I have quoted him I think. I hope you keep well. I seem to have quite got over that chill I caught in March.

Believe me

Yours sincerely
Thomas Hardy.

reproduction: Cockerell's edition of *The Gorleston Psalter: A Manuscript of the Beginning of the Fourteenth Century in the Library of C. W. Dyson Perrins* (1907). *Mr Perrins*: Charles William Dyson Perrins (1864–1958), collector of books and manuscripts; 'The Abbey Mason', the poem to which TH refers, first appeared in *Harper's Monthly Magazine*, Dec. 1912.   *the memorial*: the petition for TH to be awarded a Cambridge honorary degree, unsuccessful in 1912 but accepted the following year.   *Murray . . . dictionary*: see letter of 9 July 1903.   *Verrall*: Arthur Woollgar Verrall (1851–1912), King Edward VII Professor of English Literature at Cambridge; TH invokes him in the Preface to *The Dynasts*, Part First.

To Clement Shorter

MAX GATE, | DORCHESTER. | 8: 10: 1912

My dear Shorter:

I have not yet seen Meredith's Letters, but I don't want to tax you with sending me a copy, as I shall in the ordinary course get them from the *Times* book-club.

I don't suppose 1 shall be much in London this year, or at Aldeburgh at all, as I want to get this job of reading through proofs out of hand, though I wish half the volumes were consigned to oblivion instead of being reprinted—I mean those novels written in the past on conventional lines for magazine editors—"to keep base life afoot". However, there they are, unfortunately.

It was only influenza that was the matter with me—mild, but lingering.

Yours very truly,
Thomas Hardy.

P.S. I could not read quite all your letter, some words completely baffling me. T.H.

Meredith's Letters: Shorter had offered to send, and later did send, the two volumes of *Letters of George Meredith*, ed. W. M. Meredith (1912).   *life afoot"*: *King Lear*, II.iv.215.

To James Douglas

MG. Nov 10: 1912

Dear Mr Douglas:

I am sorry not to have replied immediately, but I have been much occupied lately.

I read your letter in the Daily News with interest. The subject is one on which my opinion is a trifle vague, owing to my having got out of touch with novels during the last 15 years or more. So I can hardly weigh it offhand, or say more than that I do not suppose any Court of Letters (if there is one) or Literary Society could interfere effectively, should such instances be a growing grievance. The R.S.L. might be induced to *discuss* it. The S. of Authors is, as you know, an almost purely business association for advising & defending authors in their commercial transactions.

The point at issue seems to be: Does such a book as "The Life of Henry Maitland" injure the dead man's memory? In this case I feel that it may possibly do so. But to set against that there is the fact (as I understand) that Gissing authorized, or half authorized, the book. Who is to tell?

What should certainly be protested against, in cases where there is no authorization, is the mixing of fact & fiction in unknown proportions. Infinite mischief would lie in that. If any statements in the dress of fiction are covertly hinted to be fact, all must be fact, & nothing else but fact, for obvious reasons. The power of telling lies about people through that channel after they are dead, by stirring in a few truths, is a horror to contemplate.

Such a development has been almost inevitable nowadays, when the novelist has ceased to be an artist, but has become a mere reporter, & is told that he must be nothing else. I have been gravely assured by a critic in full practice that to write down everything that happens in any household is the highest form of novel-construction, being the presentation of a real "slice of life" (a phrase wh. I believe I had the misfortune to originate many years ago).

I think you deserve great praise for having boldly opened up an inquiry into a matter so greatly affecting society & morals, & its ventilation may do much good. There can be no harm in yr having stated one, your own, side of the case strongly.

Yours very truly
T.H.

P.S. Of course I am leaving untouched the question whether, even if every word be truth, truth shd be presented (unauthorized) by so stealthy a means. It has a sneaking look. T.H.

Douglas: James Douglas (1867–1940), journalist and author; his 'letter' in the *Daily News* of 5 Nov. was in fact an article, 'The Grave-Worm', critical of *The Private Life of Henry Maitland: A Record Dictated by J. H.* (1912), a fictionalized life of George Gissing by Morley Roberts, a novelist and journalist who had known him well. TH allowed a shortened and slightly revised version of this present letter to be published in the *Daily News*, 15 Nov. 1912, as a contribution to the debate that Douglas had initiated. *R.S.L.*: Royal Society of Literature.   *phrase . . . originate*: it seems, in fact, to have been of French origin.

[Although Emma Hardy had grown increasingly eccentric over a period of several years and been in poor physical health for some time, her sudden death at the age of seventy-two took everyone by surprise. Hardy's regret at her loss and remorse at the erosion of their early romance were reflected in several of the letters he was obliged to write during the succeeding weeks—and, far more powerfully, in the earliest of the 'Poems of 1912–13'. Such feelings, however, were insufficient to diminish his emotional and practical dependence upon Florence Dugdale, and during the period between December 1912 and February 1914 she spent much time at Max Gate. Her role, referred to as secretarial in the vain hope of deflecting local gossip, was to a large extent actually so: Hardy made increasing use of her skill as a typist and it was at this time that he began to deal with his voluminous correspondence by drafting business and other non-personal letters in pencil and then passing them to Florence to be typed.]

To Charles Gifford

MAX GATE, | DORCHESTER. | Nov. 27. 1912

Dear Mr Gifford:

You will be grieved and shocked to hear that Emma died this morning shortly after nine o'clock. Her illness has been quite a slight one, & she was downstairs at tea on Monday evening. I was with her, fortunately, when she breathed her last. I am too distressed to write more. The funeral is fixed for Saturday at 2.30 at Stinsford Church, two miles from here. We leave this house about 1.45.

Yours sincerely
Thomas Hardy.

Gifford: Emma Hardy's first cousin Charles Edwin Gifford (1843–1922), retired paymaster-in-chief of the Royal Navy.

To Ellen Gosse

Max Gate | Dec. 12: 1912

Dear Mrs Gosse:

I was so grateful for your letter assuring me of your sympathy in my loss, for I was certain that you really felt what you so kindly said. Probably nobody in London knew her better than you did, & when I think of the innumerable times we have shared your hospitality it is sad in the extreme to feel that we shall never do so again together.

I have been full of regrets that I did not at all foresee the possibility of her passing away thus, but merely thought her few days of illness a temporary ailment which I need not be anxious about. Everybody, myself included, supposed her to have a high vitality & the soundest of constitutions.

Do you remember that you two were the first of our sleeping visitors—coming before the house was quite finished, & when all was in the roughest state.

I shall be writing to Gosse as soon as I can, & ask you to believe me

Ever sincerely yours
Thomas Hardy.

Gosse: Nellie (Ellen) Gosse, née Epps (1850–1929), wife of Edmund Gosse.

To Edward Clodd

Max Gate. | 13: 12: '12

My dear Clodd:

I would have written sooner to acknowledge your prompt letter of sympathy with me in my loss, but I could not. I feel the greatest difficulty in writing or doing anything.

Yes: what you say is true. One forgets all the recent years & differences, & the mind goes back to the early times when each was much to the other—in her case & mine intensely much.

I am disinclined to go anywhere at present, but thank you heartily for your offer of hospitality at Aldeburgh. I was at Weymouth yesterday, but could not bear to be there. My sister & Miss Dugdale attend to my wants excellently, & Mrs Hardy's niece, who has also been here, is coming to stay in a few days.

I am pleased that you liked the play, though, of course, it was amateurs' work both in writing & acting.

Yours sincerely
Thomas Hardy.

My sister: almost certainly Kate, since Mary continued to be in poor health; the niece was Lilian Gifford.   *the play*: the London performance of *The Trumpet-Major*, recently revived by the Dorchester Debating and Dramatic Society.

To Florence Henniker

Max Gate | 17: 12: '12

My dear friend:

It was a great kindness in you to write to me, & I have been going to tell you so before, but I have felt so inert that I have been able to do very little, & this will be a mere apology for a letter. Emma's death was absolutely unexpected by me, the doctor, & everybody, though not sudden, strictly speaking. She was quite well a week before, & (as I fancy) in an unlucky moment determined to motor to some friends about 6 miles off. During the night following she had a bad attack of indigestion, which I attributed to the jolting of the car. She was never well from that time, though she came down to tea with some callers on the Monday evening before her death on Wednesday morning. I was with her when she passed away. Half an hour earlier she had told the servant that she felt better. Then her bell rang violently, & when we went up she was gasping. In five minutes all was over.

I have reproached myself for not having guessed there might be some internal mischief at work, instead of blindly supposing her robust & sound & likely to live to quite old age. In spite of the differences between us, which it would be affectation to deny, & certain painful delusions she suffered from at times, my life is intensely sad to me now without her. The saddest moments of all are when I go into the garden & to that long straight walk at the top that you know, where she used to walk every evening just before dusk, the cat trotting faithfully behind her; & at times when I almost expect to see her as usual coming in from the flower-beds with a little trowel in her hand.

I think I have told you before that her *courage* in the cause of animals was truly admirable, surpassing that of any other woman I have ever known. I have nothing at all approaching it myself. In town or country she would, when quite alone among the roughest characters, beard any man ill using an animal & amaze him into a shamefaced desistence: & she would carry lost or injured cats in London into a house or to some home & insist on their being looked after.

I have her niece Lilian Gifford here with me attending to the house affairs. Florence Dugdale has also come to help me with the proofs of the American edition of my books, which happen to be in full swing. By a strange coincidence, after not having been here for a long time, she was in the train on her way down to see Mr Evans's dramatization of The Trumpet Major, at the very hour Emma died, & on her arrival at Weymouth, where she was going to stay for the sea air, was met by my telegram. So she did not see the play after all, & went back in a day or two.

I hope you are keeping well. People have been very sympathetic here. I feel so glad that you came last year to the other play. It gave her so much pleasure to have you here.

Your ever affectionate friend
Tho H.

To Dorothy Allhusen

Max Gate | 23: 12: 1912

My dear Dorothy:

It is so thoughtful of you to write a nice letter to me on my loss of poor Emma. As you know, she was peculiar & difficult in some things, but in others she was so simple & childlike as to be most winning, & I regret her now more than you can think. Indeed this very morning the vacancy she has left seemed rather to increase than to lessen.

Her death was quite unexpected. Although she had been ailing for some days we, including the doctor, thought it merely indigestion &c., when, on the morning of the 27th she was seized suddenly & died in a few minutes.

Every Christmas & New Year's wish for your happiness.

Always affectionately
Thomas Hardy.

Allhusen: Osma Mary Dorothy Allhusen, née Stanley (1877–1965), whom TH had known since her childhood; she was a daughter of Lady St Helier (Mary Jeune) by her first marriage and wife of Henry Allhusen, MP.

[Four months after Emma's death Hardy commemorated the forty-third anniversary of their first meeting in March 1870 by travelling with his brother Henry to the isolated corner of Cornwall where that encounter had taken place. Melancholy and even painful though the experience was, it clearly provided Hardy a little later on with the basis for 'After a Journey', 'Beeny Cliff', and other of the 'Poems of 1912–13'.]

To Florence Dugdale

WELLINGTON HOTEL, | BOSCASTLE, | NORTH CORNWALL. |

Sunday. [9 March 1913]

My dearest F:

I supplement my hasty post card by this note (written with a needle pointed pen). As the weather continues fair we think of going to Plymouth to-morrow, instead of straight home, sleeping there, & arriving at Dorchester Tuesday—it may be about 4 o'clock, but I don't know. Old from Stafford, who will meet H. will bring me to the gate. I am still very uneasy about your cough, & hope Dr Gowring will call early tomorrow—as I requested him.

The visit to this neighbourhood has been a very painful one to me, & I have said a dozen times I wish I had not come. What possessed me to do it! I went to St Juliot yesterday alone, & took H. there this morning. Looking back it has seemed such a cruel thing altogether that events which began so auspiciously should have turned out as they did. And now suppose that something shd happen to you, physically, as it did to her mentally! I dare not think of it, & I am sure you will not run any risk if you can help it. I have told H. I am charging you strictly to stay indoors, & he ridicules the idea that you will listen to me for a moment.

He has gone out again upon the cliffs. He went to Tintagel yesterday, but I did not go. Expect me at tea Tuesday.

Ever yr affectionate
T.

P.S. I hope Lilian is about the house as usual again. The service at St Juliot is of the extremest Ritualistic kind— elevation of the host &c—It is enough to make her poor aunt turn in her grave, though of course when E. was living there & playing the harmonium in the church she had no religious opinions whatever—was, in fact, an Agnostic. T.

Old: Robert George Old (d. 1944), blacksmith, of West Stafford, Dorset; he owned a carriage for hire.   *to the gate*: of Max Gate, where Florence Dugdale was staying.   *Gowring*: Benjamin William Nettlefold Gowring, MD, for many years the Max Gate physician.   *St Juliot*: the Cornish hamlet of which Emma Hardy's brother-in-law the Revd Caddell Holder had been the rector.   *her poor aunt*: Emma Hardy.

To Edmund Gosse

Max Gate | 18: 7: 1913

My dear Gosse:

You think too much of those MSS. The "Wessex Folk" one is a rough draft merely—all I had. I will find out when it was written.

What a stupid thing I did when sending it. In my hurry I put on it that it was afterwards published as "A Group of Noble Dames"—when I meant "A few Crusted Characters." Please make the correction.

The other, "God's Funeral", would have been enough in itself to damn me for the Laureateship, even if I had tried for or thought of it, which of course I did not. Fancy Nonconformity on the one hand, & Oxford on the other, pouring out their vials on poor Mr Asquith for such an enormity! Swinburne told me that he read in some paper: "Swinburne planteth, & Hardy watereth; & Satan giveth the increase".

Bridges is, on the whole, a very good, & what is more, a safe man.

Sincerely yours
Thomas Hardy.

"Wessex Folk": TH had given Gosse the manuscript of the stories originally published as 'Wessex Folk' in *Harper's New Monthly Magazine*, Mar.–June 1891, and later collected, as 'A Few Crusted Characters', into *Life's Little Ironies*; he also sent the manuscript of the poem 'God's Funeral', first published in Mar. 1912.   *the Laureateship*: Herbert Henry Asquith (1852–1928), prime minister 1908–16, had recently appointed Robert Bridges to the post of Poet Laureate left vacant by the death of Alfred Austin; for TH's opinion of Bridges see letter of 12 Aug. 1895.

To the Revd J. H. Dickinson

Max Gate | Dorchester | August 22: 1913

Dear Mr Dickinson:

I remember that you told me in your last letter that you were thinking of getting a suitable design for a screen in your church, & that I might give you some hints on the matter. Anything that I can do in that way is of course at your service, though, without knowing the details of the present screen—which I copied exactly from the original mediaeval one (intending a portion of the old one to be embodied, till I found that the reckless builder had destroyed it!)—I cannot very well suggest a design. I think however that a relative of mine may be going to St Juliot to inspect the tablet to my wife, in my doubt of being able to go myself, & if so I will get him to measure the details of the existing screen.

It interested me very much to learn from you that some of your parish remember my late wife when she lived there as Miss Gifford. They may perhaps recall her golden curls & rosy colour as she rode about, for she was very attractive at

that time. If they mention any incident in connection with
her I shall be glad to know it.

Believe me

Sincerely yours
Thomas Hardy.

Dickinson: the Revd John Harold Dickinson (1869–1942), rector of St Juliot
1906–25.   *relative of mine*: Emma Hardy's nephew Gordon Gifford.

To Sir George Douglas

Max Gate | 27: 8: 1913

My dear Douglas:

Your guess was to a large extent accurate, though I was
unwell for a few days just then—dyspepsia or something of
the kind—which has gone off quite, & left me very well since.
It was good of you to take the trouble to write.

The picture you draw of our imagined sojourn at Scarbor-
ough, occupied in intellectual work except when we "interpose
a little ease" by lounging & listening to the band in a
sanctuary free from trippers, is an ideal one of a fascinating
quality. But I have an immense load of inertness to overcome
nowadays before I can go anywhere, & just at present the
printers have begun sending proofs of a forthcoming volume
of short stories of mine—mostly bad—published in periodicals 20 years & more ago, which I am unhappily obliged to
include in my set of books because pirated editions of some,
vilely printed, are in circulation in America, & imported into
England by the curious. I heartily wish I could snuff out
several of them, but my hand is forced, & I shall have the
pleasure of listening to reviewers lamenting the feebleness to
which I have declined (for they always assume everything
published to have been written the preceding month.)

I paid a visit to Mrs Henniker when she was at Southwold
in April, but I see very little of her. She has just taken, or
bought, a house in Kent.

I had a delightful time at Cambridge in June, particularly

at your old college, & being now Hon. Fellow of Magdalene I am going again in Oct. or Nov.

You tell me nothing, or little, of what you are thinking about things—e.g. the new ugly school of poetry. My kindest regards to your mother & sister.

Always yours sincerely
Thomas Hardy.

little ease": quoted from Milton, *Lycidas*, l. 152.   *forthcoming volume*: *A Changed Man*, published by Macmillan in Oct. 1913.   *your old college*: Trinity; TH had been elected to an honorary fellowship at Magdalene College in July 1913.   *new ugly school*: TH is apparently referring, in terms not uncommon at the time, to such younger poets as John Masefield (1878–1967) and Rupert Brooke (1887–1915).

[Hardy's fascination with regional speech and especially with the Dorset dialect found frequent expression in both his fiction and his verse. He was also deeply interested in the derivations of words, made numerous notes in his set of the *Oxford English Dictionary*, and supplied information both to the *OED* itself and to Joseph Wright's *English Dialect Dictionary*.]

To Sir James Murray

Max Gate | Dorchester | 24: 10: '13

Dear Sir James:

"Tranter" is still, I believe, in use in the remote nooks of this county, though discontinued here near the county-town. I think the word essentially means a *carrier*—either a carrier to order, or a carrier of articles for sale not of his own manufacture). Wm Barnes defines it as "a common carrier"—but I think this definition not quite accurate; I have myself never heard the word applied to a *regular* carrier.

"He do tranty" is an expression of old peasants for the occupation of a man who habitually goes about doing jobs of carrying—the "y" at the end of the word being a termination applied to verbs to signify a continuous action, or rather series of actions.

Anyhow, the fundamental meaning of a tranter's business is that of going about with a vehicle that carries something, not of selling.

I fear that the line you quote from the ballad of Tranter Sweatly is an instance of tautology—the words "Who tranted" including the meaning that he "moved people's things".

I am unable to throw more light on the word than you have already, as you will see. I will enquire if possible of some aged persons what meaning they attach to the word, & let you know.

Yes: it was a great pleasure to meet last June. I propose being again in Cambridge at the end of this week for a day or two. My friends, too, drop around me, & render my life more & more lonely.

Yours sincerely
Thomas Hardy.

Murray: he was knighted in 1908 for his work as editor of the *Oxford English Dictionary* and he and TH received Cambridge honorary degrees at the same ceremony in June 1913.   *Barnes*: William Barnes, *A Grammar and Glossary of the Dorset Dialect* (1863).   *Tranter Sweatly*: correctly, 'The Fire at Tranter Sweatley's' (later called 'The Bride-Night Fire'); the last line of the first stanza reads, 'Who tranted, and moved people's things'.

To Frederic Harrison

Max Gate | Nov 13: 1913

My dear Harrison:

I returned here last week, & in some way or other have caught a cold in the head, which keeps me indoors, & causes other minor inconveniences. Though still rather liquid-eyed at present, I seem to be getting out of the wood by degrees. The cold anyhow has not prevented my deriving much pleasure from your thought-stirring letter, which I regret to be unable to answer as fully as I could wish—at any rate just now—but I intend to later.

Are you really a man of the West—I mean, beyond the fact

of your now living at Bath? And why did you *buy* "The Hand of Ethelberta" for Mrs Harrison. Why of course I could have given her a copy, & would have, if I had known.

As for your not being a literary man, I must argue that out with you when I see you. As the cabman said, "I wish I had half your complaint" of literary negativeness. (This frivolity is, I suppose, one of the appalling results of my cold in the head.)

I agree that the times have a strange & disturbing colour just now. I have always said that if wrong ideas & wrong doings had been withdrawn from the so-called civilized world's mind & actions gradually in the past century, catastrophes might have been avoided in its future history. But these things have been persistently bolstered up—are bolstered up every day that dawns, & they must come down "with a run" soon. I do not however suspect quite so strongly as you do that we two shall be here to see.

I am reading your book on the Evolution of Religion, but I have not finished it, though it is as limpid in style as one of our streams here. So I will leave it till another time. What a *full* man you are. But you are a trifle hard upon the Dissenters to my hurried seeming. Their horn of the revelation dilemma is not so bad as the Roman Catholic one. They did go half way across the stream towards truth & reasonableness. Why they halted there—in the middle of the plank—& why they have never moved from that utterly illogical position for erecting an edifice upon I am too ignorant to be aware.

But some of the things done & left undone by the R. C.'s— However I'll go no further this evening. . . . .

Ever yours sincerely
Thomas Hardy.

P.S. I was, as you may know, brought up as an orthodox English Churchman. T.H.

---

if I had known: Harrison had given his wife the book because she was called Ethel Bertha.   *of Religion*: Harrison's *The Positive Evaluation of Religion: Its Moral and Social Reaction* (1913).

To John Lane

MAX GATE, | DORCHESTER. | 10th. December 1913

Dear Mr Lane:

It is really more than my due that I should get a book by asking a question about the author's works. But I am not going to refuse it, so please accept my thanks. Hawker, though bigoted and superstitious to a degree, had the imagination of a true poet, and I regret that I never met him. It was by the merest chance that I did not. When Mrs Hardy before her marriage was living at the rectory of St Juliot, near Hawker's parish, with her sister and brother-in-law, Rev. C. Holder (who knew Hawker) we used often to talk of driving to Morwenstow, but unfortunately never did.

As to Lionel Johnson's book, I can, I daresay, sit to Mr Vernon Hill, if you wish me to, though of course I cannot take any active part in bringing out a book that is an "appreciation" of myself. The only thing that weighs against your reissuing it seems to me to be that it was written before my more solid work (in the opinion of academic critics) had been produced, and is therefore only a partial view. I think Johnson told me, when I got to know him afterwards, that the latest book he had seen was "Tess", and that he had only glanced at that. The only suggestion I can make is (if you are really bent on a new edition of Johnson's book) to get somebody to write a supplement bringing it up to date.

As for a list of books that has been written about my performances, I fear I cannot supply it, for I have not seen half of them. However, I will have a search made for any that I can find. The last was, I think, by a young man named Abercrombie, but I do not possess it. Mr Shorter, Editor of the Sphere collects them all I think.

Yours sincerely,
T. Hardy.

Lane: John Lane (1854–1925), publisher; his firm had recently brought out an edition of *Cornish Ballads & Other Poems* by the Revd Robert Stephen Hawker (1803–75), long the vicar of Morwenstow, about 35 miles north of St Juliot.   *Johnson's book*: Lane was planning a new edition of Lionel

Johnson's *The Art of Thomas Hardy*, first published in 1894; when it eventually appeared in 1923 it included a portrait-drawing of TH (dated 1922) by the artist Vernon Hill, a new chapter on TH's poetry by J. E. Barton, and an expanded bibliography by Lane himself.   *Abercrombie*: Lascelles Abercrombie (1881–1938), poet and critic; his *Thomas Hardy: A Critical Study* appeared in 1912.

To Florence Henniker

Max Gate | Dec 21: 1913

My dear friend:

I had reserved my reply to your last kind letter till to-day, in order to make it a Christmas greeting, & now I have a double impulse to write, having received the picture-card & words on it this morning. It seems, so far as I can judge, a very pretty place, but I cannot tell the sub-soil from the view. However I hope it is dry, & will suit you.

The new Christmas does not exhilarate me much. But of course I cannot expect it to. The worst of a sad event in middle life & beyond is that one does not recover from the shock as in earlier years; so I simply say to myself of this Christmas, "Yet another!"

The alliance with Cambridge, to which you allude, is pleasing: it gives me a fresh centre of interest, & they are all such nice friends to me there. I am intending to visit it very often, but whether I shall is doubtful.

I read Miss Wedmore's poems, that you were good enough to send, & liked best those you had marked, as was natural. The half-page of The Sphere of this week, which I enclose as a sort of Xmas card, gives a few verses I was asked for by the editor, but a periodical is a chilling atmosphere for poems: the mood induced by a newspaper is just the wrong one, & puts them out of tune.

Do you ever see a quarterly magazine called "Poetry & Drama". It is written by a group of young men whose idea of verse is that nobody has ever known how to write it in the whole history of literature till they came along to show the trick to the world; so it is amusing reading, which I think you would like.

A young lady came this week to photograph me in colour, at the request of a friend of mine. The specimens she showed me were extraordinary in their reality. But I am getting tired of it all. My niece & Miss Dugdale are here ministering to my wants: I don't know what I should do without them, & I am sorry to say that just now Florence has a bad cold. I want her to stay in bed, but cannot get her to. I do not see many people. Mrs Sheridan says she is coming, but she has not come. Lady Ilchester is at Melbury, & tells me she will be there if all's well till June. Mrs Asquith tells me she is ill, & going away—not for a "rest cure"—she is too weak for that she says. I am sorry for her. Sir H. Herkomer is doing films of "Far from the Madding Crowd," for the picture palaces: young Herkomer came here a few days ago to get local colour, & has photographed the *real* jug used in the malt-house. There: that is about all the social & artistic intelligence I can think of—a poor supply. One thing more: did you see my letter in the *Times* about performing animals? You may not have done so, & I send it on. But the words "Performing Animals" do not clearly indicate the matter: what I object to most are performances *with* animals—in which they are passive—e.g. bringing live canaries, rabbits, pigeons, &c. out of the sleeve or handkerchief. Every spectator can see that the wretched creature is in the greatest misery, & I believe that a great many are "used" in these tricks—that is, tortured to death.

I wonder when I shall see you. Not very soon I suppose; and you have many interests outside my life.

Your affectionate friend
Tho. H.

picture-card: it evidently showed the cottage in Shoreham, Kent, where Florence Henniker was then living.   *alliance with Cambridge*: his honorary fellowship at Magdalene, which had been General Henniker's college. *Wedmore's poems*: Millicent Wedmore, *Chiefly of Heroes* (1913); she was the daughter of Florence Henniker's friend Frederick Wedmore, the art critic. *a few verses*: TH's 'To Meet, or Otherwise', published within an elaborate decorative border in the *Sphere* of 20 Dec.; another poem of TH's, 'My Spirit will not Haunt the Mound', appeared in the Dec. issue of *Poetry and Drama*, edited by Harold Monro.   *young lady*: Olive Edis (1876–1955), photographer.   *Sheridan . . . Ilchester . . . Asquith*: for Mary Sheridan see letter of 1 June 1889; Lady Helen Mary Theresa Fox-Strangways (1876–1956), wife of the 6th earl of Ilchester, of Melbury House, Dorset; Margot Asquith (1864–1945), the socially and politically influential second wife of the prime minister. *Herkomer*: Sir Hubert von Herkomer (1849–1914), painter, had recently begun making a film of *Far from the Madding Crowd* in collaboration with his son Siegfried; he died before completing the project and the rights were transferred to another company. *in the Times*: the editorial staff of *The Times* had supplied the heading, 'Performing Animals', under which TH's letter appeared on 19 Dec. 1913. For an earlier expression of his passionate concern with this subject see the letter of 19 June 1906.

To the Revd H. G. B. Cowley

Max Gate | Jan 15: 1914

Dear Mr Cowley:

Possibly, as the Churchwardens & Major Balfour say, there would have been a difficulty in carrying out our idea of setting up the old font, & I am quite willing to be convinced that it cannot be done; though they seem to misapprehend our notion, which of course was not to "restore" it by designing a detailed base, &c, but merely the joining of the pieces & putting them on a square block for security. The pieces of such a highly interesting, & even valuable, parish asset ought to be made permanent by fixing them to the fabric in some way, loose stones being so apt to be moved hither & thither & ultimately lost. I trust the objectors do not fancy I have any personal wish about it, which I really have not (I was, by the way, baptized in the present marble one).

As to the date of the font, if I can get a more trustworthy opinion than my own on the point I will do so. It is probably very early Norman, or even Saxon. I think it bears some resemblance to the one at Martinstown (3 miles from here), one of a very rare kind, & very ancient. If you or Mrs Cowley should be driving in that direction any day I should like you to look at it & form an opinion.

Very truly yours
Thomas Hardy.

Cowley: the Revd Henry Guise Beatson Cowley (d. 1938), vicar of Stinsford 1911–33.   *Balfour*: Kenneth Robert Balfour (1863–1936), of Kingston Maurward house, hence the current lord of the manor.   *the old font*: discovered in seven pieces beneath some rubbish in the churchyard, it was in the end fully 'restored' and put back into use; the marble font, which TH felt should remain (see letter of 25 Apr. 1909), was then removed. *Martinstown*: an alternative name for the village of Winterborne St Martin.

[Florence Dugdale (now thirty-five) had become indispensable to Hardy (now seventy-three) during the period since Emma's death, and early in the morning of 10 February 1914 they were married at Enfield Parish Church in the presence only of Hardy's brother and Florence's father and youngest sister. It was not merely a quiet but virtually a secret marriage, only members of the immediate families having been told in advance, but many of Hardy's friends had already foreseen such a development and his own principal concern had been to minimize the publicity inevitably generated by the juxta-position of his venerability and Florence's relative youth.]

To Florence Dugdale

MAX GATE, | DORCHESTER. | Thursday [29 January 1914]
My dearest:

I am writing only a line or two, as I expect to see you so soon. Let me know if Saturday or Monday. I will try to meet you—at any rate send carriage.

If anything has happened—I hope not—to prevent your return till I fetch you, let me know that less pleasant news. Of course if you are unwell I will put up with my solitude, as you must not run any risk. A shame to take you away from E!

Katy came in yesterday, & lunched with me in the study. She was going for medicine for Mary. Dr Gowring has visited her, & is doing the best he can. He says the difficulty is the extreme weakness of her stomach.

Wessie goes up into the attics to look for you, but secretly believes you are inside your bedroom, the door of which is kept shut.

The weather here is a warm drizzle from the S.W. I live almost entirely in the study, & the house is very solitary. But I keep well—missing you however, every minute.

Our letters will probably cross, so I will not write more.

Ever your
T.

Your last letter was scarcely fastened. T.

meet you: at one of the Dorchester railway stations, on her return from visiting her parents in Enfield ('E'), Middlesex.   *Katy ... Mary*: TH's sisters; Mary suffered from emphysema and died in Nov. 1915.   *Wessie*: still a puppy at this time, Florence Dugdale's wire-haired terrier Wessex (1913–26) later became a dominant presence at Max Gate, adored by TH but notorious for the fickleness of his temper.

To Edward Clodd

MAX GATE, | DORCHESTER. | Wedny [11 February 1914]

My dear Clodd:

I wanted to let you know by letter, before you heard of it in any other way, that Miss Dugdale & I were married yesterday at Enfield. But I have been anticipated by telegraph, telephone, & other modern inventions. For reasons which will occur to your mind we thought it best to keep our intention private, & the only way to do this was to tell nobody at all— not even relations. The vicar, who is a friend of Florence's, lent his assistance, & the result was that, though the Church door was wide open, not a soul was present except her father & sister & my brother, & the officiators & contracting parties. We came straight back here, & I am going to put over my study door, "Business as usual during alterations."

Always sincerely
Thomas Hardy.

My dear Mr Clodd:

Of course I wanted you to know before anybody else, but I

was under the strictest orders not to tell anyone. I wrote you a long letter but finally decided to be obedient & not send it.

Sincerely yours,

F. H.

The vicar: the Revd Richard Howel Brown, vicar of St Andrew's, Enfield. *father & sister*: Edward Dugdale, headmaster of St Andrew's National School for Boys, and Margaret Dugdale (see letter of 4 Mar. 1917), the youngest of the five Dugdale sisters.   *My dear . . . F.H.*: this addition to the letter is in the hand of Florence Hardy (subsequently referred to as FEH).

To Florence Henniker

MAX GATE, | DORCHESTER. | Wedny. 11: 2: '14

My dear friend:

I wanted to tell you by letter before you could have learnt it from the papers that Florence Dugdale & I were married yesterday at Enfield. But somehow, although nobody seemed to know anything of it, the news was telephoned to London immediately. If I had foreseen this I would have written beforehand to you, my best friend. However, we thought it better in the circumstances to inform nobody, not even relations.

Beyond the parties & the officiators there was not a soul present but my brother & her father & sister. And although the church door stood wide open nobody walked in. It was a lovely morning, & the ceremony was over by 8.20!

You do like her I am sure, & I want you to like her better still, if you will be so kind—though as you *always* are kind I needn't have said that, & I am sure you will go on liking her.

Let me hear from you soon. I don't know when we shall go to London. I rather shun it at this time of the year because it gives me such colds. Thank you for your last nice letter. I am glad to know you are on chalk. My experience is that chalk is the healthiest subsoil of any. Believe me

Your always affectte friend

Tho. H.

on chalk: Florence Henniker, responding to an enquiry of TH's, had reported
in her letter of 17 Jan. that her cottage at Shoreham was on 'chalky' soil.

To Lady Grove

MAX GATE, | DORCHESTER. | 13: 2: 1914

My dear Lady Grove:

What a nice letter you write to me. I value good wishes
from nobody more than from you. As my wife is a literary
woman, whom I have know many years, & a connection of
my people (one of the Dugdales who, they say have been in
Wareham ever since they landed there from Denmark with
marauding intentions) we thought our affair would be rather
humdrum, especially as we came straight back here the same
evening. But the fine morning, the quiet old church, &c. were
not without romance. There were only 7 present.

Yes, do motor over, letting us know beforehand, that we
may get you some lunch ready. With kindest regards,

Ever your affectte friend

Thomas Hardy.

a connection: it was, however, of the most tenuous kind, surviving 'pedigrees'
of the Hardy and Dugdale families, drawn by TH himself, showing only a
marriage between a Thomas Dugdale and a Jane Hardy in 1777.

To the Revd J. H. Dickinson

MAX GATE, | DORCHESTER. | 16 Feb: 1914

Dear Mr Dickinson:

Warmest thanks for your kind letter & good wishes on my
marriage, in which I include Miss Dickinson. The step has
been so soberly taken, I may even say gravely, that my wife
& I hope we shall not be disappointed in it. The romance of
S. Juliot abides none the less, & will if I live to be a hundred.
Indeed one of the satisfactions of my present position is that
my wife was a great friend of my late wife, so that there is no

rupture of continuity in my life, which always seems an added sadness in a world that at the best is so transitory & full of severances.

If ever ghosts revisit old scenes I am sure mine will haunt S. Juliot by reason of the experiences I was there blest with before my first marriage, & long before the sadness came that was a result of the slight mental aberration which occasionally afflicted my wife's latter years.

I trust you will have a successful holiday. I suppose I shall never see Rome again. I recall that I was there in the spring of 1887—nearly 27 years ago. With kindest regards to Miss Dickinson, in which my wife joins, I am

Sincerely yours
Thomas Hardy.

Miss Dickinson: Dickinson's sister, living with him at St Juliot.

To Frederic Harrison

MAX GATE, | DORCHESTER. | Feb: 17: 1914

My dear Harrison:

Warmest thanks from both of us for your letter of good wishes. I felt sure the step would not surprise you greatly. Though some of the newspapers treat it (as they mostly do treat such events) gaily, & even jocosely, I can assure you that to us it has been of a sober colour enough. That the union of two rather melancholy temperaments may result in cheerfulness, as the junction of two negatives forms a positive, is our modest hope. It may seem odd to you, but the sense of continuity through her having been attached to my late wife is not the least part of my satisfaction.

We are taking little trips of two or three days each, & later on shall certainly aim to include Bath in one of them. My wife sends kindest regards, & please remember me to Mrs Harrison.

Always sincerely yours
Thomas Hardy.

include Bath: Harrison, now living in Bath, had suggested TH should bring FEH there.

To Florence Henniker

Max Gate | 6: 3: 1914

My dear friend:

I am writing again to you to answer some points on which you say you are curious (as indeed I should have guessed you were), & also because your letter was so kind as to make me wish to write.

It has been a great delight to me all through that you know Florence quite well, & like her. As you say she is very sympathetic—so much so that her own health is largely dependent upon the happiness or otherwise of her friends. One thing you may be sure of—her intense love & admiration of yourself: she often settles points by saying or thinking what *you* would do in the circumstances: assuming invariably that that is absolutely the right thing.

I rather am surprised that *you* were surprised at the step we have taken—such a course seeming an obvious one to me, being as I was so lonely & helpless. I think I told you in my last letter that I am very glad she knew Emma well, & was liked by her even during her latter years, when her mind was a little unhinged at times, & she showed unreasonable dislikes. I wonder if it will surprise you when I say that according to my own experience a second marriage does not, or need not, obliterate an old affection, though it is generally assumed that the first wife is entirely forgotten in such cases.

We are going to London next week, but only for a day or two. I will let you know when we go up later (if we do) for a longer stay, so that we may contrive to see you somehow.

Even now I have not answered your question on what people wrote about our marriage. Well: they all say they foresaw it, except one besides yourself—I forget who. Of course they *might* say so to show their penetration or to claim it. But perhaps they really did. With all affection I am,

Your sincere friend
Tho. H.

I enclose 2 little poems of mine you may like to see. They
have appeared in magazines. T.H.

As you say: Florence Henniker, writing to TH on 12 Feb., said of FEH, 'I
think she has a beautiful nature,—very full of sympathy, and she combines
(which is perhaps rare—,) the quality of enthusiasm with commonsense'.
2 little poems: one of them appears to have been 'Beyond the Last Lamp',
first published in 1911.

To Frederic Harrison

Max Gate | 23: 3: '14

My dear Harrison:

Our honeymoon—if it could be called such—was & is still
being taken in slices, or phases, as I suppose I ought to say:
three or four days in Devon; three days in London; &c, &c,
between the prosiest of home doings in the way of seeing to
repairs, the kitchen garden, getting in manure, & such like.
It will take about two years to use up the whole moon at the
rate at which we go on at present.

Oddly enough, we also struggled to grasp the meaning of
H.J.'s article in the *Times* Supplement of the 19th, & got at it
finally only by guessing what he probably was considering.
His writing beats Coleridge's talk, with its "objective & sum-
jective," quite hollow.

Please don't look at the "New Weekly"—I mean my
contribution to it. Scott-James came here one day, & I found
that poor pair of stanzas in a drawer & could find nothing
else, so I let him have them at his earnest request. Also
another little scrap like it, which I hope he won't print.

I read your letter in to-day's Times. Frankly I think
Pollard's letter unanswerable as against a Referendum.

Yes, Lady Hoare is a most agreeable woman; warm-hearted
& impulsive—which latter quality leads her to write letters
in streams.

This is a mere line. I hope Mrs Harrison is well.

Always sincerely
Thomas Hardy.

H.J.'s article: Henry James's 'The Younger Generation', *Times Literary Supplement*, 19 Mar. 1914, a signed article on some of the younger novelists; Harrison's letter of 21 Mar. described it as 'drivel'. TH's allusion to Coleridge derives from ch. 8 of Thomas Carlyle's *The Life of John Sterling* (1851). *"New Weekly"*: edited by Rolfe Arnold Scott-James (1878–1959); TH's 'The Year's Awakening' appeared in the first issue, 21 Mar., and his 'Before and After Summer' in the second, 4 Apr. *a Referendum*: in letters published in that day's *Times* Harrison argued in favour of a referendum on the issue of Home Rule for Ireland, A. F. Pollard (1869–1948), the historian, against. *Lady Hoare*: see letter of 7 Jan. 1915.

To Sir Sidney Colvin

MAX GATE, | DORCHESTER. | 14 June 1914

My dear Colvin:

We have been weighing probabilities in the question of the "splendid caverns & grottoes" of Severn, that you write about, & have come to the conclusion that he must mean "Durdle Door", close to Lulworth Cove. (You can get a post-card photograph of it—from Hills & Rowney, Dorchester: there is also an old engraving of it in Hutchins's Dorset.) Why we think it must have been Durdle Door is that it impressed my wife just in the same way when she first saw it as a girl.

To see it from the inside (which would give the impression) they would have landed in the Cove, & have walked over the Cliff to the west, & down behind the "Door". The walk would have taken them only a few minutes.

There is a smuggler's cave in Worbarrow Bay, but it is difficult to find, though in Keats's time it would most likely have been clearer. The only other cave I know about here is Cave Hole, Portland. But that is difficult of access except at low & quiet tides.

I am sending some Keats names that I jotted down when you wrote to the papers. They are useless, I fancy, which is why I did not send them earlier. However here they are. I knew personally all the persons mentioned, & used always to be struck by their resemblance to the poet.

Sincerely yours
Thomas Hardy.

P.S. I assume that Swanage would be too far east. There are, of course, the Tilly-Whim caves near that place. T.H.

Colvin: Sidney Colvin (1845–1927), art and literary critic, knighted in 1911, just prior to his retirement as Keeper of Prints and Drawings at the British Museum; he was now working on his *John Keats: His Life and Poetry, His Friends, Critics, and After-Fame* (1917) and had asked TH if he could identify, from Joseph Severn's description, the part of the Dorset coast visited by Keats during his voyage from England to Italy in Sept. 1820. &
Rowney: picture-frame makers; for Hutchins see letter of 2 Nov. 1911. *some Keats names*: those of William Keates (said to have been the 'original' of Reuben Dewy in *Under the Greenwood Tree*) and other members of the Keates family who lived in or near Higher Bockhampton during TH's childhood.

[It was a frequent source of irritation to Hardy in his later years that he was still thought and talked of as a novelist, when he had in fact been writing nothing but verse since the end of the 1890s. In responding to journalists and critics who asked him questions or sent him their books he repeatedly insisted that his later work in poetry was of greater importance and maturity than his earlier work in prose, and in discussing with Sir Frederick Macmillan the arrangements for a projected limited edition of his works his main concern was to ensure inclusion of the verse.]

To Sir Frederick Macmillan

MAX GATE, | DORCHESTER. | 15th. July 1914.

Dear Sir Frederick Macmillan:

I should much like you to publish the limited edition you write about, and as to royalty, number of copies, style, and other practical details, would agree to the arrangements you suggest.

The only point I have any misgiving about is the omission of the verse, which I confess rather surprises me; for though I have not much feeling on the matter, I fancy that if the "works" are not "complete" purchasers will be shy. There is at present a passion for having *everything* of a writer. It may have been partly the fact that the Bombay edition of Mr Kipling's works included both prose and verse (for the first time I believe) which made it so successful.

My verse has not, of course, a market like the prose, but there is the awkward circumstance that reviewers, scholars, and correspondents consider "The Dynasts" my most important and (as they put it) "greatest book" which will "live longest". America too, which at first, owing to my printing but little of the verse there, almost ignored it, is getting now to be of the same opinion. So that I fear the influence of this opinion, if not the subscribers' own tastes, will make them demand the "epic-drama" if they subscribe at all. There is also a minor difficulty in the prefaces, which refer to verse and prose both.

I imagine you feel compelled to omit the verse because of the number of volumes the whole would run into if it were included, and I have been trying to think of a plan for getting over this contingency without incurring the charge of incompleteness. The following occurred to me:—

1. To print all the verse in smaller type, as a sort of Appendix, so as to get it into two volumes, making also one volume each, of two of the shorter novels to which you have allotted two volumes each. This would still keep the whole number at 28.

(or,)

2. To keep novels under 460 pages in one volume, and only those above 460, which have also long prefaces, in two volumes. The verse in, say, four volumes. This would make 27 volumes altogether.

(or,)

3. To arrange the prose in 28 volumes under one subscription as you propose, and the verse in four or five volumes as a separate subscription, leaving it to subscribers to choose if they will include the latter or not.

By the way, I have enough more verse in M.S. to make a book about as long as "Time's Laughingstocks" whenever you like to print it. But this will go into the set as above reckoned.

I don't know if you have thought of giving the edition a

name. Would "The Casterbridge Edition" or "The Mellstock
Edition" do?

> Very truly yours,
> Thomas Hardy.

limited edition: Macmillan, writing on 13 July, proposed to follow up the
Bombay Edition of Rudyard Kipling's works with a 28-volume limited
edition of TH's prose works in essentially the same format.   *the prefaces*:
to the Wessex Edition; TH must have chiefly in mind the 'General Preface
to the Novels and Poems' included in the first volume.   *make a book*: see
next letter.   *Mellstock Edition*": this was the title chosen, but the edition
itself, including the verse and totalling 37 volumes in all, was delayed by
the outbreak of war and did not appear until 1919–20.

To Florence Henniker

MAX GATE, | DORCHESTER. | July 17: 1914

My dear friend:
   As you are kind enough to write about that little poem
called "Before & after Summer" I remember to tell you that
I am collecting the pieces in verse that I have written since
the last volume of poetry was published & looking them over
with a view of bringing them out some when towards the end
of the year. Some of them I rather shrink from printing—
those I wrote just after Emma died, when I looked back at
her as she had originally been, & when I felt miserable lest I
had not treated her considerately in her latter life. However I
shall publish them as the only amends I can make, if it were
so. The remainder of the book, & by far the greater part of it,
will be poems mostly dramatic or personative—many of
which have been printed in magazines, &c. (I have let nobody
but you & Florence know as yet that I purpose this.)
   We are going on calmly enough here as you guess. She is a
very tender companion & is quite satisfied with the quietude
of life here. But we flit about a little. Last week-end we spent
at Sir Henry Hoare's at Stour-head in Wiltshire—a beautiful
spot. Lately they have had a visitor by aeroplane; they saw
him in the air over their park, & he descended, being unable
to get further. He had come from Paris. They gave him a

night's lodging, & next morning he flew away, after entering his name in the visitors' book. He was a total stranger, & they think he must be the first entertained in that way & written down as a guest.

The Irish question is perplexing, & gloomy, but I can hardly think there will be bloodshed. I wish Mr Gladstone had never opened it up. The Irish temperament, I fear, will not be satisfied for long with *any* rule, & probably the new rule will work no better than the old.

We had a pleasant time at Lady St. Helier's. She got up a big dinner mainly on our account, & Mr & Mrs Winston Churchill came. I had her next me. He has promised her not to fly again till after a certain event, but he won't promise *never* to fly again.

I am so glad to think you mean to be more in London: I so regretted that you were not there when we were. My impression is that you would have done better by coming to the south coast instead of going to Kent, but probably you don't think so. F. still thinks you the dearest friend she has in the world.

I *may* send you a new magazine later on (if it really comes out) containing a very small poem—two stanzas only—of mine, which I think may interest you, as it refers to so long ago as 1894.

Your neighbours are probably like most country folk— rather stolid. Yet that sort of person does really feel a sincerer regard for one's welfare than town people, I consider.

Ever yr affectionate friend
Tho H.

after Summer": see letter of 23 Mar. 1914; the forthcoming volume was *Satires of Circumstance*, published in Nov. 1914.   *Hoare's*: see letter of 7 Jan. 1915. *Irish question*: the Liberal government's attempt to circumvent by parliamentary manoeuvre the defeat of its Irish home rule bill in the House of Lords was encountering fierce Ulster opposition, including threats of violence.   *Churchill*: Winston Leonard Spencer Churchill (1874–1965), currently first Lord of the Admiralty; his wife Clementine (née Hozier) give birth to their third child in Oct. 1914.   *to Kent*: Shoreham; see letter of 21 Dec. 1913.   *very small poem*: possibly 'The Difference', although it appears not to have been published before its inclusion in *Satires of Circumstance*.

[Although his letter to Frederic Harrison of 13 November
1913 might seem—like such a poem as 'Channel Firing'—to
contain anticipations of an approaching conflagration, Hardy
had in fact looked forward to a gradual disappearance of war
as a factor in human affairs. The actual outbreak of the Great
War in early August 1914 took him as much by surprise as it
did nearly everyone else, and the sheer scale and brutality of
the ensuing struggle left little scope for that romanticization of
military activity which had characterized his initial responses
to the South African War. He retained a fairly balanced
historical perspective on the war, took a pessimistic view of
the future, and was far from sharing in the more extreme and
passionate attitudes and assumptions of the hour; at the same
time, he remained firmly committed to the goal of British
survival and was glad to make the kind of gesture involved in
co-operating with Harley Granville Barker's 'patriotic' production of scenes from *The Dynasts* at the end of 1914 and with
local attempts to raise funds for wartime causes.]

To Edward Clodd

Max Gate | Tuesday [18 August 1914?]

My dear Clodd:
We wonder how you are getting on, & hope satisfactorily,
amid the shocks of this dynastic struggle just beginning.
Dorchester is teeming with soldiers, mostly drunk, Weymouth
& Portland crammed with them, ditches being dug to isolate
the latter, & we have 400 German prisoners here. Have they
begun to fortify Aldeburgh or the adjoining stretch of coast?
So much for 20th century civilization. Mrs Hardy sends kind
regards.

Sincerely yours,
Thomas Hardy.

German prisoners: these were merchant seamen and others trapped in Britain
by the sudden outbreak of hostilities.

To A. G. Gardiner

Max Gate | Dorchester. | 25 Aug. 1914.

Dear Mr Gardiner:

Many thanks for your offer of space in the D.N. for anything I may have to say on the war. But I do not feel impelled to say anything at present, the insufficiency of data apparent in all the newspaper writings on the subject being increased in my case. While as to general opinions & prophecies, they would be laughed at: e.g., such a highly rational one as that all the Churches in Europe should frankly admit the utter failure of theology, & put their heads together to form a new religion which should have at least some faint connection with morality. But as I say, I prefer to write nothing.

My friend Frederic Harrison has just sent me a letter that shows how sadly he, at 83, is affected by events.

Sincerely yours
Thomas Hardy.

P.S. We read the D.N. every day: but for some reason or other it arrives later than the other papers. T.H.

D.N.: the *Daily News*, of which Gardiner was editor.   *affected by events*: Harrison, writing on 22 Aug., spoke of 'this hour of agonising suspense' and added, 'I feel as if I was waiting for the verdict whilst my son was being tried for murder'.

To Sydney Cockerell

MAX GATE, | DORCHESTER. | 28: 8: 1914

My dear Cockerell:

I hope you have got back to Cambridge without adventure, but I suppose the northern railways are running trains more regularly than ours have been doing.

I certainly hope that you will outlive me for many a long year, & it is very good of you not to mind giving any little attention you can to such literary details of mine that may require looking after. However I think there won't be much: it will be mainly to see that nothing in the way of entries & notes obviously intended as private memoranda should be printed. As I told you I am hoping to jot down some dates, &c., that you may keep them at hand to do what you like with: e.g. to use if any preposterous stories should require contradiction, or as you choose. I do not, in truth, feel *much* interest in posthumous opinions about me, or estimates, & shall sleep quite calmly at Stinsford whatever happens. What I care most about just now is that the poems entitled, "Satires of Circumstance", (they are by no means all satires, but the title seems as good as any) should be brought out by the Macmillans at some time or other. The MS. is already in their hands—I thought it best to let them have it—& they say they think they will at any rate print it now, & perhaps keep it by them for a convenient season.

Curiously enough, a week before the war broke out, they entered into an arrangement with me for publishing an "*edition de luxe*" at about 30 guineas. I shall let this drift till the war is over, as it was to be an exact copy of the Wessex edition lately published, & will have no more value textually than that has.

The newspapers want verses or any other effusions from me, but The Times verse so far is not encouraging. My wife says that in receiving the shock of the war news she did not reckon on the additional infliction of the newspaper poets & prophets.

As for myself, the recognition that we are living in a more brutal age than that, say, of Elizabeth, or of the chivalry which could cry: "Gentlemen of the Guard, fire first!" (far more brutal, indeed: no chivalry now!) does not inspire one to write hopeful poetry, or even conjectural prose, but simply make one sit still in an apathy, & watch the clock spinning backwards, with a mild wonder if, when it gets back to the Dark Ages, & the sack of Rome, it will ever move forward again to a new Renascence, & a new literature. But people would call this pessimistic so I will stop—having inflicted on you a much longer letter than I intended. My wife tells me to give her love to Mrs Cockerell & the children. I am

Always sincerely yours
Thomas Hardy.

northern railways: Cockerell had been visiting Edinburgh.   *require looking*
after: TH had asked Cockerell to act as one of his literary executors.
exact copy: the Mellstock Edition in fact incorporated a small number of
textual revisions.   *Times verse*: *The Times* had been publishing a war poem
almost daily.   *fire first!"*: reputed to have been addressed to the French
guard ('Messieurs les gardes françaises, tirez') by Lord Charles Hay at the
battle of Fontenoy, 1745.

To Sydney Cockerell

MAX GATE, | DORCHESTER. | 26: 9: 1914

My dear Cockerell:

Many thanks for sending Cramb's book, which we have
now finished reading. He had evidently an inordinate admiration for the German idea of power, though he tries to be a
good Englishman. What a dreamer he seems to have been.
His attempts to elevate the vulgar ambition of German
Junkers to the height of a noble national aspiration shows
this: also his blindness to Napoleon's true character.

If facts bore out his theories the book would be a weighty
discourse. But it seems to me that Nietzsche, Treitske, Cramb,
& all of the school (if it can be called a school) insanely
regard life as a thing improvable by force to immaculate
gloriousness, when all the time life's inseparable conditions
allow only clumsy opportunities for amelioration by plodding
compromises & contrivances.

By the by it is rather rough on Kant, Schopenhauer, &c.,
to be swept into one net of condemnation with Nietzsche, &c,
when those philosophers & the latter are as poles asunder;
though I see this done by Christian writers in the papers. The
truth is that in ethics Kant, Schopr &c. are nearer to
Christianity than they are to Nsche.

We have had a few motor rides during the late magnificent
weather. Kind regards.

Sincerely yours
Thomas Hardy.

Cramb's book: *Germany and England* (1914) by the historian John Adam
Cramb (1862–1913). TH also refers to the German philosophers Friedrich

Wilhelm Nietzsche (1844–1900), Immanuel Kant (1724–1804), and Arthur
Schopenhauer (1780–1860), and misspells the name of the historian
Heinrich von Treitschke (1834–96).   *motor rides*: the Hardys did not own
a car but paid Hermann Lea to drive them in his.

To Sir Courtenay Ilbert

MAX GATE, | DORCHESTER. | 15 Nov: 1914

Dear Sir Courtenay Ilbert:

My reply to your interesting letter will I fear be only of the
vaguest kind, for I know of no work of fiction or drama that
deals with the militia ballot of the Napoleonic time, though
there are several I think that depict pressing for the Navy.

The effect upon the peasantry was I think rather to drive
young men into the ranks of the Volunteers than into those of
the regulars. A village would in those days have its company
of volunteers, though so far as I remember the companies
were mostly raised in towns only in the volunteer movement
of 1860.

As to the "drawing", I remember hearing old people say
that the common thing for a young man to do, if he were of
the better class of villager who could afford it, was to find a
substitute if the lot fell on him. The usual price paid the
substitute was several pounds. Malingerers of course there
were who could not afford to pay anything. One man in a
village near here bound a pennypiece (one of the old copper
ones) on to his knee "to poison his leg"—which the process
effectually did, rendering him not only too lame to go
soldiering but to do anything afterwards.

In the event of any form of conscription based on a ballot
being introduced during the present war, a point would be
whether substitution should be allowed or not.

I am delighted to find that you passed your boyhood in
South Devon, that district having much charm for me. I am
afraid it is almost too late, there or here, to find any traditions
still surviving. I have known many old soldiers in the past
who served in the Peninsula & at Waterloo, but they are all

gone. I do not recall that one of them ever spoke of having
enlisted to escape the ballot.

A system of conscription paying only half or two-thirds the
bounty that would be paid on voluntary enlistment beforehand, would probably cause a rush for voluntary enlistment.

I am so sorry to be unable to give any valuable particulars,
& am,

Sincerely yours
Thomas Hardy.

Ilbert: Sir Courtenay Peregrine Ilbert (1841–1924), clerk of the House of
Commons 1902–21; Ilbert's special responsibility was the drafting of
parliamentary legislation, and it was presumably in anticipation of some
form of wartime conscription that he had asked TH (in a letter of 12 Nov.)
whether he knew of any literary works or local traditions which might
throw light on the way in which the old Militia Ballot Acts had functioned
during the period of the Napoleonic wars.   *pressing for the Navy*: an
episode involving a naval press-gang occurs in TH's own novel *The Trumpet-
Major*.   *& at Waterloo*: TH had deliberately sought out such veterans
during visits to Chelsea Hospital in the 1870s.

To Edmund Gosse

MAX GATE, | DORCHESTER. | Dec 1: 1914

My dear Gosse:

As my wife will have told you, we were much interested in
your going to the play. It was really generous of you & Mrs
Gosse to insist on paying. I only hope G. Barker will not lose
on the production, but it seems that almost all the theatres
are starving under the present blight.

I return the playbill with the Prologue signed as you
wished. (The cold I had last week gave me rheumatism in the
shoulder & arm, which made writing painful: it has now gone
off I am happy to say). I am afraid the lines were hardly
worth signing, having nothing to do with the drama as a
whole, & being just an effusion for the nonce to help the
performance of what was staged mainly for patriotic &
practical objects.

It is, indeed, rather a comical result of the good Barker's

abridgement that I am made to appear thereby as orthodox as a church-warden, although he has, as you remark, been most loyal to the text & characterization in the parts selected. He has a wonderfully artistic instinct in drama.

Your letter on the poems was inspiriting. Certainly quote lines from the Swinburne one if you think them appropriate. I will see if I have any letters of his worth sending you.

Some—even many—of the pieces in the volume do not precisely express my attitude to certain matters nowadays— or rather they express what I would now prefer to leave unexpressed. They had, however, been printed in periodicals in past years, & I could hardly leave them out of the book, though they seem to myself harsh beside the others. There is too, in me, a little of Pilate's feeling: "What I have written I have written."

And so few of the critical trade recognize what you know well—a poem expresses a mood that sometimes ends with the very writing of it, & not a scientific conviction.

Always sincerely yours
Thomas Hardy.

I am *so* glad you like the 1912–1913 section. T.H.

the play:Harley Granville Barker's production of *The Dynasts* at the Kingsway Theatre opened on 25 Nov. 1914 and ran for 72 performances; TH's new Prologue (but not the Epilogue) was printed on the playbill.   *poems . . . Swinburne one*: Gosse had praised *Satires of Circumstance* and asked if he might quote the final stanza of 'A Singer Asleep' in his forthcoming biography of Swinburne.   *harsh beside the others*: TH refers chiefly to the group of 'Satires of Circumstance'; the quotation is from John 19: 22.   *the 1912–1913 section*: the group of poems associated with the death of Emma Hardy.

To Lucy Clifford

Max Gate | 11: 12: 1914

Dear Mrs Clifford:

I am glad to hear that the scenes from the Dynasts afforded you so much pleasure. Your own lively imagination helped the production largely, no doubt; though it is well done, as all agree. I have not been able to see it yet, except at an early rehearsal. Mr Granville Barker has done practically all, & the Prologue & Epilogue were written at his request.

I have read—not so closely as it deserved perhaps—the play you send in outline. I may as well be frank at starting, & say that I have not the vaguest idea of what effect it would have if written at length & staged. My ignorance in this respect is in accord with my having done nothing towards staging my own. To my eyes a play of anybody's from Shakespeare downwards is more vivid when read than when acted: so I am no good in such a question as this of yours.

Surely a manager is the one who knows best? But if you don't like the notion of showing it to a manager-friend I am inclined to suggest any literary friend who lives in London & often goes to plays & has therefore some power of divining the effect of this in presentation. "A woman's name"—if it were yours who have already produced plays—does not seem to be so dangerous to its consideration as you suppose.

As to the central conception—that the Krupps, or a woman-Krupp, might bring peace to the world by controlling its ordnance—it is naturally attractive in itself, especially to me; but as the theme of a practical drama which has to draw people to a theatre & make them pay: well, I am in the dark altogether.

By the way I should, if I were you, be careful to keep the plot & subject of the piece as much to yourself as possible.

I return the script, & hope it will reach you safely, & am

Sincerely yours
Thomas Hardy.

P.S. I am reminded by "Huntsman of Sheffield"—your character—that in Bulwer Lytton's novel The Last of the Barons, a poor man's invention of the steam engine is lost in a somewhat similar way, though not sufficiently similar to affect you.

Clifford: Sophia Lucy Clifford (d. 1929), novelist and playwright; she was the widow of William Kingdon Clifford, the mathematician, and usually known as Mrs W. K. Clifford. The play she outlined to TH appears not to have been completed.   *the Krupps*: the great German armaments firm founded by Albert Krupp (1812–87).   *a somewhat similar way*: in *The Last of the Barons* (1843), set in the latter half of the 15th century, both the inventor and his invention are destroyed by the power of contemporary superstition and obscurantism.

To Florence Henniker

MAX GATE, | DORCHESTER. | 23 Dec. 1914

My dear friend:

I have not written till now to thank you for your letter about the volume of poems, & I am glad that I combine with it by my delay a Christmas greeting which I wanted you to have from me. I sent the poems through the publishers because by doing so you received them 2 or 3 days sooner than they would have reached you if they had come here first. Of course I will write your name in them when I have opportunity.

At first I thought I would not send any copy to any friend owing to the harsh contrasts which the accidents of my life during the past few years had forced into the poems, & which I could not remove, so many of them having been printed in periodicals—those in fact that I liked least. And unfortunately they are the ones the papers have taken most notice of. My own favourites, that include all those in memory of Emma, have been mentioned little. The one to Florence was written when she was a mere acquaintance: I think she likes it. I am so glad that you like, "When I set out for Lyonnesse". It is exactly what happened 44 years ago.

We went to London last week to see The Dynasts. I had not seen it till then, except in an early rehearsal. It is much more impressive than I thought it would be: perhaps the present war makes one feel it more. Some people have been three times, they tell me. The actors themselves are very keen about it, & there are understudies 2 or 3 deep, on the chance of their being required. "Wessex" has developed a tendency to fight other dogs, quite to our surprise. We fancy he will get a nip from a big dog who lives near here, which will make him less bumptious.

Gosse's poem was among the few good ones that have been brought out by the war. At night here the sky is illuminated by the searchlights in Portland Roads, so we are kept in mind of the slaughter in progress. Mr Asquith went to The Dynasts one afternoon, & liked it much. I hope you keep well, & will have a cheerful Christmas.

Yr affectionate friend,
Tho H.

F. has gone to see my sisters, she wd send her love if she were here I know, & good Christmas wishes. T.H.

liked least: TH again refers to the 'Satires of Circumstance' poems within the *Satires of Circumstance* vol. The poem to FEH was 'After the Visit'; the event recorded in 'When I set out for Lyonnesse' was TH's departure from Higher Bockhampton for St Juliot (and his first meeting with Emma) in Mar. 1870.   *Gosse's poem*: 'To Our Dead', *The Times*, 20 Oct. 1914.

To Lady Hoare

[7 January 1915]

"Chuzzlewit" is, I agree, ahead of "Dombey & Son."

I certainly do not rate "Dombey & Son" as the highest of Dicken's works.

I think "David Copperfield" his best.

The Curiosity Shop is excellent in the grotesque parts relating to the wax-works, but little Nell I don't care for much—(I hate her—F.H.) Jingle is the best in the Pickwick. The much lauded Sam does not seem to me to be nearly so funny as Jingle. Pickwick would be Dickens's best if its humour did not miss fire occasionally & fall flat—at least to my sense.

I am rather shocked that you do not like Scott—though I like him in what would be called the wrong way—that is I prefer his poetry to his prose, & Kenilworth to his Scotch novels. I simply adore (*can* that be T.H. speaking? FH.) Marmion, I mean as a poem, & "The Eve of St John" has more interest than the much praised "Antiquary"—the humour of which I think forced.

Hoare: Alda Hoare, née Weston (1861–1947), wife of Sir Henry Hugh Arthur Hoare, Bt.; their house at Stourhead, with its famous gardens, is

now the property of the National Trust. This response of TH's to a request
for his views on Dickens was dictated to FEH and incorporated into one of
her own frequent letters to Lady Hoare.

To Virginia Woolf

MAX GATE, | DORCHESTER. | 20 Jan. 1915

Dear Mrs Woolf:
   I am much pleased to hear that you like the lines I wrote
in recollection of your father, & that the imperfect picture I
gave of him as editor, in Professor Maitland's book, brought
him back to you. He had a peculiar attractiveness for me, &
I used to suffer gladly his grim & severe criticisms of my
contributions & his long silences, for the sake of sitting with
him.
   As to what I am doing now, I often wonder what he would
say to it. I find that most of the present-day critics read it
very superficially, & often miss one's intention, in a way that
he certainly never did.
   Believe me, with best wishes,

Sincerely yours
Thomas Hardy.

Woolf: Adeline Virginia Woolf (1882–1941), novelist and critic, daughter of
Leslie Stephen, wife of Leonard Woolf; she had been prompted to write to
TH by the inclusion in *Satires of Circumstance* of his sonnet 'The Schreckhorn'
('the lines'), originally published together with his prose recollections of
Leslie Stephen in F. W. Maitland's *The Life and Letters of Leslie Stephen*
(1906).

To Caleb Saleeby

MAX GATE, | DORCHESTER. | Feb 2: 1915

Dear Dr Saleeby:
   Your activities are unlimited. I should like to hear your
address on "Our War for International Law".
   Personally I feel rather disheartened when I think it
probable that the War will end by the sheer exhaustion of the

combatants, & that things will be left much as they were before. But I hope not.

I have been now & then dipping into your Bergson & shall be returning the volume soon. I suppose I may assume that you are more or less a disciple, or fellow-philosopher, of his. Therefore you may be rather shocked by some views I hold about his teachings—if I may say I hold any views about anything whatever, which I hardly do.

His theories are certainly much more delightful than those they contest, & I for one would gladly believe them, but I cannot help feeling all the time that he is rather an imaginative & poetical writer than a reasoner, & that for his attractive assertions he does not adduce any proofs whatever. His use of the word "Creation" seems loose to me. Then, as to "conduct". I fail to see how, if it is not mechanism, it can be other than caprice, though he denies it (p.50). And he says that Mechanism & Finalism (I agree with him as to Finalism)— are only external views of our conduct. "Our conduct extends between them, & slips much further". Well, I hope it may, but he nowhere shows that it does. And again: "a mechanistic conception . . . treats the living as the inert . . . Let us on the contrary, trace a line of demarcation between the inert & the living", (208). Well, let us, to our great pleasure, if we can see why we should introduce an inconsistent rupture of order into uniform & consistent laws of the same.

You will see how much I want to be a Bergsonian (indeed I have for many years). But I fear that his philosophy is, in the bulk, only our old friend Dualism in a new suit of clothes—an ingenious fancy without real foundation, & more complicated, & therefore less likely, than the determinist fancy & others that he endeavours to overthrow.

You must not think me a hard-headed rationalist for all this. Half my time (particularly when I write verse) I believe—in the modern use of the word—not only in things that Bergson does, but in spectres, mysterious voices, intuitions, omens, dreams, haunted places, &c., &c. But then, I do not believe in these in the old sense of belief any more for that; & in arguing against Bergsonism I have of course, meant belief in its old sense when I aver myself incredulous.

By the way, as a kindred matter can you explain the

meaning of the paragraph I enclose? To me it seems nonsense. Please return it when writing, in case I should want to ask the author when I am at Cambridge.

Sincerely yours
Thomas Hardy.

Saleeby: Caleb Williams Saleeby (1878–1940), doctor, eugenist, and reformer.   *address . . . Law*": evidently described by Saleeby in a letter to TH which no longer survives.   *your Bergson*: Saleeby had sent TH a copy of the English translation (1911) of *Creative Evolution* by the French philosopher Henri Bergson (1859–1941); TH's quotations from it are essentially but not precisely accurate.   *paragraph I enclose*: from a brief review in the *Cambridge Review*, 30 Jan. 1915, of Alfred W. Tillett, *Spencer's Synthetic Philosophy: What It Is All About* (1914); the initials 'T.L.' on the review have not been identified.

To Edward Clodd

Max Gate | 11: 2: 1915

My dear Clodd:
    As what you don't know about money is not monetary knowledge will you be so kind as to say (quite an off hand opinion, for which I shall not bring you to book whatever happens) if you think it right to buy just now,
    Consols, or
    Liverpool Corpn 3½%, or
    Bath Corpn 3%, or
    New South Wales 4% inscribed, or
    Adelaide Electric Supply Co. debents.
My publishers, by paying up promptly, as they always do, have put me in this dilemma of not knowing what to do with a few superfluous pounds.
    I myself thought, if Europe is going scat, why not invest in America? But the brokers turn a cold shoulder to this idea apparently.
    We have not heard a sound of you lately (though I read an article of yours in the D.C. a few days ago,) & hope you are both well. We are quite dormant at present, but mean to

wake up in the spring; when, or in early summer, we hope to
see you here & Mrs Clodd.

Sincerely yours
Thomas Hardy.

To this I add affectionate greetings to you & your wife &
hope that very soon, as soon as this dismal wintery weather is
over, we may have the great pleasure of seeing you both at
Max Gate. T. is like a dormouse & loves to be curled up in
his study waiting for the spring. We have been married a year
& a day, & *really & truly* (I am not joking now) it has been a
year of *great* happiness.

F.H.

---

know about money: Clodd was secretary of the London Joint Stock Bank.
in the D.C.: a review of J. T. Mers, *A History of European Thought in the
Nineteenth Century*, *Daily Chronicle*, 6 Feb. 1915.   *Mrs Clodd*: Clodd's
second wife Phyllis (née Rope), whom he married in Dec. 1914.   *To this
. . . F.H.*: FEH has added this paragraph in her own hand, her emphatic
'*really & truly*' evidently reflecting an awareness that she had previously
written to Clodd about her marriage in more negative terms.

To Caleb Saleeby

MAX GATE, | DORCHESTER. | 16: 3: 1915

Dear Dr Saleeby:

My thanks for the revised form of "The Longest Price of
War", which I am reading.

I do not know if you mean to accept the invitation to speak
at the Temperance meeting in Dorchester; but if you do I
shall hope to see you. We live a mile from the Town, & I am
not sure if our house would be convenient for staying at, on
account of the distance at night, &c, & our not keeping a car.
But we could put you up here with pleasure if that would be
no objection.

I am returning, or shall be in a day or two, your volume of
Bergson. It is most interesting reading, & one likes to give
way to its views & assurances without criticizing them. If
however we ask for reasons & proofs (which I don't care to

do) I am afraid we do not get them. An *élan vital*—by which I understand him to mean a sort of additional & spiritual force, beyond the merely unconscious push of life—the "will" of other philosophers that propels growth & development—seems much less probable than single & simple determinism, or what he calls mechanism, because it is more complex; & where proof is impossible probability must be our guide. His partly mechanistic & partly creative theory seems to me clumsy & confused.

He speaks of "the enormous gap that separates even the lowest form of life from the inorganic world". Here again it is more probable that organic & inorganic modulate into each other, one nature & law operating throughout.

But the most fatal objection to his view of creation *plus* propulsion seems to me to lie in the existence of pain. If nature were creative she would have created painlessness, or be in process of creating it—pain being the first thing we instinctively fly from. If on the other hand we cannot introduce into life what is not already there, & are bound to mere recombination of old materials, the persistence of pain is intelligible.

Sincerely yours
Thomas Hardy.

Price of War": evidently the article published as 'The Dysgenics of War', *Contemporary Review*, Mar. 1915, in which Saleeby warned of the long-term genetic consequences of the wartime selection of the fittest to fight and die in defence of the unfit. Saleeby did speak at the temperance rally in Dorchester on 29 Mar., arguing that the intensified use of alcohol in wartime damaged the health of the nation and hence constituted 'the enemy within our gates', and he accepted the invitation to stay at Max Gate. *volume of Bergson*: see letter of 2 Feb. 1915; the passage quoted in the following paragraph is itself a quotation by Bergson from E. B. Wilson, *The Cell in Development and Inheritance* (1897).

To Florence Henniker

MAX GATE, | DORCHESTER. | 23: 3: 1915

My dear friend:

In your last letter you asked me, I remember, what I thought about the duration of the war, which question I did not answer, to my shame, though my reason was my perplexity on the point. I can only make guesses, & the one I think the most probable is that it will last till one of the combatants is exhausted & sues for peace without being beaten, or till one or more country is bankrupt, or starved, or till there is a revolution in Germany; a rupture between the dual monarchies of Austria might, too, help on peace. I hardly think it will end by the sheer victory of one side or the other in the field—unless Italy joins the allies, in which case it might.

I, too, like you, think the Germans happy & contented as a people: but the group of oligarchs & munition-makers whose interest is war, have stirred them up to their purposes—at least so it seems. I have expressed the thought in a sonnet that is coming out in the Fortnightly. I enclose a proof of it, which, as I have no other copy, you can return at your leisure.

As you say, & as it also has struck me, how can we consistently crush German militarism without reducing armaments & armies all round: & diminishing our navy?

You have no doubt read in the papers today Sir E. Grey's synopsis of the beginning of the war. England has been so often the arrogant aggressor in past wars that it would have been quite in keeping with her history if she had been in this: but really, when you honestly look at the facts marshalled by Sir E. G. England is innocent for once. They show that the war began because the Germans wanted to fight.

In this connection I am much puzzled as to the attitude of Lord Morley & John Burns in resigning office—particularly the former. When I saw him last he had aged much, & was getting deaf, so at first I thought he had given up on those accounts. But if so, it would have been stated, to strengthen his colleagues' position: on the other hand, how can he hold that we ought not to have fought? Perhaps you can solve this conundrum?

I am so glad you liked the play, which though not "The Dynasts" as I wrote it, was interesting to me also. Florence sends best love. I am sorry to say she has been confined to her bed with *sciatica*—left by some chill she caught. She is better, & would much like to see you again—as should I also.

Your affectte friend
Tho. H.

Italy joins the allies: as occurred two months later. *in the Fortnightly*: TH's 'The Pity of It', *Fortnightly Review*, Apr. 1915. *Grey's synopsis*: an account of the war's origins and causes given by Sir Edward Grey, Bt. (1862–1933), the foreign secretary, in the course of introducing a lecture by John Buchan the previous day. *Morley . . . Burns*: John Morley (now Viscount Morley) and John Burns, the former labour leader, had resigned from the Asquith government at the outbreak of war on the grounds that the conflict could and should have been averted.

[Florence Hardy was dogged by ill-health from an early date in her marriage, and in the spring of 1915 she underwent a surgical operation for the relief of 'nasal catarrh', spending a week in a London nursing-home before returning to Max Gate. She had also to endure Hardy's melancholy devotion to the memory of his first wife, his persistence in writing poems about her, and his newly increased interest in the history of her family. He began to correspond with Gifford relatives with whom neither he nor Emma had kept in touch during her lifetime and became particularly interested in the Gifford graves in the churchyard of Charles Church, Plymouth— making a special trip there with Florence in October 1917.]

To Florence Hardy

Max Gate | Monday eveng. [31 May 1915]

My dearest F:

I was so glad to have your letter by the midday post & to know that your progress is all right. But I fear that you want to get about again too quickly, & think that you ought not to leave the home till the beginning of next week. I don't at all mind paying the extra days. The wind is still east, & a cold might cause the scarcely healed wound to burst out again, which, if you were down here out of the reach of Mr Yearsley, would be serious.

I am writing to Thornycroft to know when he wants me. If by about next Sunday I could go up Saty & bring you back on the following Tuesday or so. I will await his reply.

Sir H. & Lady Hoare wired this morning that they were going to motor over & call this afternoon, & they duly came, & had tea, staying nearly an hour. (He came to Dorchr to buy a horse) They are really very nice people; & we talked of you, & the war, & all sorts. She likes very much that enlarged photogh of you by Mr Lea—says it is the best. She could not resist telling me how much she liked the cretonnes, & asked if you chose them. I think she will get some like them.

I had tea with the Popes yesterday. Their prisoner son says he is well fed (but this he may be *made* to say) & asks if they can send him some currant bread, which as Mrs P. says, seems as if he were hungry. I went to Talbotys after tea, & as I forgot the asparagus, K brought it this morning—the first time anybody has come. She also admired the cretonne covers.

I got through my gale of correspondence yesterday. It has arisen through my kindness in letting Mr Herkomer transfer his cinema rights to a company, so that he might not lose the money he had spent on the preparations. I hope it will be settled up all right.

Please don't hurry to resume activities. H. says he could not sleep the night before the operation for thinking about it. I dare say when I have closed this up I shall think of something else. I have now quite recovered the strength I had before I went to London, & did not feel my double walk yesterday. With best love

Yours ever
T.

Shall be so glad to see you gardening here again. T.

Yearsley: Percival Macleod Yearsley (d. 1951), surgeon and author.
Thornycroft: the sculptor Hamo Thornycroft (see letter of 8 Jan. 1923), who had recently begun work on a bust of TH.   *the Popes*: Alfred Pope (1842–1934), Dorchester brewer and leading citizen whom TH had known

since his schooldays, and his wife Elizabeth, née Whiting (d. 1920); Cyril, the youngest of their ten surviving sons, had been taken prisoner at Ypres in Nov. 1914.   *Herkomer . . . rights*: see letter of 21 Dec. 1913.   *double walk*: roughly a mile each way into Dorchester to visit the Popes and rather more than two miles each way in the opposite direction to Talbothays Lodge—where his brother Henry ('H.') and his sisters Mary and Kate ('K') were now living. Talbothays had been designed by TH and built by Henry in the early 1890s but then let for several years.

To Annie Watson

MAX GATE, | DORCHESTER. | June 5: 1915

Dear Miss Watson:

My best thanks for good wishes & birthday card. My wife would also send hers if she were here, but she is in London till next week.

I am glad to hear that the grave is well kept. It was very kind of your sister to go & see.

One puzzling point I should like to settle is whereabouts in that churchyard Emma's grandmother (& your great grandmother) Helen (née Davie) is buried: also your grandmother Helen Charlotte Watson, your great-aunt, great uncle, &c. From my late wife's papers I find they lie all together in a vault there somewhere; but that when the church was restored in 1889—26 years ago—the vault was cut into, or built up, or interfered with in some way, to improve the approach to the church on that side, or make new steps, so that Emma's father could not be put into it. The Gifford gravestones were then placed where they now stand, just inside the gates of the north enclosure. By unlocking the gates, which the pew-opener will do, you can go inside & read them.

If you are interested, you & your sister might like to ascertain from any old people living close to the church if they remember what was done to the entrance that side. Possibly that street running along the north side of the church was made then, or widened.

Perhaps the incumbent has a record showing what was done, how the Gifford vault was affected, &c.

Please do not take this trouble unless you are interested

yourselves in finding out where your ancestors are lying, or if their vault was much injured. No doubt there is a plan of the churchyard, with graves, vaults, &c, as they were before the alterations.

Believe me, with kind regards to your mother & sister,

Sincerely yours

T. Hardy.

Watson: Annie Carr Watson, eldest daughter of Emma Hardy's first cousin Robert Gifford Watson; since she lived in Plymouth TH had asked if she would look after the graves of Emma's parents and other members of the Gifford family in Charles Churchyard. Charles Church itself, bombed during the Second World War, is now a ruin retained as a war memorial and all traces of these graves have been obliterated.

[Lacking children or even nephews of his own—none of his siblings having married—Hardy had come to think of a distant cousin, Frank George, as a possible inheritor of Max Gate. Early in the war, however, Frank George had abandoned his legal training, volunteered for army service, and become a junior officer in the Dorset Regiment; a year later he was killed in action at Gallipoli. Although Hardy's grief seems—as he himself acknowledged—a little extreme, and was perhaps affected by a sense that he could now participate as of right in the national experience of mourning, he does indeed appear to have been deeply shocked and moved by the event. He wrote a short obituary for *The Times* and a memorial poem ('Before Marching and After') for the *Fortnightly Review*; he also visited and assisted Frank George's mother and kept in touch with other members of the family during the years that followed.]

To Florence Henniker

Max Gate | Sept 2: 1915

My dear friend:

I am sorry not to have acknowledged your letter & the enclosure sooner. As to the enclosure, upon the whole I would rather not take part in any movement of a spiritual or even ethical nature: it would in fact not quite accord with my feelings—at any rate just at present—to do so. My "faith in the good there is in humankind"—except in isolated individuals, of whom happily there are many—has been rudely shaken of late. I mention this parenthetically—not as my reason for abstention—which is purely owing to circumstances of a personal nature—

We were much distressed on Monday morning by this brief telegram:—

"Frank was killed on the 22nd."

This referred to a very dear cousin of mine, Frank George, 2d Lieut. in the 5th Dorsets, who has fallen in action in the Gallipoli peninsula—almost the only, if not the only, blood relative of the next generation in whom I have taken any interest. The death of a "cousin" does not seem a very harrowing matter as a rule, but he was such an intimate friend here, & Florence & I both were so attached to him, that his loss will affect our lives largely. His mother (who was a Hardy) is a widow, & we don't know how she is going to get over it.

We shall be glad to know when you move into your new Kensington House, though I fear we shall not be much in London for some time. I have many requests for war poetry, but what good comes of writing & publishing it I don't know, though the different charities ask for it.

We are just going to take a walk entirely for the sake of our dog "Wessie"—who *lives* for these little rambles. F. sends her love, & I am

Your affectte friend
Tho H.

"faith . . . humankind": evidently a quotation from Florence Henniker's letter or from its enclosure, neither of which has survived.   *George*: Frank William George (1880–1915), son of TH's second cousin Angelina (née Hardy) and her husband William George.

To Sydney Cockerell

Max Gate | 17 Sept. 1915

My dear Cockerell:

I am sending the "Far from the Madding Crowd" that I promised, which is a copy from the classified edition, containing both prose & verse, & has less misprints than any other. This "Wessex Edition", called in America the "Definitive Edition", will I suppose, be the last, as the Edition de luxe we intended to publish was stopped by the war. I say stopped, & not postponed, for I do not see much probability of any ventures of that sort being undertaken again for many a long year.

We went two days ago to see & bid goodbye to a brother of the boy who was killed at the Dardanelles last month. He had only 3 days leave after 11 months in France & Flanders. The third brother of the family is in the front line of trenches. All the soldiers one meets have a pathetic hope that "the war will soon be over": fortunately they do not realize the imbecility of our Ministers or the treachery of sections of the press which try to make political capital out of the country's needs.

I hope I am wrong, but at present it looks to me as if everything were tending to an indecisive issue of the war, Germany preponderating, & a huge indemnity to be paid by England to be let go in peace & quietness, as long as Germany chooses. The attitude of Labour is a very ugly one.

I read "The Daffodil Murderer"—Its fault is that it is not quite sufficiently burlesque to be understood.

Sincerely yours
Thomas Hardy.

---

that I promised: following the visit TH and Cockerell had made together in June to the old tithe barn at Cerne Abbas, Dorset; TH's inscription referred to the description of 'the great barn' in ch. 22 of *Far from the Madding Crowd*. *stopped by the war*: it was only delayed, however; see letter of 15 July 1914. *brother . . . third brother*: Charles and Cecil George, both of whom survived the war.   *"The Daffodil Murderer"*: a parody (1913) by 'Saul Kain' (Siegfried Sassoon) of John Masefield's *The Everlasting Mercy*.

To Reymond Abbott

Max Gate | 5: 11: 1915

Dear Abbott:

Although I have not written for so long a time you must not suppose I have not thought of you. I am glad to hear, or to infer from your letter, that you keep well, & are cheerful under the shadow of this war—now reaching such a critical stage.

Really I hardly think it worth while for you to read "Ethelberta" & "The Trumpet Major" over again. However you must do as you will—

I have not heard "Cutler" for ages, but I think I will get my niece, who is here for a few days, to play it over this evening.

Whether you come to Weymouth soon or later you must let us know & give us a call at least. It is quiet now, but interesting. Convalescent men are to be seen on the front. At night the place is, of course, as dark as a hedge, as is Dorchester; & every place I suppose must be so.

I have not read "Notes on Novelists"—not caring much for those personages. Though I always can read H. J.

Believe me,

Always yrs sincerely
Thomas Hardy.

Abbott: James Reymond de Montmorency Abbott (1870–1963), classicist and musician.   *"Cutler"*: a setting of Psalm 126 by the early 19th-century composer William Henry Cutler.   *my niece*: Lilian Gifford.   *must be so*: to comply with wartime 'blackout' regulations.   *H.J.*: Henry James, whose *Notes on Novelists* appeared in 1914.

[The rather stilted language of Hardy's letter to Florence's mother conveys little sense of the profundity of his grief and sense of loss at the death of his sister Mary. Not only had she been much closer to him in age and interests than any other member of the family, but she had become with the passage of the years almost the only person with whom he still shared

those childhood memories on which he had drawn for so much
of the material and imaginative temper of his work.]

To Emma Dugdale

Max Gate | Dorchester. | Nov 30: 1915

Dear Mrs Dugdale:

Just a line or two of thanks for your kind letter on our loss
of my sister Mary. We saw & talked to her the day before her
death, & I did not think it would be so soon. The funeral
yesterday was attended by many friends, though if it had not
been a drizzling rain all day there would no doubt have been
many more. The weather however did not inconvenience us
much, her grave being under the yew tree close to where the
rest of us lie.

You will remember that she painted an exceedingly pretty
portrait of Florence—the last she did at the art painting-
room in Dorchester. They were both much attached to each
other.

We shall miss her greatly as you will imagine.

Kindest regards to Mr Dugdale & the others.

Ever sincerely yours
Thomas Hardy.

Dugdale: Emma Dugdale, née Taylor, FEH's mother.   *sister Mary*: she
died on 24 Nov. and was buried at Stinsford five days later.   *art painting-
room*: a private art-school in a building since absorbed into the galleries of
the Dorset County Museum (where the portrait itself is now located).

To Edmund Gosse

Max Gate; | 15 March '16

My dear Chairman:

I am glad to find that you are still actively engaged in your
gratuitous work. It is rather barefaced of me, I confess, to be
a Committee man, & never go near the scene of my supposed
labours. However it is your fault, which is a comforting

reflection, so that I picture the unpacking of those 2400 packages by other hands than my own with comparative calm.

I am *much* interested to hear about Philip. If poverty makes strange bedfellows, war makes strange yokefellows.—I mean, how it mixes us all up. We here get men in Khaki from the camp to tea, & discover under their uniform men of every profession: lawyers, artists, bankers, &c, &c. all painted one colour for the nonce.

I hope you are economizing? We put on our coals as it were with sugartongs, drink cider only, in wineglasses, & send our ancient shoes to be mended instead of buying new ones—So you see we are getting on.

What is going to happen to English literature I don't know—if the war goes on long. I have many misgivings.

Just now I am making up a patchwork of some scenes from The Dynasts for our local actors to perform in aid of the Anglo-Russian hospital,—tedious, ephemeral labour—but what can one do else?

I wish we *could* drop in! Those Sunday evenings were indeed pleasant. But like the man in the Toccata of Galuppi's: "I feel chilly & grown old."

Always sincerely
Thomas Hardy.

gratuitous work: as chairman of the committee organizing the Red Cross Sale of books and manuscripts.   *Philip*: Gosse's son (1879–1959), who later described his wartime adventures in *Memoirs of a Camp-Follower* (1934). *scenes from The Dynasts*: they were performed in Weymouth in June 1916 and again in Dorchester that Dec.   *of Galuppi's*: the poem by Robert Browning, st. 15.

To John Galsworthy

Max Gate. | March 31, 1916.

Dear Mr. Galsworthy,

I am sorry about the influenza, though it has certainly done me an indirect service by bringing this letter from you. It has been flirting with us off and on for the last three months. The conclusion I have come to about it is that people who live away from crowds get extraordinarily susceptible to the complaint—to infection, I mean; which would explain the story that the inhabitants of St. Kilda catch cold on the landing of strangers, of which we are told somewhere in Boswell's *Johnson*. One day in London is enough to give it to me at this time of the year.

I much appreciate your tackling *The Dynasts*. Well, I suppose it would never have been finished if war had broken out when I was in the middle of it.

I am not a philosopher any more than you are, though from your letter I think I can hardly let you off the charge of at least having associated with Philosophy. The question you open up—of Free Will *versus* Determinism—is perennially absorbing, though less so when we find how much depends, in arguments on the subject, on the definition of the terms. Your own ingenious view of Free Will as a man's privileged ignorance of how he is going to act until he has acted would hardly suit the veterans who constitute the Old Guard of Free Will, but it suits me well enough.

If we could get outside the Universe and look back at it, Free Will as commonly understood would appear impossible; while by going inside one's individual self and looking at it, its difficulties appear less formidable, though I do not fancy they quite vanish.

That there seems no ultimate reason for existence, if not a staggering idea, does make most of us feel that, if there could be a reason, life would be far more interesting than it is. The mystery of consciousness having appeared in the world when apparently it would have done much better by keeping away is one of the many involved in the whole business.

Your likening Pity to the pearl in the oyster is a very beautiful idea, and, I think, a very close parallel.

As to visiting the West, I don't know, though I was full of the notion some time ago. We would, of course, let you see us, somehow.

Kindest regards to both from us.

> Always sincerely,
> Thomas Hardy.

in Boswell's Johnson: see *Life of Johnson* for spring 1768.   *not a philosopher*: Galsworthy, in his letter of 27 Mar., had confessed himself 'miserably read in Philosophy'.   *the West*: Galsworthy had expressed the hope that the Hardys would drive west during the coming summer and call in at Manaton (see letter of 26 June 1911).

To J. W. Mackail

MAX GATE, | DORCHESTER. | Aug 13: 1916

My dear Mackail:

I have been looking into your lecture on Shakespeare (which it is very kind of you to send) & it suggests all sorts of ideas about him. That Shakespeare was like putty is "a thought to look at"—as the natives say about here—& it does explain matters enormously. *That* is, in fact, the artist-nature without any other ingredient whatever—for good or for ill.

As to W.S.'s characters, he can quite stand our finding fault with some of them. It is amusing to see that he blandly exhibits to us the impossible in humanity at times—e.g. makes his villains say things that such villains never could have said; & indeed, speaking generally, puts into his ordinary folk's mouths sentiments that they would have expressed if they could, but never could have in this world. Yet when we see what the realistic writing of to-day is coming to, how blest we are that he did so.

I am glad to come across your remark that Iago is not quite a real person. I have got into hot water times & times by saying that I thought Iago the greatest failure in S.'s characters (Perhaps that shocks even you.) & it has always been a mystery to me why S. didn't blue-pencil that worthy pretty extensively. But I shouldn't wonder if he (Iago) didn't "slip idly from" S. just as a matter of potboiling.

Though you seem not to, I think the knocking scene in Macbeth *is* S.'s. But then, the only staging of it that remains with me is that of the old Drury days of Phelps. I was impressionable at that time, so may be wrong.

Alas—how one wastes one's life, even with the best intentions. I read S. more closely from 23 to 26 than I have ever
done since, or probably ever shall again.

But this will never do, as Jeffrey said about The Excursion—I mean my inflicting upon you Shakespeare-criticism
& water. I wish you would go more into that curious question
of dates that you mention in your letter. But it would be a
ticklish job—the "idolaters" are so touchy, or to use the more
genteel term, sensitive.

I have not finished reading your paper yet. This weather
has brought me a weak eye (as it mostly does, & will probably
do more & more) & I am dependent upon my wife a good
deal for reading to me.

We could not go to Tonerspuddle after all, but I believe
she has written about that. I am so pleased that you & your
household like Dorset—a poor neglected county formerly.
The weather has changed here, & it is just possible that your
daughter, & the damsels who leave with her, will be off in
time to escape dampness. I hope the harvesting won't be
interfered with.

Sincerely yours
Thomas Hardy.

Mackail: John William Mackail (1859–1945), scholar, critic, and civil
servant; he had sent TH a copy of his British Academy lecture *Shakespeare
After Three Hundred Years* (1916).   *"slip idly from"*: *Timon of Athens*, I.i.20,
quoted by Mackail in his lecture.   *Phelps*: Samuel Phelps (1804–78),
actor, whom TH had seen in London in the 1860s.   *about The Excursion*:
Francis Jeffrey (1773–1850), the Scottish judge and critic, began his
Edinburgh Review notice of Wordsworth's *The Excursion* with the sentence,
'This will never do'.   *question of dates*: Mackail had suggested that there
was something odd about the dates when Shakespeare's daughter Susannah
was married and when her daughter was born.   *Tonerspuddle*: an
alternative name for the Dorset hamlet of Turnerspuddle, south-west of
Bere Regis; it was presumably the location of the farm where Mackail's
daughter Clare had been staying.

To Sydney Cockerell

My dear Cockerell:

We shall be much pleased to see you again: I had hoped it would be this week. We went to Cornwall—& saw the tablet at St. Juliot, Boscastle; & thence to Tintagel. Alas, I fear your hopes of a poem on Iseult—the English, or British, Helen—will be disappointed: I visited the place 44 years ago with an Iseult of my own, & of course she was mixed in the vision of the other. The hotel-crowd rather jarred: but the situation of the hotel is unrivalled.

Yours ever
Thomas Hardy.

disappointed: TH did, however, publish *The Famous Tragedy of the Queen of Cornwall* in 1923; the 'Iseult of my own' was his first wife.

To Sydney Cockerell

My dear Cockerell:

I ought to have answered your very interesting letter ages ago, but I didn't.

I am rather surprised at people liking the *Sphere* poem, yourself the most trustworthy among them, for I thought it was of a middling sort. The incident of the horse galloping past precisely at the stroke of midnight between the old & new year is, by the way, true; it happened here, & we never learnt what horse it was. It is strange that you should have lighted on the Blake picture which in some respects almost matches the verses.

I am sorry to hear that Masefield has been aged by his war-experiences. Yet a man of deep feeling like him could not avoid it after coming in contact with the tragic scenes in France. It is grievous to think too that his writing of verse will probably be hindered for a time. I wish he would write more in his early style.

What a trouble you are taking with the Selected Poems. Please don't be too generous with them. I really don't deserve it.

Now as to the great nightcap question. If I begin to indulge in that apparel I shall most likely go on with it because of its comfort, whilst if I had never tried it I should have taken the colds in the head, &c., I might have got through lacking it, quite philosophically. Seriously it is too good of Mrs Cockerell to occupy herself with making it. We hope sincerely that she is mending in health.

A curious thing, in a small way, has come to my knowledge. You know I have no high opinion of American literary criticism, yet I learn from their newspapers that the verses I copied out for you—"When I set out for Lyonnesse"—because I fancied they showed something of the song-ecstasy that a lyric should have (other than an elegiac lyric) have become quite well known in the U. States & much quoted. Isn't it heaping coals of fire on my head! Not a soul in England—neither bishops, clerks, nor people of the critical hierarchy—has thought anything of them, so far as I know. Perhaps they are right, alas.

Tell Q. when you see him that I feel for him under the depression of influenza. Yes: of course you will come again & see us here later on. Last night was I think the coldest we have had in these parts this winter.

Ever yours
Thomas Hardy.

Sphere poem: 'A New Year's Eve in War Time', *Sphere*, 6 Jan. 1917; the relevant 'Blake picture' is the colour-print entitled 'Pity'.   *scenes in France*: recorded in Masefield's *The Old Front Line: or, the Beginning of the Battle of the Somme* (1917).   *Selected Poems*: *Selected Poems of Thomas Hardy*, published Oct. 1916; Cockerell was giving the volume his usual close reading. *Mrs Cockerell*: Florence Kate Cockerell, née Kingsford (d. 1949), artist and illuminator; she was becoming increasingly incapacitated by multiple sclerosis. When the nightcap arrived at Max Gate a few days later it was described (by FEH, in a letter to Cockerell) as 'so pretty and most becoming to T.H.'   *Q.*: Arthur Quiller-Couch, now knighted and occupying the King Edward VII chair of English literature at Cambridge.

To Florence Henniker

MAX GATE, | DORCHESTER. | March 4: 1917

My dear friend:

I have earned by the sale of an autograph the enclosed 1/1/- for the Blue Cross, & Florence suggests I should send it to the Fund through you, as you collect for the Society, so I do so, making it the excuse for a letter, though a poor one, as all my letters get to be somehow. We are living uneventful lives here (if the news of war events are not reckoned) feeling no enterprize for going about & seeing people while the issue of the great conflict is in the balance—& I fear that by the time the issue is reached I shall be too far on to old age to care to do so. The actual reminder in this house that the struggle is going on is that I have some German prisoners at work in the garden, cutting down some trees, & clearing the ground for more potato-room. They are amiable young fellows, & it does fill one with indignation that thousands of such are led to slaughter by the ambitions of Courts & Dynasties. If only there were no monarchies in the world, what a chance for its amelioration!

I am so glad you like some of the poems in the Golden Treasury selection. They were not, inclusively or exclusively, those I should have put there had I chosen them *entirely* for myself: but many of those I like best were included, my favourite lyric being the one called "When I set out for Lyonnesse", I think, as it has the qualities one should find in a lyric.

Florence's youngest sister Marjorie was married about a week ago to a young Lieutenant in the Royal Flying Corps, on duty every day in the air above the fighting line in France. We think it a hazardous marriage, not on account of the young people's characters, for they are much attached to each other, nor for possible lack of income, for his father is well-off, & he is an only son, but because of his dangerous post. He has only had ten days' leave for the whole business of getting home & back, marriage, & honeymoon, & it will be rather a sad parting for them next Wednesday.

Did I tell you that Sir J. Barrie came & stayed here for the play of The Dynasts. Believe me

Your affectionate friend
Th: H.

the *Blue Cross*: a charitable organization devoted to the care of horses in wartime.   *Golden Treasury selection*: TH's *Selected Poems* (see preceding letter) appeared as a volume in Macmillan's Golden Treasury series. *Marjorie*: Margaret (Marjorie) Alicia Dugdale (1893–1979); she and Reginald Henry Soundy (who survived the war) were married on 24 Feb. and spent most of their honeymoon at Max Gate.   *Barrie*: Sir James Barrie (see letter of 19 Dec. 1924); for *Wessex Scenes from The Dynasts* see letter of 15 Mar. 1916.

To Florence Henniker

Max Gate | May 20: 1917

My dear Friend:

I am so sorry to learn that you have not been at all well, & so is Florence, as you will know. Somehow you have seemed to be so much in the active world, owing to your living in London, & I to be so entirely out of it, that it never occurred to me you might be ill. I wonder if you ought not to get away from Town? We have at last discovered the ideal place for making recoveries in. It is *Dartmoor*, the air of which is really wonderful. You may remember that Louis Stevenson was on his way there, as a last hope, when he was taken ill on the road, & could not get there. Mr Eden Phillpotts, who lives near it, would find you a place if you think anything of it. Mr Galsworthy lives close to it, but he is now away in France.

The war has taken all enterprize out of me (I should add that it is partly because of the practical difficulties of getting about), & I have almost registered a vow that I will not see London till the butchery is over. Another of my cousins has been killed, & though his mother is but a distant cousin I sympathize deeply with her, as she is herself dying.

People are in strangely irritable moods I fancy. I said very harmlessly in a poem (sonnet) entitled "The Pity of It" that the Germans were a "kin folk, kin tongued" (which is

indisputable) & letters attacking me appeared, denying it!
The fact of their being our enemies does not alter their race.

Did I tell you that some time ago we had a visit from a
cousin of Emma's, who is also a cousin of our neighbours the
Hanburys here who bought the Kingston estate lately a mile
from here—& is a niece of the late Ld St. Helier? She is much
like Emma, & I felt so sorry that the Hanburys did not come
here till after Emma's death, as it wd have been pleasant for
her.

Gosse's Swinburne book has been a great success I believe,
which I am glad of, as it must have cost him much labour.

The young poets you allude to—I imagine you mean the
"Georgians" (an absurd name, as if the Georgians were not
Shelley, Scott, Byron, &c.)—are I think or some of them, on
a wrong track. They seem to forget that poetry must have
symmetry in its form, & meaning in its content.

I have read young Sassoon's book dedicated to me. I think
the poems show much promise.

We have just heard that F's sister's husband, Commander
(I think that's his title) in the Royal Flying Corps, came home
from the Front at 1.30 a.m. two nights ago to her great
surprise. He has been in a position of much danger over the
German lines & rear, & has been shot at & nearly brought
down several times, & most of his comrades have been killed.

Florence says I am to tell you that she is looking eagerly
forward to the issue of your book. She is hoping to be in
London after Whitsuntide, & to call & see you. She still keeps
up her reviewing, but will soon drop it; not having quite
sufficient spare time with the household to look after, & the
garden also, which she has taken upon herself, much to my
relief. She sends her love, & I am

Always yrs affectionately
Th: H.

Phillpotts: Eden Phillpotts (1862–1960), resident of Torquay and prolific
writer of plays and novels set in south-west England; for Galsworthy's
summer home see letter of 26 June 1911.   *Another of my cousins*: John
Francis Cheesewright died of war wounds in Mar. 1917; he and his mother
Floretta Cheesewright (née Meech) were only indirectly related to TH.
letters attacking me: the poem, first published in 1915, was criticized by a
Member of Parliament following its reprinting in the *Daily News* of 30 Jan.

1917.   *cousin of Emma's*: Evelyn Hamilton Gifford (1876–1920) had been visiting Cecil and Dorothy Hanbury of Kingston Maurward house; the latter's father, John Frederic Symons Jeune, was the brother of Evelyn Gifford's mother Margaret, the second wife of Archdeacon Edwin Hamilton Gifford.   *Swinburne book*: Gosse's *The Life of Algernon Charles Swinburne* (1917).   *Sassoon's book*: Siegfried Sassoon's *The Old Huntsman and Other Poems* (1917).   *F's sister's husband*: see preceding letter.   *your book*: Florence Henniker mentioned her 'new story' in confident terms when writing to TH in Mar. 1917, but it seems never to have been published. *her reviewing*: FEH was currently contributing unsigned reviews of new novels to the *Sphere*, edited by Clement Shorter.

To John Buchan

MAX GATE, | DORCHESTER. | June 20: 1917

Dear Colonel Buchan:

I appreciate your thought of me: & there are many things that would have led me to embrace eagerly the opportunity of visiting the fighting lines in France in such attractive company. But I remember that I am not so young as I was, & am compelled to give up almost all enterprises nowadays that comprise travelling more than a few miles, though I am as well as anybody of my age.

I am endeavouring to console myself by thinking that in the past I have studied a good many battlefields and battles of the flint-lock & touch-hole period, & that it is really not worth while for me to open up an investigation of modern scientific warfare, but to leave it for those who are young in these days, or unborn.

I must thank you for your consideration in sending the passport form, which shall be returned if required: otherwise I will keep it to show what I was on the brink of doing at 77.

Most sincerely yours
Thomas Hardy.

Buchan: John Buchan (1875–1940), author; later, as Lord Tweedsmuir, governor-general of Canada. He had written from the Foreign Office to invite TH to join Sir James Barrie and Sir Owen Seaman (editor of *Punch*) on an official visit to General Headquarters in France.

To Sir Henry and Lady Hoare

MAX GATE, | DORCHESTER. | December 26: 1917

My dear Sir Henry & Lady Hoare:

Though one should be prepared for anything in these days it never struck me what I was going to read when I opened your letter.

It is no use to offer consolation. And not even Time may be able to give that—I mean real consolation. Once a wound, always a scar left, it seems to me. Though Time can & does enlarge our vision to perceive that the one who has gone has the best of it—& that we who are left are made to look rather poor creatures by comparison with the one who has got safely to the other side—has achieved Death triumphantly & can say:

> "Nor steel nor poison—foreign levy—nothing
> Can touch me further".

You may remember what was said by Ld Clarendon in his History of the Rebellion, on the death of Ld Falkland in the Battle of Newbury:

> "If there were no other brand upon this odious & accursed War than that single loss, it must be most infamous & execrable to all posterity."

I write the above in great haste, to answer your letter quickly. Florence has been crying over her remembrance of climbing the tower with Harry. It is a satisfaction, if one may say so, to feel now that we did go to see you when you were all at home together. With deepest sympathy for both

Yours always sincerely
Thomas Hardy.

P.S. A touch of his humane character shows in that thought of the horses sufferings in his letter. Th.H.

consolation: Henry (1888–1917), the Hoares' only child, had died of war wounds on 20 Dec.   touch me further ": adapted from *Macbeth*, III. ii. 24–6. *to all posterity.* ": the quotation is accurate, apart from the deliberate omission of 'Civil' before 'War'.   climbing the tower: Stourton Tower on the Hoares' Stourhead estate, mentioned by TH in 'Channel Firing', the ominous poem he published just before the war began.

To Hall Caine

Max Gate, Dorchester, Jan. 29, 1918.

Dear Mr. Hall Caine,

My thanks for the newspaper cutting. If the mean age for the best *literary* work is thirty-seven it must be owing to the conditions of modern life; for we are told that Homer sang when old and blind, while Æschylus wrote his best tragedies when over sixty, Sophocles some of his best when nearly ninety, and Euripides did not begin to write till forty, and went on to seventy; and in these you have the pick of the greatest poets who ever lived. The philosophers, too, were nearly always old.

Yours very truly,
Th. Hardy.

Caine: Thomas Henry Hall Caine (1853–1931), novelist; the cutting from the *Observer* reported Caine as having challenged the assertion of Sir Edward Clarke, lawyer and politician, that the age of 37 marked the highest point of human intellectual development. Although TH seems not to have written this letter for publication, he did give permission for its appearance in the *Observer* of 3 Feb.

To Edmund Gosse

MAX GATE, | DORCHESTER. | Feb 4: 1918

My dear Gosse:

What you say is true enough, if you define by the word "revolutionary" my feeling that the jewelled line was what I meant to avoid in poetry, as being effeminate. Possibly I felt this as early as the date you mention, 1866, but probably not till I left London for the country in 1867, & had time to reflect a little. However, you can judge from internal evidence, & also whether this was a mere rebellious fancy that passed off, or something inherent which remained. I judge from what some sensible critics have said that a good deal of my verse is, after all, comely & finished enough. But of course this may be true, & yet the nature of the finish be bold rather than minute—like a drawing on paper with a rough surface.

As to the catalogue, "Wessex Poems, First complete edition 1898" can only mean "first edition". Only two or three had appeared before that date, not in a book but in periodicals.

We hear that submarines are round about the shore of Portland like sharks. It seems so strange that they should be so near.

Always sincerely
Thomas Hardy.

true enough: in this letter and the next TH was answering questions raised by Gosse as he worked on an article, 'Mr. Hardy's Lyrical Poems', for the Apr. number of the *Edinburgh Review*.

To Edmund Gosse

MAX GATE, | DORCHESTER. | Feb 18: 1918.

My dear Gosse:

I am puzzled about the date of "The Widow," (or as it is called in the Wessex Edn "The Widow Betrothed"). Anyhow, though I thought of it about 1867 when looking at the house described, which is near here, it must have been written after I had read Wordsworth's famous preface to Lyrical Ballads, which influenced me much, & influences the style of the poem, as you can see for yourself. I am afraid that is all I can recall.

"Moments of Vision" has run the gauntlet of the papers by now, & I feel in no bright spirits about it, though perhaps upon the whole it was just as well to print it. I don't mean that the book has not been kindly received—far from it—but the lack of grasp in the people who write "notices" is disconcerting. One wonders why they quiz the author rather than review the book. In their super-preciosity, I notice, they still think literary form of more importance to poetry than vision, & that it is more damning to show absence of "poetic diction" in a poem of which it can be said "This is Life", than to show "This is not Life" in a poem which can boast of poetic diction.

For the relief of my necessities, as the Prayer Book puts it, I began writing novels, & made a sort of trade of it; but last night I found that I had spent more years in verse-writing than at prose-writing! (prose 25½ yrs—verse 26 yrs) Yet my verses will always be considered a bye-product, I suppose, owing to this odd accident of the printing press.

We have been reading the Life of Keats, & found it very saddening. It seems to be an honest & thorough book, but Colvin has not the knack of lighting up his subject I fear. I hope you & your household are not caused shocks & shudders by the week end visits you get overhead.

Always yours
Thomas Hardy.

near here: as first published in *Poems of the Past and the Present* (1902) the poem opened with the line 'By Mellstock Lodge and Avenue', an apparent reference to Stinsford House.   *of Vision"*: TH's most recent volume of verse, published 30 Nov. 1917.   *as the Prayer Book puts it*: TH has adapted a passage from the 'Collect or Prayer for all Conditions of Men'.   *Life of Keats*: see letter of 14 June 1914.   *week end visits*: German air raids on London.

To Frederic Harrison

Max Gate | 20 June 1918

My dear Harrison:

I have been looking for evidence of hanging in chains since you wrote, & have almost concluded that your clerical friend is right in saying, as I understand he does, that it had disappeared by 1831—indeed I am inclined to think that it did not long survive the 18th Century. There were, of course, great cruelties down to 1831, but gibbets were gone: & these were not physical cruelty, as the bodies were placed on them after hanging, I believe. My grandmother told me that when she was a girl—1785 to 1790—she used to pass a gibbet in Berkshire with great terror: & the stump of a gibbet was standing near Wincanton down to 1840 or so.

Evidence of ordinary hanging(!) before 1831, too, is not wanting. My father in 1829 saw a soldier hanged over the gaol entrance here, & he was buried in the precincts where they are buried now.

Other cruelties, as I say, were still going on. Culprits were whipped in the market place continually: here it was done on Saturdays, in a farmer's waggon by the town-pump. My mother when a girl saw a child whipped at the cart-tail round Yeovil for stealing a book from a stall. Also:

"Alice C. who was tried & convicted for stealing money from her fellow-chambermaid at the King's Arms [Dorchester], & on whom judgment of death was recorded, was removed from our jail . . . on board the ———, her sentence having been commuted to transportation for life." *Dorset Chronicle* July 2. 1829.

"Burglars' execution. . . . After hanging the usual time the bodies were taken into Newgate, & will be delivered to their friends this evening." ib. Oct 22: 1829

"The gibbet . . . presents an extraordinary sight, upon which Thos Otter was hanged in chains for the murder of his wife 5 years ago . . . Under the jawbone of the skeleton a small bird has built her nest. . . ." Morning Chronicle June 4: 1811.

The last mentioned is the latest I can find of actual hanging in chains.

I must be getting rusty, I suppose, for I think we have *retrograded* in civilization since those times: such isolated cruelties were, after all, not so fiendish as the cold scientific slaughter of hundreds of thousands that we see going on now.

Hyndman the socialist was here yesterday. He takes a gloomy view of the future conduct of the masses, as they are called. He thinks they will never go back to their former docility, & that if something be not organized there will be anarchy. He is a most amiable man: I had never met him before.

Always sincerely
Thomas Hardy.

hanging in chains: Harrison wrote on 16 June to say that he had recently been reading TH's *Wessex Tales*, with its two episodes of capital punishment, and wondered whether TH could confirm that hanging in chains was still practised during Harrison's infancy in the 1830s or whether, as a clergyman friend had insisted, it ended with the judicial reforms of 1831. TH took the quotations from his 'Facts' notebook, into which he had copied them during the 1880s.   *My grandmother*: Mary Hardy (née Head), TH's paternal grandmother, came from the Berkshire village of Fawley.   *Hyndman*: Henry Mayers Hyndman (1842–1921), socialist leader and publicist.

To Florence Hardy

Max Gate: | Tuesday. 4.0 p.m. [3 September 1918]
My dearest F:

When you go away things begin to happen. Mrs Logan called this morning, & was disappointed at not seeing you. However I answered the purpose partly. She wants to know if you will give the prizes at the Church of E. Temperance Society, on Wednesday the 11th—to-morrow week, at 5 in the evening. The Bishop is to be there, & he will present the banner, & the prizes are to be given immediately after. "It is felt that Mrs T.H., the author of such beautiful books for children as Baby Birds & Baby Beasts is a more appropriate lady than any to do this for the Band of Hope—all children, especially as Mrs T.H. makes such excellent speeches". The Bishop, who has been consulted about it, says he would much like to meet Mr & Mrs T.H. (He has met me already, by the way, so it must be you he wants to see.)

He is coming to Mrs Logan's to tea on the day in question, & Mrs L. proposes that we meet him there. There will be nobody else but his Right Reverence, Mr Coote, & ourselves.

I said I would send on her message, & that I thought you would not at all object, especially as you *did* make good speeches. I said you would be back at the end of the week, so that will be soon enough to let her know, I understand, & you need not trouble to write while away.

Mrs L's manner was, I thought, in the best taste as she asked—quite as if she thought it would be a great honour.

I hope you got to Enfield without much hustling. Wess was in great misery all the morning at your absence, but he eat his dinner well, & seems much as usual this afternoon.

Unless you direct me differently by telegram or letter I shall write & send, after to-night, to the Royal York Hotel Brighton.

It was fortunate you put out that brandy. The indigestion, whatever caused it, was so acute, that the inside of my stomach seemed as if it had been scalded; but the spirit helped it much. I think when I am in Dorchester I will bring home another bottle, in case of necessity. I am going out presently with Wessie.

Your affectte hub
Th:

(I sent on a letter this morning)

This moment a letter has come from Mrs Pocock to me, saying she has used my name as a reference to the Dorset Police in her request for permission to sketch at Sea Town, & hoping that I don't mind. Th.

go away: FEH had gone to visit relatives in London and Brighton.   *Mrs Logan*: Alice Logan, wife of a Dorchester solicitor, was secretary to the local branch of the Band of Hope, the children's section of the Church of England Temperance Society; the current bishop of Salisbury was the Right Revd Frederick Edward Ridgeway, and the Revd Herbert Chidley Coote was rector of St Peter's, Dorchester.   *books for children*: FEH's *The Book of Baby Birds* (1912) and *The Book of Baby Beasts* (1911) were especially well known because illustrated by E. J. Detmold.   *Mrs Pocock*: Constance Pocock, née Osborne (d. 1942), was the wife of Reginald Innes Pocock, superintendent of the London Zoo; Sea Town, a Dorset coastal hamlet, was evidently within an area of wartime restriction.

[Arnold Bennett, the novelist and critic, had sent Hardy a copy of 'What We Are Fighting For', a set of proposals for the settlement and subsequent maintenance of the peace drawn up by the 'Writers' Group', of which Bennett was a leading member. Although Hardy, in his reply, refused to be appalled by the manifesto's threat of future wars far worse than the one then drawing to a close, his own post-war vision of the future, as expressed in letters to his friends, tended to be far from hopeful—especially after the conclusion of what he saw as the disastrous Treaty of Versailles.]

To Arnold Bennett

(Ansr)   Sept 8: 1918

Dear Arnold Bennett:

I have read the Manifesto you send, but have scruples against signing it, being, too, neither a public man nor a writer on public affairs.

If it be all true that the letter prophesies I do not think a world in which such fiendishness is possible to be worth the saving. Better let Western "Civilization" perish, & the black or yellow races have a chance. Moreover I don't see how by any sort of Mutual League such nations can prevent themselves doing what they want to do.

However, I think better of the world, as a meliorist (not a pessimist as they say). The instinct of self-preservation, & an ultimate common-sense at present obscured, will I think hinder the evils foretold from arising.

I am greatly obliged to you for letting me see the document although I am found wanting.

Yours sincerely
Th—H—

Bennett: Enoch Arnold Bennett (1867–1931), novelist, dramatist, and man of letters.   *(Ansr)*: the text is that of TH's pencil draft, from which FEH would have prepared a typed version on Max Gate stationery for TH to sign.

[During the period 1917–19 Hardy was engaged in the secret composition of the autobiographical *The Life and Work of Thomas Hardy*, which appeared after his death, as he had always intended, in the form of a two-volume official biography ostensibly written by his wife. The task—which involved, among other things, the sorting out and destruction of letters and papers of all kinds—was greatly facilitated by Florence's typing and secretarial skills, and the fact that she had done a good deal of writing of her own would later make it easier for the two published volumes to be accepted as her work.]

To Walter de la Mare

Max Gate, | Dorchester. | Nov. 1. 1918

Dear Mr de la Mare:

   I am writing this line for what is hardly a reason. I have been turning out papers from a cupboard where they have been lying many long years—press cuttings that were sent me in my active days—& among them I find a most generous review, such as only a poet could write, by you of The Dynasts in the Bookman. Well: better late than never, & I send my thanks. If I saw it at all at the time it came out—ten years ago—your name did not convey to me as it does now any of those delightful sensations of moonlight & forests & haunted houses which I myself seem to have visited, curiously enough; & that may be why I had no recollection of the article.

Believe me, yours truly,
(& not a stranger, though we have never
met except at the ghostly places aforesaid)
Thomas Hardy.

de la Mare: Walter John de la Mare (1873–1956), poet and novelist; his article, less a review than a celebration, appeared in the *Bookman*, June 1908. Following this initiative of TH's de la Mare became a friend and welcome visitor to Max Gate.

To Amy Lowell

MAX GATE, | DORCHESTER. | 26th. January 1919.

Dear Miss Lowell:

   I am truly glad to hear from you again, not only for personal reasons but because you are so staunchly zealous in the cause of poetry. The kind gift of your new book is most welcome to me, and I send warm thanks for your thought of me in presenting it.

   I have not yet mastered your argument for "polyphonic prose"—(Qy: polyphonic prosody?), but I daresay I shall discover it as I go on. I don't suppose it is what, 40 years ago, we used to call "word-painting". Curiously enough, at that time, prose having the rhythm of verse concealed in it, so to speak (e.g. in the novels of R. D. Blackmore and others) was considered a fantastic affectation. Earlier still, when used by Lytton, it was nicknamed "the ever and anon style"—I suppose because of the rhythm in those words.

This however may be quite a different thing from what you mean, and if so you must consider my mention of it an irrelevant reminiscence. I am, naturally at my age, what they call old-fashioned, and having written rhymes and metred numbers nearly fifty years ago—before you were born!—you must forgive a pedagogic tone if you find it in me.

Though of course in divine poesy there is no such thing as old fashion or new. What made poetry 2000 years ago makes poetry now.

My wife has read some of your book aloud to me, and sends her kindest regards. By the way, in taking up your book I say, Let's read some more of "Cousin Amy," (after the lady in Locksley Hall). "A great liberty!" you will say, especially as she was of a faithless nature. But you must excuse it, remembering under what strange conditions we met when you were here—when the whole world seemed to be in incipient combustion.

With best wishes and hope of seeing you again, believe me
Yours most sincerely,
Thomas Hardy.

P.S. Kind regards also to Mrs Russell. T.H.

Lowell: Amy Lowell (1874–1925), the American poet and critic, had visited Max Gate with her friend Ada Russell (Ada Dwyer, the actress) on 1 Aug. 1914, just as war was breaking out all over Europe.   *your new book*: *Can Grande's Castle* (1918); the case for 'polyphonic prose' is argued in its Preface.   *Locksley Hall*: Tennyson's poem.

To Sydney Cockerell

Max Gate | Sunday 23: 3: 1919

My dear Cockerell:

We are both so sorry to hear that you have been pulled down by this pestilence. I daresay it is the same as that the Lord offered to David—(I have been looking into the Bible, so am scriptural). I trust your hope is well founded that you are getting to the end of it, & shall be glad to know that it is really true: or in any case how you progress.

We have been free as yet, but I wont brag, for the winter is not over. We have a few flakes of snow this morning, but have had none lie this year, & the roads have got dusty the last two days.

Is Sussex a sufficient change? I think Torquay would be better—We are expecting to see you here again when spring has really come, but at present we cannot get enough firing to keep us warm, & have to do without, downstairs, for many hours, hovering over it here in the study, where we have breakfast. By "down stairs" I don't mean in the kitchen, where they of course keep a roaring fire, cooking or no cooking.

It was a great wonder that a letter from me did not cross with yours. I was going to ask you a question (in my dream that all was well with you) which you can answer better than any other man in England. Is Thomas-a-Didymus represented in old stained glass with a black beard, or in old manuscripts? There is a jingle amongst the country folk here, to which I used to be treated when a child, to my annoyance:

> ". . Thomas a-Didymus had a black beard;
> Kissed all the maidens & made 'em afeard,"

& I thought it might date from mediaeval times. But don't trouble to answer now.

My brother is better, but my sister has a violent cold, & ought really to be in bed. Their servant brought it into the house as usual.

Yes: that was very good in the *Times* suppt—"o'erleaps its selle"—I knew of the emendation before. Since I hit on the

Keats emendation somebody else has suggested it; so I hardly think it worth while to send up mine.

Thanks for the amusing note of a painting "by T.H." Who is that T.H.? A sketch "by T.H." was sold in America some time ago on the supposition that it was mine, & a print of it circulated in the papers. A collector sent the print to me (of a subject I had never seen or heard of) to know if I had done it.

Always sincerely
Thomas Hardy.

I hope the rest of the household are well or promising. Th.H.

pestilence: the great post-war influenza epidemic.   *scriptural*: the allusion is to 2 Sam. 24: 12–15 (or to 1 Chr. 21: 10–14).   *Thomas-a-Didymus*: St Thomas, referred to in John 11: 16 as 'Thomas, which is called Didymus'; Thomas and Didymus are, respectively, the Aramaic and Greek words for 'twin'.   *the emendation*: for 'o'erleaps itself', *Macbeth*, 1. vii. 27; it was mentioned in a *Times Literary Supplement* article of 20 Mar. The Keats emendation has not been identified.   *that T.H.?*: Thomas Bush Hardy (1842–97), landscape painter.

To Sir George Douglas

Max Gate | May 7: 1919

My dear Douglas:
I have been in London for a few days, so that my letter is belated. There were things to be done, so I took the bull by the horns & went up, especially as some of the things were pleasant—Private-viewing the Academy for instance, in which performance we surged about in a great crowd & could see the pictures only over people's heads, but we had luckily been looking at them in the morning when viewers were thinner. I was told that why the crowd was so great was owing to "Bolshevism having got into the Academy"—which meant that "outsiders"—non-members allowed to exhibit— were for the first time in human history invited to join the fashionables.

Yes: the end of the war was unexpected—if it has ended,

as I hope; but how it is to be prevented beginning again at some future year I do not pretend to understand. However, we will hope for the best on this point also. I was glad to know that your nephew got through without serious hurt: his gassing will enable him to appreciate Sargent's picture when he sees it.

Your turning to Spanish literature is, I think, a step of great wisdom. Very few English readers really know much about it, & you will be quite an authority on its productions. I think I told you about my having to grind up that tongue, very roughly, to get some facts about the Prince of Peace that I could not get from English books. The strange thing is that what I acquired went clean away from me afterwards. I have heard of such being the case with barristers. I hope you will keep up this line of study. Goethe has certainly sunk into neglect over here: & in fact I have heard him belittled. But that sort of thing is inevitable. I should like to see your article on him when it comes out.

I have not been doing much.—mainly destroying papers of the last 30 or 40 years, & they raise ghosts. Kipling, by the way, whom I met in London, said that we all seem ghosts nowadays. Kind regards to your brother Frank when you are writing to him. Believe me

Always yours,
Thomas Hardy.

the Academy: the Private View of the Royal Academy's Summer Exhibition; John Singer Sargent's 'Gassed', lent by the Imperial War Museum, was the 'picture of the year'.   *your nephew*: George Francis Valentine Scott Douglas (1898–1930), the son of Douglas's brother Francis, who had been a neighbour of TH's in Wimborne in the early 1880s.   *Prince of Peace*: Manuel de Godoy (1767–1851), duke of Alcudia and Prince of the Peace, Spanish minister during the Napoleonic period; he appears in *The Dynasts*, Part Second.   *your article*: 'Goethe Restudied', *Hibbert Journal*, July 1919. *Kipling*: TH had encountered him at the Royal Academy's annual dinner.

To Florence Henniker

Max Gate | 5 June 1919

Sincere thanks for your good wishes, my dear friend, which I echo back towards you. I should care more for my birthdays if at each succeeding one I could see any sign of real improvement in the world—as at one time I fondly hoped there was; but I fear that what appears much more evident is that it is getting worse & worse. All development is of a material & scientific kind—& scarcely any addition to our knowledge is applied to objects philanthropic or ameliorative. I almost think that people were less pitiless towards their fellow-creatures—human & animal—under the Roman Empire than they are now: so why does not Christianity throw up the sponge & say I am beaten, & let another religion take its place.

I suddenly remember that we had a call from our Bishop & his wife two or three days ago, so that perhaps it is rather shabby of me to write as above. By a curious coincidence we had motored to Salisbury that very day & were in his cathedral when he was in our house.

Do you mean to go to London for any length of time this summer? We are not going again till I don't know when. We squeezed a good deal into the 4 days we were there, & I got a bad throat as usual, but it has gone off. At Lady St Helier's we met the Archbishop of Dublin (English Ch:) & found him a pleasant man. We also met several young poets at Barrie's where we were staying.

We do hope you will carry out your idea of coming. We can put you up, & Anna, without trouble, & you can stay in bed half the day if you like. (I think, by the way, that Birdie will be vexed if you don't go on to her too).

I hope you are very very well—in "rude" health, as they call it. Florence sends her love, & I am

Ever affectionately
Th: H.

---

our Bishop: see letter of 3 Sept. 1918.   *of Dublin*: the Rt Revd John Henry Bernard (1860–1927).   *young poets*: Walter James Redfern Turner

(1889–1946), James Collings Squire (1884–1958), and Siegfried Sassoon (see letter of 15 Jan. 1920).   *Anna*: Anna Hirschmann, Florence Henniker's servant of many years.   *Birdie*: Lady Ilchester, of Melbury House, Dorset.

To Bishop Handley Moule

MAX GATE, | DORCHESTER. | 29 June: 1919

My dear Bishop of Durham:

You may agree with me in thinking it a curious coincidence that the evening before your letter arrived, & when it probably was just posted, we were reading a chapter in Job, & on coming to the verse: "All the days of my appointed time will I wait, till my change come," I interrupted & said: "that was the text of the Vicar of Fordington one Sunday evening about 1860." And I can hear his voice repeating the text as the sermon went on—in the way they used to repeat it in those days—just as if it were but yesterday. I wonder if you have ever preached from that text, I daresay you have. I should add that he delivered his discourse without note of any kind.

My warm thanks for your good feeling about my birthday. The thoughts of friends about one at these times take off some of the sadness they bring as one gets old.

The study of your father's life (too short, really) has interested me much. I well remember the cholera years in Fordington: you might have added many details. For instance, every morning a man used to wheel the clothing & bed linen of those who had died in the night out into the mead, where the Vicar had had a large copper set. Some was boiled there, & some burnt. He also had large fires kindled in Mill Street to carry off the infection. An excellent plan I should think.

Many thanks, too for the volume of poems which duly came. "Apollo at Pherae" seems to me remarkably well constructed in "plot", & the verse facile: I don't quite know how you could have acquired such readiness at such an early date, & the influence of Milton is not excessive—at least I think not.

I hope you will let us know when you come this way again. Our bishop tells me that he is never so happy as when he is in a cottage he has at Lulworth.

Believe me always

Sincerely yours
Thomas Hardy.

change come,": Job 14: 14.   your father's life: Handley Moule had perhaps forgotten that he had sent TH his *Memories of a Vicarage* at the time of its first publication in 1913, although the 'study' could conceivably have been the biographical notice of the Revd Henry Moule he supplied in 1880 to *'Doctrine, Manner of Life, Purpose'*, containing the texts of the sermons he and two of his brothers had preached on the occasion of their father's death. Handley Moule's *Apollo at Pherae: A Dramatic Poem after the Greek Model* was of even earlier date (1865).   *Mill Street*: the poorest area of Fordington, especially hard hit by the cholera visitations of 1849 and 1854.   *Our bishop*: see letter of 3 Sept. 1918.

To Robert Lynd

MAX GATE, | DORCHESTER. | July 30: 1919

Dear Mr Lynd:

We have been reading your essays—"Old & New Masters", & to my disappointment the article on "Moments of Vision" which appeared in The Nation, & is now reprinted, turns out to have been written by you. This has reminded me of a curious error I noticed in it when it came out anononymously in that paper, & which at the time I let pass in silence, thinking it to be not an oversight, but an evidence of the ignorance of my critic, wondering why the editor put me into such incompetent hands!!

You will be surprised probably when I mention it. The lines you quoted, & now reprint, of the poem "On Sturminster Foot-Bridge" as being as musical as a "milk-cart" are an attempt (& I am told by poets a not unsuccessful one) at *Onomatopoeia*, in which the words are made to reflect the clucking sound of water when blown up-stream into holes on the bank; so that, to those who know, your ridicule of them must have been of a reflected kind.

I write this line on the point merely because the review is recalled to me by the reprint, & not with any feeling about it (for, alas, all feeling at being misrepresented is long past for one who has been misrepresented so much as I.)

I will not dwell upon other statements in the review: e.g. that Browning invented short stories in verse. He invented the name "Dramatic Lyrics", but not the thing, which has existed for centuries.

You may resent this criticism of a brilliant professional critic; & I used to be told never to offend one, as he always takes it out of you later. That I cannot help, & after all one survives these things.

Yours very truly
Th: Hardy.

Lynd: Robert Wilson Lynd (1879–1949), journalist and essayist; his *Old and New Masters* (1919) incorporated 'Mr. Hardy in Winter' from the *Nation* of 22 Dec. 1917.   *anononymously*: so spelled by TH.

To an Unidentified Correspondent

[December 1919?]

The only practical advice I can give, and I give that with great diffidence, is to begin with *imitative* poetry, adopting the manner and views of any recent poet—say Wordsworth or Tennyson—You will thus attract the praises of the critical papers, and escape the satire and censure which they are sure to bestow on anything that strikes them as unfamiliar. Having won them by good imitations you can introduce your originalities by degrees. For if you want your book to sell it is fatal to begin with any original vein you may be blest with—to hear "some new thing", which so fascinated the Athenians, being a red rag to the English reviewer.

Be also very careful about the mechanical part of your verse—rhythms, rhymes, &c. They do not know that dissonances, and other irregularities can be produced advisedly, as art, and worked as to give more charm than strict conformities, to the mind and ear of those trained and steeped in poetry; but they assume that a poet who commits one of these irregularities does so because of his ignorance, and the inferiority of his ear to that of the critic himself. *Ars est celare artem* they have never heard of or forget it.

Unidentified: this letter appears to exist only in the form of a typed transcript, headed 'To an unnamed young poet', which is located among the materials collected for possible inclusion in *The Life and Work of Thomas Hardy*, the secretly prepared official biography. It is therefore possible that TH invented the 'young poet' in order to provide himself with an opportunity of voicing his dissatisfaction with the impoverished state of contemporary English criticism.   *"some new thing"*: Acts 17: 21.   *Ars . . . artem*: from Quintilian, *De institutione oratoria*, usually translated as 'The perfection of art is to conceal art'.

To Sydney Cockerell

Max Gate | Dec. 15: 1919.

My dear Cockerell:
    Your interesting letter would have been answered sooner if I had consulted my feelings & not submitted to be occupied with innumerable little matters of no real account.
    "She wore a wreath of roses"—an immensely popular song by T. Haynes Bayly, has always had an attraction for me— not for any poetical merit that it shows, but because it appeals to tender memories, having been sung by so many of the generation now dead & gone. The sentiment is of a sort now despised, but for which I have a weakness, &, I think, a good many more people if they had honesty enough to own it. Knight, who wrote the tune, set many of Bayly's songs to music. Bayly was also the author of "Isle of Beauty", "Gaily the Troubadour", "O no, we never mention her", "I'd be a butterfly", &c., &c.,—all songs that my mother used to sing, my late wife's mother, & my late wife from her mother's old music. All these pieces of torn & yellow old music have descended to me—a sad heritage enough.
    My dreams are not so coherent as yours. They are more

like cubist paintings & generally end by my falling down the turret stairs of an old church owing to steps being missing.

Purcell's Fairy Queen will give Mrs Cockerell a lot of labour, but if she likes doing it it will not hurt her. It will, I suppose, come on just about the time that The Dynasts—or rather scenes from it—is to be done by the Oxford U.D.C. They want us to go to the latter, but it is doubtful if I shall, even if my wife does. February is an uncertain month. Believe me, with kind regards to the household,

Always yours
Thomas Hardy.

Bayly . . . Knight: Thomas Haynes Bayly (1797–1839), a prolific writer of songs, plays, and novels; the Revd Joseph Philip Knight (1812–87), composer of popular songs.   *not so coherent as yours*: Cockerell, in his letter of 30 Nov., reported a dream about visiting Max Gate and seeing 'all the county' bow before a very grandly dressed TH.   *Fairy Queen*: Kate Cockerell was designing the costumes for a Cambridge University Musical Society production of Henry Purcell's opera *The Fairy Queen* in Feb. 1920; for the Oxford production of *The Dynasts* see letter of 28 Feb. 1920.

To J. McT. E. McTaggart

Dec 31. 1919

Dear Dr McTaggart:

It is a pleasure to get your kind letter, & we send on best wishes for the imminent New Year to you & Mrs McTaggart. I am glad to hear that your Magnum Opus (for such I take it to be) is at any rate well under way, though whether I shall live to see the end of it published is doubtful.

I have of late been getting out of patience, if not with philosophers, with men of science. You probably, or I shd say certainly, have grasped with ease all that Einstein has been telling us, which is more than I have done. Really after what he says the universe seems to be getting too comic for words. However, though one may think queerly of time & space I can see that *motion* is merely relative, & long have done so; & I feel that it is just as true to assert that the earth stands still & the rest of the universe moves as to assert the opposite: &

who knows if we may not get to despise Galileo & applaud the views of the Holy Inquisition! . . . .

Mrs McTaggart: Margaret Elizabeth McTaggart, née Bird.   *Magnum Opus*: the first volume of McTaggart's *The Nature of Existence* was published in 1921.   *Einstein*: Albert Einstein (1879–1955); a 1920 printing of an English translation of his *Relativity: The Special and the General Theory: A Popular Exposition* was in TH's library.   *Inquisition!* . . . .: the text of this letter is taken from TH's pencil draft.

[Hardy for many years felt himself isolated and unappreciated as a poet, equally out of tune with his Victorian predecessors and contemporaries and with his twentieth-century juniors. In the immediate post-war period, however, he began to discover not only that his verse was receiving a greater amount of critical attention but that for a number of the younger poets—among them Siegfried Sassoon, Robert Graves, Edmund Blunden, and Walter de la Mare—he was a major creative presence, actively contributing to the shaping of their own imaginations and literary careers. Early in 1920 he could read a similarly invigorating significance into the production of scenes from *The Dynasts* by the undergraduate members of the Oxford University Dramatic Society—a performance he was able to see when visiting Oxford to receive an honorary degree from the university itself.]

To Siegfried Sassoon

Max Gate | Jan. 15: 1920

My dear Sassoon:

I send a line to wish you may be well sped on your journey by whatever gods there be. Also to thank you for the poem, which I have hardly read yet, but shall of course.

I doubt if you will pick up many ideas over there. As a witty man once said, "it's just the same as here, except of course the language."

I am not doing much beyond keeping old things going. At this moment, by a coincidence, I am reading over proofs for a reprint of a novel suggested by an experience I had exactly 50 years ago—in its bare outline I mean—"A Pair of Blue Eyes". The people shadowed forth in the story being now all, alas, dead, I am able to give lights here & there on the locality, &c., which I had to obscure when the book was written.

Well: I repeat that we both wish you every success in your outing. Tell Turner I don't forget him.

Always yours
Thomas Hardy.

Sassoon: Siegfried Loraine Sassoon (1886–1967), poet and prose-writer, was about to embark on a two-months' lecture tour of the United States; his poem 'The Passing Show' had appeared in the *New Statesman* for 10 Jan.   *a witty man*: in Oscar Wilde's story 'The Canterville Ghost' the narrator remarks that 'we have really everything in common with America nowadays, except, of course, language'.   *Blue Eyes"*: originally published in 1873, it drew extensively upon TH's courtship in Cornwall of Emma Gifford, later his first wife; the proofs were of the Mellstock Edition, in which *A Pair of Blue Eyes* was the only novel to be significantly revised.   *Turner*: W. J. R. Turner, with whom Sassoon was sharing a house.

To Edmund Gosse

Max Gate: | Jan. 22: 1920

My dear Gosse:

We are glad to learn that you got away from the shades of George & Charlotte without misadventure.

This is very interesting that you tell me about your life in Weymouth. I had not the faintest idea that your father did so much zoological work there. The town should be proud, & would be if it knew, to have his name connected with it: perhaps the fact could be got into a guide book some day.

As nearly as I can judge, at the date you mention, 1853, I was at Mr. Last's Academy for Young Gentlemen, reading Eutropius & Caesar. Curiously enough I remember my father

driving to Weymouth on business one day about that very
year (there was no railway further than Dorchester then) &
taking me with him as a treat; so that you may certainly have
"brushed up against a boy called T.H." in the streets there—
though not a "big" boy, for I was small & delicate, & had
scarcely started off growing & reaching the robust condition
into which I plunged between then & my 21st year.

I wish I had seen your father's first Aquarium. The first
one I saw was a year or two after 1853, in a private house
near here.

I am enclosing a list of Errata for you to put into that
volume of Collected Poems. They were embodied in the
Wessex Edn but on account of the war some parts of this
book were printed at one time & some at another.

Always sincerely
Thomas Hardy.

George & Charlotte: Gosse had been staying with his wife at the Gloucester
Hotel, Weymouth, used by King George III and Queen Charlotte as a
summer residence during the early years of the 19th century, and in his
letter of 20 Jan. he recalled childhood visits to the town with his naturalist
father.   *Mr. Last's*: Isaac Glandfield Last (1814–66), Dorchester schoolmaster; TH's library contained copies of the *Breviarum historiae Romanae* of
Eutropius and Caesar's *Commentaries on the Gallic War*.   *first Aquarium*:
Philip Henry Gosse was the inventor of the marine aquarium, which he
first described in *A Naturalist's Rambles on the Devonshire Coast* (1854).

To Florence Henniker

MAX GATE, | DORCHESTER. | Feb 28: 1920

My dear friend:

Yes: you conjecture rightly: we had a very pleasant time at
Oxford. The undergrads who form the O.U.D.S. took us in
hand & treated us as their property, putting a taxi at our
disposal from morning to night all the time. There were
improvements on the London performance—notably in the
scenery; & the fact of the characters (110 in all, I think, & all
speaking ones) being young, & many of them handsome, lent
a great freshness & vivacity to their exhibition. Professional

actors might have envied the breathless silence with which some of the scenes were followed, & the large use of handkerchiefs at points of tragedy.

We did not go by motor after all. The doctor said he could not sanction it, the roads being just at that time full of holes & mud: yet a man went from here by road a few days after & said the journey was comfortable enough. We stayed at Sir W. Raleigh's, the late professor of English Literature, though we might have put up at the Giffords. However we went to see them.

So Milner requires a garage to walk about in on wet days. Our Wessex, too, is very exacting. He sleeps in a room which has an anthracite stove that burns night & day; but if it goes out by chance in the small hours he promptly comes scratching at the bedroom door to induce us to come down & light it for him, as if it were unreasonable to expect him to sleep without a fire.

I wonder if you will be a fixture at Sussex Place. It is certainly a better side of the park to live on than the South. The Gosses came about 6 weeks ago & stayed at the Gloucester Hotel Weymouth: they visited us here, & we them: I think the air strengthened Mrs Gosse, as Weyth air does many people.

We have had of late great trouble with servants: they come & picnic for a month or two, & then leave, to picnic in somebody else's house. We have been reading Ld Ilchester's book on Henry Fox which he was kind enough to send. Lady I. wanted to know what I thought of it, & I have told her. It is a very thorough & sincere piece of work, & interesting. Best love from both.

Your affectte friend
Th: H.

as their property: although TH was also in Oxford to receive an honorary degree from the university.   Raleigh's: Sir Walter Alexander Raleigh (1861–1922), critic; since he remained Merton Professor of English Literature until his death it is not clear why TH refers to him as 'the late professor', unless he simply means 'lately' or 'of late'.   Giffords: the widow and daughters of Archdeacon Edwin Hamilton Gifford, Emma Hardy's uncle.   Milner: Mrs Henniker's dog; the garage was presumably

at her new address, 3 Sussex Place, Lancaster Gate.   *Ld Ilchester's book*:
Henry Fox, First Lord Holland, His Family and Relations (1920).

To Harold Child

MAX GATE, | DORCHESTER. | 4th May. 1920.

Dear Mr Child:

(I use the universal printing-engine now, which I am sure you will excuse in one of my years.)

I am rather appalled at the prospect of my 80th. birthday—and an article thereon.—However, I daresay that in your judicious hands it may not be alarming.

As to the letter I wrote to Mr Shorter about my mother at the time of her death, I should object to it, or any other letter to him, being published or alluded to. As you will well know, one is apt at such times to write more freely than at others. I do not remember what I said in the letter, but if it concerned any facts of her life I can give you at first hand all that I should like to be mentioned—or my wife can. She will send them to you if you wish.

In respect of myself personally I am most averse to anything like an "interview," and have been for many years. Such details as it would be reasonable to print, if people want them, (would that it were impossible to print any!) she could also send you, and you could mould them into shape and good size, by warming up and adding some of the ideas that went to the making of your little book on my writings.

All this seems as if I did not wish you to come and see us—but that is not so by any means. At present, as in the perversity of things has happened before, we are in the turmoil of having repairs done to the house (postponed so many years owing to the war), but that difficulty may perhaps be overcome if you would like to run down. However a conversation with me anent the birthday does not seem to be really necessary; and I would rather you came when that date is quite past, and no newspaper copy is in question at all.

I have never printed anything about my early years of authorship &c. more than appears in Who's-Who and such publications. But absurd paragraphs have been published in the gossip-papers purporting to be my history. For instance, quite lately, an educated man at Oxford wrote to inquire if he might take it to be true, as reported, that the story of "Jude the Obscure" was my personal history. Curiously enough, that particular novel has hardly a single fact of my own life in it, or any sort of resemblance to my experiences.

If then, you say that such detail as we furnish will satisfy you for using as a skeleton of your article they shall be forwarded, on the understanding that you do not say how you came by them.

Believe me,

Yours sincerely,
Th: Hardy.

printing-engine: i.e. FEH's typewriter.   *article thereon*: 'Thomas Hardy', *Bookman*, June 1920, by Harold Child; TH also refers to Child's *Thomas Hardy* (1916).   *educated man at Oxford*: Archie Stanton Whitfield, who wrote from Exeter College in Oct. 1919 and later published a lecture entitled *Thomas Hardy: The Artist, the Man, and the Disciple of Destiny* (1921).

To Florence Henniker

Max Gate | June 4: 1920

My dear friend:

We are delighted to hear that you are coming to Weymouth on July 1. I should have written to-day in answer to your kind telegram on my birthday, even if you had not added this pleasant letter. I was going to write last night, but some people came in just at the moment. You know how I valued having it, I am sure you do!

Yes: it was amusing to have the deputation. I had never been deputated(?) before, so I was not at all dignified. But, as you know, I never am.

Yes: they *did* come to lunch. I was rather tired—not by them, for no less tiresome people can be conceived—but by the messages, & by strangers unexpectedly entering. I may tell you, since you allude to the King's message, that he has sent another to-day, thanking me for my good wishes for *his* birthday, which I expressed in my reply.

I saw the paragraph about the publishers. I wonder if it was true. Will you kindly thank Anna for her message as well. How very good of her. I am so sorry to hear of her sprained arm. I use Eliman's Embrocation for such accidents, but a relative uses a much stronger application—Jacob's Oil, or some such name. However I need not tell you of these things.

Florence has gone to Weymouth this very afternoon for an hour, taking Wessex. He so implores to be taken that it is hard to leave him at home. We will do anything to help you get there, if you will let us know. F. is splendid in managing such things. She often finds rooms for friends. Some rooms are good there, & some bad. Weymouth air is very good in summer, & probably you will not mind a few trippers beginning to come. (August is their great month.)

Lady Ir will be so glad to have you near. She always asks when we see her if we have heard lately. She & Ld I. sent a combined wire on Wedny which I must thank them for.

Barrie has just sent a note to say he is coming to morrow night for the week end. Believe me

Ever your affectionate
Tho. H.

By a curious chance the printers are reprinting just now: & you may imagine how full my hands are. Th: H.

deputation: on 2 June, TH's 80th birthday, Sir Anthony Hope Hawkins, John Galsworthy, and Augustine Birrell called at Max Gate to present him with an illuminated address from the Incorporated Society of Authors. *his birthday*: King George V was born on 3 June 1865. *paragraph about the publishers*: unidentified. *Anna*: Anna Hirschmann. *Lady Ir . . . Ld I.*: the Ilchesters. *reprinting*: TH was evidently reading proof for the verse volumes of the Mellstock Edition.

To Sir Robert Pearce Edgcumbe

MAX GATE, | DORCHESTER. | June 14: 1920
Dear Edgcumbe:

I send a line—though I am late in doing it—to thank you for your kind message on my birthday; & also for the Western Mercury with your interesting article. It reminds me that a maternal ancestor of mine established a paper in Cornwall called The West Briton, somewhere between 100 & 150 years ago. What became of the paper I never heard.

Your survey of the advance in what we call civilization since 1860 might be supplemented by a prophetic article on our probable retrogression during the next 60 years to the point from which we started (not to say further)—to turnpike-road travelling, high postage, scarce newspapers (for lack of paper to print them on), oppression of one class by another, etc., etc.

Very truly yours
Thomas Hardy.

interesting article: it has not been traced in the *Western Weekly Mercury*, however, and was perhaps published under a pseudonym; Edgcumbe was living in retirement in Torquay.   maternal ancestor: Christopher Childs, mining engineer, was the brother of TH's great-grandmother Maria Childs; the *West Briton*, founded in 1810, still continues as the *West Briton and Royal Cornwall Gazette*, a Truro weekly.

To the Revd J. H. Dickinson

MAX GATE, | DORCHESTER. | June 15: 1920
Dear Mr Dickinson:

It was a great pleasure to me to get your good wishes on my birthday, as also to my wife, who having been a friend of Emma's has naturally been always interested in St. Juliot & its associations.

It is satisfactory to learn that you have annexed Lesnewth,

& curious, inasmuch as I myself annexed it as "East Endel-
stow" when I wrote "A Pair of Blue Eyes"—that is, so far as
the story has any reality, this being confined to its topographical features. Though readers will look in vain for the mansion
I put in, the fact being, if I remember rightly, that I imported
the building bodily from some 20 miles off—Lanhydrock, I
fancy. But as it is more than 45 years ago that the romance
appeared, I am vague.

I used, of course, to know the church quite well, & have a
vivid recollection of going there on more than one Sunday
evening in summer with Miss Gifford when I was visiting at
St. J., & the churchwarden lighting the candles for the
evening hymn. But these things are passing to "the land
where all things are forgotten".

It is very kind of you to wish to see us again. But I don't
know. For though I am quite active, travelling is much slower
now than it was, so that distances have been lengthened. We
both send kind regards to your sister.

Very sincerely yours
Thomas Hardy.

Lesnewth: the parish adjoining St Juliot; the reference to the churchwarden
lighting the candles recalls TH's poem 'The Young Churchwarden'.
Lanhydrock (now the property of the National Trust) lies just south of
Bodmin.   *are forgotten"*: from the Book of Common Prayer version of Ps.
88: 12.

To Sir Henry Newbolt

MAX GATE, | DORCHESTER. | 21 June 1920

My dear Newbolt:

Hearty thanks for letter & telegram—from both of us. I am
disappointed at not being able to be present, owing to this
sudden rheumatism—not very violent, but incapacitating. I
have no idea where I caught the cold that brought it on.
However, old gents of 80 must expect such.

My interest in Salisbury Cathedral, which is of course
architectural, has lasted ever since 1860, when it began with

me, on visiting it as an architect's pupil; & I remember well my first sight of its unrivalled outline—through a driving mist that nearly hid the top of the spire. At that time the interior, as arranged by Wyatt, was still untouched by Scott, the organ being over the screen. The result was that a greater air of mystery & gloom hung over the interior than does now, & it looked much larger from the subdivision—as buildings always do.

Kindest regards to Lady Newbolt from both of us, & with renewed thanks for your offer of hospitality I am

Sincerly yours
Thomas Hardy.

to be present: Newbolt wrote on 20 June to invite the Hardys to stay with him at Netherhampton House, near Salisbury, in order to attend on 24 June a service marking the 700th anniversary of the founding of Salisbury Cathedral. The architects James Wyatt (1746–1813) and Sir George Gilbert Scott (1811–78) each carried out extensive 'restoration' work on the cathedral.

To Edward Clodd

Max Gate, | Dorchester. | June 30: 1920

My dear Clodd:

I am now sending supplementary thanks for your kind letter on my birthday—my hasty postcard having been all I was able to write at the date—as you no doubt understood: & I can also send at the same time my best wishes to you on your anniversary, & that there may be as many happy returns of it as nature with her highest efforts can allow.

We saw your article in the Daily News on the spiritualistic craze, & some so-called answers to your arguments by correspondents of the Daily Graphic. Apart from scientific & other reasons against such communications the one fact of a "medium" being necessary would, one might think, discredit them, since, in at least half these performances the medium has been proved to be an impostor.

Our ancestors used to burn these mediums—or witches as

they were then called; but we reward them—a more humane, though more mischievous, treatment. When the Witch of Endor called up Samuel we are not told what he paid her, but the case is of course an exact parallel to present practice, for one clearly gathers that Saul did not *see* Samuel, who conversed with him *through* the witch—as now. She was afraid, when she knew him: but now they are not afraid!

I daresay you go to London oftener than I do—to dinners & other genial gatherings. May you be able to go long. With kindest regards to Mrs Clodd I am

Very sincerely yours
Thomas Hardy.

your anniversary: Clodd's 80th birthday was a month after TH's, on 1 July 1920.   *your article*: Clodd's review of *The Life Beyond the Veil* (1920), by the Revd George Vale Owen, appeared in the *Daily News*, 28 June; the letters in the *Daily Graphic* were in response to two articles hostile to spiritualism which Clodd had published there on 22 and 23 June. *called up Samuel*: 1 Sam: 28. 11–14.

To Florence Henniker

MAX GATE, | DORCHESTER. | All Saints Eve. | Oct 31. 1920

My dear friend:

My thanks for your very nice letter; but before entering into it I write at this particular moment to ask if you are going to the presentation to Mr Gosse on Friday next at 3, at the Steinway Hall? Florence has to be in London the day before, & thinks she can go, as she is not coming home till the evening train of Friday. I cannot go, so she must represent me. As Ld Crewe & Mr Balfour are in it, & the recipient is Gosse, I daresay it will be an interesting ceremony. They say the bust is good, but I have not seen it.

Yes: I have thought of you in your loss of "Milner". I have gone through the same experience in respect of cats. What silly people we are to get so attached to pets whose natural lives, as we well know, must in every reasonable probability finish before our own!

I did not expect much from the electric treatment, but of course if it has made you much better my doubts are answered. I have had a bad cold, but have begun to go out again.

I do hope what you expect of the Council of Justice to be well founded. Here in this stock-breeding county one sees instances continually of what does not exactly amount to legal cruelty, & yet is cruelty.

Fancy your reading that old novel of mine Two on a Tower right through. History does not record whether Swithin married Tabitha or not. Perhaps when Lady C. was dead he grew passionately attached to her again, as people often do. I suppose the bishop did find out the secret. Or perhaps he did not.

We saw the announcement of Mr Shorter's marriage in the Times, & he has written since to us about it. We do not know anything of the lady, except from what he says, that she is young, & in his judgment pretty.

I want you to get this to-morrow morning, & must hastily wind up as the post is just going. I like this mysterious eve of saintly ghosts, & also tomorrow eve, of All Souls—

Ever affectly
Tho H.

This is a mere scrawl. I will write a better letter next time, as I hope. Th: H.

presentation: it was, in the event, on 9 rather than on 5 November ('Friday next') that Arthur James Balfour, the former prime minister, presented to Edmund Gosse the portrait bust (by Sir William Goscombe John) that had been subscribed to by more than 200 of his friends. Florence Henniker's brother, already earl of Crewe, was created marquess of Crewe in 1911.
of Justice: the Council of Justice to Animals; see letter of 3 Oct. 1911.
Swithin . . . bishop: Swithin St Cleeve, Tabitha Lark, Lady Constantine, and Bishop Helmsdale are all characters in TH's *Two on a Tower*.   *Shorter's marriage*: to Annie Doris Banfield, his second wife.

To Ford Madox Ford

Dec. 19. 1920.

Dear Mr Hueffer:

I am sorry I cannot sign the paper, or say anything about Ireland in the press. If one begins that sort of thing he must be prepared to go on, or to get the worst of it, & at my age I am not able to go on, apart from the fact that I have kept outside politics all my life.

I was faithful to Ireland for 30 years, but my views of late of that unhappy & senseless country have much changed. (I may say this as I have some Irish blood myself.)

Moreover the present Government, though it contains some stupid members, is not inhumane, & I doubt if a new Government would do much better.

Yours sincerely

Ford: although Ford had changed his surname from Hueffer (see letter of 9 Sep. 1908) six months earlier, he still signed himself 'Hueffer' (presumably to ensure recognition) when writing on 17 Dec. to solicit TH's signature to a letter to the *Manchester Guardian* urging the British government to seek mediation or arbitration of the current Irish situation. TH's claim to Irish blood rested on his belief that one of his great-great-grandmothers had come from Ireland. *Yours sincerely*: the text is that of TH's unsigned draft.

To Alfred Noyes

MAX GATE, | DORCHESTER. | December 20th. 1920.

Dear Mr Noyes:

I am much obliged for your reply, which I really ought not to have troubled you to write. I may say for myself that I very seldom do give critics such trouble, usually letting things drift, though there have been many occasions when a writer who has been so much abused for his opinions as I have been would perhaps have done well not to hold his peace.

I do not know that there can be much use in my saying

more than I did say. It seems strange that I should have to remind a man of letters of what, I should have supposed, he would have known as well as I—of the very elementary rule of criticism that a writer's opinions should be judged as a whole, and not from picked passages that contradict them as a whole—and this especially when they are scattered over a period of 50 years.

Also that I should have to remind him of the vast difference between the expression of fancy and the expression of belief. My fancy may have often run away with me; but all the same my sober opinion—so far as I have any definite one—of the Cause of Things, has been defined in scores of places, and is that of a great many ordinary thinkers:—that the said Cause is neither moral nor immoral, but *un*moral:—"loveless and hateless" I have called it; "which neither good nor evil knows"—etc, etc—(you will find plenty of these definitions in "The Dynasts" as well as in short poems, and I am surprised that you have not taken them in.) This view is quite in keeping with what you call a Pessimistic philosophy (a mere nickname with no sense in it), which I am quite unable to see as "leading logically to the conclusion that the Power behind the universe is malign."

In my fancies, or poems of the imagination, I have of course called this Power all sorts of names—never supposing they would be taken for more than fancies. I have even in prefaces warned readers to take them only as such—as mere impressions of the moment, exclamations, in fact. But it has always been my misfortune to presuppose a too intelligent reading public, and no doubt people will go on thinking that I really believe the Prime Mover to be a malignant old gentleman, a sort of King of Dahomey,—an idea which, so far from my holding it, is to me irresistibly comic. "What a fool one must have been to write for such a public!" is the inevitable reflection at the end of one's life.

The lines you allude to, "A young man's Epigram", I remember finding in a drawer, and printed them merely as an amusing instance of early cynicism. The words "Time's Laughingstocks" are legitimate imagery all of a piece with such expressions as "Life, Time's fool," and thousands in poetry, and I am amazed that you should see any *belief* in them. The other verses you mention, "New Year's Eve", "His Education", are the same fanciful impressions of the moment. The poem called "He abjures Love", ending with "and then the curtain", is a love poem, and lovers are chartered irresponsibles. A poem often quoted against me and apparently in your mind in the lecture is the one called "Nature's Questioning", containing the words "an Automaton", "Some Vast Imbecility", &c.—as if these definitions were my creed. But they are merely enumerated in the poem as fanciful alternatives to several others, and having nothing to do with my own opinion. As for "The Unborn" to which you also allude, though the form of it is imaginary, the sentiment is one which I should think, especially since the war, is not uncommon or unreasonable.

This week I have had sent me a review which quotes a poem entitled "To my father's violin", containing a Virgilian reminiscence of mine of Acheron and the Shades. The reviewer comments: "Truly this pessimism is insupportable . . . . One marvels that Hardy is not in a madhouse." Such is English criticism; and I repeat, Why did I ever write a line!

However I will go no further. And perhaps if the young ladies to whom you lectured really knew that, so far from being the wicked personage they doubtless think me at present to be, I am a harmless old character much like their own grandfathers, they would consider me far less romantic and attractive.

Yours sincerely,
Thomas Hardy.

Noyes: Alfred Noyes (1880–1958), the poet, had replied on 17 Dec. to TH's protest (of 13 Dec.) against his having said in a lecture that TH's 'philosophy' was one which held 'that the Power behind the Universe was an imbecile jester'.   *"Loveless . . . knows"*: slightly misquoted from *The Dynasts*, Part Third, After Scene, and Part Second, vi.vii.   *"leading . . . malign."*: slightly adapted from Noyes's letter.   *King of Dahomey*: popularly associated with human sacrifice on a large scale.   *Time's fool,"*: *I Henry IV*, v.iv.81.   *"His Education"*: i.e. 'God's Education'.   *and the Shades*: the dead in the poem are described as dwelling in 'Nether Glooms' and 'Mournful Meads'; the review itself has not been identified.

To Alfred Noyes

MAX GATE, | DORCHESTER. | Dec 23. 1920

Many thanks for letter. Yes: the whole scheme is incomprehensible, & there I suppose we must leave it—perhaps for the best. Knowledge might be terrible.

Th: H.

To John Galsworthy

MAX GATE, | DORCHESTER. | Feb. 7: 1921

My dear Galsworthy:

It was cheering to get good wishes of such far flight from you & Mrs Galsworthy. I can assure you that you also have the same from us. The book, too, came all right, & to judge from its matter so far as I have got in it, deserves my warm thanks, or anybody's, for it becomes more intense at every page. My wife who has read it once, is reading it again.

I almost think you ought to have put a genealogical chart at the beginning, to enable idle ones to grasp the interrelationships without trouble, since they begin to get complicated. Or perhaps you ought *not* to put a chart, for it would be encouraging the said idle people in their laziness.

How I should like to be in California all of a sudden—say for a week or two—borne thither on the magician's carpet. But to travel all the way there to see & experience its climate & beauties, & through a country where "only the language is different", as somebody says,—no, thank you. My interest in the west coast of the Continent you are on is (beyond its Spanish flavour) largely owing to its looking on the Pacific— that mysterious ocean (to me), which some say the moon came out of: at any rate I like to think it did though I believe geologists & astronomers doubt the possibility of it.

We have had a mild winter here so far (except for an early week or two), & I hope it will end as it is going on. But England & Europe do not look particularly attractive in their

political aspects. The extreme party seems to forget that the
opposite of error is error still—just as all the revolutionists of
history have forgotten it. I suppose such is inevitable: you
can't make a pendulum stop in the middle, except after
infinite swingings. A friend of mine thinks the great danger is
to art & literature, & that a new Dark Age is coming along,
in which our books will be pulped to make new paper for
football & boxing journals & cinema descriptions.

It will be pleasant to know you have got home when the
date arrives, & I hope you will have an easy return. Kindest
regards from us both to Mrs Galsworthy & yourself. I hope
the change will pick her up entirely.

Always sincerely yours
Thomas Hardy.

such far flight: Galsworthy, on an extended visit to the United States with
his wife Ada, née Cooper (d. 1956), had written on 1 Jan. from Santa
Barbara, California; he also arranged for TH to receive a copy of his *In
Chancery* (1920), one of the Forsyte series.   *as somebody says*: Oscar Wilde;
see letter of 15 Jan. 1920.   *friend of mine*: see letter of 5 Apr. 1921.

To Madeleine Rolland

MAX GATE, | DORCHESTER. | 14th. March 1921.

Dear Miss Rolland:

I have explained the words as well as I am able; but, alas,
they are old expressions rapidly dying. For instance, nobody
in Dorchester would know now the meaning of "glane",
though when I was a boy it was known quite well. I am quite
beaten over the UR. You must exercise your ingenuity in
thinking of a pattern sound. When you come here you shall
hear it—unless it is extinct, by no means an impossibility.

I think I should retain "lynchets" untranslated, unless
there is a French name for them, which I doubt. They are
also called "launches" and "lanches". They are flint slopes in
ploughed land, about 2 metres wide, forming terraces, and
their origin is unknown. Some people say they were artificially
made.

As to a photograph I have no recent one, but I send such as I have.

There was very slight foundation for the story of "Tess"— I once saw a milkmaid something like her—who had a voice also like hers—but her history was quite different—happily! Her father "Sir" John also had a prototype, and some particulars of his history were the same; but not many. A woman was hanged here more than 60 years ago for murdering her husband, but the circumstances were not similar. So I fear you must assume the novel to be but "the figment of a dream".

A translator has lately written from Paris saying he has *finished* translating "The Mayor of Casterbridge" and is about to publish it. As you know I cannot hinder him—the book having been in existence more than ten years—which is the limit of copyright in translations. So that, if I were you, I would not waste time on that novel.

By a curious coincidence I have just had sent me some translations into French prose from my *poems*—not dramatic ones, such as those I sent you, but of the more reflective sort. The translator is a stranger to me. They also have been published more than 10 years.

We both send our kindest regards and hope you keep well.

Always sincerely yours,
Th: Hardy.

P.S. "Tess d'Urberville" is best.

explained the words: Madeleine Rolland (see letter of 25 July 1899) was revising her French translation of *Tess*, originally published in 1901, and had sent TH a typed list of dialect and other words which were still giving her trouble. The list, with TH's responses, still accompanies this letter but has not been reproduced here; he explains 'glane' (in ch. 38 of *Tess*) as 'smile sneeringly' and says of the Dorset 'UR' (in ch. 2) that, in English, 'the nearest approach I can think of is "*uhr*" (It is very noticeable in the word "her", which the rustics pronounce "hurrr".)'.   *woman was hanged here*: Martha Browne; see letter of 20 Jan. 1926.   *of a dream*": perhaps an imperfect recollection of *Hamlet*, II. ii. 258–9 ('the shadow of a dream'). *publish it*: Philippe Neel's translation, *Le Maire de Casterbridge*, appeared in 1922.   *translations . . . my poems*: perhaps those of J. Fournier-Pargoire, published as *Poèmes* in 1925.   *is best*: as a title for the translation.

[Hardy's helpfulness to Madeleine Rolland provides one of several indications that he was less dismissive of his past work in fiction than might seem to be implied by his insistence on the superiority of the verse he was currently publishing. Poetry had become, however, his overwhelming concern, and while he was primarily engrossed in his own writing—to which he devoted a substantial portion of each day—he remained alert to the work of others, eager for the sound of an authentic new voice. When, in late 1920, Ezra Pound sent copies of his *Quia Pauper Amavi* (1919) and *Hugh Selwyn Mauberley* (1920), Hardy at first replied in temporizing fashion, noting that Pound's 'muse ask[ed] for considerable deliberation in estimating her', but in his letter of 18 March 1921 he made a serious and indeed successful attempt to respond with intelligent appreciativeness to unfamiliar and difficult verse, Pound himself later characterizing the suggestion for changing the title of 'Homage to Sextus Propertius' as 'impractical and infinitely valuable'.

To Ezra Pound

MAX GATE, | DORCHESTER. | March 18. 1921.

Dear Ezra Pound:

The letter you write from France contains so much that is interesting on literature, critics, etc., that I wish I could reply to it at length. But I am compelled to be brief, and am also compelled to dictate what I do send, as I have just now a weakness of the eyes which I sometimes suffer from, though perhaps not oftener than can be expected for one who has used his so cruelly as I have used mine during a long lifetime.

As to criticising the poems you so kindly sent I am afraid I cannot attempt that without knowing more clearly what you are aiming at. It is to be read only by the select few, I imagine? As I am old-fashioned, and think lucidity a virtue in poetry, as in prose, I am at a disadvantage in criticizing recent poets who apparently aim at obscurity. I do not mean that *you* do, but I gather that at least you do not care whether the many understand you or not.

Thus it is useless for me to say, for instance, as to your "S. Propertius" (on which you make an undeserved deprecatory remark) that all that seems the matter with it in my opinion—

barring perhaps a word here and there—is the lack of a few notes for the general reader. I think it really a very fine and striking poem.

By the way, since you call it "confused", don't you think that you give the reader a wrong start at the outset by naming it "Homage to S.P", and not "S.P. soliloquizes", or something of the sort? I may however, have misunderstood the word.

As to the other book "H.S.M.", I don't agree with you at all in thinking it "thin". There is so much packed away in it that it, its racy satire included, can be called very solid indeed by those who really read it. To say that it is not, any more than some other of your poetry, lucid, is as I have stated merely saying that it is not what you don't wish it to be, assuming that I don't misapprehend your aims.

So I refrain from criticising—feeling it best to leave you to the light of your own soul for guidance, and not to be bothered by my "reactions".

As to the poem I hoped to send for The Dial, I have cleared off the others I owed, and will try to have one ready soon. I need hardly say I am much flattered by the request.

I hope you will get home safely and well, and am

Sincerely yours,
Thomas Hardy.

Pound: Ezra Loomis Pound (1885–1972), American poet and critic. TH read 'Homage to Sextus Propertius' ('S. Propertius') in the *Quia Pauper Amavi* volume, received as a gift from Pound, along with *Hugh Selwyn Mauberley* ('H.S.M.'), in early Dec. 1920.   *for The Dial*: TH's 'The Two Houses' appeared in the New York *Dial* (of which Pound was the Paris editor), Aug. 1921.

To J. H. Morgan

MAX GATE, | DORCHESTER. | April 5: 1921.

Dear General Morgan:

It is not for want of remembering you that I have not replied to your letter till now, as we often wonder how you are getting on with your Berlin business. Events shift so kaleidoscopically that one can hardly reply on any change before there is another. So that I will leave out conjectures on the politics of Germany & Europe, to which you alluded in your last. I hope you will get done by August or September anyhow, but we must wait & see.

It is, at least, a fine experience for you, & may possibly result in making you a diplomat of the first water. I have said this, forgetting for a moment that diplomacy is, perhaps rightly, regarded as an error by our future masters.

We are in the middle of a coal strike as you will know, which by all accounts promises to ruin the miners no less than the rest of the community. I have no practical knowledge of the dispute whatever; but the real danger in these labour commotions, & in the Labour party's policy generally, lies less in the intention, which may be defensible, but in the method, owing to the ignorance of the majority on what results inevitably follow such & such courses of action, according to the teaching of all history. So that they are like children playing with fire, this illiterate section of the party overpowering by their numbers the thoughtful ones who know how gradually changes should be worked for to avoid a catastrophe to the whole country. A friend of mine, a Professor at Cambridge, in spite of being quite a Radical, says he thinks we are at the beginning of a New Dark Ages centuries long. Absit omen!

I did read that article on Morley in the Lit. Supt but never guessed it was yours. I believe his limited edition is going well.

I envy you your visit to Vienna. I was once on the point of going there when not far off, but something hindered. I like the Viennese love of dancing & music.

My wife is in London, or she would join with me in best wishes for you, & your mission.

Sincerely yours
Thomas Hardy.

Morgan: John Hartman Morgan (1876–1955), lawyer and author, was currently in Berlin as a member of the Inter-Allied Commission of Control for enforcement of the disarmament provisions of the Treaty of Versailles. *Labour party's policy*: the Labour Party, in opposition, supported the national

miners' strike that began on 31 Mar.   *Professor at Cambridge*: probably
John Bagnell Bury.   *limited edition*: a fifteen-volume *édition de luxe* of the
writings of Viscount Morley was currently appearing and had been
reviewed in the *Times Literary Supplement* of 10 Feb.

To Lytton Strachey

MAX GATE, | DORCHESTER. | April 20: 1921

Dear Mr Strachey:

I have just finished your Life of Queen Victoria, which
arrived as a kind gift from you, one that I shall always value.
You will by this time be rather tired of comment & criticism,
I am sure, so that I will not attempt much of the sort, but
just say that I was deeply interested in reading the book,
notwithstanding that your subject was a most uninteresting
woman, which means that my pleasure must have arisen from
your genius in the treatment. Perhaps I ought not to be quite
so absolute as to hold that she was uninteresting all through,
since during the 20 years of her married life she was certainly
more attractive.

I often wished you could have had a more adequate &
complicated woman to handle, such as Mary Stuart or
Elizabeth. However, Victoria was a good queen, well suited
to her time & circumstances, in which perhaps a smarter
woman would have been disastrous.

Your remark on her mother's domination is curiously
corroborated by what my mother once told me: that on one
of her progresses through the west of England when she was
a child (which my mother chanced to see) little Victoria stood
up in the carriage, the better to acknowledge the homage of
the people, whereupon the Duchess promptly pulled her down
into her seat by her skirts.

With my thanks for the book believe me

Yours very truly
Thomas Hardy.

Strachey: Giles Lytton Strachey (1880–1932), scholar and biographer, whose
Queen Victoria had just been published.   *mother chanced to see*: since TH's

mother lived as a child in Melbury Osmond, Dorset, this was presumably the journey from Weymouth to Melbury House which the Princess Victoria made with her mother, the Duchess of Kent, on 29 July 1833.

To Dorothy Bosanquet

MAX GATE, | DORCHESTER. | May 19: 1921.

Dear Mrs Bosanquet:

Your letter is most welcome, as it starts my writing to you, which I had put off doing for a few days—or rather writing to Mrs Moule—having thought that she would get so many letters that mine could wait. I hope she is well: please remember me to her.

I had, of course, known your dear father—off & on— nearly all my life, & the news of his death was like a bereavement. As you surmise, my thoughts went straight to the fact that he was the last of "the seven brethren"—as they used humorously to call themselves—*all* of whom I had the felicity to know, (long before you were born!): & I have many recollections of him of a personal kind. This weather brings back to me in particular one—of our hiring a boat at Weymouth, being rowed out into the Bay, diving off, swimming about, & then having great difficulty in getting back into the boat. At another time we agreed to go to Ford Abbey, which we had not seen. Reaching the place we found it was not the show day, & were turning away when the owner rushed out, said it did not matter, showed us all over the building himself, & gave us a sumptuous lunch.

However, all that is past, & I am old likewise, & the shadows are stretching out. I daresay I shall recall other experiences with him from time to time. One other, by the way, is that I happened to be at Fordington Vicarage when the news came of his fellowship.

If you ever condescend to Dorset, please come & see us. Believe me with kind regards

Sincerely yours
Thomas Hardy.

Bosanquet: Dorothy Mary Cautley Bosanquet (d. 1962), wife of Vivian Henry Courthope Bosanquet, was the daughter of TH's old but recently deceased friend Charles Walter Moule and Mary Dora Moule, née Cautley, his widow.   *Ford Abbey*: usually spelled Forde, a medieval building in north-west Dorset.   *his fellowship*: Moule was elected to his fellowship at Corpus Christi College, Cambridge, in 1858.

To Florence Henniker

Max Gate | 2 July 1921

My dear friend:

This continuous fine weather makes me think that you might do well in trying Weymouth again, before the August trippers come. We have been told this week that the Burdon Hotel, which was until lately used for war-purposes, is now restored to its original state, has had the drains overhauled, & is altogether very comfortable, while not so expensive as the Royal—which some people are beginning to complain of in point of charges.

This morning we have had an odd experience. The film-makers are here doing scenes for "The Mayor of C." & they asked us to come & see the process. The result is that I have been talking to The Mayor, Mrs Henchard, Eliz. Jane, & the rest, in the flesh. The company arrived here at 1 o'clock this morning, & leave again to-morrow. It is a strange business to be engaged in.

I believe I never have thanked you for your kind telegram on my birthday. I don't send you messages on yours, which is rather mean of me, but I send them in a lump now. I remember that you are not far from Lady Randolph Churchill, of whose accident we heard at the time, but imagined it to be one she would get over. She has had a lively life altogether, so her shade must not complain.

As you know, we did not go to London after all, & now it does not seem the sort of place to go to in the drought. We have had a few pleasant people calling—poets mostly: I am getting to know quite a lot of the Young Georgians, & have quite a paternal feeling, or grandpaternal, towards them.

Siegfried Sassoon has been, Walter de la Mare, John Masefield, & next week Mr & Mrs Galsworthy are going to call on
their way to London. We have also seen the Granville
Barkers. All this is by reason of the car fashion of travel,
which seems to make us almost suburban.

I hope Lady Crewe got over her attack of measles. Our
neighbour Mrs Hanbury is ailing, & her father Mr Jeune (Ld
St Helier's brother) is ill at her house.

We have no Sunday post now, so I must send this off to
night.

Ever yr affectionate
Th: H.

The cinema actors have just called in a body to wish us
goodbye. Th: H.

The film-makers: the director and screenwriter for the Progress Film Company
production of *The Mayor of Casterbridge* (first shown later in 1921) was
Sidney Morgan (1873–1946).   *her shade*: Lady Randolph Churchill, née
Jenny Jerome, died on 29 June; she was the widow of Lord Randolph
Churchill and the mother of Winston Spencer Churchill.   *Lady Crewe*:
the wife of Florence Henniker's brother; see letter of 15 Feb. 1899.   *her
house*: Kingston Maurward.

To Douglas Fawcett

[Ans. to Mr Douglas Fawcett]   Aug. 29. 1921
Dear Sir:

I must write my thanks to you for your book "Divine
Imagining" which you have been so kind as to send me,
although I have not as yet given it more than a general glance
over, for it is a work that I shall obviously not have read
thoroughly till acknowledgement would seem unduly delayed.

It has been very courageous of you to cast the philosophy
of the Unconscious entirely aside, the more if it should turn
out that you have not established your own more pleasing
philosophy in its place as firmly as could be wished.

As I gather, you renounce the creeds which deny life-
persistence after physical death, as being "fatuously untrue"

because they foredoom all great schemes of social betterment
to ruin. I do not follow this reasoning, failing first to see any
ground for supposing such a consequence, & second, assuming it, failing to see how it would prove the untruth of such
creeds. Thus not having grasped any evidence of the persistence of life after bodily cessation, but fancying that there is
presumptive evidence to the contrary, I am compelled to
regard your picture of the superior sentients of the world-
system coalescing into a God as a bright hypothesis merely.
But as I said, I am only beginning to get into your book.

It has, I think, been well-received by the press (if that is
worth anything!). "The Dynasts", to which you generously
allude, had a rougher reception in 1903. As an instance of
how times have changed in 18 years I remember that when in
that poem I deposed the He of theology, replacing Him by It,
as being less childishly anthropomorphic, I was mildly
scolded by the critics for such a daring innovation; but
nobody, so far as I have seen, has objected to your use of that
capital-lettered pronoun.

Believe me,

Yours very truly
T—H—

Fawcett: Edward Douglas Fawcett (1866–1960), author and sportsman, had
sent TH a copy of his *Divine Imagining: An Essay on the First Principles of
Philosophy* (1921). *[Ans. . . . Fawcett]*: the text is that of TH's draft.

To John Galsworthy

MAX GATE, | DORCHESTER. | 24 October: 1921

My dear Galsworthy:

I think I like this the best of the Forsyte chronicles, this
last one, & I ought to have written sooner to thank you for
the gift of it, but I knew you would give me time, & nowadays
my promptness, if I ever had it, is a tradition merely.

I don't pretend to estimate the novel with any critical
acuteness, but you have made me feel sorry you have finished
with the family. This is strange, considering that I do not like

any of its members *very much* personally—except perhaps
Jon—so that it must be owing to your handling of them that
I regret you are going to tell us no more about them. My wife,
by the way, has a sympathy for Soames, whom she considers
a touching figure. This I do not altogether share.

The story seems to me more of an artistic organism of
natural development than almost any of the others, which is
one reason why it appeals to me. I may mention being
particulary struck with some special scenes—one in the
summer-house at p.175: & the death of Jolyon seemed a
remarkably good dramatic stroke: the reader vaguely feels
something hanging over, yet is not clear as to the moment
when the inevitable will happen.

You have large stage schemes on hand in London, I
understand, so by this time you may have gone back there.
The Masefields called here on their way to you. We have not
heard of them since, & as they left here rather late they may
not have done the whole journey the same evening. Renewed
thanks for the book, which we have both read, & kindest
regards from both of us to Mrs Galsworthy & yourself.

Always yours
Thomas Hardy.

this last one: *To Let* (1921); TH refers specifically to Jon Forsyte (Jolyon
Forstye III), to the scene in which Soames sits alone during a thunderstorm,
reflecting upon his own emotional relationships and upon life in general,
and to the death of Young Jolyon.

To Sir Frederick Macmillan

MAX GATE, | DORCHESTER. | 8th. November 1921.

Dear Sir Frederick Macmillan:

I am writing to ask your opinion on one or two points that
have arisen. The first is that since Moments of Vision was
published in 1917 other poems have accumulated—several
being those issued in The Times, Fortnightly, and other
periodicals, American ones included, which readers say they
want in book form like the rest, and the makers of anthologies

also ask for (I don't suppose the latter means much, however). These poems with many others I have on hand would, I find, fill a volume quite as thick as Moments of Vision; and though I am by no means anxious to rush into print again—quite the reverse, indeed—the question arises whether it would not be advisable to bring them out—say early next year, or whenever you think convenient—and not leave them to the mercy of curious collectors, and people who print things privately and then coolly sell them.

What has made me pause is the consideration that the buyers of the Mellstock edition would, I suppose, want these new poems also, and that would mean a new volume in the series.

The above is the most important matter. A minor one is that several readers, "Georgian" poets, &c., say that they would gladly buy the 2 vols. (Collected Poems and Dynasts) at half-a-crown more for each volume if they could get them printed on thinner paper so as to be available for travelling, &c. I am told that the Oxford Book of English Verse doubled its sale directly it was reduced in bulk by producing it on thin paper, and I have heard of the same thing happening to other books. This is a question for your handling entirely. It seems to me that a feasible plan would be to bring out the volume of new poems, and when the time comes for incorporating them into the Collected Poems (where there is plenty of room for more at the end) the whole volume could be issued on thin paper, and the extra poems would give it a good start.

One thing more is: I have had several Professors of Literature from American Universities calling here this past summer, and they all agree in saying that the American people are getting acquainted with my poetry almost entirely through the aforesaid Collected edition, as circulated there by your American house, except for which they would hardly know anything about the poems. It therefore occurs to me to suggest that when you are writing to New York it might be well to impress them with the advisability of keeping these two green volumes, the Collected Poems and The Dynasts, before the people of the United States, who are a large and serious reading public. One shrewd Professor remarked of his own countrymen that they are like children, and that they read whatever is put before them without much judgment of their own.

This is enough for one letter, and I am,

Yours sincerely,
Thomas Hardy.

say early next year: *Late Lyrics and Earlier* was in fact published by Macmillan on 23 May 1922; the Mellstock Edition, however, was never expanded to include this or any of TH's subsequent volumes. *issued on thin paper*: Macmillan acted on this suggestion, bringing out thin-paper issues of both the one-volume *Collected Poems* and the one-volume *Dynasts* in 1923.

[Hardy had been quite seriously ill during January 1922, and this intimation of mortality perhaps affected his decision to add to his new volume of poems, *Late Lyrics and Earlier*, a preface—or, as he called it, an 'Apology'—that combined a restatement of his views on contemporary society and religion with a frank expression of personal hostility towards those (including his old friend Frederic Harrison) who continued to criticize his poetry for its excess of philosophical gloom. It is indicative of Hardy's high regard for Cockerell's judgement that he should not only have sought his advice as to the wisdom of such a gesture but accepted his recommendation that the 'Apology' be published with only minor revisions.]

To Sydney Cockerell

Private. Feb 15: 1922

My dear Cockerell:

In my hurry yesterday I did not send the enclosed as I had meant. I am sending it to ask your opinion whether I shall prefix it to the new volume or not. I don't *wish* to, & should not at all mind destroying it. It came into my mind mostly while lying in bed during the late weeks, & seemed then almost necessary.

Is it uncalled for, or, if not altogether so, is it too cantankerous in respect of reviewers, &c. for a writer whose books are fairly well received nowadays—even quite well received in general. If I cancel it I can easily print the poems without a preface.

If some parts will pass, but not all, I will cut out the undesirable parts. Please mark any paragraphs that might be so deleted, in the latter event.

I ought to have said that why I am bothering you for an opinion in this way is owing to my judgment being thrown out of balance by these household illnesses. If all were well as usual, I could reach a conclusion in a moment on such a trifling matter.

This morning I had quite made up my mind to destroy it, but I have thought since it would be advisable to consult you. The point is that I do not wish to offend staunch readers by making them suppose I think too much about the objectors who turn up from time to time.

F. is not much better, & can still hardly speak. But we are hoping she is improving.

Always yours
T.H.

I have kept no copy of the MS.
P.S. As you are well aware, a writer himself hears less of real opinion about his works, particularly of objections to his views, &c, than an outsider does. Hence my not knowing the actual weight of objections to mine. T.H.
PPS. I thought "Apology" more piquant than "Preface".

the enclosed: the draft of the 'Apology' later prefixed to *Late Lyrics and Earlier*. *not much better*: FEH was suffering from what TH called influenza but was more probably a heavy cold and sore throat.

To the Duchess of Hamilton

[Ansr]   July 5. 1922
Dear Duchess of Hamilton:
   I am unfortunately unable to be present at the meeting,

but I can say that slaughterhouse reform has my hearty support. A quick exit, with the minimum of suffering (mental & physical) is a right to which every victim is entitled, & if skilfully ensured may be less painful than the animal's natural death from age or infirmity—which is the only justification for killing such fellow-creatures at all. I fear that what among other things stands in the way in respect of many animals, such as pigs is the belief that they must "die slow" to produce a "well-blooded" carcase—which of course really impover-ishes the meat. I should welcome legislation that enforced humane killing.

Believe me

Sincerely yours
(Signed) Thomas Hardy.

Hamilton: Nina Mary Benita Douglas-Hamilton, née Poore (1878–1951), wife of the 13th duke of Hamilton; an active campaigner for slaughterhouse reform, she had, on 3 July, asked TH to send a message of support to a meeting called to protest against 'the present horrible methods of killing animals for food'. *[Ansr] . . . (Signed)*: this is another of TH's drafts.

To J. H. Morgan

MAX GATE, | DORCHESTER. | 12 Oct. 1922

Dear General Morgan:

I had already begun a reply to your interesting letter from Berlin, which opened up so many points that had engaged me 20 years ago, but had rather faded in my memory. Now that you are at home I will write it in a more succinct form, for it is not likely that amid the many details you have to attend to after your absence you will want to think much about Napoleonic times.

I cannot for my life recall where I obtained the idea of N's entry into Berlin by the Potsdamer-Strasse, though I don't think I should have written it without authority. However, you have to remember that the events generally in The Dynasts had to be pulled together into dramatic scenes, to show themselves to the mental eye of the reader as a picture viewed from one point; & hence it was sometimes necessary to see round corners, down crooked streets, & to shift buildings nearer each other than in reality (as Turner did in his landscapes); & it may possibly happen that I gave "A Public Place" in Berlin these convenient facilities without much ceremony.

You allude to Leipzig. That battle bothered me much more than Jena or Ulm (to which you also allude)—in fact more than any other battle I had to handle. I defy any human being to synchronize with any certainty its episodes from descriptions by the historians. My time-table was, I believe, as probable a one as can be drawn up at this date. But I will go no further with these stale conjectures, now you are in London.

I have quite recently been reading a yellow old letter written from Berlin in June, 1815 by a Dorset man whose daughter is a friend of ours, & who lately sent it to me. The writer says what is oddly in keeping with your remarks on the arrogance of Prussian officers.—"Buonaparte has rendered Germany completely military; at the inns & post-houses a private Gentleman exacts not half the respect exacted by a soldier. This contempt for those who wear no swords displays itself in no very pleasant shape to travellers. About 3 weeks ago I might have died of damp sheets if my German servant had not taken upon him to assure a brute of a Post-master that I was an English General travelling for my health. . . . I have since girded on a sabre, got a military cap, & let my moustache grow: soldiers now present arms as we pass."

It would be strange to find that Napoleon was really the prime cause of German militarism! What a Nemesis for the French nation!

Well, I have gone back to Boney again after all: but no more of him. I hope you find the change to London agreeable, & keep well in your vicissitudes.

Sincerely yours
Thomas Hardy.

from Berlin: see letter of 5 Apr. 1921.   *20 years ago*: i.e. when he was writing *The Dynasts*; the Potsdamer-Strasse figures in Part Second, i. vi (and see the directions at the beginning of i. v), the battle of Leipzig in Part Third, iii. i–v.   *sent it to me*: the letter (now in the Dorset County Museum) was written by George Tilley Gollop (1792–1889) and sent to TH by his daughter Jeanne Popham (d. 1946), of Bournemouth.

To Lady Grove

MAX GATE, | DORCHESTER. | 20 Oct. 1922

My dear Lady Grove:

I am glad to hear that you like the Poems, which after all are a very mixed lot, though the reviewers have been civil enough about them. As to the "Apology", one never can tell beforehand how a writer's meaning may be misapprehended, & I find some people gather from it that I have become strictly orthodox (rather funny, this!) when I thought my meaning to be clear enough that some form of Established ritual & discipline should be maintained in the interests of morality, without entering into the very large question of what that form should be: I should say offhand that it might be some ethical service based on the old liturgy.

Yes: the Romanists had a fine chance, but let it slip: & I fear the English Church may do the same if it doesn't mind. The mediaevalists are the danger: if they succeed in harking back to transubstantiation, plenary inspiration, etc. the Church becomes a sect, & all is undone. I don't know whether you are old enough to have known a friend of mine now long dead—St George Mivart—He was one of the new Catholics; but was extinguished.

Amusing things happen if you write poems: a critic—an old friend of mine by the way, who has grown cantankerous of late—Maurice Hewlett, said that "The Wood Fire" was "revolting": almost at the same time that a quite old fashioned rector near here told me he was interested in it because it was "probably what happened"—seeing nothing shocking in it at all, & thinking it the view of a sturdy Protestant that would tend to counteract any belief in fragments of the "true Cross."

I wonder if you went up to the wedding of Dorothy's daughter: Florence did, but I did not, & she saw all sorts of people there she knew.

Ever affectionately
Thomas Hardy.

the Poems: Late Lyrics and Earlier.   *a fine chance*: TH apparently means that the Roman Catholic Church had begun to move towards a more liberal theology but then reversed itself; St George Jackson Mivart (1827–1900), a distinguished biologist, was excommunicated shortly before his death for having publicly repudiated the authority of the Church.   *Hewlett*: he had reviewed *Late Lyrics*, including 'The Wood Fire', in *The Times*, 8 June. The 'old fashioned rector' has not been confidently identified.   *the wedding*: Dorothy Allhusen's elder daughter Madeleine was married to Geoffrey Cecil Congreve, RN, on 14 Oct.

To Lucy Clifford

11 November. 1922

Dear Mrs Clifford:

Alas, you are asking me to do what is mentally—& almost physically—impossible to a person of 82. It would be, in fact, beyond my powers even if I were familiar with your once much discussed book; but I am ashamed to confess that I have never read it! What you heard must have been the version of the circumstance that Lord Houghton was enthusiastic about the novel, & that I was going to read it immediately. I remember the Jeunes' dinner-party when he was eulogizing it all round. I had never heard of it till then, & my intention was to get it at once. But we know where there is a pavement of good intentions.

It is as much as I can do nowadays to find energy to put out a small poem once in a while, & I have to get the greater part of my correspondence done by another. Thus to read the story critically now for the first time would be beyond me.

So you will see that it is not a question of willingness or otherwise, but of practicability, & not one of the many requests for the same kind of thing that I get have I declined with such regret. Your publisher is probably right in saying that a preface would help a new edition, but I think he is in error in supposing that it being by myself is of any importance, as I have been outside the world of novels for more than 25 years, & know nothing of present movements in it. One of the young advanced novelists would be the man for you.

Thank you much for kind inquiries. We have been fairly

well, though with slight colds. The history of the adventures of your first book, & the Browning incident, is most interesting. In my own similar case I lost all my labour & £15 in money!

With our kind love & good wishes.

Yours very sincerely

The book & reviews shall follow in a day or two. My wife is reading the former. T.H.

never read it!: Lucy Clifford, in a letter of 8 Nov., asked TH to supply a preface for a reissue of her first novel *Mrs. Keith's Crime* (1885), explaining that her publisher believed only TH's name would be 'big enough' to ensure commercial success and that both TH and Lord Houghton were reported as having praised the novel while dining with Francis and Mary Jeune just after its original publication.　　*the Browning incident*: according to Mrs Clifford, Robert Browning had congratulated her, warmly and publicly, on having published a 'splendid book' that he wished he had written himself.　　*my own similar case*: TH had been obliged to share the costs of publication of his first novel *Desperate Remedies*, losing slightly more than £15 in the process.　　*Yours very sincerely*: the text is that of TH's unsigned draft.

To Sir Frederick Macmillan

Private.　　　　　MAX GATE, | DORCHESTER. | 22 Nov: 1922

My dear Macmillan:

Have you, in your large experience of authors, any idea of the general practice of that irritable genus in respect of autographing books for strangers? I am pestered by large parcels of my own volumes from unknown people for this purpose. For instance I have just received a package of half a dozen from Lady Sackville, a total stranger (Christian name Victoria—I fancy I recall a law-suit in connection with her) & she intends to send them *all* by degrees (!), the request being that I write in each "To Lady Sackville—Thomas Hardy", as if she were a dear friend.

In these cases the alternatives are to throw them into a cupboard & take no notice (which brings a pelting of letters of inquiry), to send them back unsigned, or to say that I will sign them (with autograph only; I could not say they are from me, as I did not present them) for a fee of a guinea, or half a guinea, each to be given to our County Hospital here, of which I am a governor, or to some other charity I choose. I have adopted each plan at various times; but as these parcels increase I have to reconsider methods, which is why I write.

There is an amusing side to it all, of course; & don't trouble to answer till you are inclined to.

Sincerely yours
Thomas Hardy.

Lady Sackville: Josephine Victoria Sackville-West (1862–1936), wife of the 3rd Baron Sackville, mother of Victoria ('Vita') Sackville-West, the writer and gardener; the case recalled by TH was probably the more recent of the two in which she was involved, a successful defence in 1913 of her right to receive money, furniture, and pictures under the will of Sir John Murray Scott.   *till you are inclined to*: Macmillan replied the next day, approving the idea of charging a fee in support of the County Hospital, and this plan was adopted in the letter—drafted by TH, typed and signed by FEH— which was sent to Lady Sackville on 25 Nov. She replied that she was only too pleased to send the two guineas, and in Mar. 1923 TH received from her another two guineas and four more books to be signed.

To Sir Hamo Thornycroft

Max Gate | 8 Jan: 1923

My dear Thornycroft:

I am much interested in the photograph of your model that you have sent—also in the illustrations showing the Memorial at Dunstable. The figure at the top is striking, & forms, of course, the best finish to such designs: but unfortunately few corporations can afford it.

Curiously enough the model of Charing Cross illustrates the part of London with which I was most familiar for between 5 & 6 years when I was a young man. I knew the spot when Hungerford Market was still standing (where Charing Cross Hotel is now,) & used to lunch there. It was quite Dickens's London in those days. I saw the iron bridge

built, from the windows of 8 Adelphi Terrace where I was, &
saw the first barge load of earth thrown into the water to form
the Embankment.

I don't gather whether your plan would sweep away that
Terrace, so familiar to me; but some plan or other will, no
doubt, before very long. Old Northumberland House went to
make room for the Avenue—destroyed unnecessarily, it was
said afterwards.

You will probably develope your model still further. If I
were you I should put in more detail, so as to make it clearer
to the man in the street. However you will know best about
that.

My wife has just come home from Surrey, & joins with me
in sending best New Years wishes to you & the household.
We have not heard from Gosse for ages, but conclude that he
is flourishing, as he always is.

> Always sincerely yrs
> Thomas Hardy.

Thornycroft: William Hamo Thornycroft (1850–1925), sculptor, knighted
1917; he was a close friend of Edmund Gosse's and had known TH for
many years.   *your model . . . Memorial*: Thornycroft had sent TH some
newspaper cuttings of a war memorial he had designed and a photograph
of his model of a proposed new layout of the entire Charing Cross area of
central London, known intimately to TH when he was working for Arthur
Blomfield in the 1860s.   *from Surrey*: she had been visiting Florence
Henniker at Epsom.

To Amy Lowell

MAX GATE, | DORCHESTER. | 7th. March 1923.

Dear Miss Amy Lowell:

"I do remember my faults this day".—Never have I
acknowledged receiving that book of American Poetry at the
end of last year with your charming inscription, although I
read as much as I could of it when it arrived. This "could"
by the way, has a sinister ambiguity that I did not mean; I
merely alluded to spare time. I read all *your* pieces anyhow,
and much like "The Swans".

Edna Millay seems the most promising of the younger poets, don't you think? As to the free verse which appears so frequently in the volume, I suppose I am too old to do it justice. You manage it best; but do you mind my saying that it too often seems a jumble of notes containing ideas striking, novel, or beautiful, as the case may be, which could be transfused into poetry, but which, as given, are not poetry? I could not undergo an examination on why (to me) they seem not. Perhaps because there is no expectation raised of a response in sound or beat, and the pleasure of its gratification, as in regular poetry; which only ancient poetry, like the English Bible, is able to dispense with because of its other character of antiquity.

As for myself, I am rather perplexed by letters I get on whether readers can have a difficulty in obtaining my books of verse in the United States, particularly "The Dynasts" complete in one volume (green, published by Macmillans). If you or any friend should be in a book store any day, and would not mind asking if they keep that edition, or if it is readily obtainable, I shall be greatly obliged. It is so difficult to get information through the publishers and booksellers themselves. With best wishes for your poetry and yourself,

Believe me,

Your affectionate friend,
Thomas Hardy.

faults this day": an apparent allusion to the version of Ps. 51: 3 in the Book of Common Prayer; the unacknowledged book was *American Poetry 1922: A Miscellany* (1922), containing seven poems by Lowell and eight sonnets by Edna St Vincent Millay (see letter of 4 Apr. 1927).

To Sydney Cockerell

MAX GATE, | DORCHESTER. | 14 April: 1923

My dear Cockerell:

The Country Dances have come, but no bill with them. I hope you have not paid for them, as they must have cost a lot, & I can't let you stand the price, which would be a poor result to you from a casual conversation. So please let me know what has happened.

I have not examined them much yet. Several of the tunes are those I used to play as a boy from my father's & grandfather's books: & several I have not seen before.

In the Folk-Song book, the one you have marked, called "The Keys of Canterbury" has much the same words as the dramatic performance for three characters that we used to call "O Jan, O Jan, O Jan", which I told you of, & have somewhere written out,
[Domestic interruption of 2 hours (a caller to lunch)]
so far as I could remember it, & will look for some day. The ending, containing the lover's last proposal, which wins her, is much tamer than ours was. Like so many of these old songs & dialogues it had a rather broad double-entendre in it, quite Shakespearean, at which the men used to laugh, some of the women smirk, others stiffen, & wh. others wd paraphrase for domestic performance. As a child I knew only the paraphrase (much like the version you send), but in after years the original dawned upon me, & I no longer wondered why my father smiled when it happened to be enacted in his presence. However I must stop this: the subject can be revived when we meet.

F. & I want to go to a meeting this afternoon to hear about ominous cracks in Salisbury Cathedral. Christopher & Mrs Moule called yesterday, with Sir R. Williams & his daughter, with whom they are staying. Many thanks for sending the books. I would finish this page but my eyes are giving out.

Always sincerely
Thomas Hardy.

Country Dances: Cockerell had visited Novello & Co., the music publishers, and arranged for TH to be sent a selection of the country-dance and folk-song music they had in print; the 'books' TH recalled from his boyhood were the old music-books used by his father and grandfather as members of the Stinsford 'quire', evoked in *Under the Greenwood Tree*.   *written out*: TH's version of 'O Jan, O Jan, O Jan', described as 'a Recension of a Wessex Folk-Piece', was performed by the Hardy Players later in the year. *Moule*: the Revd Arthur Christopher Moule (1873–1957) and his wife Mabel, née Wollaston; Moule, a grandson of the Revd Henry Moule, was vicar of Trumpington, near Cambridge, and subsequently professor of

Chinese Language and History at Cambridge University. *Williams*: Colonel Sir Robert Williams, Bt. (1848–1943), Conservative MP for West Dorset 1895–1922, and his youngest daughter Dorothy Rhoda.

To Arthur Benson

MAX GATE, | DORCHESTER. | 8 May 1923

My dear Dr Benson:

I am much pleased to see your handwriting again, & to know that your health & energies have got into their normal stride. It is very strange—that overclouding of one's mind at times—when one seems to have nothing physically the matter at all. I used to get such clouds more often than I do now. They must of course be based on something corporeal: what you tell me about the attack of neuritis bears out a suspicion I have had for a long time, that diseases transmute themselves, but don't ever take an absolute departure. I have suggested to doctors to write a book on these transmutations for the use of ordinary people; but they don't seem to warm up to the idea.

It is pleasant to hear that the Bp. of Salisbury is to be admitted to an Hon. Fellowship. I should much like to be present, for I hear delightful things about him, & it seems in every way appropriate when we think of his own personal qualifications, & his brother's too early Severance from the offices at Cambridge that he filled so well. Oddly enough, though I have known the occupants of the See of Sarum ever since I was confirmed by one of them, I don't know the new bishop.

I am, "in a manner of spaiking"—as they say here—quite well: nevertheless I feel an increasing burden in little things which have intrinsically no weight at all, & my eyes are often very weak, which is no wonder. Please don't be tempted to put on too much pace now that you feel you can do it. My wife sends her kindest regards, & I am,

Always yours
Thomas Hardy.

Benson: Arthur Christopher Benson (1862–1925), man of letters, master of Magdalene College, Cambridge, of which TH was an honorary fellow; he had been recovering slowly from a mental breakdown and suggested in his letter of 6 May that his last neuritis attack had 'shifted the poisonous elements away from the brain into the much less important leg'.　*Bp. of Salisbury*: the current bishop, St Clair George Alfred Donaldson (1863–1935), was the brother of the late Revd Stuart Alexander Donaldson, formerly master of Magdalene and vice-chancellor of the university.

To Walter de la Mare

MAX GATE, | DORCHESTER. | 28 June: 1923

My dear Mr de la Mare:

We have just returned from a sojourn in "the home of lost causes"—Oxford, & I find, among other of my negligences, that I have not yet answered your letter of the 14th—in which you very kindly point out to me a channel through which I may possibly extend the circulation of my verses in America. It happened very oddly that just after your letter had arrived a literary gentleman from the U.S. called here, & I enquired of him how my poetry books were getting on over there. He says that within the last twelvemonths their circulation has much improved, & that they are quite accessible everywhere now, though till lately they were not—a statement corroborated by Miss Amy Lowell, to whom I had put the same question a short time back. So that at present I think I may as well leave things alone & see what happens. If I should want another publisher on that side the one you mention would seem to be excellent.

We should immensely like you to be at Weymouth for a few days. A good many trippers are there in August, but after all they are a harmless folk: & we could show you some lodgings in quarters they don't frequent.

As to what friends say about "Seaton's Aunt"—well, I shouldn't listen to them. It is a *splendidly gruesome* story: & I always feel that a man should write what he can write best: if you have a bass voice they must accept bass from you, & not be perpetually wanting you to sing treble. That's my plan, anyhow.

We enjoyed ourselves at Oxford very much—living in
College (Queen's) & we went there & came back entirely by
road. My wife sends her love to Mrs de la Mare, & I am
always

Sincerely yours
Thomas Hardy.

We called on Masefield at Oxford. He lives on Boar's Hill, a
little way out, & has *a haunted house* immediately opposite him!
T.H.

lost causes": quoted—here and in Part II, ch. 1, of *Jude the Obscure*—from the
Preface to Matthew Arnold's *Essays in Criticism* (1865); the Hardys went to
Oxford as the guests of Queen's College, which had recently elected TH to
an honorary fellowship.   *a short time back*: see letter of 7 Mar. 1923.
one you mention: de la Mare had suggested that his own publisher, Alfred A.
Knopf, should bring out a selection of TH's poems in the United States.
"Seaton's Aunt": included in *The Riddle and Other Stories* (1923); de la Mare
had complained that reviewers were calling his stories 'morbid'.

[Although recent criticism has tended to ignore Hardy's one-
act verse-drama *The Famous Tragedy of the Queen of Cornwall*, it
attracted much attention upon its first appearance in November 1923 and was certainly important to Hardy himself, partly
at least because he associated its Tintagel setting with his first
wife, whom he had first met at nearby St Juliot more than fifty
years earlier. He took an active interest in the physical
appearance of the first edition, in the original stage production
by the Hardy Players, and in Rutland Boughton's adaptation
of it as a 'music-drama' performed at the Glastonbury
Festival.]

To Harold Child

MAX GATE, | DORCHESTER. | November 11. 1923.

Dear Mr Child:
    It is very good of The Times to think of sending such a
competent critic as yourself for the performance of my little

play on Nov. 28. and I only can hope that you will not be disappointed in it.

The criticism will be a comparatively easy job, as the play is to be published by Messrs Macmillan on the 15th. (three days after you get this), so that you can be familiar with it beforehand. A copy would naturally be sent to the Supplement for review—must have been, in fact, sent by this time—but I should like you to read it for your self, which will take only a quarter of an hour, being but in one act.

The points that will probably strike you are these (if any!)—that the unities are strictly preserved, whatever virtue there may be in that. (I myself am oldfashioned enough to think there *is* a virtue in it, if it can be done without artificiality. The only other case I remember attempting it in was The Return of the Native). The original events could have been enacted in the time taken by the performance, and they continue unbroken throughout. The changes of scene are denoted by the change of persons present on the stage, there being no change of background.

My temerity in pulling together into the space of an hour events that in the traditional story covered a long time will doubtless be punished by the reviewers of the book. But there are so many versions of the famous romance that I felt free to adapt it to my purposes in any way—as, in fact, the Greek dramatists did in their plays—notably Euripides.

Wishing it to be thoroughly English I have dropped the name of Chorus for the conventional onlookers, and called them Chanters, though they play the part of a Greek chorus. I have also made them ghosts (I don't for the moment recall an instance of this in a Greek play), and it will be amusing to see how our local amateurs here will acquit themselves in this very difficult business. Whether the lady ghosts will submit to have their faces whitened I don't know! They have by the way, got a very promising lady, Mrs Hirst, to take the part of the Queen, who though a cultivated woman is strictly a local amateur. They have also a very good Tristram in the person of a local doctor.

I have tried to avoid turning the rude personages of, say, the fifth century, into respectable Victorians, as was done by Tennyson, Swinburne, Arnold, &c. On the other hand it would have been impossible to present them as they really were, with their barbaric manners and surroundings.

It is the first time I have ever written a play for the Dorchester players, but I had promised them one for years, and so made this piece serve the purpose. You will see that I have flown in the face of custom by saying on the title page that no theatre is required! Our players here, however, will have none of that, as they love all the conventions of the stage, and will duly maintain them.

They tell me there is to be a full-dress rehearsal about 8 on the Tuesday evening preceding the first performance on Wednesday night the 28th. You will be welcome at either or both. I don't know which evening you will come, but my wife says I am to tell you that we shall be glad to see you here to tea on either afternoon, or to an early dinner (no dress), or both. We wish we could put you up for the night, but unfortunately our servants are in rebellion, and we are largely dependent on charwomen, added to which I am in a worse state of health than I have been in all the year, though it is nothing serious.

Any particulars that I am ignorant of will be given you privately by the Hon. Secretary Mr H. A. Martin, 4 Alexandra Villas, Dorchester—also programme—I enclose the advertisement in the local paper.

Sincerely yours
Th: Hardy.

P.S. Mr Martin has just called here. He says that there will be also a rehearsal on Monday the 26th. at 7.30. Should you be able to come to that he thinks it would be quieter than on the Tuesday, when they are invaded by photographers etc. I shall be at the Monday one. On that night, by the way, we could accommodate you without inconvenience.

He also says that if you come to a rehearsal only, and not to the first night, he could telegraph the fact that the performance actually took place, &c. T.H.

little play: Child's review of the Dorchester production of *The Queen of Cornwall* appeared in *The Times*, 29 Nov. 1923; the *Times Literary Supplement* reviewed the published text on 17 Nov.   *Mrs Hirst*: Kathleen Mary Hirst; the doctor was Edgar Wilmot Smerdon.   *Tennyson, Swinburne,*

Arnold, &c.: TH presumably has in mind Tennyson's *Idylls of the King*, Swinburne's *Tristram of Lyonesse*, and Matthew Arnold's 'Tristram and Iseult'.   *Martin*: Henry Austin Martin was a Dorchester auctioneer.

To John Middleton Murry

MAX GATE, | DORCHESTER. | 28 March 1924

Dear Mr Middleton Murry:

I am not sure whether you have started yet, or not, on your circular tour of our little lump of earth; probably not. (I remember that as a child I used to think a journey round the world, which appealed much to my imagination, meant that the traveller went in an exact circle the exact distance of 24,000 miles. What a pity that we lose these ideal views.)

However, that is not what I am sending you a line upon, which is to say that we have been much interested in your brilliant little article in The Adelphi about Mr George Moore; though it is rather like the amber enclosing the fly, for till lately I had only heard of him & his doings very vaguely, & I have not seen this book or his. Nor have I set eyes on him more than once or twice in my life; but I once answered a letter of his, about, I think, copyright, with great civility, as I supposed. Yet this attack is obviously personal. And I know hardly anything of his writings, for one makes, half unconsciously, a mental list of writers that are negligible, & I included him among them—with great relief, under the growing pressure of books that *must* be read.

I doubt if he was worth such good powder & shot as you give him!

I have occasionally wondered why the English press is so afraid of Mr Moore. It speaks of him always with bated breath, when I should have thought him to be the most tempting sport among present day detractors for robust critics. Somebody once called him a putrid literary hermaphrodite, which I thought funny, but it may have been an exaggeration.

The reviewers, so far as I have seen, have timidly waited till you came along to show at any rate that (to change the image) this lion, so great at roaring, is only Snug the Joiner: so perhaps the press will no longer be terrified.

To return to where I began, I hope you will have a good journey, whenever it may come off, & whithersoever it may be. I am,

Always sincerely yours

Thomas Hardy.

Murry: John Middleton Murry (1889–1957), critic and author; he had in fact abandoned his projected round-the-world tour.   *George Moore*: the long-standing hostility between TH and Moore had recently surfaced in the latter's *Conversations in Ebury Street* (1924), prompting Murry to defend TH in the Apr. 1924 *Adelphi*, of which he was the editor.   *lion . . . Joiner*: *A Midsummer Night's Dream*, v. i.

To Sir Henry Newbolt

MAX GATE, | DORCHESTER. | 8 April 1924

My dear Newbolt:

I don't at all mind your quoting the whole of each of the four poems you mention, in the book you are preparing— which sounds rather an interesting one by the way—& I don't think the publishers will mind either, as the pieces are among those you included in your previous book. If they say anything I will explain, but I am sure they won't.

Personally I prefer the whole of a poem to be quoted. A d—d good natured reviewer who was bent on proving me a pessimist—blessed word—at all costs, cooked up my little love-poem called "I travel as a phantom now" into one of irreligious despair by leaving out the last verse, a bit of ingenuity which did him credit if you leave honesty out of the argument.

Whenever you are motoring in this direction later in the spring you must of course call here. We are still living on in the same dull way, to outsiders, & shall be delighted to see you.

As to my views on things in general, everything is so uncertain in Politics, Literature, Religion, Science, & Art (to use the words they display at the head of Reviews) that I have forsworn opinions, & merely wait to see what happens. It saves a lot of trouble, & is a waiting that cannot, in the circumstances, be so long as to be tedious.

Our kindest remembrances to you both. I am

Always sincerely yours
Thomas Hardy.

book you are preparing: in the event, Newbolt's anthology, *The Tide of Time in English Poetry* (1925), included only two poems by TH; his previous book was *An English Anthology of Prose and Poetry* (1921).   *things in general*: Newbolt had expressed an interest in TH's political views.

To J. H. Morgan

MAX GATE, | DORCHESTER. | 21 April: 1924

Dear General Morgan:

I have read the second article, & of course was much interested in it. You raise up the shade of J.M. as vividly as the Witch of Endor did Saul's.

You will not expect me to agree with all his views & yours. For instance, there is in my opinion a real hope that the League of Nations may result in something—for a reason which, apparently (I say it with great deference) neither Lord M. nor yourself perceived, or at least cared to consider—the self-interest of mankind. Principalities & powers will discern more & more clearly that each personality in them stands himself to lose by war, notwithstanding a promise of gain at first, & this thought will damp prime movers down to moderation. Neither do I think with Ld M. that the poverty of Ireland is entirely, or mainly, owing to the English. At bottom it is the temperament of the people that has caused it, & will, I fear, perpetuate it—much as I regret my conclusion, for they are a romantic & generous people.

Many thanks for the Review. I hope you keep well, & am

Sincerely yours
Thomas Hardy.

second article: Morgan's 'The Personality of Lord Morley. II', *Quarterly Review*, Apr. 1924; the first article had appeared in the Jan. number. *Saul's*: TH means 'Samuel's'; see letter of 30 June 1920.

To Ernest Brennecke

MAX GATE, | DORCHESTER. | 21st. June 1924.

Dear Mr Brennecke:

I am sorry to find that I did not acknowledge to you the receipt of your book, as well as to the publisher. My secretary said she believed I had done so, but her memory must have been at fault.

As for the book itself, I should imagine that it had been fairly well received in this country, and probably will be in America. I saw a criticism which remarked that it was a little too much like a treatise on Schopenhauer with notes on Hardy, and though that was a humorous exaggeration, what the critic meant, I suppose, was that Schopenhauer's was too largely dwelt upon to the exclusion of other philosophies apparent in my writings to represent me truly—that, as my pages show harmony of view with Darwin, Huxley, Spencer, Comte, Hume, Mill, and others (all of whom, as a matter of fact, I used to read more than Sch.) my kinship with them should have been mentioned as well as with him. Personally I have nothing to say on this point, though I share their opinion to some extent.

You are quite right in asserting in the footnote at page 71 that I have never been influenced by Bergson. I had written a good deal before Bergson was heard of, and I have never accepted him as a thinker, his views seeming to me to be only a re-hashing of the old creed of Dualism.

By the way, a passage which struck me as odd was on page 70 where you state that I make great men "give utterance to the tendencies of the Will", and quote Pitt's words as an instance. You will be surprised to hear that those words of Pitt were literally those he used!—his last public ones—before Schopenhauer was heard of.

The paragraph on pp. 75, 76, which states that a principle

of Schopenhauer was adhered to in my use of small incidents, &c. seems an attempt to trace imitation of him in a purely accidental resemblance (if any). Such details were given because I possessed them, with no thought of any philosophy. This tendency to find influence in chance likenesses occurs frequently elsewhere, as for instance, at page 15. The "Overworld" scenes were a pure inventioon: I had no knowledge of anything of the sort in Schopenhauer. Also p. 67. "His fondness for endowing inanimate objects", &c. But every poet and every child does it!

You must not, however, suppose that I am telling you all this by way of complaint. By comparison with the extraordinary things that are said about books of mine by others, yours are venial sins. I simply mention them in case you should ever recast your volume.

I enclose a list of a few misprints which caught my eye, as you may like to have them pointed out.

If you come to England again we shall be pleased to receive a call from you, and with thanks for the book I am

Yours very truly,
Thomas Hardy.

Brennecke: Ernest Brennecke, jun. (1896–1969), American critic and university teacher; a copy of his *Thomas Hardy's Universe: A Study of a Poet's Mind* (1924) had reached TH from its English publisher in May.   *My secretary*: May O'Rourke (1897–1978), poet, and occasional secretary at Max Gate. *Bergson*: for TH's views on Bergson see letters of 2 Feb. and 16 Mar. 1915. *Pitt's words*: in *The Dynasts*, Part First, v. 5.   *principle of Schopenhauer*: defined by Brennecke (p. 75) as 'the portrayal of the smallest incident as a true mirror of the government of the universe'. On p. 15 Brennecke insists that 'the "Overworld" scenes of *The Dynasts* could not possibly have been composed if Schopenhauer had not previously written *Die Welt als Wille und Vorstellung*', and on p. 67 he links with Schopenhauer's 'teleological view of nature' TH's 'fondness for endowing even inanimate objects with personalities and making them as essential parts of his stories as the human agents'.

To Arthur Benson

MAX GATE, | DORCHESTER. | 27 Sept. 1924

My dear Benson:

I should have answered your welcome letter earlier in the week if it had not chanced to be a week of anxiety with us. My wife has to undergo a surgical operation in the next few days, which, though we are assured it is not dangerous, is serious. We had been hoping it would not be necessary, till lately the doctors have said that it must be done. They are men of the best repute in London, & it is at any rate well to think that there is no alternative, in their judgment. So we must hope for the best.

Although I know by hearsay the house you are in I have never been inside it. I remember thinking it strange that Henry James, who told me once that he could not live at Bournemouth because of the dull clubless evenings, should have gone to what I suppose from a society man's point of view, was a duller place.

Yes: Gosse is wonderfully young for his age. I hope he is not doing too much journeywork, & indeed I don't see why he should turn himself into such a journalist as he has done: his writing is too good & distinctive to be run through quickly in a newspaper.

I am glad to hear that Magdalene is flourishing: if the war had not come how many times I should have visited it! But that senseless event made all my plans gang agley, & after it was over I felt too old to get about much.

The author of the book on Ld Palmerston whom you mention as a bye-fellow, would perhaps be surprised to know that I once heard P. speak in the H. of Commons: not only so but make an atrocious pun, (to which he was much given in his later years).

The early memories of which you write are certainly not so poignant as the intermediate & nearer ones. I am close to the spots of my childish memories (though far from my middle-age scenes), & I revive them very often by going to "a slope of green access" about a mile from here, finding no pain in so doing.

I trust you will get back to Cambridge with renewed
vigour, & am

Most sincerely yours
Thomas Hardy.

the house you are in: Lamb House, Rye, formerly the home of Henry James.
Magdalene: Magdalene College, Cambridge, of which Benson was master,
and TH an honorary fellow; the bye-fellow and author of *The Triumph of
Lord Palmerston* (1924) was Basil Kingsley Martin (1897–1969), later editor
of the *New Statesman and Nation*.   *gang agley*: an allusion to Robert Burns's
'To a Mouse'.   *of green access"*: *Adonais*, st. 49; Shelley's reference is to
Keats's grave in the Protestant Cemetery in Rome, TH's to the Hardy
family graves in Stinsford churchyard.

[While Florence was away in London, undergoing an operation for the removal of a tumour in her neck, Hardy remained
at Max Gate, looking after Wessex, the troublesome dog to
which they (if not their friends and neighbours) were both
devoted, and participating in the preparations for the
Dorchester production of *Tess of the d'Urbervilles*. Since Hardy
had for the first time supplied the Hardy Players with his own
dramatization of one of his novels, and since *Tess* was both
famous and more than a little controversial, local excitement
ran extremely high. Hardy himself was unusually—and in
Florence's view, unhealthily—excited by the prospect of
seeing in performance a version that had remained unper-
formed since he first prepared it in the mid-1890s and especially by the knowledge that the heroine would be played by
Gertrude Bugler, a local actress of great beauty and consider
able talent in whom he claimed to find his original conception
of Tess Durbeyfield ideally embodied. Hardy's attraction to
Gertrude Bugler aroused great and, indeed, excessive jealousy
on Florence's part, and when it was later suggested that Mrs
Bugler should take the leading role in a London production of
the play, it was Florence who begged and bullied her into
declining the offer.]

To Florence Hardy

Sunday—noon— [5 October 1924]

My dearest F:

I have been out with Wess, who is submitting with a good grace to the force of circumstances. Did I tell you that a telegram came from the W. Dispatch asking you to give my reasons for my keeping back the Tess play for 30 years?— Miss O'R shall answer tomorrow that you are unable to reply as you are away from home. I don't know how you feel as to *when* you can return. If you feel you cannot at the end of this week (& I imagine it will be rather too early) shall I write to the gardener & his wife saying that they are not to come for a few days, but will be paid from date just the same?

K. came in to tea last evening. She thinks the idea a very good one that H. & Voss shd fetch you, & went on home to discuss it with H. There may be a letter from her by this same post telling you further what they think. She says H's car is so well springed that it wd not shake you. If this is carried out the idea of my fetching you by train wd fall through, of course.

Mr Niven called yesty aftn to inquire. I did not see him, but Nelly told him you were getting on well. Mr Tilley called in the evening to discuss Tess play. He doubts if he will not have to put it off till February, on account of possible general election, & difficulties with the parts. Gertrude B. is rather dismayed at the bigness of hers—& says she does not like the Tess of the play so well as the Tess of the book (which is intelligent criticism). Tilley says the physical strain on her will be very great, & we are thinking of the possibility of giving her some rests between.

I hope the envelope I posted yesterday with several letters &c. in it, & mine, did not burst? I ought to have used a stronger one.

I do not know whether H. & Voss cd go up for you & back in one day. T. H. Tilley says they *could* do it, but it wd be a heavy journey. They *might* go up the afternoon before, & stay at the West Central Hotel. But as they cd start from here at daybreak I think they cd do it in the same day. I will finish this later.

4.0 p.m. It has come on to be a very wet afternoon though it was a beautiful morning on Froom Hill. Nobody has called, & W. is on the hearthrug & I by the fire. There is a disabled motor-van by the gate between the cottage & the directing post. Two collided at 10 o'clock last night, but nobody seems to have been injured, though I am not sure—The leaves are beginning to come down rather fast, & Caddy has planted the little macrocarpus in the corner we looked at. I hope you sleep well. I must have an umbrella to post this.

Ever

T.

Wess: the dog Wessex, referred as 'W.' in the final paragraph; TH also abbreviates May O'Rourke, Kate Hardy, Henry Hardy, and Gertrude Bugler.   *W. Dispatch*: the *Weekly Dispatch*, a London Sunday newspaper for which FEH sometimes wrote.   *Voss . . . Niven . . . Nelly*: Harold Lionel Voss was a chauffeur often employed by the Hardys, the Revd George Cecil Niven the rector of St Peter's, Dorchester, and Ellen (Nelly) Elizabeth Titterington the Max Gate parlourmaid.   *Mr Tilley*: Thomas Henry Tilley (1864–1944), Dorchester alderman and producer for the Hardy Players; the general election of 29 Oct. seems not in fact to have affected the Dorchester performances of *Tess* in late Nov.   *Caddy*: the Max Gate gardener.

To Thomas J. Wise

MAX GATE, | DORCHESTER. | 24 Oct: 1924

Dear Mr Wise:

Many thanks for the fifth volume. It is, I think, the most interesting of the lot, including as it does such two extremes as Shelley & Sheridan. Mary's letter, with its spectral details of her home experiences when Shelley was drowned, is engrossing & moving.

You probably know that Mr Sheridan who lives near here—the direct descendant of R.B.S., has the manuscrips of all his plays.

Very truly yours

Thomas Hardy.

Wise: Thomas James Wise (1859–1937), collector, bibliographer, and forger, had for several years been sending TH copies of his publications, including the successive volumes of *The Ashley Library: A Catalogue of Printed Books, Manuscripts, and Autograph Letters*, printed in editions of 200 copies only. Mary Shelley's letter of 15 Aug. 1822 to Maria Gisborne is quoted in full in the volume TH had just received.   *manuscripts of all his plays*: Wise's prompt reply of 25 Oct., requesting (Algernon) Sheridan's full name and address (see letter of 1 June 1889), was left unanswered by TH.

To J. H. Morgan

MAX GATE, | DORCHESTER. | 1 Dec. 1924

Dear General Morgan;

The Morley book duly arrived, & I have read it through. I would not write till I had done so, &, as you may have guessed from the newspaper reports of the play just produced here, we have been much occupied with rehearsals, &c., for though I did not mean to have anything to do with the staging I was insensibly drawn in. However it was an amusing little experience, & I don't regret it.

I see Morley more clearly in your pages than I could do in his own reminiscences, which seemed to aim at keeping him invisible. There is a good deal more, I find, in this volume than in the Quarterly articles. I don't notice any error to speak of in your report of my words: I believe I said "The Sporting Times" instead of "The Pink 'Un", but that is the merest trifle. I may mention that "Frederic Harrison" is misprinted "Frederick Harrison" on p. 17.

As for Gladstone, who fills large spaces on your paper, you leave the question of his theology as much of a mystery as ever. It is almost impossible to believe a man with his intellectual curiosity & penetration to be blind to the puerilities that stare out from dogma when investigated, & yet by some sort of super-casuistry he upheld them. Even those who do not admire Mr G. can hardly think his eccelesiasticism a mask, to retain the church party politically.

Now that Morley is gone I wish I had visited him oftener. How well I remember his look—quite boyish—when I first met him in his chambers in 1868 or 1869.

With my thanks for the book & the inscription believe me
Sincerely yours
Thomas Hardy.

Morley book: Morgan's *John, Viscount Morley: An Appreciation and Some Reminiscences* (1924); for the *Quarterly Review* articles see letter of 21 Apr. 1924. TH had read Morley's own *Recollections* soon after they were published in 1917.   *merest trifle*: both were newspapers devoted to horse-racing and similar topics; on p. 31 of his book Morgan quotes TH as saying that Morley 'seemed to draw an invisible ermine about him as though he were a sporting peer who never read anything but the *Pink 'Un*'.   *first met him*: see letter of 10 Sept. 1868.

To Gertrude Bugler

MAX GATE, | DORCHESTER. | 16 Dec. 1924

My dear Mrs Bugler:

I think I ought to send you a copy of the letter I have written to Mr Harrison of the Haymarket Theatre in reply to his, which I read to you when you were here. This will let you know exactly how matters stand, in case he should write to you.

But forgive my saying that I don't quite like the idea of your going to London (if this comes to anything, which it may not). We are so proud of you down here that we wish to keep you for ourselves, so that you may be known as the Wessex actress who does not care to go away, & who makes Londoners come to her. I fancy Capt. Bugler will agree with me in this. However, you must have your own way I suppose.

Mrs Doyle Jones called next morning after Weymouth. She is coming to Kingston Russell at Easter, & will communicate with you about sitting to her. As she has a car there will be no trouble in her getting across to you. She said that why we could not find her after the performance, to introduce her to you, was that her face was so bleared with crying that she was ashamed to let us see her, & ran off to the hotel. That was your doing, young lady! There were a good many other wet handkerchiefs besides hers.

Yesterday I received a letter from the Mayor of Bournemouth informing me that he was going to lay before the General Purposes Committee the question of your giving a performance of Tess in Bournemouth. On this he says he is going to write again.

We hope to see you later on.

Your affectionate friend
Thomas Hardy.

The enclosed scrap from The Times may amuse you. Don't trouble to return either the letter or scrap. T.H.

Bugler: Gertrude Adelia Bugler, née Bugler (b. 1897); she married her cousin Ernest Frank Bugler, MC, in 1921.   *Harrison*: see next letter.
Mrs Doyle Jones: the married name of Vivien Gribble (d. 1932), the book illustrator, whose father lived in Dorset at Kingston Russell house; she was supplying the woodcuts for an illustrated edition of *Tess* and TH had suggested that she should see one of the Weymouth performances of the play and perhaps use Gertrude Bugler as her model.   *in Bournemouth*: this scheme did not materialize.   *enclosed scrap*: a photograph, cut from *The Times* of 13 Dec., showing Gertrude Bugler seated next to TH at a dinner given between the two performances of *Tess* at Weymouth on 11 Dec.

To Sir James Barrie

MAX GATE, | DORCHESTER. | 19 Dec: 1924

My dear Barrie:

Mr Frederick Harrison seems inclined to try Mrs Gertrude Bugler in *Tess* at some matinées—(Granville Barker, by the way, says he should put the play in the evening bill straight off, people being so interested in it on account of the press notices that it would be a safe venture: however, this is a point for Mr Harrison's judgment). He, F.H., asks me to refer him to my agent for terms. Now I am a child in all this, but, as you are an ancient, can you tell me of any agent? Or, if I were not ashamed to trouble you, I should say, will you pronounce *ex cathedra* whatever arrangement would be fair in the circumstances, & so make an end of it.

I don't care much what I get (if anything), so long as she

gets whatever can be expected for a novice beyond the chance of a performance in London.

As I may have told you, I have known her from girlhood, & though I don't want to begin playwriting at my time of life, & have no ambition whatever to produce a play, I feel bound to do as much for her as I can. I have told her that I don't like the idea of her trying the professional stage at all, but with little effect; & it is only natural I suppose that she should not want to hide her undoubted personal attractions under a bushel. At the same time she says that she wants to leave everything to my judgment. So there it is, & I feel frightfully responsible.

Don't answer these ruminations if they worry you, but I thought I would communicate first with you before applying to anybody else. Excuse a scrawl owing to weak eyesight.

Always sincerely
Thomas Hardy.

We were much interested in the doings at "Bonnie Dundee."

Barrie: James Matthew Barrie (1860–1937), dramatist and novelist, with whom TH had been friendly since the late 1880s; he was created a baronet in 1913.   *Harrison*: Frederick Harrison (1854–1926), manager of the Haymarket Theatre, London.   *"Bonnie Dundee"*: it was, however, the freedom not of Dundee but of Dumfries (where he once lived) that Barrie had received on 11 Dec.

To J. W. Mackail

MAX GATE, | DORCHESTER. | Christmas Eve: 1924

My dear Mackail:

It is so kind of you to send the little Bunyan book. I wish I had something new for you, but I have published nothing lately except in papers. What memories the Pilgrim's Progress wakes in me: the first time of reading it as a boy of 10 walking across a field in the dusk, in an old edition with hideous illustrations that had just been lent me by two old ladies. The picture of Apollyon fighting Christian made me so uncomfortable in that lonely spot that I was compelled to shut the book

& not open it again till I reached human society & candlelight (there were candles on earth in those days.)

During the last 2 months I have been drawn into theatrical matters quite unexpectedly, &, indeed, reluctantly, owing to the interest shown in the Tess play, which I dug out of a drawer where it had lain for 30 years, merely to please the players here. Mrs Bugler, to whom you allude, took everybody by surprise, myself not least, as I had no suspicion she could tackle tragedy in the way she did. I am afraid the attention she has drawn upon herself has given her an itch for the regular theatre, & I am old fashioned enough to feel uneasy about it, being to some extent the cause.

Our warmest wishes for Christmas & the New Year. Pardon blotted writing through weak eyesight.

Always sincerely
Thomas Hardy.

Bunyan book: the published form of Mackail's Royal Institution lecture on *The Pilgrim's Progress*, delivered in Mar. 1924.   *two old ladies*: probably Rebecca and Amelia Sparks, related to his mother by marriage, who are said to have given TH his lunch each day while he was attending school in Dorchester.

[Hardy had maintained a sparse but lively correspondence with the American poet Amy Lowell ever since she had visited Max Gate just at the outbreak of the Great War. He thought well of her work, as compared with that of the few other modern American poets he knew, and his own intense fascination with everything connected with John Keats lent a special interest to the biography she published in 1924. That did not, however, prevent him from remaining deeply suspicious of all intensive biographical investigation into creative lives, especially his own, and it was obviously a fundamental unease—not simply his justifiably low opinion of the book, nor his awareness of an 'official' biography awaiting eventual publication over his wife's name—that impelled his opposition to English publication of a *Life* of himself written by the American critic Ernest Brennecke, whose earlier book, *Thomas Hardy's Universe*, he had acknowledged with apparent equanimity just nine months previously.]

To Amy Lowell

MAX GATE, | DORCHESTER. | 6 March 1925

My dear Cousin Amy:

It has been a great pleasure to me to receive this valuable book, your life of John Keats, & I don't know how to thank you enough for it. I have not been reading it straight on—I should say we, for my wife has read it aloud on account of the weakness of my eyes. I am quite amazed at the skill & industry you have shown, & to me at any rate, every page is interesting.

Not Shakespeare himself, I should think, has been so meticulously (is that the right use of the word? I never know) examined as it has fallen at last to poor neglected Keats's lot to be. If he could only have known! How you have sifted out the legends for & against him. It was in one respect fortunate for him that his brother went to America, as it has rendered accessible to you many papers, &c., that would otherwise have been buried here in England or lost.

By the way, did it never occur to you that the words "pure serene" in the Chapman's Homer sonnet may have been an unconscious memory of the line in Gray's Elegy ending, "purest ray serene"? This seems to me more probable than Paget Toynbee's suggestion of it having come from Cary's Dante.

My wife's mother, who grew up at Enfield, Middlesex, knew the Clarke schoolbuilding of which you give an illustration. Her maiden name was Taylor, & there is every reason to believe that she & the publisher Taylor were of the same family.

Another thing: I may be wrong, but for many years I have fancied that the Grecian Urn which inspired the poem is actually one in the British Museum: at any rate I remember standing before one & concluding that it must have been the same Keat's looked at. But you have probably thought all that out.

I am sorry to say I cannot write all I would write about the book. You must not take any notice of what our funny men of

the newspaper press say about the size of it, &c. That's how
they are; & it never makes any difference.

My wife sends her love, & believe me

Affectionately yours
Thomas Hardy.

Cousin Amy: for the allusion see letter of 26 Jan. 1919.   *Toynbee's suggestion*:
Paget Jackson Toynbee (1855–1932), Dante scholar, cited by Lowell in the
biography; Henry Francis Cary's translations of Dante appeared between
1805 and 1812.   *Clarke schoolbuilding*: the Enfield school, conducted by
John Clarke, which Keats attended as a boy; John Taylor (1781–1864) was
Keats's first publisher.

To Sir Frederick Macmillan

MAX GATE, | DORCHESTER. | 4th. April 1925.

Dear Sir Frederick:

A copy of "The Life of Thomas Hardy" by Ernest Brennecke, which my wife mentioned to you, has arrived from its
New York publisher Greenberg, although I cabled to the
author my disapproval of its publication. It is a large volume,
announcing itself on the cover as: "The first biography of
England's novelist-poet; a work which will probably always
stand as the most authoritative and comprehensive book on
the subject. Mr Brennecke records every known fact of
Hardy's life. . . . This biography is the result of ten years of
research and personal contact."

The first five chapters are the biographical part (the
remainder being mostly criticism of my writings, and
although often erroneous, it is unobjectionable so far as I
have noticed). The biographical chapters are made up of: (1)
what can be learned from books of reference & newspapers;
(2) extensive assumptions that narrations in the novels and
poems are truth, though given as fiction; (3) notes taken when
the writer got into this house under the pretence of being a
student of German philosophy, and not an interviewer; (4)
what he picked up in the neighbourhood from photographers,
tradespeople, servants, etc.

The biographical part is thus mainly guesswork, and, though quite eulogistic, ridiculously incorrect; but as long as the book remains in America it does not much matter I suppose. But I have heard from Fisher Unwin & Co, who published the writer's "T.H.'s Universe", that it has just been offered to them for issuing in England, and on my informing them of its misstatements and that it is unauthorized, and contains copyright matter, they have refused it. But it will probably be offered to other firms who may not know it is so highly conjectural and without authority in its biography; so I thought I would tell you of its advent, in case anything ought to be done to caution them. The quizzing impertinence of its remarks on one's appearance, clothing, household details, &c. would warn some firms, but perhaps not all, that the apparent authorization might be untrue and would be contradicted. I should add that the book is a fairly able one from a literary point of view, & I should not have the slightest objection to the publication of the critical part without the personal details. In that case, however, the type would be so cut about that it would have to be re-set in England. T.H.

I can let you see the book whenever you may wish to, to judge upon the copyright matter (mostly poems)—in case the author should get it published here.

He has lately brought out a book through the same American publishers, entitled "Life and Art: By T.H."—as if it were a new volume by me. But it is made up of miscellaneous writings of mine before the international copyright act of 1891, with letters to newspapers at different times, &c. This he has also tried on Fisher Unwin; but here in England it is all copyright, of course.

Yours very sincerely,
Thomas Hardy.

"*T.H.'s Universe*": see letter of 21 June 1924.   *to caution them*: Macmillan and Cockerell jointly composed the letter of warning to publishers which appeared in *The Times* of 11 Apr.   *In that . . . T.H.*: added at end of letter but marked for insertion at this point.   *new volume by me*: it was published as Thomas Hardy, *Life and Art: Essays Notes and Letters Collected for the First Time*, with an introduction by Ernest Brennecke, jun. (1925).

[Hardy had been actively involved in the preparations for the first commercial production of his dramatization of *Tess of the d'Urbervilles*. Although the Barnes Theatre was in rather an out of the way corner of west London and the producer, Philip Ridgeway, little known, the play was well received when it opened on 7 September 1925 and subsequently enjoyed a successful West End run and provincial tour. Gwen Ffrangcon-Davies was cast as Tess and Hardy was much impressed, during a visit she made to Max Gate in August 1925, by her intelligent interest in all aspects of the play's structure and meaning. Hardy did not accompany Florence when she went to see the play—he had already made what proved to be his last London visit when attending the wedding of Harold Macmillan and Lady Dorothy Cavendish in April 1920—but in December 1925 the entire cast came down from London for a private performance in the Max Gate drawing room.]

To Henry Arthur Jones

MAX GATE, | DORCHESTER. | 13 Sept. 1925

Dear H. Arthur Jones:

It was with much pleasure that I received your letter telling me of your visit to the Barnes theatre for the performance of the Tess play. An experienced judgment like your own has a settling effect upon the chaos of opinions I have read in the newspapers as to the general aspect of the production, though of course I make allowance for your indulgence towards the manifold defects in the construction of the play. As you probably know, it was written thirty years ago, when both you & I were younger, & our views of the theatre—at any rate mine—were not quite the same as they are now. If I had adapted the novel in these days I daresay I should have done the job differently; but when, quite by accident, & at the request of the amateur players here, I looked it up, I found I could not get back to the subject closely enough to handle it anew. However, all independent observers agree with you in saying that it did not fail to move the emotions, which is quite as much as one could expect, though one critic, by the way, said that the audience "all went to be moved, but none were moved", a puzzling statement I pass over in the face of the other testimony. I am quite of your opinion in respect of Miss Ffrangcon Davies. She has been down here, & we liked her very much: her great intelligence, too, was striking, while she was free from the vanities one too often finds among stage people.

It is a long time since we met. I well remember your "Case of Rebellious Susan", &, of course, several of your other plays. I sometimes wonder that new plays from your hand do not appear oftener now that the terrible Victorian restrictions are removed, & events can be allowed to develope on the stage as they would in real life.

I go to London very seldom, finding that, though I am quite well while here, the least thing upsets me when I am away—which is, I suppose, not unnatural at my age.

I gather from your presence at Barnes that you keep fairly well. My wife can remember meeting you, & sends her kind regards. She went up to the Thursday matinée, but was not at the first night.

How many have disappeared for another stage since we first sat in a theatre!

Yours sincerely
Thomas Hardy.

Jones: Henry Arthur Jones (1851–1929), dramatist.   *Davies*: Gwen Ffrangcon-Davies (b. 1896), actor and singer.   *Rebellious Susan"*: first performed in 1894, though TH probably saw the revival of 1910.

To Harley Granville Barker

Max Gate, | Dorchester. | 20 October 1925.

My dear H.G.B.

I am much interested to learn that you and Helen have taken the trouble to go to the play, and seen what I shall never see— Miss Gwen F.D. in the part of Tess. It is so strange that this resurrection of the character should have come about, when a year ago I did not dream of such a thing; and it is a pity that, owing to my not foreseeing it, I had no time to revise the technicalities of the adaptation, which no doubt I should have done if I had known that my casual handing over of the old copy to the players here would have extended so far afield.

She is a charming young woman, we think, and I have had a letter from her today to say that she will drop down upon us next Sunday and talk over what has happened. She seems to live in the piece, and I hope will not wear herself out with it, for it must be a heavy strain, and she is not robust.

The real fact is, as I may have said before, to attempt to put a novel on the stage is hopeless, and altogether a mistake in art. I should never have thought of trying my hand on it nowadays; but having been tempted by many "leading ladies" of the nineties I could not resist. But the courage of managers did not equal that of the would-be Tesses, and they put the extinguisher on my effort, in the interest of propriety.

Yes: you are right in thinking the christening scene and the baby-nursing scene vital parts of the story. Not only could they not be got into the stage-action for technical reasons, but for moral reasons they were not allowed to be in the novel when it ran as a serial in 1891. Whether the gentler and more clinging quality given to the character by Miss F.D. (which I am told is most moving) than was given her in the book, is consistent with the smouldering ancestral fire in Tess's nature that broke out in the murder, I of course cannot judge: Florence says it does not strike a spectator as being out of keeping.

It must be amusing to you to see what they are all doing in London—histrionically I mean (if I may use such a dignified word in connection with stage popularities at the present day).

Later.

I have received the lecture: it is kind of you to send it. We are going to read it to-night after dinner. I am not capable of doing much just now—being only just recovering from an attack of lumbago. I was boasting a few months ago of never having anything of the sort! Best love to H., and believe me

ever yours.
Thomas Hardy.

Barker: Harley Granville Barker (1877–1946), man of the theatre; Helen, née Gates (d. 1950), was his second wife.   *F.D.*: Ffrangcon-Davies. *serial in 1891*: both scenes occur in ch. 14, omitted from the *Graphic* serialization of the novel.   *the lecture*: Barker had sent a copy of his British Academy Shakespeare Lecture *From 'Henry V' to 'Hamlet'* (1925).

To Harley Granville Barker

Max Gate, | Dorchester. | 19. Dec. 1925.

Dear H.G.B.

I have finished The Madras House which you were so kind as to send me, and though you have probably formed your own opinion about it by this time I should like to tell you how it strikes a contemporary—if I can be considered a contemporary!

I shall horrify you by saying that I am almost sorry you did not write it as a novel. I have read it as one, anyhow. Its subtleties are to my mind largely wasted on the stage which, think what you will, addresses itself to people who are not very perceptive except the few who don't count among the mass. (That's why I always feel Shakespeare is largely wasted in acting.) I think it possible that you may ultimately drift into novel writing: I don't see how otherwise you can express all the complications that you discern in life. However, I don't give advice; but bear that thought in mind.

I will only add (what is really a part of the same thing) that your acute judgements of Victorian, and other, architecture makes me hazard that guess that you would have thrived as an architect, or architectural critic.

I hope you have got to Paris without adventure either with snowstorms or anything else. We have none here. You are going on south I hear. Best wishes from us to both of you for the Christmas—not that I believe one atom in Bethlehem of Judea, though I agree with the late Dr. Cheyne in holding that much may be said for Bethlehem in Galilee. (This is a digression.)

Always yours.
Thomas Hardy.

The Madras House: the revised edition of 1925, published to coincide with a new production which opened at the Ambassadors Theatre on 30 Nov. 1925; the play was first produced in 1910.   *Dr Cheyne*: Cheyne (see letter of 18 Sep. 1909) had challenged the traditional identification of Bethlehem of Judaea as the birthplace of Christ, arguing instead for Bethlehem in Galilee—and, indeed, for still other possibilities.

To Lady Pinney

MAX GATE, | DORCHESTER. | 20 Jan. 1926

My dear Lady Pinney:

My sincere thanks for the details you have been so indefatigable as to obtain about that unhappy woman Martha Brown, whom I am ashamed to say I saw hanged, my only excuse being that I was but a youth, & had to be in the town at the time for other reasons. I gather from your description that the house of the murder has quite disappeared. I daresay it was pulled down as much on account of its tragic associations as from its dilapidated state. I wonder if there are any remains of it. I remember what a fine figure she showed against the sky as she hung in the misty rain, & how the tight black silk gown set off her shape as she wheeled half-round & back.

I hope you have not felt the cold much: we have somewhat. Young people love frost, but I for one don't. We shall be glad to see you later on.

Affectionately yours
Thomas Hardy.

Pinney: Hester Pinney (d. 1958), wife of Major-General Sir Reginald John Pinney of Racedown, Dorset—a house visited by TH in Aug. 1925 for its associations with William and Dorothy Wordsworth.   *Brown*: correctly, Browne; TH, aged 16, witnessed her public hanging in Dorchester for the murder of her husband. She came from Birdsmoorgate, near Racedown, and Lady Pinney, at TH's request, had been gathering information about her from local inhabitants.

To Marie Stopes

MAX GATE, | DORCHESTER. | 16 April 1926

Dear Dr Marie Stopes:

I have read, or rather had read to me, your play, with much interest, and sympathize with you in your troubles over it, especially as it is obviously written with great skill and care.

My knowledge of the theatre nowadays is very slight—I have only been once these seven years—and I don't at all know what is in the tradition of modern plays. So I can only judge yours as a work of literary art, and even in that may be entirely wrong.

It seems to me that the situation and events are improbable: not too improbable to have happened, but too improbable for art, which must keep far within actual truth. I cannot conceive a young woman not an imbecile who has been married three years being in such crass ignorance of physiology, especially with a young man just through the party-wall ready to teach her. If she had been married only three days, or even three months, it would not have thrown such a strain upon one's credulity. However, taking the case quite seriously, the position of the pair is painful without reaching to the tragic. I may say in passing that if you had ended it as I thought you were going to, and made her, out of kindness to her husband, and her own and her father the bishop's horror at an unchristian scandal, resign herself to a living death with her husband you would have made it a tragedy.

A play acts so differently from how it reads that I can express no opinion on the censor's refusal to license. I believe some words had to be softened when "Tess" was staged which were quite unexceptionable in the reading.

The question arises, is an abnormality ever a fit subject for a work of art, even though not immoral.

You won't want to see me in the Lighthouse after this cold douche, but will wish me at the dark house rather. But with renewed sympathy I am

Sincerely yours,
T. Hardy.

P.S. Play returned in separate parcel.

Stopes: Marie Charlotte Carmichael Stopes (1880–1958), scientist and reformer, whom TH seems first to have met in 1923, when he and FEH visited the renovated lighthouse on Portland Bill in which she often stayed. Her play *Vectia* had been refused a performance licence, and she wrote on 14 Apr. to ask if TH would publicly recommend that such a licence be granted. Despite TH's scepticism, *Vectia*'s ignorance of sexual realities even after marriage was in fact closely autobiographical.

To J. H. Morgan

MAX GATE, | DORCHESTER. | 24 April 1926

Dear General Morgan:

I have read your interesting letter about Napoleon I., but am sorry to say I am compelled to answer it by the typewriter, on account of increasing weakness of sight, which limits my handwriting to short notes only. However I must not complain, as my eyes have served me well in their time.

As to the points about Waterloo, to which you draw my attention, I fear my memory does not enable me to say what foundation I had for that legend I called "The Peasant's Confession", beyond the passage in Thiers prefixed to the verses. Of course Thiers says a great deal more about the mystery of Grouchy's movements than I quoted from him— in fact he argues it out at length if I remember, so as to prove if possible that it was not Napoleon's fault the battle was lost.

I think Napoleon himself said that, after all, the issue of a battle was a matter of chance, and that it set all foresight and calculation at defiance. Anyhow, he himself trusted far more to chance than is generally supposed. Ney's enthusiasm must have been risky, once he got out of control. It has always been a mystery to me that he did not get killed; it bears out the saying they have hereabouts: "Nought (care-not?) is never in danger."

I believe it was never exactly known how Napoleon got off, or precisely what he did, on the night after Waterloo. Probably he himself was not quite aware. I recall that the accounts were very puzzling.

Modern wars do not lend themselves to scenic drama. Old

Waterloo men have told me how close they were to the
French, and of course one can see for one's self that they were
by looking at the field. What you say about the sunken road
is quite true.

Many thanks for inquiries. My wife sends kind regards.

Sincerely yours
Th: Hardy.

that legend: Morgan's letter of 20 Apr. had asked if the episode evoked in
TH's poem 'The Peasant's Confession' was purely imaginative or based
upon some oral tradition; TH owned two sets of the massive *Histoire du
Consulat et de l'Empire de Napoléon* (1845–69) by Louis Adolphe Thiers, one
in French and one in an English translation.   *Grouchy ... Ney's*:
Emmanuel Marquis de Grouchy (1766–1847) was one of Napoleon's
generals at Waterloo; Michel Ney (1769–1815), marshal of France, personally led several charges during the course of the battle.   *Modern wars*:
Morgan had remarked that a modern battle would not be fought in so
restricted a terrain as Waterloo and that aerial reconnaissance would have
rendered impossible Napoleon's crucial ignorance of the sunken road
behind La Haye Sainte.

To Roy McKay

27 April 1926

Dear Mr McKay:

I have read your letter with interest: also the enclosure that
you & your friends sent to The Manchester Guardian,
particularly because, when I was young, I had a wish to enter
the Church.

I am now too old to take up the questions you lay open,
but I may say that it has seemed to me that a simpler plan
than that of mental reservation in passages no longer literally
accepted (which is puzzling to ordinary congregations) would
be just to abridge the creeds & other primitive parts of the
Liturgy, leaving only the essentials. Unfortunately there
appears to be a narrowing instead of a broadening tendency
among the clergy of late, which if persisted in will exclude
still more people from church. But if a strong body of young
Reformers were to make a bold stand, in a sort of New Oxford

Movement, they would have a tremendous backing from the thoughtful laity, & might overcome the retrogressive section of the Clergy.

Please don't attach much importance to these casual thoughts, & believe me

Very truly yours

R. McKay Esq. | Ripon Hall (or Magdalen Coll:) | Oxford

McKay: Roy McKay (b. 1900), candidate for ordination at Ripon Hall, Oxford, subsequently a canon of Chichester Cathedral and head of religious broadcasting for the British Broadcasting Corporation. In a letter published in the *Manchester Guardian* of 26 Apr. he and three colleagues had urged the Church of England to face the fact that many sincere members of both the clergy and the laity could not give literal consent to all elements of the regularly recited Creeds. *Very truly yours*: the text is that of TH's unsigned draft.

To J. B. Priestley

MAX GATE, | DORCHESTER. | 8 August 1926

Dear Mr Priestley:

I send my warm thanks for your kind gift of the "George Meredith" book, & should have done so before if I had not fallen into the sere, & weak eyesight did not trouble me. I have read your essay, or rather have had it read to me, & have been much interested in the bright writing of one in whom I had already fancied I discerned a coming force in letters.

I am not at all a good critic, especially *of* a critic, & when the author he reviews is a man who was, off & on, a friend of mine for 40 years; but it seems to me that you hold the scales very fairly. Meredith was, as you recognize, & might have insisted on even more strongly, & I always felt, in the direct succession of Congreve & the artificial comedians of the Restoration, & in getting his brilliancy we must put up with the fact that he would not, or could not—at any rate did not—when aiming to represent the "Comic Spirit", let himself discover the tragedy that always underlies Comedy if you only scratch it deeply enough.

I was going to tell you some passages I particularly liked in your book, but must leave off, & with renewed thanks I am

Sincerely yours,
Thomas Hardy.

Priestley: John Boynton Priestley (1894–1984), novelist, dramatist, and critic, had sent TH an inscribed copy of his *George Meredith* (1926). *fallen into the sere*: *Macbeth*, v. iii. 23.

To H. G. Wells

MAX GATE, | DORCHESTER. | 5 Sept. 1926

Dear Mr Wells:

I have a half-ashamed feeling at accepting this beautiful edition of your new book, as I have done nothing to deserve it, & an ordinary copy would have been good enough for me. However, I thank you much for such a handsome gift.

I have begun it, but perceiving it to be a book of much more solid & philosophic quality than I at first expected I find it will not be one to hurry over. No book worth reading is. Although I do not see far into it as yet, I anticipate that you will get some buffets from the thoughtless—which happily you are well able to bear.

It is a most depressing business to endeavour to advance thought ever so little along the road to rationality. Your arguments are read or listened to—sometimes with respect—& twenty years later you find you may just as well not have written a line—except, of course, for a certain satisfaction that comes of having been no hypocrite & in having expressed your views sincerely. It may not always be thus; but I don't know.

Very sincerely yours
Thomas Hardy.

Wells: Herbert George Wells (1866–1946); he had sent TH a set of the three-volume limited, signed edition of his new novel *The World of William Clissold* (1926).

To St John Ervine

MAX GATE, | DORCHESTER, | DORSET. |
9th. September 1926.

Dear Mr Ervine:

I am happy to send you the authorization you ask for—that is, that you have the sole right to dramatize "Jude" for twelve months from the beginning of November next.

I may say that I am not keen on the new mode (as I suppose it is regarded, though really Elizabethan) of giving a series of episodes in the film manner instead of set scenes. Of the outlines I sent you which suggested themselves to me many years ago, I thought the one I called (I think) "4th Scheme" most feasible. If you wanted to begin further back than the First Act of this, you could split the act up into 2 or 3 scenes.

Would not Arabella be the villain of the piece?—or Jude's personal constitution?—so far as there is any villain more than blind Chance. Christminster is of course the tragic influence of Jude's drama in one sense, but innocently so, and merely as crass obstruction. By the way it is not meant to be exclusively Oxford, but any old-fashioned University about the date of the story 1860–70, before there were such chances for poor men as there are now. I have somewhere printed that I had no feeling against Oxford in particular.

I hope you keep well as we do.

Sincerely yours,
Th: Hardy.

Ervine: St John Greer Ervine (1883–1971), playwright and author; his proposed dramatization of *Jude the Obscure* did not materialize. *"4th Scheme"*: it was the one which followed most closely the action of the novel itself.

To Harley and Helen Granville Barker

Max Gate, | Dorchester. | 29 Dec. 1926.
Dear H.G.B. and Helen.

This is intended to be a New Year's letter, but I don't know if I have made a good shot at it. How kind of you to think of sending me Raymond Guyot's *Napoleon*. I have only glanced at it, at the text that is, as yet, but what an interesting collection of records bearing on the life of the man who finished the Revolution with "a whiff of grapeshot," and so crushed not only its final horrors but all the worthy aspirations of its earlier time, made them as if they had never been, and threw back human altruism scores, perhaps hundreds of years.

We have had a sad aftering to our Christmas. Our devoted (and masterful) dog Wessex died on the 27th, and last night had his bed outside the house under the trees for the first time for 13 years. We miss him greatly, but he was in such misery with swelling and paralysis that it was a relief when a kind breath of chloroform administered in his sleep by 2 good-natured Doctors (not vets) made his sleep an endless one—A dog of such strong character required human doctors!

Best wishes for the coming year that the scheme, or no scheme, of the universe will permit from both and with many thanks believe me

Very sincerely yours
Thomas Hardy.

P.S. Sight bad: accounting for this scrawl of a letter. T.H.

Napoleon: published in Paris in 1921, it was a folio volume largely consisting of plates and facsimiles of documents. *of grapeshot,"*: from Thomas Carlyle, *Frederick the Great*, bk. v, ch. 3. *under the trees*: in the pets' cemetery at Max Gate.

To Sir Frederick Macmillan

MAX GATE, | DORCHESTER, | DORSET. | 27 September 1927.
Dear Sir Frederick:

I think I had better read through the proofs of the Selected Poems, new edition, in case of any oversight, and I will therefore be ready for them at any time.

In respect to your suggestion of a volume of my short stories at 7/6, I quite agree to such a volume on the terms you mention, since it seems likely to do well, and I am willing for you to put it in hand whenever convenient. The order in which you have written them down is as good as any I think. The text of the Wessex Edition is the most correct to print from, and I hope the printers will be able to use that. If any expression in either of the Prefaces or Introductory notes should not apply to the intended edition I will put it right on receiving a proof of the page on which it occurs.

Another matter. I enclose herewith a letter that has just been sent me by Mr John Drinkwater, which explains itself. I don't myself see that his proposed inclusion in his book of the six short poems of mine that he names will do any harm though I think that Messrs Houghton & Mifflin ought to pay something, which indeed they appear quite ready to do. I remember your telling me that John O'London is paying £100 for the 25 poems they are printing, and it has occurred to me that the same ratio might not be too high for Messrs Houghton,—so that the amount would be £24 for the six poems, if they want to sell the book in England as well as America. However I don't much mind what it is, and will ask you to settle the matter. I will let Mr Drinkwater have a line telling him that he will hear from you on the point. Our best regards, & believe me,

Yours Sincerely
Th: Hardy.

new edition: both *Chosen Poems*, as TH decided to call it, and *The Short Stories of Thomas Hardy* were published posthumously.   *Drinkwater*: John Drinkwater (1882–1937), poet and playwright, was one of the editors of *Twentieth-Century Poetry* (1929), an anthology published by the American firm of

Houghton Mifflin; the magazine *John O'London's Weekly* had recently
contracted to print a TH poem each week for 25 weeks.

To William Maxwell

MAX GATE, | DORCHESTER, | DORSET. | 18 Oct. 1927

Dear Mr Maxwell:

I don't think I have acknowledged the reccipt of your
"Annie Laurie" versions & researches—for which I thank
you now. The very interesting details that you have been able
to muster show that my idea of somebody writing an article
called "The truth about Annie Laurie" was not such a bad
one after all. It would certainly attract the public. How one
would like to know more of the unhappy Douglas of Fingland,
& his love-making, & his end: also of Annie's life with her
husband Ferguson of Craigdarroch. Possibly it was a prosy
commonplace life, which if known would spoil our romantic
tradition of her: still, I shd like to know it. Alicia, Lady John
Scott, must have been a gifted woman, not only in music, but
as a poetess, for the 3rd verse of the song is a beautiful one.

I daresay the impression we have of Annie as being
something of a coquette—if not a heartless flirt—has some
basis of truth. A faithful woman would not have become
famous: that's how things are! My vision of her & her lover
Fingland was derived mainly from James Grant's romance,
"The Scottish Cavalier" which I read in my boyhood. You
are probably familiar with it.

I am greatly obliged to you for letting me have these
particulars, which may lead to more. But possibly the present
day Lauries (if there are any) would object to having them
raked up—people are so queer sometimes, though not always.

Sincerely yours
Thomas Hardy.

Maxwell: William Maxwell (1873–1957), master printer and managing
director of the Edinburgh firm of R. & R. Clark, printers of almost all of
TH's books from 1902 onwards; during a recent visit of Maxwell's to Max

Gate TH had expressed curiosity as to the origins of the song 'Annie Laurie', and Maxwell had sent him the text of the poem as contained in Allan Ramsay's *Scots Songs* together with a more modern version by Alicia, Lady John Scott (1810–1900), who had altered the two existing verses and added a third verse of her own.   *Scottish Cavalier"*: *The Scottish Cavalier: An Historical Romance* (1850), by the Scottish novelist James Grant (1822–87); its somewhat sketchy account of the Annie Laurie story identifies Richard Douglas, laird of Fingland, as having composed the famous ballad after losing Annie to his rival, Fergusson of Craigdarroch.

To Sir Frederick Macmillan

MAX GATE, | DORCHESTER, | DORSET. | 30 Nov. 1927

My dear Macmillan:

I am delighted to receive the two copies of The Dynasts. There was great excitement here when they came, & they are all that I expected. Leslie Stephen used to say that all modern books & newspapers would have perished in 100 years, but I fancy these volumes will hold out. I notice that you have embodied all the latest corrections, & I hope the booksellers will do well with their stock.

I hope you are getting through these fogs without discomfort.

With kind regards

Yours sincerely
Thomas Hardy.

The Dynasts: the three-volume limited, signed edition just published by Macmillan; Sir Frederick reported that the entire edition had already been subscribed for by booksellers.

[Hardy's last illness began, almost without warning, on 11 December 1927. Though Hardy was greatly weakened, his life did not at first seem to be threatened, and he managed to send off his poem 'Christmas in the Elgin Room' for publication in *The Times* of 24 December. On Christmas Day itself he summoned the strength—and humour—to pencil one last letter to Edmund Gosse, the oldest and closest of his surviving friends, but his condition steadily declined thereafter and in the evening of 11 January 1928 he died.]

To Sir Edmund Gosse

MAX GATE, | DORCHESTER, | DORSET. | Xmas Day 1927

Dear Edmund Gosse:

I must thank you for your very kind letter as well as I can. I am in bed on my back, living on butter-broth & beef tea, the servants being much concerned at my not being able to eat any Christmas pudding, though I am rather relieved.

As to those verses in the *Times* you inquire about & gratify me by liking, I can only go by the dates attached in fixing their history: the poem having been begun in 1905 (possibly when I was in the Elgin Room, though I don't remember being there) & then abandoned, & not finished till last year.

I am sorry to hear of your cold on the chest—whatever you do, don't go out against an east wind. I think my aches are diminishing. J.M.M. called here last week, but I did not see him. F. says he is much more cheerful, & he & his young wife are both hoping she will get well again, but the doctors say it is next to impossible—

Best wishes to you & your house for the New Year—& believe m

Always your sincere
T.H.

very kind letter: Gosse wrote 24 Dec., congratulating TH on 'Christmas in the Elgin Room' and asking when it was written; the room itself, in the British Museum, houses the 'Elgin Marbles' from the Parthenon.   *J.M.M.*: John Middleton Murry was living in a Dorset cottage with his seriously ill second wife Violet (née le Maistre, d. 1931), and experiencing severe financial difficulties; Gosse, prompted by TH and FEH, had just persuaded Stanley Baldwin, the prime minister, to make him an immediate grant of £250 from the Privy Purse.   *believe m*: TH did not complete the intended 'me'.

INDEX

The titles of Hardy's works are dispersed alphabetically throughout the index; all other works are indexed under their authors. Where several footnote entries are listed for a single person an asterisk is used to identify the one providing the principal biographical details; the abbreviation 'c.' indicates a reference to one of the editorial commentaries which appear at intervals throughout the volume. Topical entries appear in bold-face.